The Modern
Student's Library

PHILOSOPHY SERIES

THE Modern Student's Library has been enlarged to include a series of volumes containing writings of the great philosophers.
These volumes are edited by the most competent
authorities at home and abroad. The selections
are comprehensive and suited to the special needs
of students and the general reading public. Each
volume contains an introduction giving a brief
outline of the system of the author and indicating
his place in the history of thought.

The Philosophy Series is under the general editorship of Ralph Barton Perry, Professor of Philosophy, Harvard University.

[*For a complete list of* THE MODERN STUDENT'S
LIBRARY *see the pages following the text*]

CHARLES SCRIBNER'S SONS

SPINOZA
Selections

SPINOZA
SELECTIONS

EDITED BY

JOHN WILD

INSTRUCTOR IN PHILOSOPHY, HARVARD UNIVERSITY

CHARLES SCRIBNER'S SONS
NEW YORK   CHICAGO   ATLANTA
SAN FRANCISCO   DALLAS

For permission to reprint selections from the correspondence of Spinoza the editor is indebted to The Dial Press.

CONTENTS

CONTENTS

INTRODUCTION

It is perhaps impossible to understand any philosophy without a knowledge of the life and personality of which it is the expression. Of Spinozism this is especially the case, for, whether we view it from the standpoint of the thought or that of the thinker of the thought, the two fuse into one organic and consistent whole. One of the most characteristic doctrines of the system is the identity of intellect and will, of thought and action. For Spinoza thinking was in no sense the exploration of a dream-world but a way of life. And when we view the man himself certainly there is no figure in the whole history of thought who in his concrete actions has so whole-heartedly devoted himself to the search for truth, and literally lived the philosophic life.

Baruch or Benedict Spinoza was born on the 24th of November, 1632, at Amsterdam. His parents belonged to a group of Spanish and Portuguese Jews who had fled from the persecutions of the Inquisition and had finally found a refuge in the United Provinces, at that time in the midst of their inspiring eighty-year struggle for independence, which lasted up to the fifteenth year of Spinoza's life. Michael Spinoza, the father, was a well-to-do merchant evidently held in high esteem by the Jewish community in Amsterdam since he was four times Warden of his Synagogue and also one of the Wardens of the Amsterdam Jewish School. His second wife, the mother of Benedict, died in 1638. There were three other children, only one of whom, a sister, survived the father who died in 1654. Benedict was, of course, sent to the Rabbinical school where he received the most thorough training in the Hebrew language and literature, and finally read the works of Jewish philosophical writers such as Ibn Ezra and Maimonides who unquestionably exercised a permanent influence over Spinoza's mind. One of his teachers was the Rabbi Manasseh ben Israel, quite widely but rather superficially read, with mystical tendencies and a host of friends both Jewish and Christian. Among the latter was the painter Rembrandt who made several studies of the Rabbi and, since he lived in the very heart of the Jewish quarter for sixteen years, possibly knew Spinoza himself. The Rabbi Manasseh was a very sincere and eloquent preacher, and he may have passed on some of his moral earnestness to his pupil. He went to England in 1655 on a special mission to Cromwell for the readmission of the Jews into England. But all his dreams collapsed and he returned to the Netherlands two years later bringing with him the corpse of his eldest son. He himself died soon after, a broken man. We may well imagine that his moral integrity and his cosmopolitan point of view at least strengthened the tendencies that were already drawing Spinoza away from the orthodox tradition.

The Hebrew religious and legal codes are full of subtle problems and distinctions whose value, at least as mental discipline, is unquestionable. No doubt at an early age Spinoza was doing his own thinking and drawing his own conclusions concerning the problems opened up by the great Jewish literature of the Spanish period. As his mind developed beyond the confines of the tradition which nurtured him, he thirsted for more knowledge, and the treasures which only a command of Latin could give him. This language was viewed askance by the Jews at the time from its associations with Catholicism and the Inquisition, and called "the priest's language"; so Spinoza was forced to seek instruction from a certain Francis van den Enden who had just opened a fashionable school in Amsterdam and was reputed to be a free-thinker. To him Spinoza probably owes his classical knowledge as well as his acquaintance with physical science and the philosophy of Descartes. This move undoubtedly further alienated him from the Jewish orthodoxy, and we may suppose that his attendance at the synagogue became more and more irregular. Spinoza's brilliance as a student made him a marked man, and as the news of his heresies spread, the crisis became more imminent till in June, 1656 he was summoned before the court of the Rabbis and one month later publicly banned. This public excommunication was probably made necessary by the precarious position of the newly-established Jewish community and its fear that rumors of atheism might lead to persecution by the dominant Calvinistic clergy. When it is remembered that even twenty years after, various Synods of the Reformed Church tried to induce the government to adopt strong measures for the forcible conversion of the Jews, it becomes possible to understand the delicate position of the Amsterdam community and its desire to avoid all scandal, which had led some years before to the anathematizing and ultimate suicide of another free-thinking though far-inferior radical, Uriel da Costa. If Judaism alone had been concerned, probably more leniency would have been shown. This is confirmed by the fact that before his summons Spinoza was offered 1000 florins if he would keep silent and outwardly conform. Such a blunder could only have the opposite effect on his sensitive spirit. But the banishment was probably something of a blessing since it utterly freed him from sectarian considerations and allowed him to become henceforth a universal thinker.

Spinoza was now cast upon his own resources at the age of 24. At the death of his father two years before, his sister had attempted to keep him from inheriting his share of the estate probably on the basis of his religious delinquencies. Spinoza resented this and appealed to the law of the land. But after winning the case Spinoza voluntarily gave up everything but a bedstead. For some time he was an assistant to van den Enden at the latter's school, but the excommunication made it necessary for him to leave Amsterdam temporarily. So he moved to Ouwerkerk a little village just south of the city, and took up the trade of grinding lenses which he had mastered previously, in accordance with the Rabbinical tradition which demands that every student must learn a manual trade. This must have been a period of trial and suffering during which many possible careers opened up before him, and during which he must have definitely decided to renounce worldly ambition and devote himself to the pursuit of knowledge and those "eternal things" of which he speaks in the first pages of "The Improvement of the Understanding." Among his friends at this time were Jarig Jelles who later persuaded Spinoza to publish the version of Descartes' *Principia* at his expense, Ludwig Meyer who wrote the introduction to this treatise and gave Spinoza medical assistance throughout his life, Jan Rieuwartsz a book-seller who was very liberal in his views, and published Spinoza's works, and Simon de Vries, a medical student a year younger than Spinoza who always revered him as a disciple and later, when he realized that his own death was imminent tried to make Spinoza his heir but was finally dissuaded by the latter. With these friends Spinoza probably held many a philosophical discussion in the course of which the substance of his treatise on the *Improvement of the Understanding*, and the *Short Treatise on God, Man, and His Well-Being* were formulated.

In order to work out his thoughts which had now far outgrown Descartes just as they had previously outgrown the Jewish tradition, Spinoza in 1660 moved to the quiet little village of Rijnsburg where he lived in a cottage on a narrow lane with a surgeon named Homan who belonged to the Collegiant sect. The formation of this sect dated from 1619 when the Synod of Dordrecht excommunicated the non-Calvinists (Arminians), closed their churches, and executed Barneveldt, the political head of the Remonstrants, and one of the greatest statesmen of the Netherlands. Certain groups at this time banded together and resolved to live without clerical officers, simply holding informal meetings (collegia) for prayers and religious discussion. One such group settled at Rijnsburg. Spinoza always numbered friends among this sect and thoroughly sympathized with their peaceful and tolerant way of life. It is easy to understand from this association Spinoza's hatred of religious bigotry and the polemics of the *Tractatus Theologico-Politicus* against the temporal power of the church. The four years spent among these peaceful surroundings were probably the happiest of Spinoza's life and among the most fruitful. During them he carried on an important correspondence with his friends at Amsterdam who met together in a sort of seminary to discuss the letters and treatises he sent them, (e. g. Letter VIII) among which was the now completed *Short Treatise* and probably the *Treatise on the Improvement of the Understanding*. It was during this time also that Spinoza, through some of his Collegiant friends, met Henry Oldenburg, soon to become Secretary of the newly established Royal Society, with whom Spinoza carried on a long and interesting correspondence.

Indeed his circle of friends had so widened that again he felt it imperative to move. So in 1663 he decided to move to Voorburg, a little village near the Hague. But on his way he went first to Amsterdam to visit his friends who persuaded him during his visit to publish his geometrical version of Descartes' *Principia*. Then he retired to Voorburg where he immersed himself for the first two years in preparation for a work which was to embody his complete system—the *Ethics*. But he found time to carry on a wide correspondence with such friends as Oldenburg and Blyenburgh, the well-meaning merchant of Dordrecht who later wrote denunciations of the *Tractatus Theologico-Politicus* and the *Ethics* attributing their contents to the inspiration of Hell. But in 1665 Spinoza suddenly laid the *Ethics* aside and started work on the *Tractatus Theologico-Politicus*. In a letter to Oldenburg Spinoza gives three reasons for his taking up this new treatise. In the first place he wished to attack the prejudices of the theologians which he felt at that time to be the chief obstacle in the path of true philosophy. Then he wished to refute the charges of atheism which even at that time were being levelled against him. Finally and most essentially he wished to fight with all the intellectual resources at his disposal for the defence of freedom of thought and of speech (see especially his great plea in the twentieth chapter of the *Tractatus*) which was being jeopardized by the tyranny of the reformed church clergy. Only the most intense feeling could have drawn Spinoza from the speculative heights of the *Ethics* and embroiled him in the turmoil of contemporary issues. It is a great mistake to think of Spinoza as a mere spectator of life, entirely lost in the clouds of mystical abstraction. Like Plato he felt that it was the philosopher's duty to redescend into the cave and to struggle for earthly light. Indeed for him philosophy and life were one. Undoubtedly one of the factors that drew him into political controversy was his friendship with Jan de Witt the great Grand Pensionary of Holland whom he came to know at this time. De Witt was the leader of the liberal, anti-Orange and anti-clerical party of the time and he must have encouraged Spinoza as he encouraged other writers notably Spinoza's friend, Dr. Ludwig Meyer, to use his pen in support of the policy of enlightenment and tolerance.

It was probably his friendship with de Witt that finally after four years of tireless labor on the *Tractatus Theologico-Politicus*, published in 1670, led him to move from Voorburg and settle in the Hague itself, first in the boarding house of the widow van Velden but finally in the more economical lodgings of the artist van der Spyck where he was able to do his own housekeeping on a very modest scale. His great *Treatise* went through five editions in a very short time, and exercised a vast contemporary influence. It was, of course, condemned on all sides by the orthodox clergy but as long as de Witt was in authority it could not be suppressed. Eventually, however, with the ascendancy of the Orange party it was strictly banned in 1674. In his quiet lodgings in the Hague Spinoza was now able to devote himself again to the *Ethics*, and during the completion and perfection of this work his ideas led him on and on to the projection of a scientific treatise on the Hebrew language in which of course he had become deeply interested in the development of the treatise, a translation of the Old Testament based on this, a separate treatise on political theories (*Tractatus Politi-*

cus), and, in closer connection with the *Ethics* itself, a work on natural science and an exposition of the principles of Algebra. But Spinoza was by no means well. For more than ten years he had been suffering from consumption aggravated by the effects of the fine glass inhaled in the laborious process of lense-polishing. But in spite of his physical feebleness his indomitable courage enabled him to get well along on the *Hebrew Grammar* and the Dutch translation of the Bible, and he almost finished the *Political Treatise*. The other works remained entirely beyond his strength. Political events also saddened the last years of his life and undoubtedly hastened its end.

In 1672 England and France declared war against the Netherlands and an army of 120,000 invaded the United Provinces, sweeping all before it. In the crisis that ensued the reactionary party took the ascendancy, and de Witt became the scapegoat. On the 20th of August 1672 a mob broke into the prison at the Hague where Jan de Witt was visiting his imprisoned brother and brutally murdered both of them. Spinoza was completely overcome by this ghastly tragedy. He burst into tears and had to be forcibly restrained from rushing to the scene and posting placards against "the very lowest of barbarians" who had committed the crime. Shortly after this Spinoza was invited to the camp of Prince Condé in command of the French army, a man of liberal views and interested in science and philosophy, who had heard of the author of the famous *Tractatus*. After long deliberation Spinoza finally decided to make the trip in the hope of possibly being able to do something in the way of re-establishing peace. Condé himself was unable to see him, but Spinoza's simple grace made him completely at home in any surroundings whether that of the simple peasants at Rijnsburg or that of the

French courtiers. Indeed on the latter he made such an impression that he was offered a pension if he would dedicate a work to Louis XIV. But Spinoza was not ready, like his friend Christian Huyghens, to serve any master,—above all the great enemy of his country. So he returned to the Hague and his modest lodgings with the van der Spycks. Rumor had it that Spinoza was a spy and in the evening a mob collected in front of the house. The landlord feared an attack but Spinoza reassured him saying, "At the slightest sign of danger I will go out to the people even if they do to me what they did to the good de Witts."

In 1673 Spinoza received an even greater compliment than that of the French from Karl Ludwig, Elector Palatine, who offered him the Professorship of Philosophy at the University of Heidelberg. Spinoza considered this invitation carefully for six weeks but finally decided that he was unwilling to give up his habitual quietude and retirement for the distracting demands of public teaching. Also he was somewhat afraid of academic limitations on the freedom of his philosophical teaching. But in spite of his declining health he gave himself unsparingly to his many friends and carried on his persistently wide correspondence. The most important letters written at this time were those to Tschirnhaus, a German gentleman, mathematically inclined, who had met Spinoza at Rijnsburg, and who now offered Spinoza the most intelligent criticism of his system he had yet received.

In 1673 he journeyed to the Hague to arrange for the publication of his *Ethics*. What happened is best revealed in his own words:

"At the time when I received your letter of 22 July, I was setting out for Amsterdam with the intention of getting printed the work about which I had written to

you. While I was engaged on this matter, a rumour
was spread everywhere that a book of mine about God
was in the press, and that in it I endeavoured to show
that there is no God. This rumour was believed by
many. Therefore certain Theologians (perhaps the authors of this rumour) seized the opportunity of bringing
complaints against me before the Prince and the Magis-
trates; moreover the dull-witted Cartesians, because they
are believed to be in my favour, and in order to free
themselves from suspicion, continued and even now
continue to denounce my opinions and writings everywhere. When I heard all this from certain trustworthy
men, who also said that the Theologians were intriguing
against me everywhere I decided to postpone the publication I was preparing, until I saw how the matter
turned out, and I also intended to inform you what
plan I would then follow. But the business seems to
grow daily worse, and I am yet uncertain what to do."

And so he continued to write and reflect in his lonely
retreat, working far into the night as his habit was till
two and three, and often not moving from his lodgings
for months at a time, though he used often to come
downstairs for a friendly word in the afternoons with
the van der Spycks. Once, his hostess, who was a
simple woman with the most profound respect for his
wisdom, sensing his aloofness, asked if she could really
be saved in her religion. Spinoza answered, "Your
religion is a good one. You should not seek any other
nor doubt that you will procure salvation if in attaching
yourself to piety you lead at the same time a peaceful
and tranquil life." On Saturday afternoon the 20th of
February he chatted as usual with the van der Spycks,
but he was feeling very ill, and retired early after
sending for his friend Dr. Schuller. Sunday morning

he was up and received the Doctor. The van der Spycks went to church believing there was no immediate danger. On their way home, they were told that he had died at three o'clock. He was buried near Jan de Witt in the new church on the Spuy.

Through the century subsequent to his death and during his life Spinoza was vilified as an amoral atheist and since the swinging of the pendulum there has developed an all too unmistakable tendency to regard him as an ascetic saint. Of course he was neither. Although he hated mere salvation-seeking his whole approach to philosophy was ethical and religious. His modest means made abstemiousness a necessity but he was no ascetic. He said "the wise man should use the things of this life and enjoy them as much as possible." In a remarkable passage of the *Ethics* (IV 45 Note) he who had never himself been able to enjoy such advantages advises the rational man to make the most of music, the beauty of nature, sports, the theatre and the other innocent amusements of life. Still he saw that nothing mattered but the inner life; so he was rather careless about the rest. When a friend wanted him to accept a better coat he asked, "What is the use of costly covering for a worthless thing?" The dominant trait in his character was his absolute devotion to the search for truth. To this he willingly sacrificed everything, worldly goods, preferment, even health. And yet what he sought was not mere abstract knowledge but the sort of wisdom that vivifies life. Indeed as he saw them life and the search for wisdom were one and the same,—the gradual expression of God the infinite in us the finite. For him God was no transcendant negative to be proved by miracles and worshipped by self-mutilation, but an immanent God here in us, proved by the eternal laws of reason, and adequately worshipped only by those who understand with an understanding merging into love.

METHOD

Spinoza's thought is so often associated with the rather rigid and forbidding form in which he chose to embody it that a discussion of his method is called for. How the mind may best achieve truth is the subject of the important treatise on the Improvement of the Understanding. Spinoza here takes Descartes as his point of departure. For Descartes the universe was essentially irrational. Not only was God's intellect subordinate to his infinite will so that he could, for example, will a circle to be square, but there was an essential discontinuity in things which made it possible to conceive legitimately of any number of things and nothing at all occurring at any moment. Thus the Cartesian universe was, so to speak, unable to stand on its own feet, and required, as Descartes himself saw and the Occasionalists later emphasized, the creative super-rational activity of God to maintain it perpetually. This is why in the end Descartes' clear and distinct ideas have to be justified by a super-rational faith; the universe is not intrinsically rational. Clear and distinct ideas are not their own guarantee. Some demon may be deceiving us! Spinoza clearly saw the circularity in the Cartesian position, and the utter impossibility of attempting to condemn or justify reason by anything except itself. He saw that reason must be its own guarantee, that truth must bear its own sign. For him the universe was inherently continuous and rational, and it was the very nature of the mind to know this order. It is indeed difficult to see how this assumption can be avoided if one agrees to think at all. Certainly it underlies all scientific investigation, since the scientist, no matter how

open-minded he may be concerning what he shall discover, nevertheless whatever it may turn out to be,
necessarily assumes it to be discoverable. Even though
he hold before himself the possibility that reality should
be opaque to reason, by his very act of investigation he
assumes that this fact is at least discoverable by mind,
and therefore that the universe is not ultimately opaque.
Now this assumption of the ultimate and necessary
rationality of things is the very basis of Spinoza's
thought. For him the universe is intrinsically rational
and it is the nature of the mind to know. Instead of
following Descartes in making the universe a chaos and
trying to justify God by what little order there is,
Spinoza saw clearly that out of chaos only chaos could
be derived, that if God cannot be justified by reason
there is no justification. As he so clearly shows in
his famous chapter six of the *Tractatus Theologico-
Politicus*, from our human point of view at least,—to the
human philosopher, reason is the basis of God, not God
of reason, for if reason in the broad sense cannot be
trusted, then nothing can be trusted, and we may as
well not think. Faith has its sphere in the practical life
of man as an instiller of obedience (chapter XV of the
Tractatus T-P) but it cannot give us truth.

On the basis of this fundamental assumption of an
inherently orderly and rational universe certain modern
conceptions of truth would appear absurd to Spinoza.
For example the idea that truth must be tested by something external to itself such as its "working" would
seem naïve, since what, it may be at once asked, is to
be the test of the working? Of course *ultimately* we
must come to the insights of the rational mind. This
must be always the court of final appeal. So we may
as well admit once and for all that the final test of
truth lies simply in the clear and distinct ideas that we

immediately perceive. If we cannot trust these, then all theories and all thinking fall into meaningless chaos, including our very distrust. There is nothing positive in error or falsity, since in the more inclusive standpoint from which it is seen *to have been* error it *becomes* true. Our minds naturally and inevitably know. It is only their finiteness and limitation that leads to such confusion that we fail to grasp the broader reality which includes ourselves. But when the larger view is achieved it becomes impossible to confuse our ideas just as it is impossible to confuse a circle with a square. Nor do we need to know that we know before knowledge and so on in infinite regress, since to know that we know we must *first* know. So the universe is rational and it is the very nature of the mind to know and know truly.

Now to know a thing is to know its cause or reason. It is important to remember that Spinoza does not use the word "cause" in the ordinary sense, but as the logical essence or reason of a thing, though this is also an active efficient principle like the rule or formula which as mathematicians say "generates" a series. If the universe is rational then everything must have such an active reason, and this reason can be known, and there are two sorts of reason. Either a thing may contain its own reason or essence, or it may have a proximate reason outside itself. Now ordinary things all have proximate causes outside themselves, but unless we are content with an infinite regress which leaves reality ultimately incomprehensible, we must finally come to something which is its own reason, which, in Spinoza's language, is "cause of itself" or "whose essence involves existence." Only if we can find such an object will the universe be *perfectly* rational. The very core of Spinoza's philosophy is his discovery and proof of such an object or "substance" which can exist in and through itself without depending on any outside principle and the scheme of the Ethics is precisely the scheme of the perfectly rational universe, starting as it does with the one self-caused substance and tracing all finite existence back to it, just as in reality all things (or modes) must be ultimately traced back to the single substance which is the cause of itself and thus does not have to be traced back to anything.

Now the era of Spinoza was the era of the beginnings of physical science and modern mathematics, and the whole world was impressed deeply with the success of the deductive method which viewed everything mechanically, and made everything follow with the same rigid necessity that we suppose *makes* a billiard ball move when hit by another, or *makes* 4 when we add two units to two. This also impressed Spinoza. This is why he constructed his *Ethics* on the geometrical model and sometimes seems to try to make one proposition follow from another with the same rigid necessity as a mathematical whole, which is nothing but the combination of its parts, follows from the nature of the parts. His thought, however, was constantly escaping from the rigid framework, and in various prefaces, appendices, and scholia which are among the most interesting parts of the *Ethics* he steps out of the system altogether and discusses the method and its results (E II App., and III pref), takes occasion to criticize current views (EI App. V pref. I 15 S, I 33 S, II 48 and 49, V 41S) or develops special interests of his own (IV pref Good and Evil, II 17 S error, II 40 S Common Notions, IV 35 S Asceticism, IV 39 S Alternations of Personality, V 10 S Value of Ethical Maxims, V 36 S Beatitude). The *Ethics* itself is certainly very much more than a mere deductive system in which the great mass of the work is nothing more than the various permutations and combinations of certain simple elements presented on the first few pages. And there are reasons for believing that Spinoza himself meant more by "logical necessity" than mechanical or mathematical compulsion. The very title of the *ethics*, for example, says "proved in geometrical order" not proved with geometrical *necessity*. Also in his rendition of Descartes' *Principia* Spinoza had used the geometrical method to *prove* propositions he did not in the least hold to be true, which surely indicates that he did not believe geometry to be the infallible way to truth. One of Spinoza's reasons for employing the technical machinery of proofs and propositions is undoubtedly its impersonality. Mathematics neither laughs nor weeps at its objects but seeks only to understand. This surely is the spirit of the *Ethics*. But it is very important to realize that the necessity which holds the propositions together and which Spinoza speaks so much of is *not* a mere mechanical necessity in which the whole is determined by the parts. The *Ethics,* as well as the universe it describes, is not a mere set of parts which combine to form a mechanical whole. The God which lies at the basis of the system does not determine the parts the way one billiard ball is supposed to determine another, but rather determines them the way the living purposes of an organism determine the actions of the hands, for instance, or the eyes by living freely in them. Thus, as Spinoza himself informs us, (E I 17) his necessity is perfectly compatible with freedom. And also I think it must be granted that in his mature thought at least his determinism is perfectly compatible with an immanent teleology or purposiveness (E V 35 and 36). This is certainly implied by his identifying Man's essence with "conatus" or striving, as well as by his constant use of the term "perfection" in connection with God (I 17 Cor. 1). The sort of purposes Spinoza argues against (Eth I Appendix) are the external purposes fulfilled by machines, for example, which lie altogether outside themselves, rather than the immanent purposes of an organism. From the ultimate standpoint of God the *Ethics* and the Spinozistic universe are free products, organic or purposive wholes rather than mathematical combinations. And finally reason for Spinoza is *not* the narrow geometrical process he sometimes makes it, but the *whole* of man's inner life. It is by means of the self-complete spirit that we must interpret the universe, not merely by one of its abstract phases.

GOD

Thus that the universe is rational in the sense of being assimilable by the human mind is Spinoza's basic assumption just as it is the basic assumption of all scientific activity. This rationality demands that everything must have a reason or a ground either in itself or in something else. We are all aware of the distinction between substances which stand alone and the properties which depend upon or inhere in them. Thus the blueness of the eye cannot exist apart from the eye which is a substance. But if we really think the matter through we soon see that the eye itself is only relatively able to exist alone, and that it in turn is dependent for its existence upon the whole organism or is in Spinoza's terminology not a substance at all but a mere mode. And then if we consider the human individual he turns out to be obviously dependent upon the existence of other organisms which are dependent upon the climate of the earth which is dependent upon the sun which is dependent upon the motions of the other stars et cetera, until we reach the whole universe. Only then do we seem to have a reality truly self-dependent. Anything we could fasten upon, short of the whole of things, would turn out to be intertwined with other things themselves interconnected with others until we should have the whole again. Now as Spinoza pointed out, this vast totality of things *must* exist because it is by definition all-inclusive. There is nothing else for it to be dependent upon. Therefore it must be its own reason for existing,—its own "cause." As Spinoza says (Bk. I prop VII) "its essence necessarily involves existence." What Spinoza is pointing to is the essential continuity of experience, the fact that reality is really one, that the sharp lines we draw between things are as a matter of fact artificial, that if we properly understand them we shall find them all to be interdependent and parts of one great interlocking system which *must* exist, since there is nothing outside it to limit it, or make it dependent. This result may be achieved by anyone no matter where he starts in reality, if he merely asks himself what may be supposed to be completely independent. He will find that he cannot logically stop short of the whole of things.

But so far Spinoza has only shown that *if* there is a self-dependent substance, its essence must involve existence. He has not proved that there is any such thing. This very fundamental proof is given in *Ethics* I 11. The first proof asks us to suppose that God does not exist, but such a God would be a contradiction since existence has been shown to be the essence of God or the *whole* of reality. Either there is no substance at all,— no reality, or God exists. This is the first proof. The second proof, like the first, depends on the fundamental assumption of rationality. If God does not exist there must be a reason why he does not exist. But this reason cannot lie outside of God since he is all-inclusive. Also it cannot lie in God since his essence is existence. It will be noted that both these proofs can be denied if we are prepared to assert that absolutely nothing exists. In the third proof we get Spinoza's thought in a form which protects it against Kant's criticism of the ontological argument, for this proof is *a posteriori*. *Something,* namely the inner process of thought we usually call ourselves does actually in any case exist. Spinoza here probably has Descartes in mind. *Something* must exist because in doubting or denying it I do thereby assert it. Suppose I deny myself. Then I exist because I am denying. Hence the finite self exists. But since a mere finite reality can exist, God must exist, since existence is a sign of power and the infinite Being is infinitely more powerful. The fourth proof given in the Scholium is merely the third stated in *a priori* form,— if any finite mode exists, then God must exist since he is infinite in power. Spinoza himself probably felt the *a priori* proofs sufficient, but to be invulnerable against later criticisms, the *a posteriori* proof is required. Spinoza's full proof then depends upon the existence of something finite. If one admits the existence of finite, dependent reality, the existence of God follows necessarily. But one cannot deny one's own existence since in doing so one asserts it. Hence God exists.

Furthermore, since the existence of God thus follows *necessarily,* he must exist eternally and not merely for a limited period of time, just as it is *always* true and *never* false that the interior angles of a triangle must equal 180 degrees. In other words, as Spinoza phrases it, "the existence of God is an eternal truth." And there is a whole realm of such eternal truths, for in so far as our intellect is able to know things as included in the nature of the whole of reality, we see them as embodied in his necessary perfection and therefore, as Spinoza says, "under the aspect of eternity" (V 29 Note). This is one of the most important of his conceptions. Time

is really an artificial barrier that arises from our finite
imagination and keeps us from seeing things properly
as qualifications or "modes" of the whole. Instead of
being given all at once, things are presented to the
imagination in the past or the future and separated from
us by seconds, years or æons. Instead of coming to
us in one great tidal wave, as they should, the waters
of reality are held back by the dams of our puny imaginations and only allowed to dribble over in a tiny
stream of time. But the intellect is able to transcend such
barriers and glimpse things as contained in God and
therefore as eternal. What could seem more evanescent
and perishable than a minute snow crystal melting on
the glass? And yet when we understand it, we see it not
as an isolated event but as bound up with an infinite
number of other such occurrences exemplifying certain
natural laws which express the nature of the universe
as a whole. Always as we come to understand a thing
we see it in relation to wider and wider perspectives
until finally we glimpse it as belonging to the very essence of the whole of things, or as eternal. This fleeting
moment, as belonging to the absolute totality of things,
can never die. Caesar as a necessary element in the
infinite organization of things is not dead, although
from the standpoint of our limited imaginations and the
minute portions of reality they have access to, it may
seem as if he has passed irrevocably. And so he has
from *our* worlds. But our worlds are only fragments of
the infinite whole. For us things come into existence and
pass away. For God they never die. All events are expressions of his infinite perfection. Like ancient dia-
monds they may be strung together in all manner of
finite combinations in our lives. But the jewels outlast
the finite strings and shine with an eternal light.

The absolute totality of things is not only eternally

existent but perfect or infinite. Spinoza means by infinity not the innumerable or uncountable but the self-contained or self-limited. Since reality is all-inclusive, therefore it must exist in the completest and fullest sense. There is no mere possibility, what we call the possible being a mere result of our ignorance. In actuality everything that could possibly overflow into being must do so, since there is nothing outside of reality as a whole to hinder it. This offers Spinoza a solution of the problem of evil (last page of I App.). The imperfect as well as the perfect must be included in the all-inclusive or ultimately perfect universe,—that is the universe would not be truly infinite did it not include within itself the finite.

Spinoza's God is also utterly unique (I 5) for since it is all-inclusive there can be no substance different from it in nature. And yet also indivisible (I 12) because either the parts into which substance would be divided would be infinite or finite. In the first case there would be many infinite, all-inclusive wholes, which is absurd. In the second case the infinite whole would be deprived of its essential characters and dissolve away into nothingness.

The whole first book of the *Ethics* deals with these and other properties of the infinite and eternal being which must embody all of reality, if the universe be thinkable in any sense. Such a being must exist if anything at all exists, and that something exists is asserted by the very denial. Since God thus exists necessarily, he exists eternally not merely now or then, and as all things exist in him, they also, when properly understood as embodied in the systematic whole of being, exist under the aspect of eternity. This great universal being is unique and indivisible rather than *one*, since number like time is only a convenient "mode of imagin-

ing" (Letter XII). It is infinitely rich in existence since
there is nothing to hinder or limit it. Therefore it has
poured out from itself as pure creative activity (natura
naturans) a complete and perfect world of things or
modes (natura naturata) in which every conceivable possibility is actualized. Although Spinoza often seems to
speak in the first book as if God remained outside his
modes and mechanically "determined" them (I 27, 28,
29, 33) this is not his real thought, for God is the
immanent, and not the transitive cause of all things
(I 18). He lives and moves in all his creatures and
is one with them. Their action is his action and "God
acts from the laws of His own nature only, and is compelled by no one" (prop 17); so that, though all things
are necessary in the sense that they arise from God's
infinite perfection, they are not *mechanically* necessary
in the sense of being determined by something outside
themselves (Letters LXXIII and LXXV).

ATTRIBUTES

From the discussion so far it will be seen that God
seems to exist in two ways, finitely in individual things
and infinitely in his all-inclusive self-sufficient totality.
The infinite aspect of God in which he exists perfectly
or self-sufficiently is his very essence or what Spinoza
calls "attribute." The finite, dependent aspect of reality
he calls "mode." Since God is perfectly inclusive or
unlimited it follows that he will be infinite in both attribute and mode. Hence Spinoza supposes that not only
are there an infinite number of finite dependent things,
but an infinite number of self-sufficient aspects in which
he makes these manifest, although only two of these,
extension and thought are known to our finite imagination. Every finite mode or thing such as a tree is thus
expressed under an infinite number of attributes or

aspects of which two only, thought and extension, are known to us. The tree, therefore, is not a mere object in space, but also expresses itself just as we do in thought and in feeling. Today Spinoza would be called a panpsychist, since he believed that mind is everywhere, not simply in the comparatively few and insignificant creatures we call men. This view is often called anthropomorphic as tending to read into other things merely human traits. No thinker in the whole history of thought has attacked anthropomorphism more vigorously than Spinoza (see especially I App.) or more assiduously guarded himself against it. And yet the idea of a low order of consciousness in such a thing as a rock, for example, seemed to him not only not anthropomorphic but thoroughly self-evident. For him the true anthropomorphism was the arrogation of such an altogether isolating uniqueness on the part of human beings. For him matter and consciousness, "outside" and "inside" were simply two aspects of God in both of which he equally expressed his essential nature. Each attribute is distinct in itself—muscle-twitches are not the same thing as feelings, but the attributes run parallel to each other, and everything that is expressed in one is expressed in the others, each attribute, since it is essentially God, being infinite or self-complete. Thus when we are in the realm of matter we must stay in the realm of matter, and when we start in the realm of mind we must stay in the realm of mind. It would seem perfectly nonsensical to Spinoza to try to explain feelings, for example, by muscle-twitches. The best sort of parallel is perhaps an infinite set of planes each expressing an identical but infinite modal pattern. But our finite imagination confines us to an existence in only two of these planes or attributes.

An infinite number of infinitely diverse worlds stretches out beyond our ken. Such is Spinoza's view of attributes.

And it is here certainly that the weak spot in Spinoza's system lies. In the first place, God is infinite or self-complete, and so each of the attributes must be infinite or self-complete or unlimited by anything outside itself. But each attribute must in a sense be outside the other attributes, limited by them, and hence will not express God's full essence. In other words, what Spinoza called attributes are really modes, for nothing short of God himself in the unlimited fulness of his being can really be supposed to express his essence. In addition to this point the complete parallelism which Spinoza supposes to exist between the attributes (II 7) breaks down. In particular there are certain crucial modes, in the attribute of thought which have no exact correlate in extension. For example, Spinoza implies that ideas of non-extensional, non-actualized objects exist in the mind of God (II 8). Also there is the "conatus" or "striving" which Spinoza defines man to be in essence. This seems to belong only to the attribute of thought, for extended things merely move, they do not "strive." Finally there is the unique fact of self-consciousness which belongs to mind (II 22) and mind alone. Spaces do not know, nor know that they know. It is only in thought that we find modes bound up into that sustaining unity which Spinoza identifies with God (V 24). In spite of what Spinoza says to the contrary (I 15) space remains a sum of parts, rather than an active, organic whole. Self-conscious thought is just such a unity in diversity. We must attribute the exaggerated importance given to space in Spinoza's system to the tremendous influence exerted by the growth of physical science on the mind of the time, which as we have also pointed out contributed to his use of the geometrical method. Why not a geometrical philosophy indeed, if space is one of the essential attributes of God, and the geometrical method works so well here? But as we have seen, Spinoza's philosophy simply did not allow itself to become incarcerated in a rigid mould. Thought is an active, creative principle (III 3) which lives in all its phases without compelling them. There is certainly something inconsistent in paralleling an organic process of this sort with the static diversity of space.

As is usually the case with Spinoza we find here that he himself at least implicitly recognized the difficulty and at least indicated the path to a solution, for it was precisely such difficulties as we have been discussing that his acute friend Tschirnhaus brought against the doctrine of the attributes (Letters LXV and LXX). How does it happen, asks Tschirnhaus, that thought which runs parallel to all attributes knows only that of extension? Spinoza replies that the divine thought (idea Dei) *does* comprehend all other attributes since the essence of thought is knowledge, and God's knowledge must be perfect (Eth. II 3 and 5). But then, as Tschirnhaus points out (Letter LXVIIIA), "the attribute of thought is pronounced to extend much more widely than other attributes." Thought comes to occupy a central position in the system of reality, and just as the whole realm of extension is contained in our knowledge of it, so are all the other attributes apprehended in the infinite mind of God (idea Dei). That Spinoza really did recognize the supremacy of thought as compared with the other attributes is further evidenced by the decreasing interest shown in extension, which certainly fades further and further into the background as the *Ethics* proceeds. Indeed, after the lemmas of Book II 13 the physical "attribute" receives no extended treatment. The interest shifts altogether to the inner drama, for the major concerns of the later books of the *Ethics* is the achievement of oneness with God, and this is obviously a spiritual process involving reason alone and the exfoliation of its own essence into other essences till the whole Divine system is grasped. For this there is no physical correlate, since the realm of extension is not made up of rational, eternal essences, but particular enduring things. There is no proper sense in which our body can become one with all space. Union with God is attained through thought alone.

MODES

Mode is defined by Spinoza as "that which is in another thing through which it is conceived." What he means will always be more adequately grasped if "modes" are read as "things," for as we have seen what we ordinarily consider things are not really things at all, but, like the eye, connected in the most inextricable fashion with the rest of the organism, with the atmosphere, the sunshine and ultimately, of course, with the whole universe. So that really there is only one "thing," the absolute totality of being, which is able to exist self-sufficiently. Everything else is dependent on this in the sense that we cannot adequately understand it till we have seen it in the light of the whole system of reality. It is most important to realize, however, that Spinoza does not in the least mean that the things we see around us are unreal. What he means is simply that their reality is dependent in nature. The eye, for example, is just as real as the organism on which it depends and without which it would not be an eye. Everything is at least to a certain *degree* real. But of course some things are much *more* real than others in so far as they come to embrace more being in their nature.

Thus we call a dream unreal when we awaken and reach a point of view broad enough to include the whole dream world together with many other things it cannot include. But nothing is lost. The dream world is not denied. It is simply placed in a larger context which subsumes it. Therefore what we call falsity or unreality is simply what Spinoza calls "privation" (II 35) and is nothing positive in itself. It is simply the lack of fulness or completeness which characterizes everything in various degrees, short of the infinite being of God which alone is perfectly and completely real.

The point cannot be too often stressed that Spinoza's God is really an immanent God who exists only in and through his modes and includes them rather than simply transcends them, like the Neo-Platonic God which was defined merely as the negation of all finite attributes. Spinoza is primarily the philosopher of rationalism, and there is no place in his thinking for transcendant or super-rational entities. How, he maintains, could such beings if truly inconceivable be even denied? But in spite of himself there are times when the differences between God himself and the finite modes become so impressive to Spinoza that he speaks of God as if he were something existing independently or in some way external to his modes and acting on them from the outside as in I 26. But as we have already said this is not Spinoza's real drift. His God is not outside things but always active and immanent in them to the degree in which they themselves embody reality. Even in the realm of extension, when one thing determines another, God is the *real* determiner for, though we trace the chain of causation back as far as we like, we shall never come to an end. We shall always find a particular cause for the first cause and so on. But there *is* an ultimate cause running through the whole chain of physical events.

something constant in the flux—namely the total amount
of energy (motion and rest) in the universe. This is
back of all events and remains always the same. It is
self-terminated and hence infinite—what Spinoza calls
an infinite mode. And the same is true of thought. Any
individual thought seems to have another thought as a
cause, and so on, but as a matter of fact God himself,
as the creative intellectual activity involved in all thinking, is the real cause (II 9). By his doctrine of infinite
modes which is treated in Propositions I 21, 22 and 23
which can only be adequately understood in connection
with Letters LXIII and LXIV and especially Short
Treatise (Part I. Ch. 9), Spinoza shows that he thinks
of God not as a passive abstraction but as a dynamic, active process moving in the world of matter and thinking
in the world of thought. This doctrine offers a striking
contrast to that of Descartes who held matter at least to
be purely passive so that all motion has to come outside
the world from the transcendant will of the deity. But
Spinoza's God can embody himself in the world as an
active, infinite mode and work in it, so that the world itself is not dead but alive with God. Letter XXXII contains perhaps the clearest and simplest exposition of Spinoza's organic view of the universe. A human being is
like a tiny cell in the blood-stream, thinking of the lymph
and the chyle and the other components of the blood as
being utterly separate and distinct entities, and taking
the changes of temperature and pressure around him as
ultimate inexplicable facts. Just so we live in our
environment and take the earth and stars and so on
to be separate entities changing and interacting in ultimately inexplicable ways. But this way of looking at
things is simply a result of our being tiny cells. If
we were only able to see the whole of things we should
see that the barriers we have created are artificial, that

all the seemingly separate things are parts of one great life and the seemingly inexplicable changes are all guided by its immanent action, which works through all for the realization of its perfection. This is undoubtedly the manner in which Spinoza conceived God to be related to his modes.

MAN

Of course of all the infinite modes in which the creative activity of God (*natura naturans*) expresses itself, the most interesting and important to us is man. Indeed as Spinoza tells us in the first part of his *Treatise on the Improvement of the Understanding,* the real motivation back of his philosophy is the practical interest as to how to live well, and so as the *Ethics* progresses we find the finite mode man coming to occupy a more and more prominent place in the discussion. Like all other things in our universe, though man is essentially one he is expressed under the two aspects of thought and extension, inner consciousness or idea and physical behavior or body. Spinoza often speaks as in II 13, of the body as "the object of the idea constituting the human mind," as if thought was a mere sequence of subjective conscious states running parallel to the central nervous system. But this is *not* Spinoza's view. It is the whole psychic life of the mind involving *both* subject and object which constitute the attribute of thought. And furthermore, what parallels this is not merely the human body. At first, in the early confused stages of thought this may be the case, but as our thought advances in scope, as we come to think clearly, we become independent of the body and our thought becomes one with the infinite thought of God ("idea of God") which is paralleled only by the whole extended world. Thus Spinoza would say that the body of him who truly understands things is really the whole physical universe, and his mind is the mind of God. But even though Spinoza thus clung to his early conception of a parallel extension, his discussion clearly shows that it is the inner life in which he is primarily interested, and from which he draws his leading conceptions. Thus after laying down the general principles of parallelism in II 7 he proceeds *first* to discuss the mental aspect and only secondarily its "object" or extended correlate. The parallelism of mind and body is really only formally adhered to. The body, or the objective "outside" of things is by no means able to duplicate the manifold oneness of our creative self-consciousness. It is like a shadow reflecting only the gross features of the original, after-effect rather than cause.

This becomes quite obvious when Spinoza comes to give the actual essence of man (III 6 and 7). This is the conatus or "the effort by which each thing endeavors to persevere in its own being." It is only from the inner standpoint that things can be said to "endeavor." This inner urge or will-to-live constitutes the essence of man and like God is thus not only a rational principle but an active one as well. Indeed, it is a part of the omnipresent activity of God as expressed through the active infinite modes of Intellect and Will, and Motion. In so far, therefore, as we express this inner urge, we realize our essential nature and live directly in God. But in so far as our action is not perfect or self-caused, —in so far, that is, as we are passive and determined by the external influences of other urges than our own, in so far is our essence negated and we fall lower in the scale of reality and goodness. Of course whatever happens is in God, and whatever happens in so far as it is real is an expression of God's perfection. But a mode may express more or less reality. In so far as its action is determined not by its own divine essence but by other essences, its own reality is negated and it becomes less real as compared with other modes. Spinoza's interesting correspondence with Blyenburgh gives the clearest statement of his ethical views. Here he explains that our human notions of good and bad arise solely from imaginative limitations which lead us artificially to separate things and to compare them with one another. From this standpoint some things obviously include more reality in their nature and are therefore referred to by us as "better than" things which embody less reality. Thus a blind man *from our point of view* is imperfect, but not when we see him as belonging to the infinite whole of reality, for this whole cannot be lacking in anything. The blind man is simply one of the possibilities that the universe in its infinite creative power has individualized. As such he is part of its perfection. Of course this is not to say that we may refrain from making moral judgments, for we are human modes, and thus must always, at least to a certain extent, imagine things in isolated chopped-up ways, and thus make comparisons between them. Thus from Spinoza's point of view we should not waste time lamenting over criminals and immoral persons who are as much a part of God's perfection as we. But we should pity them for being enslaved or negated by external things and for living in such a paltry way. Man's good is to express his essential nature, —to be most wholly and thoroughly himself. In so far as his own essence or "will to live" is subjected to other essences in so far is his life stunted and he himself evil or immoral.

Thus, for Spinoza, life itself is good, and the more life or reality we succeed in embracing in our essence, the more fully and richly we express ourselves, the higher are we in the scale of reality, and the better and more Godlike do we become. At first this theory sounds like a ruthless evolutionism. If life itself is the good, and the good for any single man is to realize his own essence or "will to live" and not be dominated by other wills, then is not life a sort of mad scramble in which we must pit ourselves against all others and fight to win with the Devil taking the hindmost? Is not all activity inherently selfish, and the whole purpose of life to dominate others as much as possible? Spinoza answers all these questions with a definite negative. The whole question hinges of course on just what this essence is whose expression is man's highest good. If the essence is a bare unconscious appetite then life is nothing but a blind struggle for existence. But we are soon informed (III 9 Schol.) that what he means by appetite is really conscious desire, and conscious desire, although Spinoza glosses over the difference, is a very different thing from mere blind appetite. The highest good of the mind is knowledge rather than the expression of mere impulse (IV 23 and 28). Only in thought does the mind really become free from external restraint and express itself. What Spinoza means is that no amount of animal action can help us to achieve our*selves*. We do not become free by merely squirming and writhing. Indeed a passionate action, whether successful or no but more in the degree in which it is successful, enslaves us to external things, for the passions are all directed outwardly. So the traditional "strong man" who believes that he has conquered the outer world by subordinating it to his passions has really himself been enslaved, for instead of expressing himself, his life is merely an arduous round of tasks imposed upon him by outer stimuli. Not he but the outer objects of his passion call the turn. Like the bully who inevitably absorbs the cringing attitudes of his victim, the "strong man" is conquered by the things he conquers physically, and in reality becomes not himself but only a partially diluted version of *them*. By blind interaction with outside things we only become confused and mixed. Not even in the imagination which seems to lead us to a thoroughly private world do we become completely free, for the imagination simply recombines together images that things have impressed upon us. It is only in perfectly rational, non-pictorial thinking that we truly escape from all converse with the finite modes around us and express our essential selves.

When we achieve such freedom we no longer act from "confused perceptions," representing a chaotic mixture of ourselves and other modes surrounding us, but from "adequate ideas" representing our own undiluted essence which is part of God. All our inner states (emotions) become transformed. We do not cease to act but we act rationally, and since our feelings are no longer the passive by-products of physical stimuli but part of our own creative thought, they are "active emotions" rather than "passions." And this free, rational action which is *our* essence is not in any sense particular or private. Indeed, the very form of thought is universality. The goods of the spirit are not like economic goods. It is not true that the more truth I possess the less truth somebody else possesses. The life of reason is necessarily a common life. "The highest good of those who follow after virtue is common to all, and all may equally enjoy it," (IV 36). The State, therefore, which renders men "mutually secure" and able to "feel mutual trust," arises from the rational recognition that for men to live in harmony it is necessary that they should forego the unlimited right to follow their desires which they possess in the state of nature. If men were solely guided by passion each would follow the direction of his own particular "conatus" and there would be no State. But men are rational. Hence they set up the State as a supreme power in order to curb the anti-social passions. Spinoza was certainly influenced by Hobbes in his political theory. But he differed from Hobbes in his clear realization of the fact that the State owes its existence to reason alone and serves solely as a means to the rational life. The State is thus in no sense an alien force imposed on individuals from without, but a consequence of their true, intrinsic nature; the Sovereign is not an external power, but an objectification of our deeper selves. A conflict between an individual and a State, therefore, is a conflict between the deeper rational side of our nature and passion, between illusion and reality. But as Spinoza says (Tract. Theo. Pol. Ch. XVI) the State is "only made valid by its utility," so that if the State ceases to perform its rational functions, "everyone has by virtue a right to break his compacts." Hence the great plea for freedom of speech which terminates the Tractatus. A State which fails to foster reason and the rational life ceases to be a State and becomes merely an organized passion. Revolution in this case becomes a necessity of reason which must always lead to a society of persons cooperating together for the sake of living the rational life.

Such a life whose realization is our highest good is not the externally dependent life of passion. This is not a life at all, but a mere medley of outside influences. Our true self is the rational self, and the whole purpose of life is to shake off the bondage of the passions, the pleasures and pains belonging to the narrow and chaotic self, so that we are determined by the rational good which is common to all men. The final and most complete stage of self-expression is the utter absorption of the finite self in God, when the State becomes the universe and there arises such a complete perfection of action as is sometimes achieved by the saint or citizen of God. At this stage all finite limits are left behind and all things are not only thought but also felt in the light of the Absolute. Love is no longer directed to anything external, for there is no longer any external. One simply loves God, and there is no question of a return, for "this is the very love with which he loves himself" (V 36).

In the *Ethics* it will be noted that thought, action, and feeling seem to merge. Spinoza saw clearly that the various faculties into which psychologists are apt to divide the mind are really artificial, that in reality our inner life is one. The essence of the whole, in so far as we can hope to describe it, is what he called "conatus" or the inner urge to action. Pleasure and pain are simply the heightening of pitch or lowering of pitch of this creative urge (III 59 Schol. defs. II and III), and all the passions are in book III derived from these components. Our psychic life is an organic stream of action, which may either be free and self-determined or a mere series of responses. It will be seen that Spinoza not only does not deny freedom but makes its achievement the goal of the moral life, for the essence of man is true thinking and only active thinking is true. We all know the difference between a reasoned opinion and a mere prejudice, which is not an expression of ourselves at all but merely of some hereditary or environmental influence which happened to have impinged upon us. The former only is an expression of our own unhindered action and is therefore free. Spinoza's polemic against "free will" (I 17, 32 and II 48 and 49 Cor.) is not a polemic against freedom, but against the special view of Descartes which separated the Will from all the other faculties and made it an ultimate, irrational force. Against this view Spinoza's whole system is really a polemic, for as we have seen, reality is for him rational through and through. So there can be no separation of thought and will in man. All action is purposive or ideational in character. There is no such thing as an act without any idea or purpose back of it, any more than there is any such thing as a sensation without any meaning or interpretation. The ideas back of our acts, the reasons we do things may be very confused, but there is always *some* reason. Similarly all thought is active. There is no such thing as a pure suspense of judgment, for the very suspense is an act. The logician or mathematician who thinks he is contemplating a purely abstract system without judging it to be either true or false is mistaken, for he is at least judging the *connections* to be true. These units he is asserting are such as must stand or fall together. There is no thought that is not assertion. Ideas are not mere pictures floating in and out of our mental atmosphere, but creative acts of judgment.

Thus for Spinoza thought and will are simply two aspects of the same identical reality. The sort of willing that we say is mere blind will, is not *altogether* blind, but is the sort of willing that goes with confused, inadequate ideas. And the sort of thought that does not seem to move us to action is again confused. If we *really* know the good we ipso facto *will* the same. And similarly the sort of knowledge which is purely abstract and has no feeling is again not *really* knowledge. We all recognize this in the case of the knowledge of human beings, for we call the comprehension of another human being "sympathy," something that implies feeling as well as thought. For Spinoza we cannot *fully* understand anything without will and also feeling. The highest knowledge is tinged with love. The aim of all our faculties is to extend ourselves and make ourselves one with God. In the moral life we project ourselves actively into the world and try to suffuse it with our inner selves. In feeling we are more passive, absorbing the outer influences into ourselves and so becoming one with them. But thought is the union of the two, for in thought we not only project ourselves actively into reality, but also reflect its essential nature. In thought the process is completed. Inner and outer are synthesized and we become one with God.

HUMAN BONDAGE

During the first part of the *Ethics* while we are being assured that man as well as the universe is essentially rational, it seems as if the path to blessedness ought to be fairly easy of achievement, as if we need only cast aside the veils that cover us and step out our true selves. But in the course of the fourth book the process is no such easy one. The road to freedom is no open highway but an arduous ascent and fraught with peril. It may be that this change represents the result of the fateful four years in which the *Ethics* was interrupted by Spinoza's entrance into the turmoil of contemporary politics and his tragic association with de Witt. Be that as it may, it is certain that a change had come over Spinoza and that the author of the fourth book was deeply convinced of the fatal weaknesses that so infallibly keep men from the way of reason.

Man after all is only finite man, and inevitably sees things confusedly by the flickering torch of his unsteady imagination. He is thus inevitably part of "the common order of nature," not the eternal system of reality, but the tiny little piece of reality, torn out of its context which is all that the finite imagination can know. As part of this "common order of nature" man is only one finite mode among many and "any individual thing being given, another and a stronger is also given, by which the former can be destroyed" (IV axiom). Hence the world of nature in which we are entangled keeps stimulating us and generating passions in us which are commensurate not with our natures but with the forces outside. And the only way in which we can control or counteract the enslaving passions is by means of other passions equal to these or stronger (IV 7). Of course our knowledge has an emotional side which can be used in this way for the achievement of freedom but the strength of this intellectual emotion depends upon our physical nature and not upon the truth of our knowledge (IV 14).

Also our knowledge as applied to ourselves, "the knowledge of good and evil" inevitably takes the imaginative form of time, so that many "good" things lie in the future and appear contingent, but our nature is such that we are far less strongly affected by remote and dubious objects than by those immediately confronting us. Thus it often happens that we have a confused conception of what we ought to do, nevertheless the forces around us are strong enough to overcome the recommendations of reason. In this way "the knowledge of good and evil" instead of leading us to freedom may simply generate in us an endless, useless conflict in which the better is ceaselessly overwhelmed by the worse. Indeed so agonizing may this struggle become, that men may even welcome philosophies of naturalism which simply abandon "the knowledge of good and evil" and allow men to follow their passions without painful qualms. In any case men become inevitably the slave of alien forces which play upon them with no rhyme or reason, igniting them to purposeless passions which tear them asunder and lead them on to war and hate

(IV 22 and 23). Buffeted about by such reasonless forces man ceases to be himself and becomes a mere plaything of fate. Losing control of his destiny he falls prey to the reckless caprices of nature and is led on to his lasting destruction.

THE WAY TO BLESSEDNESS

After all, this whole chaotic confusion is a mere product of the finite mind. In reality there is no mere dribbling stream of time, no "common order of nature." The "outside forces" which seem to overcome us are figments of the imagination, for in God there is no outside. "The knowledge of good and evil" may be inadequate. But the remedy is not no knowledge but more. We must come to see things in the light of pure reason (ratio). This is the first stage in the difficult but possible upward ascent of the soul toward blessedness.

At the level of imagination we merely combine pictures together in an abstract and eccentric way depending upon the haphazard associations of our private experience. Two things happening to fall together in our experience become associated so that the one leads us to think of the other although there may be no rational connection between the two. The imaginative pictures we form are merely due to the impact of external things on our bodies. Since there is room in our limited imaginations for only a finite number of distinct impressions, similar images blur together into what we call "universals" (II 18), such as "dog" or "horse." But such merely mechanical coalescences are bound to be confused and eccentric. Thus each man will have a different imaginative picture of the universal dog or man. Imagination gives us only a private, subjective world dependent upon impacts which chance to impinge on our bodies. But now suppose that there is a property present in each and every part of the material system, which is common to all bodies including our own. This we *must* perceive adequately since the fusion of external with internal will in *this* case not lead to distortion but mutual reinforcement (II 38 and 39). Thus in the case of extension, for example, the idea arising from perceptive interaction is adequate, because both our body and the outside object are extended. In this way the mind can, through intellectual effort, become cognizant of true universals or "common notions" as Spinoza calls them, which become the basis for true knowledge of the "second kind" which enables us to transcend the private and confused world of imagination. It is therefore a great mistake to suppose that Spinoza was a nominalist. It is only *abstract* universals formed by the mere fusion or loss of individual differences that he denies. The universals which are actually "properties of things" (II 40 s 2 part 3) which are "equally in the part and the whole" like "extension" and "substance" (II 37) form the foundation for that universal knowledge which is capable of lifting man above the subjective flux of imagination.

The second stage in the release of man is what Spinoza calls "ratio," or what we would call science. Here we are freed from our finite individuality and see things under "a certain form of eternity." In mathematics and physics there are no before or after and no finite, private entities, only a number of universal constants and variables related in various ways. It has no meaning to say, for example, that yesterday at two P.M. the interior angles of a triangle equalled 180 degrees. We are simply not moving in the realm of time but in the realm of eternal essences and laws. Starting with the "common notions" it intuits, the intellect deduces systems and systems of systems, unfolding itself according to the laws of its own nature, gradually building its world by its timeless proofs and demonstrations for "demonstrations are the eye of the mind through which it sees things" (V 23 s). Nor can there be any error in this self-development of the mind, for deduction is its own guarantee. Is not the mind itself a part of reality, and in thinking does it not realize its own essential nature? Furthermore at the level of ratio or science we have transcended our finite individuality, for intellect, like substance and extension, is a true universal or "common notion" actually living in all things, so that in so far as we think rationally or clearly and distinctly we think not with our mere private minds but with the mind of all men. At the level of science our mind is the mind of all intelligences and our body the physical system of things (facies totius universi). And thus we have transcended time and become eternal, for it is only individuals that come into existence and pass away. The universal remains.

But there is still something incomplete about scientific knowledge. The mind moves surely and unfalteringly, it is true, among its timeless essences, from one to another, but there is no sense of the system of universals as a whole. And also individuality must be given some place, for even an illusion *as* an illusion, *as* embraced in a larger *reality* must be explained. This concrete element the scientist of necessity ignores. He is interested in the common characters of all roses, while the concrete individual rose that blooms before us escapes his attention. It is really the synthesis of the last two stages, of imagination and science, that constitutes philosophy, or what Spinoza calls "the third stage of knowledge,"—"scientia intuitiva." This knowledge is more than imaginative perception for we now see the

individual in the light of the whole of reality which
science outlines but does not concretely fulfill. And it is
more than science because we see more than the common
properties, even more than the common properties which
actually live in persons and things. In philosophy one
sees the common properties *as living in* the particulars
which are in *no way* lost sight of. We see the whole in
the parts, and the parts in the whole. As Spinoza says
"as each person therefore becomes stronger in this kind
of knowledge, the more he is conscious of himself and
of God, of himself that is in God, and of God as in himself" (V 31 8). The science of abstract essences has left
the world of imagination for a higher world, but it is
not conscious of this fact. The individual scientist is not
sufficiently conscious of himself, and his own relationship with the intricate reality he knows. It is the task
of philosophy to make knowledge conscious not only of
the outside world but of itself, to bring back science
to the common life, to infuse science with the light of
concrete intuition. What Spinoza has in mind is the
difference between knowledge and wisdom, between technique and creative interpretation, between the virtuoso
and the master who has made his universal technique
breathe with the life of his own individual personality.
The scientist understands the universe as the thoughtful
and skilled physician understands a person. The philosopher understands as an artist understands. This is what
Spinoza has in mind in making the distinction between ratio and "scientia intuitiva," "the third kind
of knowledge."

Thinking is the very essence of the mind, but we may
also look at the ascent to freedom from the standpoint
of the Will, as the two are simply two aspects of the
same identical process. The level of imagination is,
of course, the level of passion. Just as our perceptions

do not proceed from ourselves but contain all manner
of external adulterations, so do our acts, instead of
expressing our own individual essence, proceed from
external stimuli to which we merely react. We are thus
the sport of circumstances and simply drift in passive
response to the tides of reality. But by becoming conscious of them thought is ultimately able to master the
passions in spite of the enormous difficulties which have
made such a conquest impossible for the vast majority.
By its ability to form clear and adequate ideas of
things, especially of the passions themselves, the mind
in the end can conquer. This does not mean that we will
cease to have feelings and emotions but simply that the
feelings and emotions will be *ours* rather than mere
stimulations from outside forces. Such emotions since
they depend on the free exercise of universal reason
will be constant and stable rather than in continuous
flux and will hence have an advantage over the inconstant passions (V 8, 11, 20). Furthermore, reason will
lay down moral principles in calm moments, applying
them, to imaginary situations, thus steeling the will
against catastrophe (V 10). Action at this second level
will be strictly subject to rational rule. But at the third
stage the self transcends such rigid maxims through
having completely mastered them. We are one with God,
but through this oneness we are most perfectly and
poignantly ourselves, for Spinoza's God is really an
infinite God in the positive sense rather than something
merely non-finite. His God is only infinite by expressly
becoming the finite,—hence in so far as we are truly at
one with God we become most truly ourselves. Thus at
the third level of action our conduct transcends all rigid
principles and we play on life as a great musician plays
on his instrument, using all rules and principles when
he needs them to embody the living essence of his per-

sonality, synthesizing concreteness and universality, in a oneness which sustains the two. At the third level we are more than finite modes for we have become one with God. Thus we are capable of neither jealousy nor envy. Indeed, as Spinoza says, "God loves no one and hates no one." And yet God loves, for love is an aspect of thinking, and therefore really the essence of God. So at the third level we do not cease to love, but we cease to love finite objects. We love objects not as mere objects but as expressions of the infinite, and we love persons not as men and women here and now but as embodiments of the Eternal. Thus our love is not extinguished, but pried loose from all mere finite objects, so that instead of this or that virtuous action we love virtue, and rather than this or that person we love God. Such love is that "amor intellectualis Dei" in which men find their highest blessedness.

Those who have reached this state of ultimate peace make no demand for a return of their love, any more than God makes a demand for a return, for love is of his very essence.[1] Blessedness itself is the achievement of all perfection in God, and hence it is senseless to talk of anything beyond it,—any reward. Blessedness is its own reward. One of the few angry passages in Spinoza's writings is in his letter to Orobio in defence of the Tractatus, where he refers to him who "abstains from evil actions and obeys the divine commands like a slave with unwillingness and hesitation, expecting as the reward of his bondage to be recompensed by God with gifts far more pleasing than Divine love, and greater in proportion to his dislike to goodness and consequent unwillingness to practise it." Such views

[1] Note. It will be understood that throughout this discussion the last part of the fifth book is being referred to especially 19-38.

were so odious to Spinoza that he could never speak of them without emotion. For Spinoza, as we have seen, Life itself in all its phases and manifestations was altogether good, and the idea that there could be any blessedness higher than achieving one's essential nature by becoming one with reality, could not but be repellent to him. The free man's wisdom is "not a meditation upon death but upon life." Consequently the eager searching for goods beyond life is not only foolish but immoral, since it leads to the stultification of ourselves at this moment where our opportunity lies. The free man who achieves blessedness has no need for a hereafter for he has already transcended time. Immortality is not mere everlastingness but a state of being. The genius is no longer constrained within his finite organism. Through his reason he has joined himself to the timeless order of the universe. He has freed himself from his earthly passions, and by attaching himself only to infinite objects he has himself become infinite. By becoming one with God the free man is himself eternal (Sh. Tr. II ch. 22).

ETERNAL LIFE

Spinoza is primarily the philosopher of immanence. God lives and moves in all things as their active rational cause. Thus for each existent object in space there is an eternal essence which may be apprehended by the mind as its moving principle. Thus the Platonic universals are brought down from their transcendent heaven, individualized and injected into things (See Imp. of Understanding, p. 37). The external essence of the body is what we call the individual soul or consciousness. The key to the understanding of human life really lies in the ambiguous position of this essence which participates both in the nature of extension and thought. On the one hand it is the essence of a particular body and must respond as it responds to the impact of external things. But on the other hand the essence of our body is connected with other essences in the infinite mind of God and by exfoliating itself according to its own laws (Ratio) may identify itself with this eternal system. Thus there arises the moral struggle in each individual soul between the passions which bind it to external things that partially negate it, and the urge to follow its own intrinsic nature and to identify itself with the mind of God which is outside time. If God were temporal his existence would increase from day to day. But he is complete and wholly actual. So he does not have to become. He is given all at once, as it were, and not piecemeal as mere modes. And the true essences of things are also eternal *in* God. It is only our finite imaginations that separate modes from their enduring and sustaining reality, and conceive of them as independent things. But such confusion does not arise from our true selves. It emanates only from the connection of our essence with a finite corpuscular body, which is subject to all manner of external influences. We become our true selves only through the agency of pure creative thought. If we could only shake ourselves free from the finite bonds that enchain us with matter, our minds would be adequate and able to stand by themselves. And death is precisely what so shakes us free. "The mind can imagine nothing nor recollect past things save while in the body." (V 21.) At death our body is destroyed and with it all connection with external body. Hence the private confused realm of the imagination is destroyed.

No longer are we confronted by the blurred and shifting panorama of the senses. No longer is the blessed man subject to the discordant reign of passion. The bonds which attach him to all the finite objects which he loves or hates are severed. Thus the finite, earth-bound self is destroyed at death. But the mind endures. The active rational self which is truly ours endures, for this is our very essence which is one with God. Death is like a purifying fire which devours every finite, material element in us, leaving only the pure spirit. Thus, just as there are various degrees of life, so are there various degrees of death. Those who have become inextricably intertwined with the things of time, have reason to fear it, for they will most certainly perish. But the wise man cannot die. For he has freed himself from the love of external things. His life, like that of Socrates, has really been a long continuous death in which he has completely freed himself from the temporal body and its connections. So that there is nothing left for what we call death to consume. Instead of joining himself with the body and its lusts, the wise man through his reason unites himself only with eternal things (Sh. Tr. App. II). He does not love finite things, but loves them only in so far as they belong to God. Finally he becomes one with the object of his thought and love which cannot perish (Tractatus T-P. ch. 4, p. 60).

There is no one who becomes so enmeshed in the body that he does not share at least infinitesimally in the clear consciousness of himself and all things. But there are infinite grades in the reality of different men, or in the degree in which they achieve free expression of themselves in God. We need the third kind of knowledge, Scientia Intuitiva, to answer this question of degree. Usually we realize immediately upon being confronted with a person whether he is higher or lower than we in the scale of being, whether his mind penetrates through ours and includes it, together with myriad other insights seeming at first strange and foreign to us but bearing in them the unmistakable stamp of truth, or whether his mind is merely a part of our own. Thus there is an infinite hierarchy of eternal minds, each mode being included in another which is included in another so that each occupies its appointed place in the divine system, and all taken together form the eternal and infinite mind of God (V 40 Schol.).

Such then is the hard and lonely way which the soul must take in order to loose itself from the trammels of finitude which bind it to the body, in order to realize its own essential nature and find its place in the eternal community of rational intellects which make up God. The person whose self is most real, whose eternal individuality is most concrete and valuable, is he who devotes himself most thoroughly and unswervingly to the search for truth—not mere theory but the knowledge that vitalizes conduct, not a life of mystic contemplation, but a life of intense activity filled with duties and pleasures. Such a mind which thinks truly becomes one with the real which it thinks. It does not lose itself in the absolute, but through its intimate relations with the rest of reality becomes more uniquely itself, just as ordinary words become ennobled by the functions they play in a glorious poem, and mean much more than when we see them in the pages of a dictionary. The isolated things we seem to see in the common-sense or imaginary world are torn from their context in precisely this way. We do not really understand them until we refit them together into the whole, any more than we can understand a language until we hear the living speech. For the man who achieves such understanding through the unhampered use of his reason, there is no longer any sense of increasing vitality (pleasure), for we have reached the goal of blessedness. We become no more. We simply are. Pleasure becomes "felicity" (beatitudo) and time eternity, not simply the going on for ever and ever, but a *state of being* which transcends time altogether. The wise man is not eternal in a remote hereafter. He is eternal here and now.

Such was the teaching of Spinoza. The deepest aim of his life was to discover something concerning the path to that "supreme human perfection" (Imp. of Und.) which it is the aim of all science to achieve. Not by any sort of passionate experience may we attain the goal, nor yet by abstract contemplation, but only through a unity of the two, in rational insight or intuition. But such intuition is not any more opposed to reason than it is opposed in the end to imagination, for without it reason becomes a sterile threshing of dead essences. It is only through the harmonious interplay of all our faculties under the guidance of creative thought that we free ourselves from the chains of matter and become blessed. In this state we do not cease to feel and love, but we feel and love only the eternal, for we are at one with God.

JOHN WILD

BIBLIOGRAPHY

A. Spinoza's known writings.

    I. Complete Books.

        a. the *Principles of Descartes' Philosophy*, with the *Metaphysical Thoughts*. Amsterdam, 1663.

        b. the *Theological-Political Treatise*. Amsterdam, 1670.

        c. the *Ethics* (first published in *Opera Posthuma*, 1677).

        d. the *Short Treatise* (the Dutch version of an original manuscript not meant for publication. First published in 1862).

    II. Correspondence (published in *Opera Posthuma*, 1677).

    III. Fragments (all published in *Opera Posthuma*, 1677).

        a. *On the Improvement of the Understanding*.

        b. the *Political Treatise*.

        c. the *Hebrew Grammar*.

B. English Translations of Spinoza's Works.

    I. *The Principles of Descartes' Philosophy*, H. H. Britan, Open Court, 1905.

    II. *Theologico-Political Treatise and Political Treatise*, R. H. M. Elwes, London, Routledge and Sons, 1895.

    III. *Ethics*, W. H. White and A. H. Stirling, Oxford, 1927.

    IV. *Short Treatise*, A. Wolf, London, A. and C. Black, 1910 (including an excellent biography).

    V. *Treatise on the Correction of the Understanding*, A. Boyle, New York, Dutton, 1925.

    VI. *Correspondence*, A. Wolf, New York, the Dial Press, 1927.

C. Commentaries in English.

    Joachim, H. H., *A Study of the Ethics of Spinoza* (Oxford, Clarendon Press, 1901).

    Knight, W., *Spinoza: Four Essays* (by Land, Fischer, Van Vloten and Renan. London, Williams and Norgate, 1882).

McKeon, R., *The Philosophy of Spinoza*. (New York, Longmans, 1928).

Pollock F., *Spinoza* (London, Duckworth, 1912).

Roth, L., *Spinoza, Descartes and Maimonides* (Oxford, Clarendon Press, 1924).

Roth, L., *Spinoza*. (Boston, Little Brown, 1929).

Wolfson, H. A., *Articles in Chronicon Spinozanum* (Hague, 1921 ff.)

SPINOZA
Selections

NOTE

IN THESE Selections the *Ethic* is printed entire (W. H. White translation), as is the *Improvement of the Understanding* (Elwes, Bohn translation). In the case of the *Short Treatise* (Wolf translation), most of the second part, which consists of an immature and largely Cartesian account of the passions, is omitted. It is believed that all the letters (Wolf translation) of real philosophic importance have been included. Although parts of the *Tractatus Theologico-politicus* are of great philosophic interest, this work together with the *Tractatus Politicus* is primarily of social and political significance, and is therefore omitted from this volume.

ON THE IMPROVEMENT OF THE UNDER-STANDING

AFTER experience has taught me that all the usual surroundings of social life are vain and futile; seeing that none of the objects of my fears contained in themselves anything either good or bad, except in so far as the mind is affected by them, I finally resolved to inquire whether there might be some real good having power to communicate itself, which would affect the mind singly, to the exclusion of all else; whether, in fact, there might be anything of which the discovery and attainment would enable me to enjoy continuous, supreme, and unending happiness. I say "I FINALLY resolved," for at first sight it seemed unwise willingly to lose hold on what was sure for the sake of something then uncertain. I could see the benefits which are acquired through fame and riches, and that I should be obliged to abandon the quest of such objects, if I seriously devoted myself to the search for something different and new. I perceived that if true happiness chanced to be placed in the former I should necessarily miss it; while if, on the other hand, it were not so placed, and I gave them my whole attention, I should equally fail.

I therefore debated whether it would not be possible to arrive at the new principle, or at any rate at a certainty concerning its existence, without changing the conduct and usual plan of my life; with this end in view I made many efforts, but in vain. For the ordinary surroundings of life which are esteemed by men (as their actions testify) to be the highest good, may be classed under the three heads—Riches, Fame, and the Pleasures of Sense: with these three the mind is so absorbed that it has little power to reflect on any different good. By sensual pleasure the mind is enthralled to the extent of quiescence, as if the supreme good were actually attained, so that it is quite incapable of thinking of any other object; when such pleasure has been gratified it is followed by extreme melancholy, whereby the mind, though not enthralled, is disturbed and dulled.

The pursuit of honors and riches is likewise very absorbing, especially if such objects be sought simply for their own sake, inasmuch as they are then supposed to constitute the highest good. In the case of fame the mind is still more absorbed, for fame is conceived as always good for its own sake, and as the ultimate end to which all actions are directed. Further, the attainment of riches and fame is not followed as in the case of sensual pleasures by repentance, but, the more we acquire, the greater is our delight, and, consequently, the more we are incited to increase both the one and the other; on the other hand, if our hopes happen to be frustrated we are plunged into the deepest sadness. Fame has the further drawback that it compels its votaries to order their lives according to the opinions of their fellow-men, shunning what they usually shun, and seeking what they usually seek.

When I saw that all these ordinary objects of desire would be obstacles in the way of a search for something different and new—nay, that they were so opposed thereto, that either they or it would have to be abandoned, I was forced to inquire which would prove the most useful to me: for, as I say, I seemed to be willingly losing hold on a sure good for the sake of something uncertain. However, after I had reflected on the matter, I came in the first place to the conclusion that by abandoning the ordinary objects of pursuit, and betaking myself to a new quest, I should be leaving a good, uncertain by reason of its own nature, as may be gathered from what has been said, for the sake of a good not uncertain in its nature (for I sought for a fixed good), but only in the possibility of its attainment.

Further reflection convinced me, that if I could really get to the root of the matter, I should be leaving certain evils for a certain good. I thus perceived that I was in a state of great peril, and I compelled myself to seek with all my strength for a remedy, however uncertain it might be; as a sick man struggling with a deadly disease, when he sees that death will surely be upon him unless a remedy be found, is compelled to seek such a remedy with all his strength, inasmuch as his whole hope lies therein. All the objects pursued by the multitude, not only bring no remedy that tends to preserve our being, but even act as hindrances, causing the death not seldom of those who possess them, and always of those who are possessed by them. There are many examples of men who have suffered persecution even to death for the sake of their riches, and of men who in pursuit of wealth have exposed themselves to so many dangers, that they have paid away their life as a penalty for their folly. Examples are no less numerous for men, who have endured the utmost wretchedness for the sake of gaining or preserving their reputation. Lastly, there are innumerable cases of men, who have hastened their death through over-indulgences in sensual pleasure. All these evils seem to have arisen from the fact, that happiness or unhappiness is made wholly to depend on the quality of the object which we love. When a thing is not loved, no quarrels will arise concerning it—no sadness will be felt if it perishes—no envy if it is possessed by another—no fear, no hatred, in short no disturbances

of the mind. All these arise from the love of what is
perishable, such as the objects already mentioned. But
love toward a thing eternal and infinite feeds the mind
wholly with joy, and is itself unmingled with any sadness, wherefore it is greatly to be desired and sought
for with all our strength. Yet it was not at random
that I used the words, "If I could go to the root of the
matter," for, though what I have urged was perfectly
clear to my mind, I could not forthwith lay aside all
love of riches, sensual enjoyment, and fame. One thing
was evident, namely, that while my mind was employed
with these thoughts it turned away from its former
objects of desire, and seriously considered the search
for a new principle; this state of things was a great
comfort to me, for I perceived that the evils were not
such as to resist all remedies. Although these intervals
were at first rare, and of very short duration, yet afterward, as the true good became more and more discernible
to me, they became more frequent and more lasting;
especially after I had recognized that the acquisition of
wealth, sensual pleasure, or fame, is only a hindrance,
so long as they are sought as ends not as means; if they
be sought as means they will be under restraint, and, far
from being hindrances, will further not a little the end
for which they are sought, as I will show in due time.

I will here only briefly state what I mean by true
good, and also what is the nature of the highest good.
In order that this may be rightly understood, we must
bear in mind that the terms good and evil are only
applied relatively, so that the same thing may be called
both good and bad, according to the relations in view,
in the same way as it may be called perfect or imperfect. Nothing regarded in its own nature can be called
perfect or imperfect; especially when we are aware that
all things which come to pass, come to pass according to

the eternal order and fixed laws of nature. However, human weakness cannot attain to this order in its own thoughts, but meanwhile man conceives a human character much more stable than his own, and sees that there is no reason why he should not himself acquire such a character. Thus he is led to seek for means which will bring him to this pitch of perfection, and calls everything which will serve as such means a true good. The chief good is that he should arrive, together with other individuals if possible, at the possession of the aforesaid character. What that character is we shall show in due time, namely, that it is the knowledge of the union existing between the mind and the whole of nature. This, then, is the end for which I strive, to attain to such a character myself, and to endeavor that many should attain to it with me. In other words, it is part of my happiness to lend a helping hand, that many others may understand even as I do, so that their understanding and desire may entirely agree with my own. In order to bring this about, it is necessary to understand as much of nature as will enable us to attain to the aforesaid character, and also to form a social order such as is most conducive to the attainment of this character by the greatest number with the least difficulty and danger. We must seek the assistance of Moral Philosophy [1] and the Theory of Education; further, as health is no insignificant means for attaining our end, we must also include the whole science of Medicine, and, as many difficult things are by contrivance rendered easy, and we can in this way gain much time and convenience, the science of Mechanics must in no way be despised. But, before all things, a means must be devised for improving the understanding and purifying it, as far as may

---

[1] I do no more here than enumerate the sciences necessary for our purpose; I lay no stress on their order.

be at the outset, so that it may apprehend things without error, and in the best possible way.

Thus it is apparent to every one that I wish to direct all sciences to one end and aim, so that we may attain to the supreme human perfection which we have named; and, therefore, whatsoever in the sciences does not serve to promote our object will have to be rejected as useless.[1] To sum up the matter in a word, all our actions and thoughts must be directed to this one end. Yet, as it is necessary that while we are endeavoring to attain our purpose, and bring the understanding into the right path, we should carry on our life, we are compelled first of all to lay down certain rules of life as provisionally good, to wit, the following:

I. To speak in a manner intelligible to the multitude, and to comply with every general custom that does not hinder the attainment of our purpose. For we can gain from the multitude no small advantages, provided that we strive to accommodate ourselves to its understanding as far as possible: moreover, we shall in this way gain a friendly audience for the reception of the truth.

II. To indulge ourselves with pleasures only in so far as they are necessary for preserving health.

III. Lastly, to endeavor to obtain only sufficient money or other commodities to enable us to preserve our life and health, and to follow such general customs as are consistent with our purpose.

Having laid down these preliminary rules, I will betake myself to the first and most important task, namely, the amendment of the understanding, and the rendering it capable of understanding things in the manner necessary for attaining our end.

[1] This primary, ethical motivation utterly separates Spinoza from Descartes in whom nothing of this sort is conceivable. [Ed.]

In order to bring this about, the natural order demands that I should here recapitulate all the modes of perception, which I have hitherto employed for affirming or denying anything with certainty, so that I may choose the best, and at the same time begin to know my own powers and the nature which I wish to perfect.

Reflection shows that all modes of perception or knowledge may be reduced to four:

I. Perception arising from hearsay or from some sign which everyone may name as he pleases.

II. Perception arising from mere experience—that is, from experience not yet classified by the intellect, and only so called because the given event has happened to take place, and we have no contradictory fact to set against it, so that it therefore remains unassailed in our mind.

III. Perception arising when the essence of one thing is inferred from another thing, but not adequately; this comes when from some effect we gather its cause, or when it is inferred from some general proposition that some property is always present.

IV. Lastly, there is the perception arising when a thing is perceived solely through its essence, or through the knowledge of its proximate cause.

All these kinds of perception I will illustrate by examples. By hearsay I know the day of my birth, my parentage, and other matters about which I have never felt any doubt. By mere experience I know that I shall die, for this I can affirm from having seen that others like myself have died, though all did not live for the same period, or die by the same disease. I know by mere experience that oil has the property of feeding fire, and water of extinguishing it. In the same way I know that a dog is a barking animal, man a rational animal, and in fact nearly all the practical knowledge of life.

We deduce one thing from another as follows: when we clearly perceive that we feel a certain body and no other, we thence clearly infer that the mind is united to the body, and that their union is the cause of the given sensation; but we cannot thence absolutely understand the nature of the sensation and the union. Or, after I have become acquainted with the nature of vision, and know that it has the property of making one and the same thing appear smaller when far off than when near, I can infer that the sun is larger than it appears, and can draw other conclusions of the same kind.

Lastly, a thing may be perceived solely through its essence; when, from the fact of knowing something, I know what it is to know that thing, or when, from knowing the essence of the mind, I know that it is united to the body. By the same kind of knowledge we know that two and three make five, or that two lines each parallel to a third, are parallel to one another, etc. The things which I have been able to know by this kind of knowledge are as yet very few.

In order that the whole matter may be put in a clearer light, I will make use of a single illustration as follows: Three numbers are given—it is required to find a fourth, which shall be to the third as the second is to the first. Tradesmen will at once tell us that they know what is required to find the fourth number, for they have not yet forgotten the rule which was given to them arbitrarily without proof by their masters; others construct a universal axiom from their experience with simple numbers, where the fourth number is self-evident, as in the case of 2, 4, 3, 6; here it is evident that if the second number be multiplied by the third, and the product divided by the first, the quotient is 6; when they see that by this process the number is produced which they knew beforehand to be the proportional, they infer that the process

always holds good for finding a fourth number proportional. Mathematicians, however, know by the proof of
the nineteenth proposition of the seventh book of Euclid,
what numbers are proportionals, namely, from the nature
and property of proportion it follows that the product
of the first and fourth will be equal to the product of
the second and third: still they do not see the adequate
proportionality of the given numbers or, if they do see
it, they see it not by virtue of Euclid's proposition, but
intuitively, without going through any process.

In order that from these modes of perception the best
may be selected, it is well that we should briefly enumerate the means necessary for attaining our end.

I. To have an exact knowledge of our nature which
we desire to perfect, and to know as much as is needful
of nature in general.

II. To collect in this way the differences, the agreements, and the oppositions of things.

III. To learn thus exactly how far they can or cannot
be modified.

IV. To compare this result with the nature and power
of man. We shall thus discern the highest degree of
perfection to which man is capable of attaining. We
shall then be in a position to see which mode of perception we ought to choose.

As to the first mode, it is evident that from hearsay
our knowledge must always be uncertain, and, moreover,
can give us no insight into the essence of a thing, as is
manifest in our illustration; now one can only arrive at
knowledge of a thing through knowledge of its essence,
as will hereafter appear. We may, therefore, clearly conclude that the certainty arising from hearsay cannot be
scientific in its character. For simple hearsay cannot
affect anyone whose understanding does not, so to speak,
meet it half way.

The second mode of perception [1] cannot be said to give us the idea of the proportion of which we are in search. Moreover its results are very uncertain and indefinite, for we shall never discover anything in natural phenomena by its means, except accidental properties, which are never clearly understood, unless the essence of the things in question be known first. Wherefore this mode also must be rejected.

On the third mode of perception we may say in a manner that it gives us the idea of the thing sought, and that it enables us to draw conclusions without risk of error; yet it is not by itself sufficient to put us in possession of the perfection we aim at.

The fourth mode alone apprehends the adequate essence of a thing without danger of error. This mode, therefore, must be the one which we chiefly employ. How, then, should we avail ourselves of it so as to gain the fourth kind of knowledge with the least delay concerning things previously unknown? I will proceed to explain.

Now that we know what kind of knowledge is necessary for us, we must indicate the way and the method whereby we may gain the said knowledge concerning the things needful to be known. In order to accomplish this, we must first take care not to commit ourselves to a search, going back to infinity—that is, in order to discover the best method for finding out the truth, there is no need of another method to discover such method; nor of a third method for discovering the second, and so on to infinity. By such proceedings, we should never arrive at the knowledge of the truth, or, indeed, at any knowledge at all. The matter stands on the same footing

---

[1] I shall here treat a little more in detail of experience, and shall examine the method adopted by the Empirics, and by recent philosophers.

as the making of material tools, which might be argued
about in a similar way. For, in order to work iron, a
hammer is needed, and the hammer cannot be forth-
coming unless it has been made; but, in order to make
it, there was need of another hammer and other tools,
and so on to infinity. We might thus vainly endeavor to
prove that men have no power of working iron. But as
men at first made use of the instruments supplied by
nature to accomplish very easy pieces of workmanship,
laboriously and imperfectly, and then, when these were
finished, wrought other things more difficult with less
labor and greater perfection; and so gradually mounted
from the simplest operations to the making of tools, and
from the making of tools to the making of more complex tools, and fresh feats of workmanship, till they
arrived at making, with small expenditure of labor, the
vast number of complicated mechanisms which they now
possess. So, in like manner, the intellect, by its native
strength,[1] makes for itself intellectual instruments,
whereby it acquires strength for performing other intellectual operations, and from these operations gets
again fresh instruments, or the power of pushing its
investigations further, and thus gradually proceeds till
it reaches the summit of wisdom.

That this is the path pursued by the understanding
may be readily seen, when we understand the nature of
the method for finding out the truth, and of the natural
instruments so necessary for the construction of more
complex instruments, and for the progress of investigation. I thus proceed with my demonstration.

A true idea (for we possess a true idea) is something
different from its correlate (*ideatum*); thus a circle is
different from the idea of a circle. The idea of a circle

[1] By native strength, I mean that not bestowed on us by
external causes, as I shall afterwards explain in my philosophy.

is not something having a circumference and a centre,
as a circle has; nor is the idea of a body that body itself.
Now, as it is something different from its correlate, it is
capable of being understood through itself; in other
words, the idea, in so far as its actual essence (*essentia
formalis*) is concerned, may be the subject of another
subjective essence (*essentia objectiva*). And, again, this
second subjective essence will, regarded in itself, be
something real, and capable of being understood; and
so on, indefinitely. For instance, the man Peter is something real; the true idea of Peter is the reality of Peter
represented subjectively, and is in itself something real,
and quite distinct from the actual Peter. Now, as this
true idea of Peter is in itself something real, and has
its own individual existence, it will also be capable of
being understood—that is, of being the subject of another idea, which will contain by representation (*objective*) all that the idea of Peter contains actually
(*formaliter*). And, again, this idea of the idea of Peter
has its own individuality, which may become the subject
of yet another idea; and so on, indefinitely. This every
one may make trial of for himself, by reflecting that
he knows what Peter is, and also knows that he knows,
and further knows that he knows that he knows, etc.
Hence it is plain that, in order to understand the
actual Peter, it is not necessary first to understand the
idea of Peter, and still less the idea of the idea of
Peter. This is the same as saying that, in order to know,
there is no need to know that we know, much less to
know that we know that we know. This is no more
necessary than to know the nature of a circle before
knowing the nature of a triangle. But, with these ideas,
the contrary is the case: for, in order to know that I
know, I must first know. Hence it is clear that certainty
is nothing else than the subjective essence of a thing:

in other words, the mode in which we perceive an actual reality is certainty. Further, it is also evident that, for the certitude of truth, no further sign is necessary beyond the possession of a true idea:[1] for, as I have shown, it is not necessary to know that we know that we know. Hence, again, it is clear that no one can know the nature of the highest certainty, unless he possesses an adequate idea, or the subjective essence of a thing: for certainty is identical with such subjective essence. Thus, as the truth needs no sign—it being sufficient to possess the subjective essence of things, or, in other words, the ideas of them, in order that all doubts may be removed—it follows that the true method does not consist in seeking for the signs of truth after the acquisition of the idea, but that the true method teaches us the order in which we should seek for truth itself, or the subjective essences of things, or ideas, for all these expressions are synonymous. Again, method must necessarily be concerned with reasoning or understanding— I mean, method is not identical with reasoning in the search for causes, still less is it the comprehension of the causes of things: it is the discernment of a true idea, by distinguishing it from other perceptions and by investigating its nature in order that we may thus know our power of understanding, and may so train our mind that it may, by a given standard, comprehend whatsoever is intelligible, by laying down certain rules as aids, and by avoiding useless mental exertion.

Whence we may gather that method is nothing else than reflective knowledge, or the idea of an idea; and that as there can be no idea of an idea—unless an idea exists previously—there can be no method without a

[1] This unmitigated rationalism is stated with peculiar cogency here and elsewhere in this treatise. It is implied in all of Spinoza's thought. [Ed.]

pre-existent idea. Therefore, that will be a good method which shows us how the mind should be directed, according to the standard of the given true idea.

Again, seeing that the ratio existing between two ideas is the same as the ratio between the actual realities corresponding to those ideas, it follows that the reflective knowledge which has for its object the most perfect being is more excellent than reflective knowledge concerning other objects—in other words, that method will be most perfect which affords the standard of the given idea of the most perfect being whereby we may direct our mind. We thus easily understand how, in proportion as it acquires new ideas, the mind simultaneously acquires fresh instruments for pursuing its inquiries further. For we may gather from what has been said, that a true idea must necessarily first of all exist in us as a natural instrument; and that when this idea is apprehended by the mind, it enables us to understand the difference existing between itself and all other perceptions. In this, one part of the method consists.

Now it is clear that the mind apprehends itself better in proportion as it understands a greater number of natural objects; it follows, therefore, that this portion of the method will be more perfect in proportion as the mind attains to the comprehension of a greater number of objects, and that it will be absolutely perfect when the mind gains a knowledge of the absolutely perfect being or becomes conscious thereof. Again, the more things the mind knows, the better does it understand its own strength and the order of nature; by increased self-knowledge it can direct itself more easily, and lay down rules for its own guidance; and, by increased knowledge of nature, it can more easily avoid what is useless.

And this is the sum total of method, as we have

already stated. We may add that the idea in the world of thought is in the same case as its correlate in the world of reality. If, therefore, there be anything in nature which is without connection with any other thing, and if we assign to it a subjective essence, which would in every way correspond to the objective reality, the subjective essence would have no connection with any other ideas—in other words, we could not draw any conclusion with regard to it. On the other hand, those things which are connected with others—as all things that exist in nature—will be understood by the mind, and their subjective essences will maintain the same mutual relations as their objective realities—that is to say, we shall infer from these ideas other ideas, which will in turn be connected with others, and thus our instruments for proceeding with our investigation will increase. This is what we are endeavoring to prove. Further, from what has just been said—namely, that an idea must, in all respects, correspond to its correlate in the world of reality—it is evident that, in order to reproduce in every respect the faithful image of nature, our mind must deduce all its ideas from the idea which represents the origin and source of the whole of nature, so that it may itself become the source of other ideas.

It may, perhaps, provoke astonishment that, after having said that the good method is that which teaches us to direct our mind according to the standard of the given true idea, we should prove our point by reasoning, which would seem to indicate that it is not self-evident. We may, therefore, be questioned as to the validity of our reasoning. If our reasoning be sound, we must take as a starting point a true idea. Now, to be certain that our starting point is really a true idea, we need a proof. This first course of reasoning must be supported by a second, the second by a third, and so on to infinity. To

this I make answer that, if by some happy chance anyone had adopted this method in his investigations of
nature—that is, if he had acquired new ideas in the
proper order, according to the standard of the original
true idea, he would never have doubted of the truth of
his knowledge, inasmuch as truth, as we have shown,
makes itself manifest, and all things would flow, as it
were, spontaneously toward him. But as this never, or
rarely, happens, I have been forced so to arrange my
proceedings, that we may acquire by reflection and fore-
thought what we cannot acquire by chance, and that it
may at the same time appear that, for proving the truth,
and for valid reasoning, we need no other means than
the truth and valid reasoning themselves: for by valid
reasoning I have established valid reasoning, and, in like
measure, I seek still to establish it. Moreover, this is
the order of thinking adopted by men in their inward
meditations. The reasons for its rare employment in
investigations of nature are to be found in current misconceptions, whereof we shall examine the causes hereafter in our philosophy. Moreover, it demands, as we
shall show, a keen and accurate discernment. Lastly, it
is hindered by the conditions of human life, which are,
as we have already pointed out, extremely changeable.
There are also other obstacles, which we will not here
inquire into.

If any one asks why I have not at the starting point
set forth all the truths of nature in their due order,
inasmuch as truth is self-evident, I reply by warning
him not to reject as false any paradoxes he may find
here, but to take the trouble to reflect on the chain of
reasoning by which they are supported; he will then
be no longer in doubt that we have attained to the
truth. This is why I have begun as above.

If there yet remains some sceptic, who doubts of our

primary truth, and of all deductions we make, taking such truth as our standard, he must either be arguing in bad faith, or we must confess that there are men in complete mental blindness either innate or due to misconceptions—that is, to some external influence.

Such persons are not conscious of themselves. If they affirm or doubt anything, they know not that they affirm or doubt; they say that they know nothing, and they say that they are ignorant of the very fact of their knowing nothing. Even this they do not affirm absolutely, they are afraid of confessing that they exist, so long as they know nothing; in fact, they ought to remain dumb, for fear of haply supposing something which should smack of truth. Lastly, with such persons, one should not speak of sciences; for, in what relates to life and conduct, they are compelled by necessity to suppose that they exist, and seek their own advantage, and often affirm and deny, even with an oath. If they deny, grant, or gainsay, they know not that they deny, grant, or gainsay, so that they ought to be regarded as automata, utterly devoid of intelligence.

Let us now return to our proposition. Up to the present we have, first, defined the end to which we desire to direct all our thoughts; secondly, we have determined the mode of perception best adapted to aid us in attaining our perfection; thirdly, we have discovered the way which our mind should take, in order to make a good beginning—namely, that it should use every true idea as a standard in pursuing its inquiries according to fixed rules. Now, in order that it may thus proceed, our method must furnish us, first, with a means of distinguishing a true idea from all other perceptions, and enabling the mind to avoid the latter; secondly, with rules for perceiving unknown things according to the standard of the true idea; thirdly, with an order which enables us to avoid useless labor. When we became acquainted with this method, we saw that, fourthly, it would be perfect when we had attained to the idea of the absolutely perfect Being. This is an observation which should be made at the outset, in order that we may arrive at the knowledge of such a being more quickly.

Let us then make a beginning with the first part of the method, which is, as we have said, to distinguish and separate the true idea from other perceptions, and to keep the mind from confusing with true ideas those which are false, fictitious, and doubtful. I intend to dwell on this point at length, partly to keep a distinction so necessary before the reader's mind, and also because there are some who doubt of true ideas, through not having attended to the distinction between a true perception and all others. Such persons are like men who, while they are awake, doubt not that they are awake, but afterward in a dream, as often happens, thinking that they are surely awake, and then finding that they were in error, become doubtful even of being awake. This state of mind arises through neglect of the distinction between sleeping and waking.

Meanwhile, I give warning that I shall not here give the essence of every perception, and explain it through its proximate cause. Such work lies in the province of philosophy. I shall confine myself to what concerns method—that is, to the character of fictitious, false, and doubtful perception, and the means of freeing ourselves therefrom. Let us then first inquire into the nature of a fictitious idea.

Every perception has for its object either a thing considered as existing, or solely the essence of a thing. Now "fiction" is chiefly occupied with things considered as existing. I will, therefore, consider these first—I mean cases where only the existence of an object is

feigned, and the thing thus feigned is understood, or
assumed to be understood. For instance, I feign that
Peter, whom I know to have gone home, is gone to see
me, or something of that kind. With what is such an
idea concerned? It is concerned with things possible,
and not with things necessary or impossible. I call a
thing IMPOSSIBLE, when its existence would imply a contradiction; NECESSARY, when its non-existence would
imply a contradiction; POSSIBLE, when neither its existence nor its non-existence imply a contradiction, but
when the necessity or impossibility of its nature depends
on causes unknown to us, while we feign that it exists.
If the necessity or impossibility of its existence depending on external causes were known to us, we could not
form any fictitious hypothesis about it; whence it follows
that if there be a God or omniscient Being, such an
one cannot form fictitious hypotheses. For, as regards
ourselves, when I know that I exist, I cannot hypothesize
that I exist or do not exist, any more than I can hypothesize an elephant that can go through the eye of a
needle; nor when I know the nature of God, can I hypothesize that he exists or does not exist. The same
thing must be said of the Chimæra, whereof the nature
implies a contradiction. From these considerations, it is
plain, as I have already stated, that fiction cannot be
concerned with eternal truths.

But before proceeding further, I must remark, in passing, that the difference between the essence of one
thing and the essence of another thing is the same as
that which exists between the reality or existence of one
thing and the reality or existence of another; therefore,
if we wished to conceive the existence, for example, of
Adam, simply by means of existence in general, it would
be the same as if, in order to conceive his existence, we
went back to the nature of being, so as to define Adam

as a being. Thus, the more existence is conceived generally, the more is it conceived confusedly, and the more
easily can it be ascribed to a given object. Contrariwise,
the more it is conceived particularly, the more is it
understood clearly, and the less liable is it to be ascribed, through negligence of Nature's order, to anything
save its proper object. This is worthy of remark.

We now proceed to consider those cases which are
commonly called fictions, though we clearly understand
that the thing is not as we imagine it. For instance, I
know that the earth is round, but nothing prevents my
telling people that it is a hemisphere, and that it is like
a half apple carved in relief on a dish; or, that the sun
moves round the earth, and so on. However, examina-
tion will show us that there is nothing here inconsistent
with what has been said, provided we first admit that
we may have made mistakes, and be now conscious of
them; and, further, that we can hypothesize, or at least
suppose, that others are under the same mistake as ourselves, or can, like us, fall under it. We can, I repeat,
thus hypothesize so long as we see no impossibility.
Thus, when I tell anyone that the earth is not round,
etc., I merely recall the error which I perhaps made
myself, or which I might have fallen into, and afterward
I hypothesize that the person to whom I tell it is still,
or may still fall under the same mistake. This I say,
I can feign so long as I do not perceive any impossibility or necessity; if I truly understood either one or
the other I should not be able to feign, and I should be
reduced to saying that I had made the attempt.

It remains for us to consider hypotheses made in
problems, which sometimes involve impossibilities. For
instance, when we say—let us assume that this burning
candle is not burning, or, let us assume that it burns in
some imaginary space, or where there are no physical

objects. Such assumptions are freely made, though the last is clearly seen to be impossible. But, though this be so, there is no fiction in the case. For, in the first case, I have merely recalled to memory another candle not burning, or conceived the candle before me as without a flame, and then I understand as applying to the latter, leaving its flame out of the question, all that I think of the former. In the second case, I have merely to abstract my thoughts from the objects surrounding the candle, for the mind to devote itself to the contemplation of the candle singly looked at in itself only; I can then draw the conclusion that the candle contains in itself no cause for its own destruction, so that if there were no physical objects the candle, and even the flame, would remain unchangeable, and so on. Thus there is here no fiction, but true and bare assertions.

Let us now pass on to the fictions concerned with essences only, or with some reality or existence simultaneously. Of these we must specially observe that in proportion as the mind's understanding is smaller, and its experience multiplex, so will its power of coining fictions be larger, whereas, as its understanding increases, its capacity for entertaining fictitious ideas becomes less. For instance, in the same way as we are unable, while we are thinking, to feign that we are thinking or not thinking, so, also, when we know the nature of body we cannot imagine an infinite fly; or, when we know the nature of the soul, we cannot imagine it as square, though anything may be expressed verbally. But, as we said above, the less men know of nature the more easily can they coin fictitious ideas, such as trees speaking, men instantly changed into stones, or into fountains, ghosts appearing in mirrors, something issuing from nothing, even gods changed into beasts and men, and infinite other absurdities of the same kind.

Some persons think, perhaps, that fiction is limited by fiction, and not by understanding; in other words, after I have formed some fictitious idea, and have affirmed of my own free will that it exists under a certain form in nature, I am thereby precluded from thinking of it under any other form. For instance, when I have feigned (to repeat their argument) that the nature of body is of a certain kind, and have of my own free will desired to convince myself that it actually exists under this form, I am no longer able to hypothesize that a fly, for example, is infinite; so, when I have hypothesized the essence of the soul, I am not able to think of it as square, etc. But these arguments demand further inquiry. First, their upholders must either grant or deny that we can understand anything. If they grant it, then necessarily the same must be said of understanding as is said of fiction. If they deny it, let us, who know that we do know something, see what they mean. They assert that the soul can be conscious of, and perceive in a variety of ways, not itself nor things which exist, but only things which are neither in itself nor anywhere else, in other words, that the soul can, by its unaided power, create sensations or ideas unconnected with things. In fact, they regard the soul as a sort of god. Further, they assert that we or our soul have such freedom that we can constrain ourselves, or our soul, or even our soul's freedom. For, after it has formed a fictitious idea, and has given its assent thereto, it cannot think or feign it in any other manner, but is constrained by the first fictitious idea to keep all its other thoughts in harmony therewith. Our opponents are thus driven to admit, in support of their fiction, the absurdities which I have just enumerated; and which are not worthy of rational refutation.

While leaving such persons in their error, we will

take care to derive from our argument with them a truth serviceable for our purpose, namely, that the mind, in paying attention to a thing hypothetical or false, so as to meditate upon it and understand it, and derive the proper conclusions in due order therefrom, will readily discover its falsity; and if the thing hypothetical be in its nature true, and the mind pays attention to it, so as to understand it, and deduce the truths which are derivable from it, the mind will proceed with an uninterrupted series of apt conclusions; in the same way as it would at once discover (as we showed just now) the absurdity of a false hypothesis, and of the conclusions drawn from it.

We need, therefore, be in no fear of forming hypotheses, so long as we have a clear and distinct perception of what is involved. For, if we were to assert, haply, that men are suddenly turned into beasts, the statement would be extremely general, so general that there would be no conception, that is, no idea or connection of subject and predicate, in our mind. If there were such a conception we should at the same time be aware of the means and the causes whereby the event took place. Moreover, we pay no attention to the nature of the subject and the predicate. Now, if the first idea be not fictitious, and if all the other ideas be deduced therefrom, our hurry to form fictitious ideas will gradually subside. Further, as a fictitious idea cannot be clear and distinct, but is necessarily confused, and as all confusion arises from the fact that the mind has only partial knowledge of a thing either simple or complex, and does not distinguish between the known and the unknown, and, again, that it directs its attention promiscuously to all parts of an object at once without making distinctions, it follows, FIRST, that if the idea be of something very simple, it must necessarily be clear and distinct. For a very simple object cannot be known in part, it must either be known altogether or not at all. SECONDLY, it follows that if a complex object be divided by thought into a number of simple component parts, and if each part be regarded separately, all confusion will disappear. THIRDLY, it follows that fiction cannot be simple, but is made up of the blending of several confused ideas of diverse objects or actions existent in nature, or rather is composed of attention [1] directed to all such ideas at once, and unaccompanied by any mental assent.

Now a fiction that was simple would be clear and distinct, and therefore true, also a fiction composed only of distinct ideas would be clear and distinct, and therefore true. For instance, when we know the nature of the circle and the square, it is impossible for us to blend together these two figures, and to hypothesize a square circle, any more than a square soul, or things of that kind. Let us shortly come to our conclusion, and again repeat that we need have no fear of confusing with true ideas that which is only a fiction. As for the first sort of fiction of which we have already spoken, when a thing is clearly conceived, we saw that if the existence of that thing is in itself an eternal truth, fiction can have no part in it; but if the existence of the thing conceived be not an eternal truth, we have only to be careful that such existence be compared to the thing's essence, and to consider the order of nature. As for the second sort of fiction, which we stated to be the result of simultaneously directing the attention, without the

[1] Observe that fiction regarded in itself, differs only from dreams in that in the latter we do not perceive the external causes which we perceive through the senses while awake. It has hence been inferred that representations occurring in sleep have no connection with objects external to us. We shall presently see that error is the dreaming of a waking man; if it reaches a certain pitch it becomes delirium.

assent of the intellect, to different confused ideas representing different things and actions existing in nature, we have seen that an absolutely simple thing cannot be feigned, but must be understood, and that a complex thing is in the same case if we regard separately the simple parts whereof it is composed; we shall not even be able to hypothesize any untrue action concerning such objects, for we shall be obliged to consider at the same time the causes and the manner of such action.

These matters being thus understood, let us pass on to consider the false idea, observing the objects with which it is concerned, and the means of guarding ourselves from falling into false perceptions. Neither of these tasks will present much difficulty, after our inquiry concerning fictitious ideas. The false idea only differs from the fictitious idea in the fact of implying a mental assent—that is as we have already remarked, while the representations are occurring, there are no causes present to us, wherefrom, as in fiction, we can conclude that such representations do not arise from external objects, in fact it is much the same as dreaming with our eyes open, or while awake. Thus a false idea is concerned with (or to speak more correctly), attributable to the existence of a thing whereof the essence is known, or the essence itself, in the same way as a fictitious idea. If attributable to the existence of the thing, it is corrected in the same way as a fictitious idea under similar circumstances. If attributable to the essence, it is likewise corrected in the same way as a fictitious idea. For if the nature of the thing known implies necessary existence, we cannot possibly be in error with regard to its existence; but if the nature of the thing be not an eternal truth, like its essence, but contrariwise, the necessity or impossibility of its existence depends on external causes, then we must follow the same course as we adopted in the case of fiction, for it is corrected in the same manner. As for false ideas concerned with essences, or even with actions, such perceptions are necessarily always confused, being compounded of different confused perceptions of things existing in nature, as, for instance, when men are persuaded that deities are present in woods, in statues, in brute beasts, and the like; that there are bodies which, by their composition alone, give rise to intellect; that corpses reason, walk about and speak; that God is deceived, and so on. But ideas which are clear and distinct can never be false: for ideas of things clearly and distinctly conceived are either very simple themselves, or are compounded from very simple ideas—that is, are deduced therefrom. The impossibility of a very simple idea being false is evident to every one who understands the nature of truth or understanding and of falsehood.

As regards that which constitutes the reality of truth, it is certain that a true idea is distinguished from a false one, not so much by its extrinsic object as by its intrinsic nature. If an architect conceives a building properly constructed, though such a building may never have existed, and may never exist, nevertheless the idea is true; and the idea remains the same, whether it be put into execution or not. On the other hand, if any one asserts, for instance, that Peter exists, without knowing whether Peter really exists or not, the assertion, as far as its asserter is concerned, is false, or not true, even though Peter actually does exist. The assertion that Peter exists is true only with regard to him who knows for certain that Peter does exist. Whence it follows that there is in ideas something real, whereby the true are distinguished from the false. This in reality must be inquired into, if we are to find the best standard of truth (we have said that we ought to determine our thoughts by the given standard of a true idea, and that method is reflective knowledge), and to know the properties of our understanding. Neither must we say that the difference between true and false arises from the fact that true knowledge consists in knowing things through their primary causes, wherein it is totally different from false knowledge, as I have just explained it: for thought is said to be true, if it involves subjectively the essence of any principle which has no cause, and is known through itself and in itself. Wherefore the reality (*forma*) of true thought must exist in the thought itself, without reference to other thoughts; it does not acknowledge the object as its cause, but must depend on the actual power and nature of the understanding. For, if we suppose that the understanding has perceived some new entity which has never existed, as some conceive the understanding of God before He created things (a perception which certainly could not arise from any object), and has legitimately deduced other thoughts from the said perception, all such thoughts would be true, without being determined by any external object; they would depend solely on the power and nature of the understanding. Thus, that which constitutes the reality of a true thought must be sought in the thought itself and deduced from the nature of the understanding. In order to pursue our investigation, let us confront ourselves with some TRUE idea, whose object we know for certain to be dependent on our power of thinking, and to have nothing corresponding to it in nature. With an idea of this kind before us, we shall, as appears from what has just been said, be more easily able to carry on the research we have in view. For instance, in order to form the conception of a sphere, I invent a cause at my pleasure—namely, a semicircle revolving round its centre, and thus producing a sphere. This is indisputably

a true idea; and, although we know that no sphere in
nature has ever actually been so formed, the perception
remains true, and is the easiest manner of conceiving
a sphere. We must observe that this perception asserts
the rotation of a semicircle—which assertion would be
false, if it were not associated with the conception
of a sphere, or of a cause determining a motion of
the kind, or absolutely, if the assertion were isolated.
The mind would then only tend to the affirmation of
the sole motion of a semicircle which is not contained in
the conception of a semicircle, and does not arise from the
conception of any cause capable of producing such
motion.

Thus FALSITY consists only in this, that something is
affirmed of a thing, which is not contained in the conception we have formed of that thing, as motion or rest
of a semicircle. Whence it follows that simple ideas cannot be other than TRUE—e.g., the simple idea of a semicircle, of motion, of rest, of quantity, etc.

Whatsoever affirmation such ideas contain is equal to
the concept formed, and does not extend further. Wherefore we may form as many simple ideas as we please,
without any fear of error. It only remains for us to
inquire by what power our mind can form true ideas,
and how far such power extends. It is certain that such
power cannot extend itself infinitely. For when we affirm
somewhat of a thing, which is not contained in the concept we have formed of that thing, such an affirmation
shows a defect of our perception, or that we have formed
fragmentary or mutilated ideas. Thus we have seen that
the motion of a semicircle is false when it is isolated
in the mind, but true when it is associated with the
concept of a sphere, or of some cause determining
such a motion. But if it be the nature of a thinking
being, as seems, *prima facie*, to be the case, to form

true or adequate thoughts, it is plain that inadequate ideas arise in us only because we are parts of a thinking being, whose thoughts—some in their entirety, others in fragments only—constitute our mind.

But there is another point to be considered, which was not worth raising in the case of fiction, but which gives rise to complete deception—namely, that certain things presented to the imagination also exist in the understanding—in other words, are conceived clearly and distinctly. Hence, so long as we do not separate that which is distinct from that which is confused, certainty, or the true idea, becomes mixed with indistinct ideas. For instance, certain Stoics heard, perhaps, the term "soul," and also that the soul is immortal, yet imagined it only confusedly; they imagined, also, and understood that very subtle bodies penetrate all others, and are penetrated by none. By combining these ideas, and being at the same time certain of the truth of the axiom, they forthwith became convinced that the mind consists of very subtle bodies; that these very subtle bodies cannot be divided, etc. But we are freed from mistakes of this kind, so long as we endeavor to examine all our perceptions by the standard of the given true idea. We must take care, as has been said, to separate such perceptions from all those which arise from hearsay or unclassified experience.

Moreover, such mistakes arise from things being conceived too much in the abstract; for it is sufficiently self-evident that what I conceive as in its true object I cannot apply to anything else. Lastly, they arise from a want of understanding of the primary elements of nature as a whole; whence we proceed without due order, and confound nature with abstract rules, which, although they be true enough in their sphere, yet, when misapplied, confound themselves, and pervert the order of nature. However, if we proceed with as little abstraction as possible, and begin from primary elements—that is, from the source and origin of nature, as far back as we can reach,—we need not fear any deceptions of this kind. As far as the knowledge of the origin of nature is concerned, there is no danger of our confounding it with abstractions. For when a thing is conceived in the abstract, as are all universal notions, the said universal notions are always more extensive in the mind than the number of individuals forming their contents really existing in nature.

Again, there are many things in nature, the difference between which is so slight as to be hardly perceptible to the understanding; so that it may readily happen that such things are confounded together, if they be conceived abstractedly. But since the first principle of nature cannot (as we shall see hereafter) be conceived abstractedly or universally, and cannot extend further in the understanding than it does in reality, and has no likeness to mutable things, no confusion need be feared in respect to the idea of it, provided (as before shown) that we possess a standard of truth. This is, in fact, a being single and infinite; in other words, it is the sum total of being, beyond which there is no being found.

Thus far we have treated of the false idea. We have now to investigate the doubtful idea—that is, to inquire what can cause us to doubt, and how doubt may be removed. I speak of real doubt existing in the mind, not of such doubt as we see exemplified when a man says that he doubts, though his mind does not really hesitate. The cure of the latter does not fall within the province of method, it belongs rather to inquiries concerning obstinacy and its cure. Real doubt is never produced in the mind by the thing doubted of. In other words, if there were only one idea in the mind, whether that idea were true or false, there would be no doubt of certainty present, only a certain sensation. For an idea is in itself nothing else than a certain sensation; but doubt will arise through another idea, not clear and distinct enough for us to be able to draw any certain conclusion with regard to the matter under consideration; that is, the idea which causes us to doubt is not clear and distinct. To take an example. Supposing that a man has never reflected, taught by experience, or by any other means, that our senses sometimes deceive us, he will never doubt whether the sun be greater or less than it appears. Thus rustics are generally astonished when they hear that the sun is much larger than the earth. But from reflection on the deceitfulness of the senses [1] doubt arises, and if, after doubting, we acquire a true knowledge of the senses, and how things at a distance are represented through their instrumentality, doubt is again removed. Hence we cannot cast doubt on true ideas by the supposition that there is a deceitful Deity, who leads us astray even in what is most certain. We can only hold such an hypothesis so long as we have no clear and distinct idea—in other words, until we reflect on the knowledge which we have of the first principle of all things, and find that which teaches us that God is not a deceiver, and until we know this with the same certainty as we know from reflecting on the nature of a triangle that its three angles are equal to two right angles. But if we have a knowledge of God equal to that which we have of a triangle, all doubt is removed. In the same way as we can arrive at the said knowledge of a triangle, though not absolutely sure that there is not some arch-deceiver leading us astray, so can we come

[1] That is, it is known that the senses sometimes deceive us. But it is only known confusedly, for it is not known how they deceive us.

to a like knowledge of God under the like condition, and when we have attained to it, it is sufficient, as I said before, to remove every doubt which we can possess concerning clear and distinct ideas. Thus, if a man proceeded with our investigations in due order, inquiring first into those things which should first be inquired into, never passing over a link in the chain of association, and with knowledge how to define his questions before seeking to answer them, he will never have any ideas save such as are very certain, or, in other words, clear and distinct; for doubt is only a suspension of the spirit concerning some affirmation or negation which it would pronounce upon unhesitatingly if it were not in ignorance of something, without which the knowledge of the matter in hand must needs be imperfect. We may, therefore, conclude that doubt always proceeds from want of due order in investigation.

These are the points I promised to discuss in this first part of my treatise on method. However, in order not to omit anything which can conduce to the knowledge of the understanding and its faculties, I will add a few words on the subject of memory and forgetfulness.

The point most worthy of attention is, that memory is strengthened both with and without the aid of the understanding. For the more intelligible a thing is, the more easily it is remembered, and the less intelligible it is, the more easily do we forget it. For instance, a number of unconnected words is much more difficult to remember than the same number in the form of a narration. The memory is also strengthened without the aid of the understanding by means of the power wherewith the imagination or the sense called common is affected by some particular physical object. I say PARTICULAR, for the imagination is only affected by particular objects. If we read, for instance, a single romantic comedy, we shall remember it very well, so long as we do not read many others of the same kind, for it will reign alone in the memory. If, however, we read several others of the same kind, we shall think of them altogether, and easily confuse one with another. I say, also PHYSICAL. For the imagination is only affected by physical objects. As, then, the memory is strengthened both with and without the aid of the understanding, we may conclude that it is different from the understanding, and that in the matter considered in itself there is neither memory nor forgetfulness. What, then, is memory? It is nothing else than the actual sensation of impressions on the brain, accompanied with the thought of a definite duration of the sensation. This is also shown by reminiscence. For then we think of the sensation, but without the notion of continuous duration; thus the idea of that sensation is not the actual duration of the sensation or actual memory. Whether ideas are or are not subject to corruption will be seen in my philosophy. If this seems too absurd to any one, it will be sufficient for our purpose, if he reflect on the fact that a thing is more easily remembered in proportion to its singularity, as appears from the example of the comedy just cited. Further, a thing is remembered more easily in proportion to its intelligibility; therefore we cannot help remembering that which is extremely singular and sufficiently intelligible.

Thus, then, we have distinguished between a true idea and other perceptions, and shown that ideas fictitious, false, and the rest, originate in the imagination—that is, in certain sensations fortuitous (so to speak) and disconnected, arising not from the power of the mind, but from external causes, according as the body, sleeping or waking, receives various motions.

But one may take any view one likes of the imagination so long as one acknowledges that it is different from the understanding, and that the soul is passive with regard to it. The view taken is immaterial, if we know that the imagination is something indefinite, with regard to which the soul is passive, and that we can by some means or other free ourselves therefrom with the help of the understanding. Let no one then be astonished that before proving the existence of body, and other necessary things, I speak of imagination of body, and of its composition. The view taken is, I repeat, immaterial, so long as we know that imagination is something indefinite, etc. As regards a true idea, we have shown that it is simple or compounded of simple ideas; that it shows how and why something is or has been made; and that its subjective effects in the soul correspond to the actual reality of its object. This conclusion is identical with the saying of the ancients, that true science proceeds from cause to effect; though the ancients, so far as I know, never formed the conception put forward here that the soul acts according to fixed laws; and is, as it were, an immaterial automaton. Hence, as far as is possible at the outset, we have acquired a knowledge of our understanding, and such a standard of a true idea that we need no longer fear confounding truth with falsehood and fiction. Neither shall we wonder why we understand some things which in nowise fall within the scope of the imagination, while other things are in the imagination but wholly opposed to the understanding, or others, again, which agree therewith. We now know that the operations, whereby the effects of imagination are produced, take place under other laws quite different from the laws of the understanding, and that the mind is entirely passive with regard to them. Whence we may also see how easily men may fall into grave errors through not distinguishing accurately between the imagination and the understanding; such as believing that extension must be localized, that it must be finite, that its parts are really distinct one from the other, that it is the primary and single foundation of all things, that it occupies more space at one time than at another, and other similar doctrines, all entirely opposed to truth, as we shall duly show.

Again, since words are a part of the imagination—that is, since we form many conceptions in accordance with confused arrangements of words in the memory, dependent on particular bodily conditions—there is no doubt that words may, equally with the imagination, be the cause of many and great errors, unless we keep strictly on our guard. Moreover, words are formed according to popular fancy and intelligence, and are, therefore, signs of things as existing in the imagination, not as existing in the understanding. This is evident from the fact that to all such things as exist only in the understanding, not in the imagination, negative names are often given, such as incorporeal, infinite, etc. So, also, many conceptions really affirmative are expressed negatively, and *vice versa*, such as uncreate, independent, infinite, immortal, etc., inasmuch as their contraries are much more easily imagined, and, therefore, occurred first to men, and usurped positive names. Many things we affirm and deny, because the nature of words allows us to do so, though the nature of things does not. While we remain unaware of this fact, we may easily mistake falsehood for truth.

Let us also beware of another great cause of confusion, which prevents the understanding from reflecting on itself. Sometimes, while making no distinction between the imagination and the intellect, we think that what we more readily imagine is clearer to us; and also we think that what we imagine we understand. Thus, we put first that which should be last; the true order of progression is reversed, and no legitimate conclusion is drawn.

Now, in order at length to pass on to the second part of this method, I shall first set forth the object aimed at, and next the means for its attainment. The object aimed at is the acquisition of clear and distinct ideas, such as are produced by the pure intellect, and not by chance physical motions. In order that all ideas may be reduced to unity, we shall endeavor so to associate and arrange them that our mind may, as far as possible, reflect subjectively the reality of nature, both as a whole and as parts.

As for the first point, it is necessary (as we have said) for our purpose that everything should be conceived, either SOLELY THROUGH ITS ESSENCE, OR THROUGH ITS PROXIMATE CAUSE. If the thing be self-existent, or as is commonly said, the cause of itself, it must be understood through its essence only; if it be not self-existent, but requires a cause for its existence, it must be understood through its proximate cause.[1] For, in reality, the knowledge of an effect is nothing else than the acquisition of more perfect knowledge of its cause. Therefore, we may never, while we are concerned with inquiries into actual things, draw any conclusions from abstractions; we shall be extremely careful not to confound that which is only in the understanding with that which is in the thing itself. The best basis for drawing a conclusion will be either some particular affirmative essence, or a true and legitimate definition. For the understanding can not descend from universal axioms by themselves

---

[1] And if the thing cannot be understood in either of these ways it is utterly irrational and the universe in which it occurs is chaotic and absurd. See also Letter 12 (Rab Chasdai's view) and Letter 40. [Ed.]

to particular things, since axioms are of infinite extent, and do not determine the understanding to contemplate one particular thing more than another. Thus the true method of discovery is to form thoughts from some given definition. This process will be the more fruitful and easy in proportion as the thing given be better defined. Wherefore, the cardinal point of all this second part of method consists in the knowledge of the conditions of good definition, and the means of finding them. I will first treat of the conditions of definition.

A definition, if it is to be called perfect, must explain the inmost essence of a thing, and must take care not to substitute for this any of its properties. In order to illustrate my meaning, without taking an example which would seem to show a desire to expose other people's errors, I will choose the case of something abstract, the definition of which is of little moment. Such is a circle. If a circle be defined as a figure, such that all straight lines drawn from the center to the circumference are equal, every one can see that such a definition does not in the least explain the essence of a circle, but solely one of its properties. Though, as I have said, this is of no importance in the case of figures and other abstractions, it is of great importance in the case of physical beings and realities: for the properties of things are not understood so long as their essences are unknown. If the latter be passed over, there is necessarily a perversion of the succession of ideas which should reflect the succession of nature, and we go far astray from our object.

In order to be free from this fault, the following rules should be observed in definition:

I. If the thing in question be created, the definition must (as we have said) comprehend the proximate cause. For instance, a circle should, according to this rule, be defined as follows: the figure described by any line

whereof one end is fixed and the other free. This definition clearly comprehends the proximate cause.

II. A conception or definition of a thing should be
such that all the properties of that thing, in so far as
it is considered by itself, and not in conjunction with
other things, can be deduced from it, as may be seen in
the definition given of a circle: for from that it clearly
follows that all straight lines drawn from the center to
the circumference are equal. That this is a necessary
characteristic of a definition is so clear to any one, who
reflects on the matter, that there is no need to spend
time in proving it, or in showing that, owing to this
second condition, every definition should be affirmative.
I speak of intellectual affirmation, giving little thought
to verbal affirmations which, owing to the poverty of the
language, must sometimes, perhaps, be expressed negatively, though the idea contained is affirmative.

The rules for the definition of an uncreated thing are
as follows:

I. The exclusion of all idea of cause—that is, the
thing must not need explanation by anything outside
itself.

II. When the definition of the thing has been given,
there must be no room for doubt as to whether the thing
exists or not.

III. It must contain, as far as the mind is concerned,
no substantives which could be put into an adjectival
form; in other words, the object defined must not be explained through abstractions.

IV. Lastly, though this is not absolutely necessary, it
should be possible to deduce from the definition all the
properties of the thing defined.

All these rules become obvious to any one giving
strict attention to the matter.

I have also stated that the best basis for drawing a

conclusion is a particular affirmative essence. The more specialized the idea is, the more is it distinct, and therefore clear. Wherefore a knowledge of particular things should be sought for as diligently as possible.

As regards the order of our perceptions, and the manner in which they should be arranged and united, it is necessary that as soon as is possible and rational, we should inquire whether there be any being (and, if so, what being) that is the cause of all things, so that its essence, represented in thought, may be the cause of all our ideas, and then our mind will to the utmost possible extent reflect nature. For it will possess, subjectively, nature's essence, order, and union. Thus we can see that it is before all things necessary for us to deduce all our ideas from physical things—that is, from real entities proceeding, as far as may be, according to the series of causes, from one real entity to another real entity, never passing to universals and abstractions, either for the purpose of deducing some real entity from them, or deducing them from some real entity. Either of these processes interrupts the true progress of the understanding. But it must be observed that, by the series of causes and real entities, I do not here mean the series of particular and mutable things, but only the series of fixed and eternal things. It would be impossible for human infirmity to follow up the series of particular mutable things, both on account of their multitude, surpassing all calculation, and on account of the infinitely diverse circumstances surrounding one and the same thing, any one of which may be the cause for its existence or non-existence. Indeed, their existence has no connection with their essence, or (as we have said already) is not an eternal truth. Neither is there any need that we should understand their series, for the essences of particular mutable things are not to be gathered

from their series or order of existence, which would
furnish us with nothing beyond their extrinsic denomi-
nations, their relations, or, at most, their circumstances,
all of which are very different from their inmost essence.[1] This inmost essence must be sought solely from
fixed and eternal things, and from the laws, inscribed
(so to speak) in those things as in their true codes, according to which all particular things take place and
are arranged; nay, these mutable particular things depend so intimately and essentially (so to phrase it)
upon the fixed things, that they cannot either be or be
conceived without them.

Whence these fixed and eternal things, though they
are themselves particular, will nevertheless, owing to
their presence and power everywhere, be to us as universals, or genera of definitions of particular mutable
things, and as the proximate causes of all things.

But, though this be so, there seems to be no small
difficulty in arriving at the knowledge of these particular
things, for to conceive them all at once would far surpass
the powers of the human understanding. The arrangement whereby one thing is understood before another, as
we have stated, should not be sought from their series of
existence, nor from eternal things. For the latter are all
by nature simultaneous. Other aids are therefore needed
besides those employed for understanding eternal things
and their laws; however, this is not the place to recount
such aids, nor is there any need to do so, until we have
acquired a sufficient knowledge of eternal things and
their infallible laws, and until the nature of our senses
has become plain to us.

Before betaking ourselves to seek knowledge of par-

[1] Thus each particular thing in the realm of space and time
has its eternal essence inherent in it. The similarity to Bacon's
"forms" has been often noted. [Ed.]

ticular things, it will be seasonable to speak of such aids, as all tend to teach us the mode of employing our senses, and to make certain experiments under fixed rules and arrangement which may suffice to determine the object of our inquiry, so that we may therefrom infer what laws of eternal things it has been produced under, and may gain an insight into its inmost nature, as I will duly show. Here, to return to my purpose, I will only endeavor to set forth what seems necessary for enabling us to attain to knowledge of eternal things, and to define them under the conditions laid down above.

With this end, we must bear in mind what has already been stated, namely, that when the mind devotes itself to any thought, so as to examine it and to deduce therefrom in due order all the legitimate conclusions possible, any falsehood which may lurk in the thought will be detected; but if the thought be true, the mind will readily proceed without interruption to deduce truths from it. This, I say, is necessary for our purpose, for our thoughts may be brought to a close by the absence of a foundation. If, therefore, we wish to investigate the first thing of all, it will be necessary to supply some foundation which may direct our thoughts thither. Further, since method is reflective knowledge, the foundation which must direct our thoughts can be nothing else than the knowledge of that which constitutes the reality of truth, and the knowledge of the understanding, its properties, and powers. When this has been acquired we shall possess a foundation wherefrom we can deduce our thoughts, and a path whereby the intellect, according to its capacity, may attain the knowledge of eternal things, allowance being made for the extent of the intellectual powers.

If, as I stated in the first part, it belongs to the nature of thought to form true ideas, we must here inquire what is meant by the faculties and power of the understanding. The chief part of our method is to understand as well as possible the powers of the intellect, and its nature; we are, therefore, compelled (by the considerations advanced in the second part of the method) necessarily to draw these conclusions from the definition itself of thought and understanding. But, so far, we have not got any rules for finding definitions, and, as we cannot set forth such rules without a previous knowledge of nature, that is without a definition of the understanding and its power, it follows either that the definition of the understanding must be clear in itself, or that we can understand nothing. Nevertheless this definition is not absolutely clear in itself; however, since its properties, like all things that we possess through the understanding, cannot be known clearly and distinctly, unless its nature be known previously, the definition of the understanding makes itself manifest, if we pay attention to its properties, which we know clearly and distinctly. Let us, then, enumerate here the properties of the understanding, let us examine them, and begin by discussing the instruments for research which we find innate in us.

The properties of the understanding which I have chiefly remarked, and which I clearly understand, are the following:—

I. It involves certainty—in other words, it knows that a thing exists in reality as it is reflected subjectively.

II. That it perceives certain things, or forms some ideas absolutely, some ideas from others. Thus it forms the idea of quantity absolutely, without reference to any other thoughts; but ideas of motion it only forms after taking into consideration the idea of quantity.

III. Those ideas which the understanding forms absolutely express infinity; determinate ideas are derived from other ideas. Thus in the idea of quantity, perceived by means of a cause, the quantity is determined, as when a body is perceived to be formed by the motion of a plane, a plane by the motion of a line, or, again, a line by the motion of a point. All these are perceptions which do not serve toward understanding quantity, but only toward determining it. This is proved by the fact that we conceive them as formed as it were by motion, yet this motion is not perceived unless the quantity be perceived also; we can even prolong the motion so as to form an infinite line, which we certainly could not do unless we had an idea of infinite quantity.

IV. The understanding forms positive ideas before forming negative ideas.

V. It perceives things not so much under the condition of duration as under a certain form of eternity, and in an infinite number; or rather in perceiving things it does not consider either their number or duration, whereas, in imagining them, it perceives them in a determinate number, duration, and quantity.

VI. The ideas which we form as clear and distinct, seem so to follow from the sole necessity of our nature, that they appear to depend absolutely on our sole power; with confused ideas the contrary is the case. They are often formed against our will.

VII. The mind can determine in many ways the ideas of things, which the understanding forms from other ideas: thus, for instance, in order to define the plane of an ellipse, it supposes a point adhering to a cord to be moved round two centres, or, again, it conceives an infinity of points, always in the same fixed relation to a given straight line, or a cone cut in an oblique plane, so that the angle of inclination is greater than the angle of the vertex of the cone, or in an infinity of other ways.

VIII. The more ideas express perfection of any object, the more perfect are they themselves; for we do not admire the architect who has planned a chapel so much as the architect who has planned a splendid temple.

I do not stop to consider the rest of what is referred to thought, such as love, joy, etc. They are nothing to our present purpose, and cannot even be conceived unless the understanding be perceived previously. When perception is removed, all these go with it.

False and fictitious ideas have nothing positive about them (as we have abundantly shown) which causes them to be called false or fictitious; they are only considered as such through the defectiveness of knowledge. Therefore, false and fictitious ideas as such can teach us nothing concerning the essence of thought; this must be sought from the positive properties just enumerated; in other words, we must lay down some common basis from which these properties necessarily follow, so that when this is given, the properties are necessarily given also, and when it is removed, they too vanish with it.

[*The rest of the treatise is wanting.*]

SPINOZA'S SHORT TREATISE ON GOD, MAN, AND HIS WELL-BEING [1]

FIRST PART

On God

CHAPTER I

THAT GOD EXISTS

As REGARDS the first, namely, whether there is a God, this, we say, can be proved.

I. In the first place, *a priori* thus:

    1. Whatever we clearly and distinctly know to belong to the nature [2] of a thing, we can also truly affirm of that thing. Now we can know clearly and distinctly that existence belongs to the nature of God;

    Therefore . . .

    Otherwise also thus:

    2. The essence of things are from all eternity, and unto all eternity shall remain immutable;

    The existence of God is essence;

    Therefore . . .

---

[1] Note. Words in brackets are those of the translator.

[2] Understand the definite nature through which a thing is what it is, and which can by no means be removed from it without at the same time destroying that thing: thus, for instance, it belongs to the essence of a mountain that it should have a valley, or the essence of a mountain is that it has a valley; this is truly eternal and immutable, and must always be included in the concept of a mountain, even if it never existed, or did not exist now.

II. *A posteriori*, thus:

> If a man has an idea of God, then God must
> exist *formaliter*;
>
> Now, man has an idea of God;
>
> Therefore . . .

The first we prove thus:

> If there is an idea of God, then the cause thereof
> must exist *formaliter*, and contain in itself all
> that the idea has *objective*;
>
> Now there is an idea of God;
>
> Therefore . . .

In order to prove the first part of this argument we state the following principles, namely:

1. That the number of knowable things is infinite;
2. That a finite understanding cannot apprehend the infinite;
3. That a finite understanding, unless it is determined by something external, cannot through itself know anything; because, just as it has no power to know all things equally, so little also has it the power to begin or to commence to know this, for instance, sooner than that, or that sooner than this. Since, then, it can do neither the one nor the other it can know nothing.

The first (or the major premise) is proved thus:

> If the imagination of man were the sole cause of
> his ideas, then it would be impossible that he
> should be able to apprehend anything, but he
> can apprehend something;
>
> Therefore . . .

The first is proved by the first principle, namely, *that the knowable things are infinitely numerous.* Also, following the second principle, man cannot know all, because the human understanding is finite, and if not determined by external things to know this sooner than that, and that sooner than this, then according to the third principle it should be impossible for it to know anything.[1]

---

[1] Further, to say that this idea is a fiction, this also is false: for it is impossible to have this [idea] if it [the *ideatum*] does not exist; this is shown on page 46, and we also add the following:

It is quite true that when an idea has first come to us from a particular thing, and we have generalised it *in abstracto*, then our understanding may fancy various things about it, and we can add to it many other attributes abstracted from other things. But it is impossible to do this without a prior knowledge of the things themselves from which these abstractions have been made. Once, however, it is assumed that this idea [of God] is a fiction, then all *other ideas* that we have must be fictions no less. If this is so, *whence* comes it that we find such a great difference among them? For as regards *some* we see that it is impossible they should exist; *e.g.,* all monsters supposed to be composed of two natures, such as an animal that should be both a bird and a horse, and the like, for which it is impossible to have a place in Nature, which we find differently constituted; *other ideas* may, but need not, exist; whether, however, they exist or do not exist, their essence is always necessary; such is the idea of a triangle, and that of the love in the soul apart from the body, &c.; so that even if I at first thought that I had imagined these, I am nevertheless compelled afterwards to say that they are, and would be, the same no less even if neither I nor anybody had ever thought about them. They are, consequently, not merely imagined by me, and must also have outside me a *subjectum* other than myself, without which *subjectum* they cannot be. In addition to these there is yet *a third idea*, and it is an only one; this one carries with it necessary existence, and not, like the foregoing, the mere possibility of existence: for, in the case of those, their essence was indeed necessary, but not their existence, while in its case, both its existence and its essence are necessary, and it is nothing without them. I therefore see now that the truth, essence, or existence of anything never depends on me: for, as was shown with reference to the second kind of ideas, they are what they are independently of me, whether as regards their essence alone, or as regards both essence and existence. I find this to be true also, indeed much more so, of this third unique idea; not only does it not depend on me, but, on the contrary, he alone must be the *subjectum* of that which I affirm of him. Consequently if he

From all this the second point is proved, namely, *that the cause of a man's ideas is not his imagination but some external cause, which compels him to apprehend one thing sooner than another*, and it is no other than this, that the things whose *essentia objectiva* is in his understanding exist *formaliter*, and are nearer to him than other things. If, then, man has the idea of God, it is clear that God must exist *formaliter*, though not *eminenter*, as there is nothing more real or more excellent beside or outside him. Now, that man has the idea of God, this is clear, because he knows his attributes,[1] which attributes cannot be derived from [man] himself, because he is imperfect. And that he knows these attributes is evident from this, namely, that he knows

did not exist, I should not be able to assert anything at all about him; although this can be done in the case of other things, even when they do not exist. He must also be, indeed, the *subjectum* of all other things.

From what has been said so far it is clearly manifest that the idea of infinite attributes in the perfect being is no fiction; we shall, however, still add the following:

According to the foregoing consideration of Nature, we have so far not been able to discover more than two attributes only which belong to this all-perfect being. And these give us nothing adequate to satisfy us that this is all of which this perfect being consists, quite the contrary, we find in us *a something* which openly tells us not only of more, but of infinite perfect attributes, which must belong to this perfect being before he can be said to be perfect. And whence comes this idea of perfection? This *something* cannot be the outcome of these two [attributes]: for two can only yield two, and not an infinity. Whence then? From myself, never; else I must be able to give what I did not possess. Whence, then, but from the infinite attributes themselves which tell us *that* they are, without however telling us, at the same time, *what* they are: for only of two do we know what they are.

[1] *His attributes*; it is better [to say], because he knows what is proper to God; for these things [infinity, perfection, &c.] are no attributes of God. Without these, indeed, God could not be God, but it is not through them [that he is God], since they show nothing substantial, but are only like adjectives which require substantives or their explanation.

that the infinite cannot be obtained by putting together divers finite parts; that there cannot be two infinites, but *only one*; that it is perfect and immutable, for we know that nothing seeks, of itself, its own annihilation, and also that it cannot change into anything better,[1] because it is perfect, which it would not be in that case, or also that such a being cannot be subjected to anything outside it, since it is omnipotent, and so forth.

From all this, then, it follows clearly that we can prove both *a priori* and *a posteriori* that God exists. Better, indeed, *a priori*. For things which are proved in the latter way [*a posteriori*] must be proved through their external causes, which is a manifest imperfection in them, inasmuch as they cannot make themselves known through themselves, but only through external causes. God, however, who is the first cause of all things, and also the cause of himself [*causa sui*], makes himself known through himself. Hence one need not attach much importance to the saying of Thomas Aquinas, namely, that God could not be proved *a priori* because he, forsooth, has no cause.

CHAPTER II

WHAT GOD IS

Now that we have proved above *that* God is, it is time to show *what* he is. Namely, we say that he is a

---

[1] The cause of this change would have to be either outside, or in it. It cannot be outside, because no substance which, like this, exists through itself depends on anything outside it; therefore it is not *subject to change through it*. Nor can it be in it: because no thing, much less this, desires its own undoing; all undoing comes from outside. Again, that there can be no finite substance is clear from this, because in that case it would necessarily have to have something which it had from nothing: which is impossible; for whence has it that wherein it differs from God? Certainly not from God; for he has nothing imperfect or finite, &c.: whence, therefore, but from nothing?

being of whom all or infinite attributes are predicated,[1] *of which attributes every one is infinitely perfect in its kind.* Now, in order to express our views clearly, we shall premise the four following propositions:

1. That there is no finite substance,[2] but that every substance must be infinitely perfect in its kind, that

[1] The reason is this, since *Nothing* can have no attributes, the *All* must have all attributes; and just as *Nothing* has no attribute because it is *Nothing*, so that which is *Something* has attributes because it is *Something*. Hence, the more it is *Something*, the more attributes it must have, and consequently God being the most perfect, and all that is Anything, he must also have infinite, perfect, and all attributes.

[2] Once we can prove that there can be no *Finite Substance*, then all *substance* must without limitation belong to the divine being. We do it thus: 1. It must either have limited itself or *some other* must have limited it. It could not have done so itself, because having been infinite it would have had to change its whole essence. Nor can it be limited by another: for this again must be either finite or infinite; the former is impossible, therefore the latter; therefore it [*i.e.,* the other thing] is God. He must, then, have made it finite because he lacked either the power or the will [to make it infinite]: but the first [supposition] is contrary to his omnipotence, the second is contrary to his goodness. 2. That *there can be no finite substance* is clear from this, namely, that, if so, it would necessarily have something which it would have from Nothing, which is impossible. For whence can it derive that wherein it differs from God? Certainly not from God, for he has nothing imperfect or finite, &c. So, whence then but from Nothing? Therefore there is no substance other than infinite. Whence it follows, *that there cannot be two like infinite substances;* for to posit such necessitates limitation. And from this, again, it follows *that one substance cannot produce another;* thus: The cause that we might suppose to produce this substance must have the same attribute as the one produced, and also either just as much perfection or more or less. The first supposition is not possible, because there would then be two like [substances]. The second also not, because in that case there would be a finite [substance]. Nor the third, because something cannot come from nothing.—Moreover, if the finite came from the infinite, then the infinite would also be finite, &c. Therefore one substance can not produce another. And from this, again, it follows *that all substance must exist "formaliter"*: for if it did not exist, there would be no possibility for it to come into existence.

is to say, that in the infinite understanding of God no substance can be more perfect than that which already exists in Nature.

2. That there are not two like substances.

3. That one substance cannot produce another.

4. That in the infinite understanding of God there is no other substance than that which is *formaliter* in Nature.

As regards the first, namely, that there is no finite substance, &c., should any one want to maintain the opposite, we would ask the following question, namely, whether this substance is finite through itself, whether it has made itself thus finite and did not want to make itself less finite; or whether it is thus finite through its cause, which cause either could not or would not give more? The first [alternative] is not true, because it is impossible that a substance should have wanted to make itself finite, especially a substance which had come into existence through itself. Therefore, I say, it is made finite by its cause, which is necessarily God. Further, if it is finite through its cause, this must be so either because its cause could not give more, or because it would not give more. That he should not have been able to give more would contradict his omnipotence; [1]

[1] To say to this *that the nature of the thing required such [limitation] and that it could not therefore be otherwise,* that is no reply: for the nature of a thing can require nothing while it does not exist. Should you say that one may, nevertheless, see what belongs to the nature of a thing which does not exist: that is true as regards its existence, but by no means as regards its essence. And herein lies the difference between *creating* and *generating*. To create is to posit a thing *quo ad essentiam et existentiam simul* [i.e., to give a thing both essence and existence]; while in the case of generation a thing comes forth *quo ad existentiam solam* [i.e., it only receives existence]. And therefore there is now in Nature no creation but only generation. So that when God creates he creates at once the nature of the thing with the thing itself. He would therefore show ill-will if (from lack of will, and not of power) he

that he should not have been willing to give more, when he could well do so, savours of ill-will, which is nowise in God, who is all goodness and perfection.

As regards the second, *that there are not two like substances*, we prove this on the ground that each substance is perfect in its kind; for if there were two alike they would necessarily limit one another, and would consequently not be infinite, as we have already shown before.

As to the third, namely, *that one substance cannot produce another*: should any one again maintain the opposite, we ask whether the cause, which is supposed to produce this substance, has or has not the same attributes as the produced [substance]. The latter is impossible, because something cannot come from nothing; therefore the former. And then we ask whether in the attribute which is presumed to be the cause of this produced [substance], there is just as much perfection as in the produced substance, or less, or more. Less, we say, there cannot be, for the reasons given above. More, also not, we say, because in that case this second one would be finite, which is opposed to what has already been proved by us. Just as much, then; they are therefore alike, and are two like substances, which clearly conflicts with our previous demonstration. Further, that which is created is by no means produced from Nothing, but must necessarily have been produced from something existing. But that something should have come forth from this, and that it should none the less have this something even after it has issued from it, that we cannot grasp with our understanding. Lastly, if we would seek the cause of the substance which is the

---

created the thing in such a way that it should not agree with its cause in essence and existence. However, what we here call creation can really not be said ever to have taken place, and it is only mentioned to indicate what we can say about it, if we distinguish between *creating* and *generating*.

origin of the things which issue from its attribute, then it behoves us to seek also the cause of that cause, and then again the cause of that cause, *et sic in infinitum*; so that if we must necessarily stop and halt somewhere, as indeed we must, it is necessary to stop at this only substance.

As regards the fourth, *that there is no substance or attribute in the infinite understanding of God other than what exists "formaliter" in Nature*, this can be, and is, proved by us: (1) from the infinite power of God, since in him there can be no cause by which he might have been induced to create one sooner or more than another; (2) from the simplicity of his will; (3) because he cannot omit to do what is good, as we shall show afterwards; (4) because it would be impossible for that which does not now exist to come into existence, since one substance cannot produce another. And, what is more, in that case there would be more infinite substances not in existence than there are in existence, which is absurd. From all this it follows then: that of Nature all in all is predicated, and that consequently Nature consists of infinite attributes, each of which is perfect in its kind. And this is just equivalent to the definition usually given of God.

Against what we have just said, namely, that there is no thing in the infinite understanding of God but what exists *formaliter* in Nature, some want to argue in this way: if God has created all, then he can create nothing more; but that he should be able to create nothing more conflicts with his omnipotence; therefore . . .

Concerning the first, we admit that God can create nothing more. And with regard to the second, we say that we own, if God were not able to create all that could be created, then it would conflict with his omnipotence; but that is by no means the case if he cannot create what is self-contradictory; as it is, to say that he has created all, and also that he should be able to create still more. Assuredly it is a far greater perfection in God that he has created all that was in his infinite understanding than if he had not created it, or, as they say, if he had never been able to create it. But why say so much about it? Do they not themselves argue thus,[1] or must they not argue thus from God's omniscience: If God is omniscient then he can know nothing more; but that God can know nothing more is incompatible with his perfection; therefore . . . ? But if God has all in his understanding, and, owing to his infinite perfection, can know nothing more, well then, why can we not say that he has also created all that he had in his understanding, and has made it so that it exists or should exist *formaliter* in Nature?

Since, then, we know that all alike is in the infinite understanding of God, and that there is no cause why he should have created this sooner and more than that, and that he could have produced all things in a moment, so let us see, for once, whether we cannot use against them the same weapons which they take up against us; namely, thus:

If God can never create so much that he cannot create more, then he can never create what he can create; but that he cannot create what he can create is self-contradictory. Therefore . . .

Now the reasons why we said that all these attributes, which are in Nature, are but one single being, and by no means different things (although we can know them clearly and distinctly the one without the other, and the other without another), are these:

[1] That is, whenever we make them argue from this admission, namely, *that God is omniscient*, then they cannot but argue thus.

1. Because we have found already before that there must be an infinite and perfect being, by which nothing else can be meant than such a being of which all in all must be predicated. Why? [Because] to a being which has any essence attributes must be referred, and the more essence one ascribes to it, the more attributes also must one ascribe to it, and consequently if a being is infinite then its attributes also must be infinite, and this is just what we call a perfect being.

2. Because of the unity which we see everywhere in Nature. If there were different beings in it[1] then it would be impossible for them to unite with one another.

3. Because although, as we have already seen, one substance cannot produce another, and if a substance does not exist it is impossible for it to begin to exist, we see, nevertheless, that in no substance (which we none the less know to exist in Nature), when considered separately, is there any necessity to be real, since existence does not pertain to its separate essence.[2] So it must

[1] That is, if there were different substances which were not connected in one only being, then their union would be impossible, because we see clearly that they have nothing at all in common, it is so with thought and extension of which we nevertheless consist.

[2] That is, if no substance can be other than real, and yet existence does not follow from its essence, when it is considered by itself, it follows that it is not something independent, but must be something, that is, an attribute, of another thing, namely, the one, only, and universal being. Or thus: All substance is real, and when a substance is considered by itself its existence does not follow from its essence; therefore, no existing substance can be known through itself, but it must belong to something else. That is, when with our understanding we consider "substantial" Thought and ["substantial"] Extension, then we consider them only in their essence and not as existing, that is [we do not consider] that their existence necessarily pertains to their essence. When, however, we prove [of each] that it is an attribute of God, we thereby prove a priori that it exists, and a posteriori (as regards extension alone) [we prove its existence] from the modes which must necessarily have it for their subjectum.

necessarily follow that Nature, which results from no causes, and which we nevertheless know to exist, must necessarily be a perfect being to which existence belongs.

From all that we have so far said it is evident, then, that we posit extension as an attribute of God; and this seems not at all appropriate to a perfect being: for since extension is divisible, the perfect being would have to consist of parts, and this is altogether inapplicable to God, because he is a simple being. Moreover, when extension is divided it is passive, and with God (who is never passive, and cannot be affected by any other being, because he is the first efficient cause of all) this can by no means be the case.

To this we reply: (1) that "part" and "whole" are not true or real entities, but only "things of reason," and consequently there are in Nature [1] neither whole nor parts. (2) A thing composed of different parts must be

---

[1] In Nature, that is, in "substantial" Extension; for if this were divided its nature and being would be at once annihilated, as it exists only as infinite extension, or, which comes to the same, it exists only as a whole.

But should you say: is there, in extension, no part prior to all its modes? I say, certainly not. But you may say, since there is motion in matter, it must be in some part of matter, for it cannot be in the whole, because this is infinite; and whither shall it be moved, when there is nothing outside it? Therefore it must be in a part. My answer is: Motion alone does not exist, but only motion and rest together; and this is in the whole, and must be in it, because there is no part in extension. Should you, however, say that there is, then tell me: if you divide the whole of extension then, as regards any part which you cut off from it in thought, can you also separate it in nature from all [other] parts; and supposing this has been done, I ask, what is there between the part cut off and the rest? You must say, a vacuum, or another body, or something of extension itself; there is no fourth possibility. The first will not do, because there is no vacuum, something positive and yet no body; nor the second, because then there would exist a mode, which cannot be, since extension as extension is without and prior to all modes. Therefore the third; and then there is no part but only the whole of extension.

such that the parts thereof, taken separately, can be conceived and understood one without another. Take, for
instance, a clock which is composed of many different
wheels, cords, and other things; in it, I say, each wheel,
cord, &c., can be conceived and understood separately,
without the composite whole being necessary thereto.
Similarly also in the case of water, which consists of
straight oblong particles, each part thereof can be conceived and understood, and can exist without the whole;
but extension, being a substance, one cannot say of it
that it has parts, since it can neither diminish nor increase, and no parts thereof can be understood apart,
because by its nature it must be infinite. And that it
must be such, follows from this, namely, because if it
were not such, but consisted of parts, then it would not
be infinite by its nature, as it is said to be; and it is
impossible to conceive parts in an infinite nature, since
by their nature all parts are finite. Add to this still: if
it consisted of different parts then it should be intelligible that supposing some parts thereof to be annihilated, extension might remain all the same and not
be annihilated together with the annihilation of some
of its parts; this is clearly contradictory in what is
infinite by its own nature and can never be, or be conceived, as limited or finite. Further, as regards the parts
in Nature, we maintain that division, as has also been
said already before, never takes place in substance, but
always and only in the mode of substance. Thus, if I
want to divide water, I only divide the mode of substance, and not substance itself. And whether this mode
is that of water or something else it is always the same.

Division, then, or passivity, always takes place in
the mode; thus when we say that man passes away or
is annihilated, then this is understood to apply to man
only in so far as he is such a composite being, and a

mode of substance, and not the substance on which he depends.

Moreover, we have already stated, and we shall repeat it later, that outside God there is nothing at all, and that he is an *Immanent Cause*. Now, passivity, whenever the agent and the patient are different entities, is a palpable imperfection, because the patient must necessarily be dependent on that which has caused the passivity from outside; it has, therefore, no place in God, who is perfect. Furthermore, of such an agent who acts in himself it can never be said that he has the imperfection of a patient, because he is not affected by another; such, for instance, is the case with the understanding, which, as the philosophers also assert, is the cause of its ideas, since, however, it is an immanent cause, what right has one to say that it is imperfect, howsoever frequently it is affected by itself? Lastly, since substance is [the cause] and the origin of all its modes, it may with far greater right be called an agent than a patient. And with these remarks we consider all adequately answered.

It is further objected, that there must necessarily be a first cause which sets body in motion, because when at rest it is impossible for it to set itself in motion. And since it is clearly manifest that rest and motion exist in Nature, these must, they think, necessarily result from an external cause. But it is easy for us to reply to this; for we concede that, if body were a thing existing through itself, and had no other attributes than length, breadth, and depth, then, if it really rested there would be in it no cause whereby to begin to move itself; but we have already stated before *that Nature is a being of which all attributes are predicated*, and this being so, it can be lacking in nothing wherewith to produce all that there is to be produced.

Having so far discussed what God is, we shall say but

a word, as it were, about his attributes: that those which are known to us consist of two only, namely, *Thought* and *Extension*; for here we speak only of attributes which might be called the *proper attributes* of God, through which we come to know him [as he is] in himself, and not [merely] as he acts [towards things] outside himself. All else, then, that men ascribe to God beyond these two attributes, all that (if it otherwise pertains to him) must be either an "extraneous denomination," such as *that he exists through himself*, is *Eternal, One, Immutable*, &c., or, I say, has reference to his activity, such as that he is a *cause, predestines*, and *rules* all things: all which are properties of God, but give us no information as to what he is. But how and in what manner these attributes can nevertheless have a place in God we shall explain in the following chapters. But, for the better understanding of this and in further exposition thereof, we have thought it well and have decided to add the following arguments consisting of a [Dialogue].

[FIRST] DIALOGUE

BETWEEN THE LOVE, UNDERSTANDING, REASON, AND DESIRE

LOVE. I see, Brother, that both my essence and perfection depend on your perfection; and since the perfection of the object which you have conceived is your perfection, while from yours again mine proceeds, so tell me now, I pray you, whether you have conceived such a being as is supremely perfect, not capable of being limited by any other, and in which I also am comprehended.

UNDERSTANDING. I for my part consider Nature only in its totality as infinite, and supremely perfect, but you, if you have any doubts about it, ask Reason, she will tell you.

REASON. To me the truth of the matter is indubitable, for if we would limit Nature then we should, absurdly enough, have to limit it with a mere Nothing; we avoid this absurdity by stating that it is *One Eternal Unity, infinite, omnipotent,* &c., that is, that Nature is infinite and that all is contained therein; and the negative of this we call Nothing.

DESIRE. Ah indeed! it is wondrously congruous to suppose that *Unity* is in keeping with the *Difference* which I observe everywhere in Nature. But how? I see that thinking substance has nothing in common with *extended substance,* and that the one limits [not] the other; and if, in addition to these substances, you want to posit yet a third one which is perfect in all respects, then look how you involve yourself in manifest contradictions; for if this third one is placed outside the first two, then it is wanting in all the attributes which belong to those two, but this can never be the case with a whole outside of which there is nothing. Moreover if this being is omnipotent and perfect, then it must be such because it has made itself, and not because another has made it; that, however, which could produce both itself and yet another besides would be even more omnipotent. And lastly, if you call it omniscient then it is necessary that it should know itself; and, at the same time, you must know that the knowledge of oneself alone is less than the knowledge of oneself together with the knowledge of other substances. All these are manifest contradictions. I would, therefore, have advised Love to rest content with what I show her, and to look about for no other things.

LOVE. What now, O dishonourable one, have you shown me but what would result in my immediate ruin.

For, if I had ever united myself with what you have shown me, then from that moment I should have been persecuted by the two archenemies of the human race, namely, *Hatred* and *Remorse*, and sometimes also by *Oblivion*; and therefore I turn again to Reason only to proceed and stop the mouths of these foes.

REASON. What you say, O Desire, that there are different substances, that, I tell you, is false; for I see clearly that there is but *One, which exists through itself, and is a support to all other attributes*. And if you will refer to the material and the mental as substances, in relation to the modes which are dependent on them, why then, you must also call them modes in relation to the substance on which they depend: for they are not conceived by you as existing through themselves. And in the same way that willing, feeling, understanding, loving, &c., are different modes of that which you call a thinking substance, in which you bring together and unite all these in one, so I also conclude, from your own proofs, that *Both Infinite Extension and Thought together with all other infinite attributes* (or, according to your usage, other *substances*) are only modes of the *One, Eternal, Infinite Being, who exists through himself*; and from all these we posit, as stated, *An Only One* or a *Unity* outside which nothing can be imagined to be.

DESIRE. Methinks I see a very great confusion in this argument of yours; for, it seems you will have it that *the whole must be something outside of or apart from its parts*, which is truly absurd. For all philosophers are unanimous in saying that *"whole" is a second notion, and that it is nothing in Nature apart from human thought*. Moreover, as I gather from your example, you confuse *whole* with *cause*: for, as I say, the whole only consists of and [exists] through its parts, and so it comes that you represent the *thinking power* as a thing on which the Understanding, Love, &c., depend. But you cannot call it a *Whole*, only a *Cause of the Effects* just named by you.

REASON. I see decidedly how you muster all your friends against me, and that, after the method usually adopted by those who oppose the truth, you are designing to achieve by quibbling what you have not been able to accomplish with your fallacious reasoning. But you will not succeed in winning Love to your side by such means. Your assertion, then, is, *that the cause (since it is the Originator of the Effects) must therefore be outside these.* But you say this because you only know of the *transeunt* and not of the *immanent cause*, which by no means produces anything outside itself, as is exemplified by the Understanding, which is the cause of its ideas. And that is why I called the understanding (in so far as, or because, its ideas depend on it) a *cause*; and on the other hand, since it consists of its ideas, a *whole*: so also *God is both an Immanent Cause with reference to his works or creatures, and also a whole, considered from the second point of view.*

SECOND DIALOGUE

BETWEEN

ERASMUS AND THEOPHILUS

RELATING PARTLY TO THE PRECEDING, PARTLY TO THE FOLLOWING SECOND PART

ERASMUS. I have heard you say, Theophilus, that God is a *cause of all things*, and, at the same time, that he can be *no other* than an *Immanent* cause. Now, if he is an *immanent cause* of *all things*, how then can you call him a *remote cause*? For, that is impossible in the case of an Immanent cause.

THEOPHILUS. When I said that God is a remote cause, I only said it with reference to the things [which God has produced mediately, and not with reference to those] which God (without any other conditions beyond his mere existence) has produced immediately; but on no account did I mean to call him a remote cause absolutely: as you might also have clearly gathered from my remarks. For, I also said that in some respects we can call him a remote cause.

ERASMUS. I understand now adequately what you want to say; but I note also that you have said, *that the effect of the immanent cause remains united with its cause in such a way that together they constitute a whole.* Now, if this is so, then, methinks, God cannot be an immanent cause. For, if he and that which is produced by him together form a whole, then you ascribe to God at one time more essence than at another time. I pray you, remove these doubts for me.

THEOPHILUS. If, Erasmus, you want to extricate yourself from this confusion, then mark well what I am going to tell you now. The essence of a thing does not increase through its union with another thing with which it constitutes a whole; on the contrary, the first remains unchanged. I will give you an illustration, so that you may understand me the better. An image-carver has made from wood various forms after the likeness of the parts of the human body; he takes one of these, which has the form of a human breast, joins it to another, which has the form of a human head, and of these two he makes a whole, which represents the upper part of a human body; would you therefore say that the essence of the head has increased because it has been joined to the breast? That would be erroneous, because it is the same that it was before. For the sake of greater clearness let me give you another illustration, namely, an idea that I have of a triangle, and another resulting from an extension of one of the angles, which extended or extending angle is necessarily equal to the two interior opposite angles, and so forth. These, I say, have produced a new idea, namely, that the three angles of the triangle are equal to two right angles. This idea is so connected with the first, that it can neither be, nor be conceived without the same. Mark well now that although the new idea is joined to the preceding one, the essence of the preceding idea does not undergo any change in consequence; on the contrary, it remains without the slightest change. The same you may also observe in every idea which produces love in itself: this love in no way adds to the essence of the idea. But why multiply illustrations? since you can see it clearly in the subject which I have been illustrating and which we are discussing now. I have distinctly stated that all attributes, which depend on no other cause, and whose definition requires no genus pertain to the essence of God; and since the created things are not competent to establish an attribute, they do not increase the essence of God, however intimately they become united to him. Add to this, that "whole" is but a thing of Reason, and does not differ from the general except in this alone that the general results from various Disconnected individuals, the Whole, from various United individuals; also in this, that the General only comprises parts of the same kind, but the Whole, parts both the same and different in kind.

ERASMUS. So far as this is concerned you have satisfied me. But, in addition to this, you have also said, that *the effect of the inner cause cannot perish so long as its cause lasts*; this, I well see, is certainly true, but if this is so, then how can God be an inner cause of all things, seeing that many things perish? After your previous distinction you will say, that *God is really a cause of the effects which he has produced immediately, without any other conditions except his attributes alone; and that these cannot perish so long as their cause endures; but that you do not call God an inner cause of the effects whose existence does not depend on him immediately, but which have come into being through some other thing, except in so far as their causes do not operate and cannot operate, without God, nor also outside him;* and that for this reason also, since they are not produced immediately by God, they can perish. But this does not satisfy me. For I see that you conclude, that the human understanding is immortal, because it is a product which God has produced in himself. Now it is impossible that more than the attributes of God should have been necessary in order to produce such an understanding; for, in order to be a being of such supreme perfection, it must have been created from eternity, just like all other things which depend immediately on God. And I have heard you say so, if I am not mistaken. And this being so, how will you reconcile this without leaving over any difficulties?

THEOPHILUS. It is true, Erasmus, that the things (for the existence of which no other thing is required, except the attributes of God) which have been created immediately by him have been created from eternity. It is to be remarked, however, that although in order that a thing may exist there is required a special modification and a thing beside the attributes of God, for all that, God does not cease to be able to produce a thing immediately. For, of the necessary things which are required to bring things into existence, some are there in order that they should produce the thing, and others in order that the thing should be capable of being produced. For example, I want to have light in a certain room; I kindle a light, and this lights up the room through itself; or I open a window [shutter], now this act of opening does not itself give light, but still it brings it about that the light can enter the room. Likewise in order to set a body in motion another body is required that shall have all the motion that is to pass from it to the other. But in order to produce in us an idea of God there is no need for another special thing that shall have what is to be produced in us, but only such a body in *Nature* whose idea is necessary in order to represent God immediately. This you could also have gathered from my remarks: for I said that God is only known through himself, and not through something else. However, I tell you this, that so long as we have not such a clear idea of God as shall unite us with him in such a way that it will not let us love anything beside him, we cannot truly say that we are united with God, so as to depend immediately on him. If there is still anything that you may have to ask, leave it for another time; just now circumstances require me to attend to other matters. Farewell.

ERASMUS. Nothing at present, but I shall ponder what you have just told me till the next opportunity. God be with you.

CHAPTER III

THAT GOD IS A CAUSE OF ALL THINGS

WE SHALL now begin to consider those attributes [of God] which we called *Propria*.[1] And, first of all, how God *is a cause of all things*.

[1] The [attributes] following are called *Propria*, because they are only Adjectives, which cannot be understood without their Substantives. That is to say, without them God would

Now, we have already said above *that one substance cannot produce another*; and *that God is a being of whom all attributes are predicated*; whence it clearly follows that all other things can by no means be, or be understood, apart from or outside him. Wherefore we may say with all reason *that God is a cause of all things.*

As it is usual to divide the efficient cause in eight divisions, let me, then, inquire how and in what sense *God* is a cause.

First, then, we say that he is an *emanative* or *productive cause of his works*; and, in so far as there is activity, *an active or operating cause*, which we regard as one and the same, because they involve each other.

Secondly, he is an *immanent*, and not a *transeunt cause*, since all that he produces is within himself, and not outside him, because there is nothing outside him.

Thirdly, God is a *free cause*, and not a *natural* cause, as we shall make clear and manifest when we come to consider *whether God can omit to do what he does*, and then it will also be explained wherein *true freedom* consists.

Fourthly, God is a cause *through himself*, and not *by accident*; this will become more evident from the discussion on Predestination.

Fifthly, God is a *principal cause of his works which he has created immediately*, such as movement in matter, &c.; in which there is no place for a subsidiary [instrumental] cause, since this is confined to particular things; as when he dries the sea by means of a strong wind, and so forth in the case of all particular things in Nature.

The subsidiary provoking cause is not [found] *in*

---

indeed be no God, but still it is not they that constitute God; for they reveal nothing of the character of a Substance, through which alone God exists.

God, because there is nothing outside him to incite him. The *predisposing cause*, on the other hand, is his perfection itself; through it he is a cause of himself, and, consequently, of all other things.

Sixthly, God alone is *the first or Initial cause*, as is evident from our foregoing proof.

Seventhly, God is also *a Universal cause*, but only in so far as he produces various things; otherwise this can never be predicated of him, as he needs no one in order to produce any results.

Eighthly, God is the *proximate cause* of the things that are infinite, and immutable, and which we assert to have been created immediately by him, but, in one sense, he is the remote cause of all particular things.

CHAPTER IV

On God's Necessary Activity

WE DENY that God can omit to do what he does, and we shall also prove it when we treat of Predestination; when we will show that all things necessarily depend on their causes. But, in the second place, this conclusion also follows from the perfection of God; for it is true, beyond a doubt, *that God can make everything just as perfect as it is conceived in his Idea*; and just as things that are conceived by him cannot be conceived by him more perfectly than he conceives them, so all things can be made by him so perfect that they cannot come from him in a more perfect condition. Again, when we conclude that God could not have omitted to do what he has done, we deduce this from his perfection; because, in God, it would be an imperfection to be able to omit to do what he does; we do not, however, suppose that there is a subsidiary provoking cause in God that might have moved him to action, for then he were no God.

But now, again, there is the controversy whether, namely, of all that is in his Idea, and which he can realise so perfectly, whether, I say, he could omit to realise anything, and whether such an omission would be a perfection in him. Now, we maintain that, since all that happens is done by God, it must therefore necessarily be predetermined by him, otherwise he would be mutable, which would be a great imperfection in him. And as this predetermination by him must be from eternity, in which eternity there is no before or after, it follows irresistibly that God could never have predetermined things in any other way than that in which they are determined now, and have been from eternity, and that God could not have been either before or without these determinations. Further, if God should omit to do anything, then he must either have some cause for it, or not; if he has, then it is necessary that he should omit doing it; if he has not, then it is necessary that he should not omit to do it; this is self-evident. Moreover, in a created thing it is a perfection to exist and to have been produced by God, for, of all imperfection, non-existence is the greatest imperfection; and since God desires the welfare and perfection of all things, it would follow that if God desired that a certain thing should not exist, then the welfare and perfection of this thing must be supposed to consist in its non-existence, which is self-contradictory. That is why we deny *that God can omit to do what he does*. Some regard this as blasphemy, and as a belittling of God; but such an assertion results from a misapprehension of what constitutes *true freedom*; this is by no means what they think it is, namely, the ability to do or to omit to do something good or evil; but *true freedom is only, or no other than* [the status of being] *the first cause,* which is in no way constrained or coerced by anything else, and which through its perfection alone is the cause of all perfection; consequently, if God could omit to do this, he would not be perfect: for the ability to omit doing some good, or accomplishing some perfection in what he does, can have no place in him, except through defect.

That God alone is the only free cause is, therefore, clear not only from what has just been said, but also from this, namely, that there is no external cause outside him to force or constrain him; all this is not the case with created things.

Against this it is argued thus: The good is only good because God wills it, and this being so, he can always bring it about that evil should be good. But such reasoning is about as conclusive as if I said: It is because God wills to be God that he is God; therefore it is in his power not to be God, which is absurdity itself. Furthermore, when people do anything, and they are asked why they do it, their answer is, because it is what justice demands. If the question is then put, why justice, or rather the first cause of all that is just, makes such a demand, then the answer must be, because justice wills it so. But, dear me, I think to myself, could Justice really be other than just? By no means, for then it could not be Justice. Those, however, who say that God does all that he does because it is good in itself, these, I say, may possibly think that they do not differ from us. But that is far from being the case, since they suppose that there is something before God to which he has duties or obligations, namely, a cause [through] which [God] desires that this shall be good, and, again, that that shall be just.

Then comes the further controversy, namely, whether

God, supposing all things had been created by him in some other way from eternity, or had been ordered and predetermined to be otherwise than they now are, whether, I say, he would then be just as perfect as he is now. To this it may serve as an answer, that if Nature had, from all eternity, been made different from what it is now, then, from the standpoint of those who ascribe to God will and understanding, it would necessarily follow that God had a different will and a different understanding then, in consequence of which he would have made it different; and so we should be compelled to think that God has a different character now from what he had then, and had a different character then from what he has now; so that, if we assume he is most perfect now, we are compelled to say that he would not have been so had he created all things differently. All these things, involving as they do palpable absurdities, can in no way be attributed to God, who now, in the past, and unto all eternity, is, has been, and will remain immutable. We prove this also from the definition that we have given of a free cause, which is not one that can do or omit to do anything, but is only such as is not dependent on anything else, so that whatever God does is done and carried into effect by him as the freest cause. If, therefore, he had formerly made things different from what they are now, it would needs follow that he was at one time imperfect, which is false. For, since God is the first cause of all things, there must be something in him, through which he does what he does, and omits not to do it. Since we say that *Freedom* does not consist in [having the choice of] doing or not doing something, and since we have also shown that that which makes him [God] do anything can be nothing else than his own perfection, we conclude *that, had it not been that his perfection made him do all this, then the things would not exist, and could not come into existence, in order to be what they are now.* This is just like saying: *if God were imperfect then things would be different from what they are now.*

So much as regards the first; we shall now pass on to the second attribute, which we call a *proprium* of God, and see what we have to say about it, and so on to the end.

CHAPTER V

ON DIVINE PROVIDENCE

THE second attribute, which we call a *proprium* [of God] is his Providence, which to us is nothing else than the *striving* which we find in the whole of Nature and in individual things to maintain and preserve their own existence. For it is manifest that no thing could, through its own nature, seek its own annihilation, but, on the contrary, that every thing has in itself a striving to preserve its condition, and to improve itself. Following these definitions of ours we, therefore, posit a *general* and a *special providence*. The general [providence] is that through which all things are produced and sustained in so far as they are parts of the whole of Nature. The *special providence* is the striving of each thing separately to preserve its existence [each thing, that is to say], considered not as a part of Nature, but as a whole [by itself]. This is explained by the following example: All the limbs of man are provided for, and cared for, in so far as they are parts of man, this is *general providence*; while *special* [providence] is the striving of each separate limb (as a whole in itself, and not as a part of man) to preserve and maintain its own well-being.

CHAPTER VI

On Divine Predestination

THE third attribute, we say, is divine predestination.

1. We proved before that God cannot omit to do what he does; that he has, namely, made everything so perfect that it cannot be more perfect.

2. And, at the same time, that without him no thing can be, or be conceived.

It remains to be seen now whether there are in Nature any accidental things, that is to say, whether there are any things which may happen and may also not happen. Secondly, whether there is any thing concerning which we cannot ask why it is.

Now that there are no accidental things we prove thus: That which has no cause to exist cannot possibly exist; that which is accidental has no cause: therefore . . .

The first is beyond all dispute; the second we prove thus: If any thing that is accidental has a definite and certain cause why it should exist, then it must necessarily exist; but that it should be both accidental and necessary at the same time, is self-contradictory; Therefore . . .

Perhaps some one will say, that *an accidental thing* has indeed no definite and certain cause, but an accidental one. If this should be so, it must be so either *in sensu diviso* or *in sensu composito,* that is to say, either the existence of the cause is accidental, and not its being a cause; or it is accidental that a certain thing (which indeed must necessarily exist in Nature) should be the cause of the occurrence of that accidental thing. However, both the one and the other are false.

For, as regards the first, if the accidental something is accidental because [the existence of] its cause is accidental, then that cause must also be accidental, because the cause which has produced it is also accidental, *et sic in infinitum.*

And since it has already been proved, *that all things depend on one single cause,* this cause would therefore also have to be accidental: which is manifestly false.

As regards the second: if the cause were no more compelled to produce one thing than another, that is, [if the cause were no more compelled] to produce this something than not to produce it, then it would be impossible at once both that it should produce it and that it should not produce it, which is quite contradictory.

Concerning the second [question raised] above, *whether there is no thing in Nature about which one cannot ask why it is,* this remark of ours shows that we have to inquire through what cause a thing is real; for if this [cause] did not exist it were impossible that the thing should exist. Now, we must look for this cause either in the thing or outside the thing. If, however, any one should ask for a rule whereby to conduct this inquiry, we say that none whatever seems necessary. For if existence pertains to the nature of a thing, then it is certain that we must not look outside it for its cause; but if such is not the case, then we must always look outside the thing for its cause. Since, however, the first pertains to God alone, it is thereby proved (as we have already also proved before) that God alone is the first cause of all things. From this it is also evident that this or that will of man (since the existence of the will does not pertain to its essence) must also have an external cause, by which it is necessarily caused; that this is so is also evident from all that we have said in this chapter; and it will be still more evident when, in the second part, we come to consider and discuss the freedom of man.

Against all this others object: how is it possible that God, who is said to be supremely perfect, and the sole cause, disposer, and provider of all, nevertheless permits such *confusion* to be seen everywhere in Nature? Also, why has he not *made man so as not to be able to sin?*

Now, in the first place, it cannot be rightly said that there is *confusion in Nature,* since nobody knows all the causes of things so as to be able to judge accordingly. This objection, however, originates in this kind of ignorance, namely, that they have set up general Ideas, with which, they think, particular things must agree if they are to be perfect. These *Ideas*, they state, are in the understanding of God, as many of *Plato's* followers have said, namely, that these *general Ideas* (such as Rational, Animal, and the like) *have been created by God*; and although those who follow *Aristotle* say, indeed, that these things are not *real* things, only things of Reason, they nevertheless regard them frequently as [real] things, since they have clearly said that his providence does not extend to particular things, but only to kinds; for example, God has never exercised his providence over Bucephalus, &c., but only over the whole genus Horse. They say also that God has no knowledge of particular and transient things, but only of the general, which, in their opinion, are imperishable. We have, however, rightly considered this to be due to their ignorance. For it is precisely the particular things, and they alone, that have a cause, and not the general, because they are nothing.

God then is the cause of, and providence over, particular things only. If particular things had to conform to some other Nature, then they could not conform to their own, and consequently could not be what they truly are. For example, if God had made all human beings like Adam before the fall, then indeed he would only have created Adam, and no Paul nor Peter; but no, it is just perfection in God, that he gives to all things, from the greatest to the least, their essence, or, to express it better, that he has all things perfectly in himself.

As regards the other [objection], *Why God has not made mankind so that they should not sin,* to this it may serve [as an answer], that whatever is said about sin is only said with reference to us, that is, as when we compare two things with each other, or [consider one thing] from different points of view. For instance, if some one has made a clock precisely in order to strike and to show the hours, and the mechanism quite fulfils the aims of its maker, then we say that it is good, but if it does not do so, then we say that it is bad, notwithstanding that even then it might still be good if only it had been his intention to make it irregular and to strike at wrong times.

We say then, in conclusion, that Peter must, as is necessary, conform to the Idea of Peter, and not to the Idea of *Man;* good and evil, or sin, these are only modes of thought, and by no means things, or any thing that has reality, as we shall very likely show yet more fully in what follows. For all things and works which are in Nature are perfect.

CHAPTER VII

ON THE ATTRIBUTES WHICH DO NOT PERTAIN TO GOD

HERE we shall take up the consideration of those attributes [1] which are commonly attributed to God, but

[1] As regards the attributes of which God consists, they are only infinite substances, each of which must of itself be infinitely perfect. That this must necessarily be so, we are

which, nevertheless, do not pertain to him; as also of those through which it is sought to prove the existence of God, though in vain; and also of the rules of accurate definition.

For this purpose, we shall not trouble ourselves very much about the ideas that people commonly have of God, but we shall only inquire briefly into what the Philosophers can tell us about it. Now these have defined God as *a being existing through or of himself, cause of all things, Omniscient, Almighty, eternal, simple, infinite, the highest good, of infinite compassion,* &c. But before we approach this inquiry, let us just see what admissions they make to us.

In the first place, they say that it is impossible to give a true or right definition of God, because, according to their opinion, there can be no definition except *per genus et differentiam,* and as God is not a species of any genus, he cannot be defined rightly, or according to the rules.

In the second place, they say that God cannot be defined, because the definition must describe the thing itself and also positively; while, according to their standpoint, our knowledge of God cannot be of a positive, but only of a negative kind; therefore no proper definition can be given of God.

They also say, besides, that God can never be proved

---

convinced by clear and distinct reasons. It is true, however, that up to the present only two of all these infinites are known to us through their own essence; and these are thought and extension. All else that is commonly ascribed to God is not any attribute of his, but only certain modes which may be attributed to him either in consideration of all, that is, *all* his attributes, or in consideration of *one* attribute. In consideration of *all* [it is said], for instance, that he is eternal, self-subsisting, infinite, cause of all things, immutable. In consideration of *one* [*it is said*], for instance, that he is omniscient, wise, &c., which pertains to thought, and, again, that he is omnipresent, fills all, &c., which pertains to extension.

a priori, because he has no cause, but only by way of probability, or from his effects.

Since by these assertions of theirs they admit sufficiently that their knowledge of God is very little and slight, let us now proceed to examine their definition.

In the first place, we do not see that they give us in it any *attribute* or attributes through which it can be known what the thing (God) is, but only some *propria* or properties which do, indeed, belong to a thing, but never explain what the thing is. For although *self-subsisting, being the cause of all things, highest good, eternal and immutable,* &c., are peculiar to God alone, nevertheless, from those properties we cannot know what that being, to whom these properties pertain is, and what attributes he has.

It is now also time for us to consider the things which they ascribe to God, and which do not, however, pertain to him,[1] such as *omniscient, merciful, wise,* and so forth, which things, since they are only certain modes of the thinking thing, and can by no means be, or be understood without the substances whose modes they are, can, consequently, also not be attributed to him, who *is a Being subsisting without the aid of anything, and solely through himself.*

Lastly, they call him *the highest good*; but if they understand by it something different from what they have already said, namely, that God *is immutable, and a cause of all things,* then they have become entangled in their own thought, or are unable to understand themselves. This is the outcome of their misconception of good and evil, for they believe that man himself, and not God, is the cause of his sins and wickedness—which, according to what we have already proved, cannot be

---

[1] That is to say, when he is considered as all that he is, or with regard to all his attributes; *see* on this point pp. 76 and 77 *n.*

the case, else we should be compelled to assert that man is also the cause of himself. However, this will appear yet more evident when we come to consider the will of man.

It is necessary that we should now unravel their specious arguments wherewith they seek to excuse their ignorance in Theology.

First of all, then, they say *that a correct definition must consist of a "genus" and "differentia."* Now, although all the Logicians admit this, I do not know where they get it from. And, to be sure, if this must be true, then we can know nothing whatever. For if it is through a definition consisting of *genus* and *differentia* that we can first get to know a thing perfectly, then we can never know perfectly the highest *genus*, which has no *genus* above it. Now then: If the highest *genus*, which is the cause of our knowledge of all other things, is not known, much less, then, can the other things be understood or known which are explained by that *genus*. However, since we are free, and do not consider ourselves in any way tied to their assertions, we shall, in accordance with true logic, propose other rules of definition, namely, on the lines of our division of Nature.

Now we have already seen that the attributes (or, as others call them, substances) are things, or, to express ourselves better and more aptly, [constitute] a being which subsists through itself, and therefore makes itself known and reveals itself through itself.

As to the other things, we see that they are but modes of the attributes, without which also they can neither be, nor be understood. Consequently definitions must be of two kinds (or sorts):

1. The first, namely, are those of attributes, which pertain to a self-subsisting being, these need no genus, or anything, through which they might be better under-

stood or explained: for, since they exist as attributes of a self-subsisting being, they also become known through themselves.

2. The second [kind of definitions] are those [of things] which do not exist through themselves, but only through the attributes whose modes they are, and through which, as their *genus*, they must be understood.

And this is [all that need be said] concerning their statement about definitions. As regards the other [assertion], namely, that God can [not] be known by us adequately, this has been sufficiently answered by D. des Cartes in his answers to the objections relating to these things.

And the third [assertion], namely, that God cannot be proved *a priori*, has also already been answered by us. Since God is the cause of himself, it is enough that we prove him through himself, and such a proof is also much more conclusive than the *a posteriori* proof, which generally rests only on external causes.

CHAPTER VIII

ON NATURA NATURANS

HERE, before we proceed to something else, we shall briefly divide the whole of Nature—namely, into *Natura naturans* and *Natura naturata*. By *Natura naturans* we understand a being that we conceive clear and distinctly through itself, and without needing anything beside itself (like all the attributes which we have so far described), that is, God. The Thomists likewise understand God by it, but their *Natura naturans* was a being (so they called it) beyond all substances.

The *Natura naturata* we shall divide into two, a general, and a particular. The *general* consists of all the modes which depend immediately on God, of which we shall treat in the following chapter; the *particular* consists of all the particular things which are produced by the general mode. So that the *Natura naturata* requires some substance in order to be well understood.

On Natura Naturata

Now, as regards the *general Natura naturata*, or the modes, or creations which depend on, or have been created by, God immediately, of these we know no more than two, namely, *motion* in matter,[2] and the *understanding* in the thinking thing. These, then, we say, have been from all eternity, and to all eternity will remain immutable. A work truly as great as becomes the greatness of the work-master.

All that specially concerns *Motion*, such as that it *has been from all eternity, and to all eternity will remain immutable; that it is infinite in its kind; that it can neither be, nor be understood through itself*, but only by means of Extension,—all this, I say, since it [Motion] more properly belongs to a treatise on Natural Science rather than here, we shall not consider in this place, but we shall only say this about it, that it is *a Son, Product, or Effect* created immediately by God.

As regards the *Understanding* in the thinking thing, this, like the first, is also a *Son, Product, or immediate Creation* of God, also created by him from all eternity,

---

[1] This chapter is especially important as elucidating Spinoza's conception of "infinite modes." See Letters 63 and 64. [Ed.]

[2] *Note.*—What is here said about motion in matter is not said seriously. For the Author still intends to discover the cause thereof, as he has already done to some extent *a posteriori*. But it can stand just as it is, because nothing is based upon it, or dependent thereon.

and remaining immutable to all eternity. It has but one function, namely, to understand clearly and distinctly all things at all times; which produces invariably an infinite or most perfect satisfaction, which cannot omit to do what it does. Although what we have just said is sufficiently self-evident, still, we shall prove it more clearly afterwards in our account of the Affects of the Soul, and shall therefore say no more about it here.

CHAPTER X

WHAT GOOD AND EVIL ARE

IN ORDER to explain briefly what good and evil are in themselves, we shall begin thus:

Some things are in our understanding and not in Nature, and so they are also only our own creation, and their purpose is to understand things distinctly: among these we include all relations, which have reference to different things, and these we call *Entia Rationis* [things of reason]. Now the question is, whether good and evil belong to the *Entia Rationis* or to the *Entia Realia* [real things]. But since good and evil are only relations, it is beyond doubt that they must be placed among the *Entia Rationis*; for we never say that something is good except with reference to something else which is not so good, or is not so useful to us as some other thing. Thus we say that a man is bad, only in comparison with one who is better, or also that an apple is bad, in comparison with another which is good or better.

All this could not possibly be said, if that which is better or good, in comparison with which it [the bad] is so called, did not exist.

Therefore, when we say that something is good, we

only mean that it conforms well to the general Idea which we have of such things. But, as we have already said before, the things must agree with their particular Ideas, whose essence must be a perfect essence, and not with the general [Ideas], since in that case they would not exist.

As to confirming what we have just said, the thing is clear to us; but still, to conclude our remarks, we will add yet the following proofs:

All things which are in Nature, are either things or actions. Now good and evil are neither things nor actions. Therefore good and evil do not exist in Nature.

For, if good and evil are things or actions, then they must have their definitions. But good and evil (as, for example, the goodness of Peter and the wickedness of Judas) have no definitions apart from the essence of Judas or Peter, because this alone exists in Nature, and they cannot be defined without their essence. Therefore, as above—it follows that good and evil are not things or actions which exist in Nature.

SECOND PART

ON MAN AND WHAT PERTAINS TO HIM

PREFACE

HAVING, in the first part, discoursed on God, and on the universal and infinite things, we shall proceed now, in the second part, to the treatment of particular and finite things; though not of all, since they are innumerable, but we shall only treat of those which concern man; and, in the first place, we shall consider here what man is, in so far as he consists of certain modes (contained in the two attributes which we have remarked

in God). I say of certain *modes,* for I by no means
think that man, in so far as he consists of spirit, soul,[1]

[1] 1. Our soul is either a *substance* or a *mode*; it is not a
substance, because we have already shown that there can be
no finite substance; it is therefore a *mode.*

2. Being a mode then, it must be such either of "substantial"
extension or of "substantial" *thought*; not of *extension*, because, &c.; therefore of *thought.*

3. *"Substantial" Thought,* since it cannot be finite, is infinitely perfect in its kind, and an attribute of God.

4. *Perfect thought* must have a *Knowledge,* Idea, or mode of
thought of all and everything *that is real,* of substances as well
as of modes, without exception.

5. We say, *that is real,* because we are not speaking here of
a Knowledge, Idea, &c., which completely knows the nature of
all things as involved in their essence, apart from their individual existence, but only of the Knowledge, Idea, &c., of the
particular things which are constantly coming into existence.

6. This Knowledge, Idea, &c., of each particular thing which
happens to be real is, we say, the *soul* of this particular thing.

7. All and sundry particular things that are real, have become such through motion and rest, and this is true of all the
modes of "substantial" extension which we call *bodies.*

8. The differences among these result solely from the varying
proportions of motion and rest, through which this is *so,* and
not so—this is *this,* and not *that.*

9. From such proportion of motion and rest comes also the
existence of *our body*; of which, consequently, no less than of
all other things, there must be a Knowledge, an Idea, &c., in
the thinking thing, and hence at once also *our soul.*

10. This body of ours, however, had a different proportion
of motion and rest when it was an unborn embryo; and in due
course, when we are dead, it will have a different proportion
again; none the less there was at that time [before our
birth], and there will be then [after death] an idea, knowledge,
&c., of our body in the thinking thing, just as there is now:
but by no means the same [idea, &c.], since it is now differently proportioned as regards motion and rest.

11. To produce, in "substantial" thought, such an idea,
knowledge, mode of thought as ours now is, what is required
is, not any body you please (then it would have to be known
differently from what it is), but just such a body having this
proportion of motion and rest, and no other: for as the body
is, so is the Soul, Idea, Knowledge, &c.

12. As soon, then, as a body has and retains this proportion
[which our body has], say, *e.g.*, of 1 to 3, then that soul and
that body will be like ours now are, being indeed constantly

or body, is a *substance*. Because, already at the beginning of this book, we proved (1) that no substance can have a beginning; (2) that one substance cannot produce another; and lastly (3), that there cannot be two like substances.

As man has not been in existence from eternity, is finite, and is like many men, he can be no substance; so that all that he has of thought are only *modes of the attribute thought* which we have attributed to God. And, again, all that he has of form, motion, and other things, are likewise [modes] of *the other attribute which is attributed by us to God.*

And although from this, [namely,] that the nature of man can neither be, nor be understood without the attributes which we ourselves admit to constitute substance, some try to prove that man is a substance, yet this has no other ground than false suppositions. For, since the nature of matter or body existed before the form of this human body existed, that nature cannot be

---

subject to change, but to none so great that it will exceed the limits of 1 to 3; though as much as it changes, so much also does the soul always change.

13. And this change in us, resulting from other bodies acting upon us, cannot take place without the soul, which always changes correspondingly, becoming aware of the change. And [the consciousness of] this change is really what we call feeling.

14. But when other bodies act so violently upon ours that the proportion of motion [to rest] cannot remain 1 to 3, that means death, and the annihilation of the Soul, since this is only an Idea, Knowledge, &c., of this body having this proportion of motion and rest.

15. Still, since it [the soul] is a mode in the thinking substance it could also know, and love this [substance] as well as that of extension, and by uniting with substances (which remain always the same) it could make itself eternal.[a]

[a] These passages show clearly the ambiguous state of the human soul and the two divergent paths that lie before it. Cf. Tr. T-P. Ch. 4, p. 60. [Ed.]

peculiar to the human body, because it is clear that during the time when man was not, it could never belong to the nature of man.

And what they set up as a fundamental principle, [namely,] *that that pertains to the nature of a thing, without which the thing can neither be, nor be understood,* we deny. For we have already shown *that without God no thing can be or be understood.* That is, God must first be and be understood before these particular things can be and be understood. We have also shown that *genera* do not belong to the nature of definition, but that only such things as cannot exist without others, can also not be understood without these. This being so, what kind of a rule shall we, then, state, whereby it shall be known what belongs to the nature of a thing?

Well, the rule is this: That belongs to the nature of a thing, without which the thing can neither be, nor be understood; not merely so, however, but in such wise that the judgment must be convertible, that is, that the predicate can neither be, nor be understood without the thing. . . .

CHAPTER XXII

ON TRUE KNOWLEDGE, REGENERATION, &c.

SINCE, then, Reason has no power to lead us to the attainment of our well-being, it remains for us to inquire whether we can attain it through the fourth, and last, kind of knowledge. Now we have said that this kind of knowledge does not result from something else, but from a direct revelation of the object itself to the understanding. And if that object is glorious and good, then the soul becomes necessarily united with it, as we have also remarked with reference to our body. Hence it follows incontrovertibly that it is this knowledge which evokes love. So that when we get to know God after this manner then (as he cannot reveal himself, nor become known to us otherwise than as the most glorious and best of all) we must necessarily become united with him. And only in this union, as we have already remarked, does our blessedness consist.

I do not say that we must know him just as he is, or adequately, for it is sufficient for us to know him to some extent, in order to be united with him. For even the knowledge that we have of the body is not such that we know it just as it is, or perfectly; and yet, what a union! what a love!

That this fourth [kind of] knowledge, which is the knowledge of God, is not the consequence of something else, but immediate, is evident from what we have proved before, [namely,] that he is the cause of all knowledge that is acquired through itself alone, and through no other thing; moreover, also from this, that we are so united with him by nature that without him we can neither be, nor be known. And for this reason, since there is such a close union between God and us, it is evident that we cannot know him except directly.

We shall endeavour to explain, next, this union of ours with him through nature and love.

We said before that in Nature there can be nothing of which there should not be an Idea in the soul of that same thing.[1] And according as the thing is either more or less perfect, so also is the union and the influence of the Idea with the thing, or with God himself, less or more perfect. For as the whole of Nature is but one only

---

[1] This also explains what we said in the first part, namely, that the infinite understanding must exist in Nature from all eternity, and why we called it the son of God. For, as God existed from eternity, his Idea must also be in the thinking thing, that is, in himself from eternity, *objective* this Idea coincides with himself; see Chap. IX.

substance, and one whose essence is infinite, all things are united through Nature, and they are united into one [being], namely, God. And now, as the body is the very first thing of which our soul becomes aware (because as already remarked, no thing can exist in Nature, the Idea of which is not in the thinking thing, this Idea being the soul of that thing) so that thing must necessarily be the first cause of the Idea.[1]

But, as this Idea can by no means find rest in the knowledge of the body without passing on to the knowledge of that without which the body and Idea could neither be, nor be understood, so (after knowing it first) it becomes united with it immediately through love. This union is better understood, and one may gather what it must be like, from its action with the body, in which we see how through knowledge of, and feelings towards corporeal things, there arise in us all the effects which we are constantly becoming aware of in the body, through the movements of the [vital] spirits; and therefore (if once our knowledge and love come to embrace that without which we can neither be, nor be understood, and which is in no way corporeal) how incomparably greater and more glorious will and must be the kind of effects resulting from this union; for these must necessarily be commensurate with the thing with which it is united. And when we become aware of these excellent effects, then we may say with truth, *that we have been born again.* For our first birth took place when we were united with the body, through which the activities and movements of the [vital] spirits have arisen; but this our other or second birth will take place when we become aware in us of entirely different effects of

[1] That is, our soul being an Idea of the body derives its first being from the body, but it is only a representation of the body, both as a whole and in its parts, in the thinking thing.

love, commensurate with the knowledge of this incorporeal object, and as different from the first as the corporeal is different from the incorporeal, spirit from flesh. And this may, therefore, all the more justly and truly be called Regeneration, inasmuch as only from this love and union does Eternal and unchangeable existence ensue, as we shall prove.[1]

[APPENDIX II]

On the Human Soul

As MAN is a created finite thing, &c., it necessarily follows that what he has of Thought, and what we call the Soul, is a mode of the attribute which we call Thought, and that nothing else except this mode belongs to his essence: so much so that when this mode comes to naught, the soul perishes also, although the above attribute remains unchanged. Similarly as regards what he has of Extension; what we call Body is nothing else than a mode of the other attribute which we call Extension; when this is destroyed, the human body also ceases to be, although the attribute Extension remains unchanged.

Now in order to understand what this mode is, which we call Soul, and how it derives its origin from the body, and also how its change (only) depends on the body (which to me constitutes the union of soul and body) it must be observed:

1. That the most immediate mode of the attribute which we call thought contains *objective* the formal essence of all things; so much so, that if one could posit a real thing whose essence was not *objective* in the above-named attribute, then this would not be infinite, nor supremely perfect in its kind; contrary to what has already been proved in the third proposition.

[1] Vide preface, and also Tr. T-P. ch. 4, p. 60. [Ed.]

And since, as a matter of fact, Nature or God is one being of which infinite attributes are predicated, and which contains in itself all the essences of created things, it necessarily follows that of all this there is produced in Thought an infinite Idea, which comprehends *objective* the whole of Nature just as it is *realiter*.

2. It is to be observed that all the remaining modes, such as Love, Desire, Joy, &c., derive their origin from this first immediate mode; and that, too, in such wise, that if it did not precede, then there could be no love, desire, nor joy, &c. Whence it clearly follows that the natural love which prompts everything to preserve its body (I mean the mode) cannot have any other origin than in the Idea or the *"objective"* essence of such body which is in the thinking attribute. Further, since for the real existence of an Idea (or "objective" essence) no other thing is required than the thinking attribute and the object (or "formal" essence), it is certain, as we have said, that the Idea, or the "objective" essence, is the most immediate [1] mode of the thinking attribute. And, consequently, there can be in the thinking attribute no other mode, that should belong to the essence of the soul of every thing, except only the Idea, which must be in the thinking attribute when its object exists: for such an idea brings with it the remaining modes of Love, Desire, Joy, &c. Now as the Idea comes from the existence of the object, therefore according as the object changes or perishes, so its Idea must change or perish, and such being the case, it is that which is united with the object.

Lastly, if we should want to proceed and ascribe to the essence of the soul that through which it can be real, we shall be able to find nothing else than the at-

[1] I call that mode the most immediate mode, which, in order to exist, requires no other mode in the same attribute.

tribute [Thought] and the object of which we have just been speaking; and neither of these can belong to the essence of the Soul, as the object has nothing of Thought, and is *realiter* different from the Soul. And with regard to the attribute, we have also proved already that it cannot pertain to the above-mentioned essence, as appears even more clearly from what we said subsequently; for the attribute as attribute is not united with the object, since it neither changes nor perishes, although the object changes or perishes.

Therefore the essence of the soul consists in this alone, namely, in the existence of an Idea or "objective" essence in the thinking attribute, arising from the essence of an object which in fact exists in Nature. I say, *of an object which in fact exists, &c.*, without more particulars, so as to include under this not only the modes of extension, but also the modes of all the infinite attributes, which have also each its soul, just as in the case of extension. And in order that this definition may be somewhat more fully understood, it should be borne in mind what I have already said when speaking about the attributes, which, I said, are not different as regards their existence, for they are themselves the "subjects" of their essences; also that the essence of every one of the modes is contained in the above-named attributes, and, lastly, that all the attributes are attributes of One infinite Being. Wherefore also, in the ninth chapter of the First Part, I called this Idea *a creation created immediately by God*; since it contains *objective* the "formal" essence of all things without omission or addition. And this is necessarily but one, considering that all the essences of the attributes, and the essences of the modes comprehended in these attributes, are the essence of one only infinite being. But it has still to be remarked that these modes, now under consideration, [even when] none of them exists, are nevertheless equally comprehended in their attributes; and as there is no inequality whatever in the attributes, nor yet in the essences of the modes, there can be no particularity in the idea when there is none in Nature. But as soon as ever some of these modes take on their particular existence, and thereby become in some way different from their attributes (because then their particular existence, which they have in the attribute, is the "subject" of their essence), then there shows itself a particularity in the essences of the modes, and consequently in the "objective" essences of these which are necessarily comprehended in the Idea. And this is the reason why we said, in the definition, that the Idea *arises from an object, which really exists in Nature.* And with this we think we have sufficiently explained what kind of a thing the soul is in general, understanding by this expression not only the Ideas which arise from the existence of corporeal modes, but also those which arise from the existence of every mode of the remaining attributes.

But, since we have no such knowledge of the remaining attributes as we have of extension, let us just see whether, having regard to the modes of extension, we can discover a more special definition, and one that shall be more appropriate to express the essence of our souls, for this is the real task before us. Now we shall presuppose here, as something already demonstrated, that extension contains no other modes than motion and rest, and that every particular material thing is nothing else than a certain proportion of motion and rest, so much so indeed that, even if extension contained nothing else except motion only or rest only, then no particular thing could be shown or exist in the whole of extension; the human body, therefore, is nothing else than a certain proportion of motion and rest. Now the "objective essence" of this actual ration of motion and rest which is in the thinking attribute, this (we say) is the soul of the body; so that whenever one of these two modes changes into more or less (motion or rest) the Idea or the soul also changes accordingly. For example, when the [amount of] rest happens to increase, while the [quantity of] motion is diminished, then there is produced thereby that pain or sorrow which we call *cold*; but if, on the contrary, this [increase] takes place in the [amount of] motion, then there is produced thereby that pain which we call *heat.* And so when it happens that the degrees of motion and rest are not equal in all the parts of our body, but that some have more motion and rest than others, there arises therefrom a difference of feeling (and thence arises the different kind of pain which we feel when we are struck in the eyes or on the hands with a cane). And when it happens that the external causes, which bring about these changes, are different from one another, and have not all the same effect, then there results from this a difference of feeling in one and the same part (and from this results the difference of feeling according as one and the same hand is struck with a piece of wood or of iron). And, again, if the change which occurs in a part restores it to its first proportion of motion and rest, there arises from this that joy which we call repose, pleasurable activity, and cheerfulness. Lastly, now that we have explained what feeling is, we can easily see how this gives rise to an *Idea reflexiva*, or the knowledge of oneself, Experience and Reasoning. And from all this (as also because our soul is united with God, and is a part of the infinite Idea, arising immediately from God) there can also be clearly seen the origin of clear knowledge, and the immortality of the soul. But, for the present, what we have said must be enough.

ETHIC

FIRST PART

OF GOD

DEFINITIONS

I. By CAUSE of itself, I understand that, whose essence involves existence; or that, whose nature cannot be conceived unless existing.

II. That thing is called finite in its own kind (*in suo genere*) which can be limited by another thing of the same nature. For example, a body is called finite, because we always conceive another which is greater. So a thought is limited by another thought; but a body is not limited by a thought, nor a thought by a body.

III. By substance, I understand that which is in itself and is conceived through itself;[1] in other words, that, the conception of which does not need the conception of another thing from which it must be formed.

IV. By attribute, I understand that which the intellect perceives of substance, as if constituting its essence.[2]

V. By mode, I understand the affections of substance, or that which is in another thing through which also it is conceived.

VI. By God, I understand Being absolutely infinite,

[1] The phrase "conceived through itself" distinguishes this from the ordinary mediaeval definition of substance. Also Descartes *Principles of Phil.* Principle LI. [Ed.]

[2] This definition is sometimes taken to indicate the subjective character of the attributes. Cf., however, Book I, Prop. XIX [Ed.]

that is to say, substance consisting of infinite attributes, each one of which expresses eternal and infinite essence.

Explanation.—I say absolutely infinite but not infinite in its own kind (*in suo genere*); for of whatever is infinite only in its own kind (*in suo genere*), we can deny infinite attributes; but to the essence of that which is absolutely infinite pertains whatever expresses essence and involves no negation.

VII. That thing is called free which exists from the necessity of its own nature alone, and is determined to action by itself alone. That thing, on the other hand, is called necessary, or rather compelled, which by another is determined to existence and action in a fixed and prescribed manner.

VIII. By eternity, I understand existence itself, so far as it is conceived necessarily to follow from the definition alone of the eternal thing.

Explanation.—For such existence, like the essence of the thing, is conceived as an eternal truth. It cannot therefore be explained by duration or time, even if the duration be conceived without beginning or end.

AXIOMS

I. Everything which is, is either in itself or in another

II. That which cannot be conceived through another must be conceived through itself.

III. From a given determinate cause an effect necessarily follows; and, on the other hand, if no determinate cause be given, it is impossible that an effect can follow.

IV. The knowledge (cognitio) of an effect depends upon and involves the knowledge of the cause.

V. Those things which have nothing mutually in common with one another cannot through one another be mutually understood, that is to say, the conception of the one does not involve the conception of the other.

VI. A true idea must agree with that of which it is the idea (*cum suo ideato*).

VII. The essence of that thing which can be conceived as not existing does not involve existence.

PROP. I.—*Substance is by its nature prior to its affections.*

Demonst.—This is evident from Defs. 3 and 5.

PROP. II.—*Two substances having different attributes have nothing in common with one another.*

Demonst.—This is also evident from Def. 3. For each substance must be in itself and must be conceived through itself, that is to say, the conception of one does not involve the conception of the other.—Q.E.D.

PROP. III.—*If two things have nothing in common with one another, one cannot be the cause of the other.*[1]

Demonst.—If they have nothing mutually in common with one another, they cannot (Ax. 5) through one another be mutually understood, and therefore (Ax. 4) one cannot be the cause of the other.—Q.E.D.

PROP. IV.—*Two or more distinct things are distinguished from one another, either by the difference of the attributes of the substances, or by the difference of their affections.*

[1] In this proposition as well as in Prop. VI Spinoza probably has the Neo-Platonic theory of emanation in mind. According to this view, widely current in the Middle Ages, the world has been produced by God as a transcendent cause. [Ed.]

Demonst.—Everything which is, is either in itself or in another (Ax. 1), that is to say (Defs. 3 and 5), outside the intellect there is nothing but substances and their affections. There is nothing therefore outside the intellect by which a number of things can be distinguished one from another, but substances or (which is the same thing by Def. 4) their attributes and their affections.—Q.E.D.

PROP. V.—*In nature there cannot be two or more substances of the same nature or attribute.*

Demonst.—If there were two or more distinct substances, they must be distinguished one from the other by difference of attributes or difference of affections (Prop. 4). If they are distinguished only by difference of attributes, it will be granted that there is but one substance of the same attribute. But if they are distinguished by difference of affections, since substance is prior by nature to its affections (Prop. 1), the affections therefore being placed on one side, and the substance being considered in itself, or, in other words (Def. 3 and Ax. 6), truly considered, it cannot be conceived as distinguished from another substance, that is to say (Prop. 4), there cannot be two or more substances, but only one possessing the same nature or attribute.—Q.E.D.

PROP. VI.—*One substance cannot be produced by another substance.*

Demonst.—There cannot in nature be two substances of the same attribute (Prop. 5), that is to say (Prop. 2), two which have anything in common with one another. And therefore (Prop. 3) one cannot be the cause of the other, that is to say, one cannot be produced by the other.—Q.E.D.

Corol.—Hence it follows that there is nothing by which substance can be produced, for in nature there is nothing but substances and their affections (as is evident from Ax. 1 and Defs. 3 and 5). But substance cannot be produced by substance (Prop. 6). Therefore absolutely there is nothing by which substance can be produced.—Q.E.D.

Another Demonst.—This corollary is demonstrated more easily by the *reductio ad absurdum.* For if there were anything by which substance could be produced, the knowledge of substance would be dependent upon the knowledge of its cause (Ax. 4), and therefore (Def. 3) it would not be substance.

PROP. VII.—*It pertains to the nature of substance to exist.*

Demonst.—There is nothing by which substance can be produced (Corol. Prop. 6). It will therefore be the cause of itself, that is to say (Def. 1), its essence necessarily involves existence, or in other words it pertains to its nature to exist.—Q.E.D.

PROP. VIII.—*Every substance is necessarily infinite.*

Demonst.—Substance which has only one attribute cannot exist except as one substance (Prop. 5), and to the nature of this one substance it pertains to exist (Prop. 7). It must therefore from its nature exist as finite or infinite. But it cannot exist as finite substance, for (Def. 2) it must (if finite) be limited by another substance of the same nature, which also must necessarily exist (Prop. 7), and therefore there would be two substances of the same attribute, which is absurd (Prop. 5). It exists therefore as infinite substance.—Q.E.D.

Schol. 1.—Since finiteness is in truth partly negation, and infinitude absolute affirmation of existence of some kind, it follows from Prop. 7 alone that all substance must be infinite.

Schol. 2.—I fully expect that those who judge things confusedly, and who have not been accustomed to cognise things through their first causes, will find it difficult to comprehend the demonstration of the 7th Proposition, since they do not distinguish between the modifications of substances and substances themselves, and are ignorant of the manner in which things are produced. Hence it comes to pass that they erroneously ascribe to substances a beginning like that which they see belongs to natural things; for those who are ignorant of the true causes of things confound every thing, and without any mental repugnance represent trees speaking like men, or imagine that men are made out of stones as well as begotten from seed, and that all forms can be changed the one into the other. So also those who confound human nature with the divine, readily attribute to God human affects,[1] especially so long as they are ignorant of the manner in which affects are produced in the mind. But if men would attend to the nature of substance, they could not entertain a single doubt of the truth of Proposition 7; indeed this proposition would be considered by all to be axiomatic, and reckoned amongst common notions. For by "substance" would be understood that which is in itself and is conceived through itself, or, in other words, that, the knowledge of which does not need the knowledge of another thing.

[1] *Affectus* is translated by "affect" and *affectio* by "affection." There seems to be no other way in the English language of marking the relationship of the two words and preserving their exact meaning. *Affectus* has sometimes been translated "passion," but Spinoza uses *passio* for passion, and means something different from *affectus*. See Def. III, part 3.

But by "modifications" would be understood those things which are in another thing—those things, the conception of which is formed from the conception of the thing in which they are. Hence we can have true ideas of non-existent modifications, since although they may not actually exist outside the intellect, their essence nevertheless is so comprehended in something else, that they may be conceived through it. But the truth of substances is not outside the intellect unless in the substances themselves, because they are conceived through themselves. If any one, therefore, were to say that he possessed a clear and distinct, that is to say, a true idea of substance, and that he nevertheless doubted whether such a substance exists, he would forsooth be in the same position as if he were to say that he had a true idea and nevertheless doubted whether or not it was false (as is evident to any one who pays a little attention). Similarly if any one were to affirm that substance is created, he would affirm at the same time that a false idea had become true, and this is a greater absurdity than can be conceived. It is therefore necessary to admit that the existence of substance, like its essence, is an eternal truth. Hence a demonstration (which I have thought worth while to append) by a different method is possible, showing that there are not two substances possessing the same nature. But in order to prove this methodically it is to be noted: 1. That the true definition of any one thing neither involves nor expresses anything except the nature of the thing defined. From which it follows, 2. That a definition does not involve or express any certain number of individuals, since it expresses nothing but the nature of the thing defined. For example, the definition of a triangle expresses nothing but the simple nature of a triangle, and not any certain number of triangles. 3. It is to be observed that of every existing thing there is some certain cause by reason of which it exists. 4. Finally, it is to be observed that this cause, by reason of which a thing exists, must either be contained in the nature itself and definition of the existing thing (simply because it pertains to the nature of the thing to exist), or it must exist outside the thing. This being granted, it follows that if a certain number of individuals exist in nature, there must necessarily be a cause why those individuals, and neither more nor fewer, exist. If, for example, there are twenty men in existence (whom, for the sake of greater clearness, I suppose existing at the same time, and that no others existed before them), it will not be sufficient, in order that we may give a reason why twenty men exist, to give a cause for human nature generally; but it will be necessary, in addition, to give a reason why neither more nor fewer than twenty exist, since, as we have already observed under the third head, there must necessarily be a cause why each exists. But this cause (as we have shown under the second and third heads) cannot be contained in human nature itself, since the true definition of a man does not involve the number twenty, and therefore (by the fourth head) the cause why these twenty men exist, and consequently the cause why each exists, must necessarily lie outside each one; and therefore we must conclude generally that whenever it is possible for several individuals of the same nature to exist, there must necessarily be an external cause for their existence.

Since now it pertains to the nature of substance to exist (as we have shown in this scholium), its definition must involve necessary existence, and consequently from its definition alone its existence must be concluded. But from its definition (as we have already shown under the second and third heads) the existence of more sub-

stances than one cannot be deduced. It follows, therefore, from this definition necessarily that there cannot
be two substances possessing the same nature.

PROP. IX.—*The more reality or being a thing possesses,
the more attributes belong to it.*

Demonst.—This is evident from Def. 4.

PROP. X.—*Each attribute of a substance must be conceived through itself.*

Demonst.—For an attribute is that which the intellect perceives of substance, as if constituting its essence
(Def. 4), and therefore (Def. 3) it must be conceived
through itself.—Q.E.D.

Schol.—From this it is apparent that although two
attributes may be conceived as really distinct—that is to
say, one without the assistance of the other—we cannot
nevertheless thence conclude that they constitute two
beings or two different substances; for this is the nature
of substance, that each of its attributes is conceived
through itself, since all the attributes which substance
possesses were always in it together, nor could one be
produced by another; but each expresses the reality or
being of substance. It is very far from being absurd,
therefore, to ascribe to one substance a number of
attributes, since nothing in nature is clearer than that
each being must be conceived under some attribute, and
the more reality or being it has, the more attributes it
possesses expressing necessity or eternity and infinity.
Nothing consequently is clearer than that Being absolutely infinite is necessarily defined, as we have shown
(Def. 6), as Being which consists of infinite attributes,
each one of which expresses a certain essence, eternal
and infinite. But if any one now asks by what sign,

therefore, we may distinguish between substances, let him read the following propositions, which show that in nature only one substance exists, and that it is absolutely infinite. For this reason that sign would be sought for in vain.

PROP. XI.—*God, or substance consisting of infinite attributes, each one of which expresses eternal and infinite essence, necessarily exists.*

Demonst.—If this be denied, conceive, if it be possible, that God does not exist. Then it follows (Ax. 7) that His essence does not involve existence. But this (Prop. 7) is absurd. Therefore God necessarily exists.—Q.E.D.

Another proof.—For the existence or non-existence of everything there must be a reason or cause. For example, if a triangle exists, there must be a reason or cause why it exists; and if it does not exist, there must be a reason or cause which hinders its existence or which negates it. But this reason or cause must either be contained in the nature of the thing or lie outside it. For example, the nature of the thing itself shows the reason why a square circle does not exist, the reason being that a square circle involves a contradiction. And the reason, on the other hand, why substance exists follows from its nature alone, which involves existence (see Prop. 7). But the reason why a circle or triangle exists or does not exist is not drawn from their nature, but from the order of corporeal nature generally; for from that it must follow, either that a triangle necessarily exists, or that it is impossible for it to exist. But this is self-evident. Therefore it follows that if there be no cause nor reason which hinders a thing from existing, it exists necessarily. If, therefore, there be no reason nor cause which hinders God from existing, or which negates His existence, we must conclude absolutely that He necessarily exists. But if there be such a reason or cause, it must be either in the nature itself of God or must lie outside it, that is to say, in another substance of another nature. For if the reason lay in a substance of the same nature, the existence of God would be by this very fact admitted. But substance possessing another nature could have nothing in common with God (Prop. 2), and therefore could not give Him existence nor negate it. Since, therefore, the reason or cause which could negate the divine existence cannot be outside the divine nature, it will necessarily, supposing that the divine nature does not exist, be in His Nature itself, which would therefore involve a contradiction. But to affirm this of the Being absolutely infinite and consummately perfect is absurd. Therefore neither in God nor outside God is there any cause or reason which can negate His existence, and therefore God necessarily exists.—Q.E.D.

#3 *Another proof.*—Inability to exist is impotence, and, on the other hand, ability to exist is power, as is self-evident. If, therefore, there is nothing which necessarily exists excepting things finite, it follows that things finite are more powerful than the absolutely infinite Being, and this (as is self-evident) is absurd; therefore either nothing exists or Being absolutely infinite also necessarily exists. But we ourselves exist, either in ourselves or in something else which necessarily exists (Ax. 1 and Prop. 7). Therefore the Being absolutely infinite, that is to say (Def. 6), God, necessarily exists.—Q.E.D.

#4 *Schol.*—In this last demonstration I wished to prove the existence of God *a posteriori*, in order that the demonstration might be the more easily understood, and not because the existence of God does not follow *a priori* from the same grounds. For since ability to exist is power, it follows that the more reality belongs to the nature of anything, the greater is the power for existence it derives from itself; and it also follows, therefore, that the Being absolutely infinite, or God, has from Himself an absolutely infinite power of existence, and that He therefore necessarily exists. Many persons, nevertheless, will perhaps not be able easily to see the force of this demonstration, because they have been accustomed to contemplate those things alone which flow from external causes, and they see also that those things which are quickly produced from these causes, that is to say, which easily exist, easily perish, whilst, on the other hand, they adjudge those things to be more difficult to produce, that is to say, not so easy to bring into existence, to which they conceive more properties pertain. In order that these prejudices may be removed, I do not need here to show in what respect this saying, "What is quickly made quickly perishes," is true, nor to inquire whether, looking at the whole of nature, all things are or are not equally easy. But this only it will be sufficient for me to observe, that I do not speak of things which are produced by external causes, but that I speak of substances alone which (Prop. 6) can be produced by no external cause. For whatever perfection or reality those things may have which are produced by external causes, whether they consist of many parts or of few, they owe it all to the virtue of an external cause, and therefore their existence springs from the perfection of an external cause alone and not from their own. On the other hand, whatever perfection substance has is due to no external cause. Therefore its existence must follow from its nature alone, and is therefore nothing else than its essence. Perfection consequently does not prevent the existence of a thing, but

establishes it; imperfection, on the other hand, prevents
existence, and so of no existence can we be more sure
than of the existence of the Being absolutely infinite or
perfect, that is to say, God. For since His essence shuts
out all imperfection and involves absolute perfection,
for this very reason all cause of doubt concerning His
existence is taken away, and the highest certainty concerning it is given,—a truth which I trust will be evident to any one who bestows only moderate attention.

PROP. XII.—*No attribute of substance can be truly conceived from which it follows that substance can be
divided.*

Demonst.—For the parts into which substance thus
conceived would be divided will or will not retain the
nature of substance. If they retain it, then (Prop. 8)
each part will be infinite, and (Prop. 6) the cause of
itself, and will consist of an attribute differing from
that of any other part (Prop. 5), so that from one substance more substances could be formed, which (Prop.
6) is absurd. Moreover the parts (Prop. 2) would have
nothing in common with their whole, and the whole
(Def. 4 and Prop. 10) could be, and could be conceived
without its parts, which no one will doubt to be an
absurdity. But if the second case be supposed, namely,
that the parts will not retain the nature of substance,
then, since the whole substance might be divided into
equal parts, it would lose the nature of substance and
cease to be, which (Prop. 7) is absurd.

PROP. XIII.—*Substance absolutely infinite is indivisible.*

Demonst.—For if it were divisible, the parts into
which it would be divided will or will not retain the

nature of substance absolutely infinite. If they retain it, there will be a plurality of substances possessing the same nature, which (Prop. 5) is absurd. If the second case be supposed, then (as above), substance absolutely infinite can cease to be, which (Prop. 11) is also absurd.

Corol.—Hence it follows that no substance, and consequently no bodily substance in so far as it is substance, is divisible.

Schol.—That substance is indivisible is more easily to be understood from this consideration alone, that the nature of substance cannot be conceived unless as infinite, and that by a part of substance nothing else can be understood than finite substance, which (Prop. 8) involves a manifest contradiction.

PROP. XIV.—*Besides God, no substance can be nor can be conceived.*

Demonst.—Since God is Being absolutely infinite, of whom no attribute can be denied which expresses the essence of substance (Def. 6), and since He necessarily exists (Prop. 11), it follows that if there were any substance besides God, it would have to be explained by some attribute of God, and thus two substances would exist possessing the same attribute, which (Prop. 5) is absurd; and therefore there cannot be any substance excepting God, and consequently none other can be conceived. For if any other could be conceived, it would necessarily be conceived as existing, and this (by the first part of this demonstration) is absurd. Therefore besides God no substance can be, nor can be conceived.—Q.E.D.

Corol. 1.—Hence it follows with the greatest clearness, firstly, that God is one, that is to say (Def. 6), in nature there is but one substance, and it is absolutely infinite, as (Schol. Prop. 10) we have already intimated.

Corol. 2.—It follows, secondly, that the thing extended (*rem extensam*) and the thing thinking (*rem cogitantem*) are either attributes of God or (Ax. 1) affections of the attributes of God.

PROP. XV.—*Whatever is, is in God, and nothing can either be or be conceived without God.*

Demonst.—Besides God there is no substance, nor can any be conceived (Prop. 14), that is to say (Def. 3), nothing which is in itself and is conceived through itself. But modes (Def. 5) can neither be nor be conceived without substance; therefore in the divine nature only can they be, and through it alone can they be conceived. But besides substances and modes nothing is assumed (Ax. 1). Therefore nothing can be or be conceived without God.—Q.E.D.

Schol.—There are those who imagine God to be like a man, composed of body and soul and subject to passions; but it is clear enough from what has already been demonstrated how far off men who believe this are from the true knowledge of God. But these I dismiss, for all men who have in any way looked into the divine nature deny that God is corporeal. That He cannot be so they conclusively prove by showing that by "body" we understand a certain quantity possessing length, breadth, and depth, limited by some fixed form; and that to attribute these to God, a being absolutely infinite, is the greatest absurdity. But yet at the same time, from other arguments by which they endeavour to confirm their proof, they clearly show that they remove altogether from the divine nature substance itself corporeal or extended, affirming that it was created by God. By what divine power, however, it could have been created they are altogether ignorant, so that it is clear they do not understand what they themselves say. But I have demonstrated, at least in my own opinion, with sufficient clearness (see Corol. Prop. 6 and Schol. 2, Prop. 8), that no substance can be produced or created by another being (*ab alio*). Moreover (Prop. 14), we have shown that besides God no substance can be nor can be conceived; and hence we have concluded that extended substance is one of the infinite attributes of God. But for the sake of a fuller explanation, I will refute my adversaries' arguments, which, taken altogether, come to this. First, that corporeal substance, in so far as it is substance, consists, as they suppose, of parts, and therefore they deny that it can be infinite, and consequently that it can pertain to God. This they

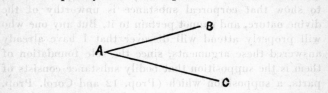

illustrate by many examples, one or two of which I will adduce. If corporeal substance, they say, be infinite, let us conceive it to be divided into two parts; each part, therefore, will be either finite or infinite. If each part be finite, then the infinite is composed of two finite parts, which is absurd. If each part be infinite, there is then an infinite twice as great as another infinite, which is also absurd. Again, if infinite quantity be measured by equal parts of a foot each, it must contain an infinite number of such parts, and similarly if it be measured by equal parts of an inch each; and therefore one infinite number will be twelve times greater than another infinite number. Lastly, if from one point of any infinite quantity it be imagined that two lines, AB, AC, which at first are at a certain and determinate distance from one another, be infinitely extended, it is plain that the distance between B and C will be continually increased, and at length from being determinate will be indeterminable. Since therefore these absurdities follow, as they think, from supposing quantity to be infinite, they conclude that corporeal substance must be finite, and consequently cannot pertain to the essence of God. A second argument is assumed from the absolute perfection of God. For God, they say, since He is a being absolutely perfect, cannot suffer; but corporeal substance, since it is divisible, can suffer: it follows, therefore, that it does not pertain to God's essence. These are the arguments which I find in authors, by which they endeavour to show that corporeal substance is unworthy of the divine nature, and cannot pertain to it. But any one who will properly attend will discover that I have already answered these arguments, since the sole foundation of them is the supposition that bodily substance consists of parts, a supposition which (Prop. 12 and Corol. Prop. 13) I have shown to be absurd. Moreover, if any one will rightly consider the matter, he will see that all these absurdities (supposing that they are all absurdities, a point which I will now take for granted), from which these authors attempt to draw the conclusion that substance extended is finite, do not by any means follow from the supposition that quantity is infinite, but from the supposition that infinite quantity is measurable, and that it is made up of finite parts. Therefore, from the absurdities to which this leads nothing can be concluded, excepting that infinite quantity is not measurable, and that it cannot be composed of finite parts. But this is what we have already demonstrated (Prop. 12, &c.), and the shaft therefore which is aimed at us turns against those who cast it. If, therefore, from these absurdities any one should attempt to conclude that substance extended must be finite, he would, forsooth, be in the position of the man who supposes a circle to have the properties of a square, and then concludes that it has no centre, such that all the lines drawn from it to the circumference are equal. For corporeal substance, which cannot be conceived except as infinite, one and indivisible (Props. 8, 5, and 12), is conceived by those against whom I argue to be composed of finite parts, and to be multiplex and divisible, in order that they may prove it finite. Just in the same way others, after they have imagined a line to consist of points, know how to discover many arguments, by which they show that a line cannot be divided *ad infinitum*; and indeed it is not less absurd to suppose that corporeal substance is composed of bodies or parts than to suppose that a body is composed of surfaces, surfaces of lines, and that lines, finally, are composed of points. Every one who knows that clear reason is infallible ought to admit this, and especially those who deny that a vacuum can exist. For if corporeal substance could be so divided that its parts could be really distinct, why could not one part be annihilated, the rest remaining, as before, connected with one another? And why must all be so fitted together that there can be no vacuum? For of things which are really distinct the one from the other, one can be and remain in its own position without the other. Since, therefore, it is supposed that there is no vacuum in nature (about which I will speak at another time), but that all the parts must be united, so that no vacuum can exist, it follows that they cannot be really separated; that is to say, that corporeal substance, in so far as it is substance, cannot be divided. If, nevertheless, any one should now ask why there is a natural tendency to consider quantity as capable of division, I reply that quantity is conceived by us in two ways: either abstractly or superficially; that is to say, as we imagine it, or else as substance, in which way it is conceived by the intellect alone. If, therefore, we regard quantity (as we do very often and easily) as it exists in the imagination, we find it to be finite, divisible, and composed of parts; but if we regard it as it exists in the intellect, and conceive it in so far as it is substance, which is very difficult, then, as we have already sufficiently demonstrated, we find it to be infinite, one, and indivisible. This will be plain enough to all who know how to distinguish between the imagination and the intellect, and more especially if we remember that matter is everywhere the same, and that, except in so far as we regard it as affected in different ways, parts are not distinguished in it; that is to say, they are distinguished with regard to mode, but not with regard to reality. For example, we conceive water as being divided, in so far as it is water, and that its parts are separated from one another; but in so far as it is corporeal substance we cannot thus conceive it, for as such it is neither separated nor divided. Moreover, water, in so far as it is water, is originated and destroyed; but in so far as it is substance, it is neither originated nor destroyed. By this reasoning I think that I have also answered the second argument, since that too is based upon the assumption that matter, considered as substance, is divisible and composed of parts. And even if what I have urged were not true, I do not know why matter should be unworthy of the divine nature, since (Prop. 14) outside God no substance can exist from which the divine nature could suffer. All things, I say, are in God, and everything which takes place takes place by the laws alone of the infinite nature of God, and follows (as I shall presently show) from the necessity of His essence. Therefore in no way whatever can it be asserted that God suffers from anything, or that substance extended, even if it be supposed divisible, is unworthy of the divine nature, provided only it be allowed that it is eternal and infinite. But enough on this point for the present.[1]

PROP. XVI.—*From the necessity of the divine nature infinite numbers of things in infinite ways (that is to say, all things which can be conceived by the infinite intellect) must follow.*

Demonst.—This proposition must be plain to every one who considers that from the given definition of anything a number of properties necessarily following from it (that is to say, following from the essence of the thing itself) are inferred by the intellect, and just in proportion as the definition of the thing expresses a greater reality, that is to say, just in proportion as the essence of the thing defined involves a greater reality, will more properties be inferred. But the divine nature possesses absolutely infinite attributes (Def. 6), each one of which expresses infinite essence in its own kind (*in suo genere*), and therefore, from the necessity of the divine nature, infinite numbers of things in infinite ways (that is to say, all things which can be conceived by the infinite intellect) must necessarily follow.—Q.E.D.

Corol. 1.—Hence it follows that God is the efficient cause of all things which can fall under the infinite intellect.

Corol. 2.—It follows, secondly, that God is cause

[1] See Letter 12 for an interesting version of this argument. [Ed.]

through Himself, and not through that which is contingent (*per accidens*).

Corol. 3.—It follows, thirdly, that God is absolutely the first cause.

Prop. XVII.—*God acts from the laws of His own nature only, and is compelled by no one.*

Demonst.—We have just shown (Prop. 16) that from the necessity, or (which is the same thing) from the laws only of the divine nature, infinite numbers of things absolutely follow; and we have demonstrated (Prop. 15) that nothing can be, nor can be conceived, without God, but that all things are in God. Therefore, outside Himself, there can be nothing by which He may be determined or compelled to act; and therefore He acts from the laws of His own nature only, and is compelled by no one.—Q.E.D.

Corol. 1.—Hence it follows, firstly, that there is no cause, either external to God or within Him, which can excite Him to act except the perfection of His own nature.

Corol. 2.—It follows, secondly, that God alone is a free cause; for God alone exists from the necessity alone of His own nature (Prop. 11, and Corol. 1, Prop. 14), and acts from the necessity alone of His own nature (Prop. 17). Therefore (Def. 7) He alone is a free cause.—Q.E.D.

Schol.—There are some who think that God is a free cause because He can, as they think, bring about that those things which we have said follow from His nature —that is to say, those things which are in His power— should not be, or should not be produced by Him. But this is simply saying that God could bring about that it should not follow from the nature of a triangle that its three angles should be equal to two right angles, or that from a given cause an effect should not follow, which is absurd. But I shall show farther on, without the help of this proposition, that neither intellect nor will pertain to the nature of God.

I know, indeed, that there are many who think themselves able to demonstrate that intellect of the highest order and freedom of will both pertain to the nature of God, for they say that they know nothing more perfect which they can attribute to Him than that which is the chief perfection in ourselves. But although they conceive God as actually possessing the highest intellect, they nevertheless do not believe that He can bring about that all those things should exist which are actually in His intellect, for they think that by such a supposition they would destroy His power. If He had treated, they say, all things which are in His intellect, He could have created nothing more, and this, they believe, does not accord with God's omnipotence so then they prefer to consider God as indifferent to all things, and creating nothing excepting that which He has decreed to create by a certain absolute will. But I think that I have shown with sufficient clearness (Prop. 16) that from the supreme power of God, or from His infinite nature, infinite things in infinite ways, that is to say, all things, have necessarily flowed, or continually follow by the same necessity, in the same way as it follows from the nature of a triangle, from eternity and to eternity, that its three angles are equal to two right angles. The omnipotence of God has therefore been actual from eternity, and in the same actuality will remain to eternity. In this way the omnipotence of God, in my opinion, is far more firmly established. My adversaries, indeed (if I may be permitted to speak plainly), seem to deny the omnipotence of God, inasmuch as they are forced to

admit that He has in His mind an infinite number of
things which might be created, but which, nevertheless,
He will never be able to create, for if He were to create
all things which He has in His mind, He would, according to them, exhaust His omnipotence and make Himself
imperfect. Therefore, in order to make a perfect God,
they are compelled to make Him incapable of doing all
those things to which His power extends, and anything
more absurd than this, or more opposed to God's omnipotence, I do not think can be imagined. Moreover—to
say a word, too, here about the intellect and will which
we commonly attribute to God—if intellect and will
pertain to His eternal essence, these attributes cannot
be understood in the sense in which men generally use
them, for the intellect and will which could constitute
His essence would have to differ entirely from our
intellect and will, and could resemble ours in nothing
except in name. There could be no further likeness than
that between the celestial constellation of the Dog and
the animal which barks. This I will demonstrate as
follows. If intellect pertains to the divine nature, it
cannot, like our intellect, follow the things which are
its object (as many suppose), nor can it be simultaneous in its nature with them, since God is prior to
all things in causality (Corol. 1, Prop. 16); but, on
the contrary, the truth and formal essence of things is
what it is, because as such it exists objectively in God's
intellect. Therefore the intellect of God, in so far as
it is conceived to constitute His essence, is in truth the
cause of things, both of their essence and of their
existence,—a truth which seems to have been understood
by those who have maintained that God's intellect, will,
and power are one and the same thing. Since, therefore,
God's intellect is the sole cause of things, both of their
essence and of their existence (as we have already

shown), it must necessarily differ from them with regard
both to its essence and existence; for an effect differs
from its cause precisely in that which it has from its
cause. For example, one man is the cause of the existence but not of the essence of another, for the essence is
an eternal truth; and therefore with regard to essence
the two men may exactly resemble one another, but
with regard to existence they must differ. Consequently
if the existence of one should perish, that of the other
will not therefore perish; but if the essence of one could
be destroyed and become false, the essence of the other
would be likewise destroyed. Therefore a thing which is
the cause both of the essence and of the existence of any
effect must differ from that effect both with regard to
its essence and with regard to its existence. But the
intellect of God is the cause both of the essence and
existence of our intellect; therefore the intellect of
God, so far as it is conceived to constitute the divine
essence, differs from our intellect both with regard to
its essence and its existence, nor can it coincide with
our intellect in anything except the name, which is
what we essayed to prove. The same demonstration may
be applied to the will, as anyone may easily see for
himself.

PROP. XVIII.—*God is the immanent, and not the transitive* [1] *cause of all things.*

Demonst.—All things which are, are in God and must
be conceived through Him (Prop. 15), and therefore
(Corol. 1, Prop. 16) He is the cause of the things
which are in Himself. This is the first thing which was
to be proved. Moreover, outside God there can be no
substance (Prop. 14), that is to say (Def. 3), outside

[1] *Transiens,* passing over and into from the outside.

Him nothing can exist which is in itself. This was the second thing to be proved. God, therefore, is the immanent, but not the transitive cause of all things.—Q.E.D.

PROP. XIX.—*God is eternal, or, in other words, all His attributes are eternal.*

Demonst.—For God (Def. 6) is substance, which (Prop. 11) necessarily exists, that is to say (Prop. 7), a substance to whose nature it pertains to exist, or (which is the same thing) a substance from the definition of which it follows that it exists, and therefore (Def. 8) He is eternal. Again, by the attributes of God is to be understood that which (Def. 4) expresses the essence of the divine substance, that is to say, that which pertains to substance. It is this, I say, which the attributes themselves must involve. But eternity pertains to the nature of substance (Prop. 7). Therefore each of the attributes must involve eternity, and therefore all are eternal.—Q.E.D.

Schol.—This proposition is as clear as possible, too, from the manner in which (Prop. 11) I have demonstrated the existence of God. From that demonstration I say it is plain that the existence of God, like His essence, is an eternal truth. Moreover (Prop. 19 of the "Principles of the Cartesian Philosophy"), I have demonstrated by another method the eternity of God, and there is no need to repeat the demonstration here.

PROP. XX.—*The existence of God and His essence are one and the same thing.*

God (Prop. 19) and all His attributes are eternal, that is to say (Def. 8), each one of His attributes expresses existence. The same attributes of God, therefore, which (Def. 4) manifest the eternal essence of God, at the same time manifest His eternal existence;

that is to say, the very same thing which constitutes the essence of God constitutes at the same time His existence, and therefore His existence and His essence are one and the same thing.—Q.E.D.

Corol. 1.—Hence it follows, 1. That the existence of God, like His essence, is an eternal truth.

Corol. 2.—It follows, 2. That God is immutable, or (which is the same thing) all His attributes are immutable; for if they were changed as regards their existence, they must be changed also as regards their essence (Prop. 20); that is to say (as is self-evident), from being true, they would become false, which is absurd.

PROP. XXI.—*All things which follow from the absolute nature of any attribute of God must for ever exist, and must be infinite; that is to say, through that same attribute they are eternal and infinite.*[1]

Demonst.—Conceive, if possible (supposing that the truth of the proposition is denied), that in some attribute of God something which is finite and has a determinate existence or duration follows from the absolute nature of that attribute; for example, an idea of God in thought.[2] But thought, since it is admitted to be an attribute of God, is necessarily (Prop. 11) in its nature infinite. But so far as it has the idea of God it is by supposition finite. But (Def. 2) it cannot be conceived as finite unless it be determined by thought itself. But it cannot be determined by thought itself so far as it constitutes the idea of God, for so far by supposition it is finite.

[1] In this proposition and the next succeeding two Spinoza is referring to the "infinite modes." Cf. Letters 63 and 64 and especially Sh. Treatise Part I chap. 9. [Ed.]

[2] Not the idea which man forms of God, but rather one of God's ideas. The original "idea Dei" admits either interpretation when taken without the context.—TR.

Therefore it must be determined by thought so far as it does not constitute the idea of God, but which, nevertheless (Prop. 11), necessarily exists. Thought, therefore, exists which does not form the idea of God, and therefore from its nature, in so far as it is absolute thought, the idea of God does not necessarily follow (for it is conceived as forming and as not forming the idea of God), which is contrary to the hypothesis. Therefore, if an idea of God in thought, or anything else in any attribute of God, follow from the necessity of the absolute nature of that attribute (for the demonstration being universal will apply in every case), that thing must necessarily be infinite, which was the first thing to be proved.

Again, that which thus follows from the necessity of the nature of any attribute cannot have a determinate duration. For, if the truth of this be denied, let it be supposed that in some attribute of God a thing exists which follows from the necessity of the nature of the attribute—for example, an idea of God in thought—and let it be supposed that at some time it has either not existed or will not exist. But since thought is supposed to be an attribute of God, it must exist both necessarily and unchangeably (Prop. 11, and Corol. 2, Prop. 20). Therefore, beyond the limits of the duration of the idea of God (for it is supposed that at some time it has either not existed or will not exist), thought must exist without the idea of God; but this is contrary to hypothesis, for the supposition is that thought being given, the idea of God necessarily follows. Therefore neither an idea of God in thought, nor anything else which necessarily follows from the absolute nature of any attribute of God, can have a determinate duration, but through the same attribute is eternal; which was the second thing to be proved. Observe that what we have affirmed here is true of everything which in any attribute of God necessarily follows from the absolute nature of God.

PROP. XXII.—*Whatever follows from any attribute of God, in so far as it is modified by a modification which through the same attribute exists necessarily and infinitely, must also exist necessarily and infinitely.*

Demonst.—This proposition is demonstrated in the same manner as the preceding proposition.

PROP. XXIII.—*Every mode which exists necessarily and infinitely must necessarily follow either from the absolute nature of some attribute of God, or from some attribute modified by a modification which exists necessarily and infinitely.*

Demonst.—Mode is that which is in something else through which it must be conceived (Def. 5), that is to say (Prop. 15), it is in God alone and through God alone can be conceived. If a mode, therefore, be conceived to exist necessarily and to be infinite, its necessary existence and infinitude must be concluded from some attribute of God or perceived through it, in so far as it is conceived to express infinitude and necessity of existence, that is to say (Def. 8), eternity, or, in other words (Def. 6 and Prop. 19), in so far as it is considered absolutely. A mode, therefore, which exists necessarily and infinitely must follow from the absolute nature of some attribute of God, either immediately (Prop. 21), or mediately through some modification following from His absolute nature, that is to say (Prop. 22), a modification which necessarily and infinitely exists.—Q.E.D.

Prop. XXIV.—*The essence of things produced by God does not involve existence.*

This is evident from the first Definition; for that thing whose nature (considered, that is to say, in itself) involves existence, is the cause of itself and exists from the necessity of its own nature alone.

Corol.—Hence it follows that God is not only the cause of the commencement of the existence of things, but also of their continuance in existence, or, in other words (to use scholastic phraseology), God is the *causa essendi rerum.* For if we consider the essence of things, whether existing or non-existing, we discover that it neither involves existence nor duration, and therefore the essence of existing things cannot be the cause of their existence nor of their duration, but God only is the cause, to whose nature alone existence pertains (Corol. 1, Prop. 14).

Prop. XXV.—*God is not only the efficient cause of the existence of things, but also of their essence.*

Demonst.—Suppose that God is not the cause of the essence of things; then (Ax. 4) the essence of things can be conceived without God, which (Prop. 15) is absurd. Therefore God is the cause of the essence of things.—Q.E.D.

Schol.—This proposition more clearly follows from Prop. 16. For from this proposition it follows that, from the existence of the divine nature, both the essence of things and their existence must necessarily be concluded, or, in a word, in the same sense in which God is said to be the cause of Himself He must be called the cause of all things. This will appear still more clearly from the following corollary.

Corol.—Individual things are nothing but affections or modes of God's attributes, expressing those attributes in a certain and determinate manner. This is evident from Prop. 15 and Def. 5.

PROP. XXVI.—*A thing which has been determined to any action was necessarily so determined by God, and that which has not been thus determined by God cannot determine itself to action.*

Demonst.—That by which things are said to be determined to any action is necessarily something positive (as is self-evident); and therefore God, from the necessity of His nature, is the efficient cause both of its essence and of its existence (Props. 25 and 16), which was the first thing to be proved. From this also the second part of the proposition follows most clearly. For if a thing which has not been determined by God could determine itself, the first part of the proposition would be false, and to suppose this possible is an absurdity, as we have shown.

PROP. XXVII.—*A thing which has been determined by God to any action cannot render itself indeterminate.*

Demonst.—This proposition is evident from the third Axiom.

PROP. XXVIII.—*An individual thing, or a thing which is finite and which has a determinate existence, cannot exist nor be determined to action unless it be determined to existence and action by another cause which is also finite and has a determinate existence; and again, this cause cannot exist nor be determined to action unless by another cause which is also finite and determined to existence and action, and so on* ad infinitum.

Demonst.—Whatever is determined to existence and action is thus determined by God (Prop. 26 and Corol. Prop. 24). But that which is finite and which has a determinate existence could not be produced by the absolute nature of any attribute of God, for whatever follows from the absolute nature of any attribute of God is infinite and eternal (Prop. 21). The finite and determinate must therefore follow from God, or from some attribute of God, in so far as the latter is considered to be affected by some mode, for besides substance and modes nothing exists (Ax. 1, and Defs. 3 and 5), and modes (Corol. Prop. 25) are nothing but affections of God's attributes. But the finite and determinate could not follow from God, or from any one of His attributes, so far as that attribute is affected with a modification which is eternal and infinite (Prop. 22). It must, therefore, follow or be determined to existence and action by God, or by some attribute of God, in so far as the attribute is modified by a modification which is finite, and which has a determinate existence. This was the first thing to be proved. Again, this cause or this mode (by the same reasoning by which we have already demonstrated the first part of this propositon) must be determined by another cause, which is also finite, and which has a determinate existence, and this last cause (by the same reasoning) must, in its turn, be determined by another cause, and so on continually (by the same reasoning) *ad infinitum.*

Schol.—Since certain things must have been immediately produced by God, that is to say, those which necessarily follow from His absolute nature; these primary products being the mediating cause for those things which, nevertheless, without God can neither be nor can be conceived; it follows, firstly, that of things immediately produced by God He is the proximate cause absolutely, and not in their own kind (*in suo genere*), as we say; for effects of God can neither be nor be conceived without their cause (Prop. 15, and Corol. Prop. 24).

It follows, secondly, that God cannot be properly called the remote cause of individual things, unless for the sake of distinguishing them from the things which He has immediately produced, or rather which follow from His absolute nature. For by a remote cause we understand that which is in no way joined to its effect. But all things which are, are in God, and so depend upon Him that without Him they can neither be nor be conceived.

PROP. XXIX.—*In nature there is nothing contingent, but all things are determined from the necessity of the divine nature to exist and act in a certain manner.*

Demonst.—Whatever is, is in God (Prop. 15); but God cannot be called a contingent thing, for (Prop. 11) He exists necessarily and not contingently. Moreover, the modes of the divine nature have followed from it necessarily and not contingently (Prop. 16), and that, too, whether it be considered absolutely (Prop. 21), or as determined to action in a certain manner (Prop. 27). But God is the cause of these modes, not only in so far as they simply exist (Corol. Prop. 24), but also (Prop. 26) in so far as they are considered as determined to any action. And if they are not determined by God (by the same proposition), it is an impossibility and not a contingency that they should determine themselves:

and, on the other hand (Prop. 27), if they are determined by God, it is an impossibility and not a contingency that they should render themselves indeterminate. Wherefore all things are determined from a necessity of the divine nature, not only to exist, but to exist and act in a certain manner, and there is nothing contingent.—Q.E.D.

Schol.—Before I go any farther, I wish here to explain, or rather to recall to recollection, what we mean by *natura naturans* and what by *natura naturata*.[1] For, from what has gone before, I think it is plain that by *natura naturans* we are to understand that which is in itself and is conceived through itself, or those attributes of substance which express eternal and infinite essence, that is to say (Corol. 1, Prop. 14, and Corol. 2, Prop. 17), God in so far as He is considered as a free cause. But by *natura naturata* I understand everything which follows from the necessity of the nature of God, or of any one of God's attributes, that is to say, all the modes of God's attributes in so far as they are considered as things which are in God, and which without God can neither be nor can be conceived.

PROP. XXX.—*The actual intellect,[2] whether finite or infinite, must comprehend the attributes of God and the affections of God, and nothing else.*

Demonst.—A true idea must agree with that of which it is the idea (Ax. 6), that is to say (as is self-evident), that which is objectively contained in the intellect must necessarily exist in nature. But in nature (Corol. 1,

---

[1] These are two expressions derived from a scholastic philosophy which strove to signify by the same verb the oneness of God and the world, and yet at the same time to mark by a difference of inflexion that there was not absolute identity.—TR.

[2] Distinguished from potential intellect, Schol. Prop. 31.—TR.

Prop. 14) only one substance exists, namely, God, and no affections (Prop. 15) excepting those which are in God, and which (by the same proposition) can neither be nor be conceived without God. Therefore the actual intellect, whether finite or infinite, must comprehend the attributes of God and the affections of God, and nothing else.—Q.E.D.

PROP. XXXI.——*The actual intellect, whether it be fin-*
ite or infinite, together with the will, desire, love,
&c., must be referred to the natura naturata *and not*
to the natura naturans.

Demonst.—For by the intellect (as is self-evident) we do not understand absolute thought, but only a certain mode of thought, which mode differs from other modes, such as desire, love, &c., and therefore (Def. 5) must be conceived through absolute thought, that is to say (Prop. 15 and Def. 6), it must be conceived through some attribute of God which expresses the eternal and infinite essence of thought in such a manner that without that attribute it can neither be nor can be conceived. Therefore (Schol. Prop. 29) the actual intellect, &c., must be referred to the *natura naturata,* and not to the *natura naturans,* in the same manner as all other modes of thought.—Q.E.D.

Schol.—I do not here speak of the *actual* intellect because I admit that any intellect *potentially* exists, but because I wish, in order that there may be no confusion, to speak of nothing excepting of that which we perceive with the utmost clearness, that is to say, the understanding itself, which we perceive as clearly as we perceive anything. For we can understand nothing through the intellect which does not lead to a more perfect knowledge of the understanding.

PROP. XXXII.—*The will cannot be called a free cause. but can only be called necessary.*

Demonst.—The will is only a certain mode of thought, like the intellect, and therefore (Prop. 28) no volition can exist or be determined to action unless it be determined by another cause, and this again by another, and so on *ad infinitum*. And if the will be supposed infinite, it must be determined to existence and action by God, not in so far as He is substance absolutely infinite, but in so far as He possesses an attribute which expresses the infinite and eternal essence of thought (Prop. 23). In whatever way, therefore, the will be conceived, whether as finite or infinite, it requires a cause by which it may be determined to existence and action, and therefore (Def. 7) it cannot be called a free cause but only necessary or compelled.—Q.E.D.

Corol. 1.—Hence it follows, firstly, that God does not act from freedom of the will.

Corol. 2.—It follows, secondly, that will and intellect are related to the nature of God as motion and rest, and absolutely as all natural things, which (Prop. 29) must be determined by God to existence and action in a certain manner. For the will, like all other things, needs a cause by which it may be determined to existence and action in a certain manner, and although from a given will or intellect infinite things may follow, God cannot on this account be said to act from freedom of will, any more than He can be said to act from freedom of motion and rest by reason of the things which follow from motion and rest (for from motion and rest infinite numbers of things follow). Therefore, will does not appertain to the nature of God more than other natural things, but is related to it as motion and rest and all other things are related to it; these all following, as we have shown, from the necessity of the divine nature, and being determined to existence and action in a certain manner.

PROP. XXXIII.—*Things could have been produced by God in no other manner and in no other order than that in which they have been produced.*

Demonst.—All things have necessarily followed from the given nature of God (Prop. 16), and from the necessity of His nature have been determined to existence and action in a certain manner (Prop. 29). If, therefore, things could have been of another nature, or could have been determined in another manner to action, so that the order of nature would have been different, the nature of God might then be different to that which it now is, and hence (Prop. 11) that different nature would necessarily exist, and there might consequently be two or more Gods, which (Corol. 1, Prop. 14) is absurd. Therefore, things could be produced by God in no other manner and in no other order than that in which they have been produced.—Q.E.D.

Schol. 1.—Since I have thus shown, with greater clearness than that of noonday light, that in things there is absolutely nothing by virtue of which they can be called contingent, I wish now to explain in a few words what is to be understood by *contingent,* but firstly, what is to be understood by *necessary* and *impossible.* A thing is called necessary either in reference to its essence or its cause. For the existence of a thing necessarily follows either from the essence and definition of the thing itself, or from a given efficient cause. In the same way a thing is said to be impossible either because the essence of the thing itself or its definition involves a contradiction, or because no external cause exists determinate to the production of such a thing. But a thing cannot be called contingent unless with reference to a deficiency in our knowledge. For if we do not know that the essence of a thing involves a contradiction, or if we actually know that it involves no contradiction, and nevertheless we can affirm nothing with certainty about its existence because the order of causes is concealed from us, that thing can never appear to us either as necessary or impossible, and therefore we call it either contingent or possible.

Schol. 2.—From what has gone before it clearly follows that things have been produced by God in the highest degree of perfection, since they have necessarily followed from the existence of a most perfect nature. Nor does this doctrine accuse God of any imperfection, but, on the contrary, His perfection has compelled us to affirm it. Indeed, from its contrary would clearly follow, as I have shown above, that God is not absolutely perfect, since, if things had been produced in any other fashion another nature would have had to be assigned to Him, different from that which the consideration of the most perfect Being compels us to assign to Him. I do not doubt that many will reject this opinion as ridiculous, nor will they care to apply themselves to its consideration, and this from no other reason than that they have been in the habit of assigning to God another liberty widely different from that absolute will which (Def. 7) we have taught. On the other hand, I do not doubt, if they were willing to study the matter and properly to consider the series of our demonstrations, that they would altogether reject this liberty which they now assign to God, not only as of no value, but as a great obstacle to knowledge. Neither is there any need that I should here repeat those things which are said in the scholium to Prop. 17. But for the sake of those who differ from me, I will here show that although it be granted that will pertains to God's essence, it follows nevertheless from His perfection that things could be created in no other mode or order by Him. This it will be easy to show if we first consider that which my opponents themselves admit, that it depends upon the decree and will of God alone that each thing should be what it is, for otherwise God would not be the cause of all things. It is also admitted that all God's decrees were decreed by God Himself from all eternity, for otherwise imperfection and inconstancy would be proved against Him. But since in eternity there is no *when* nor *before* nor *after*, it follows from the perfection of God alone that He neither can decree nor could ever have decreed anything else than that which He has decreed; that is to say, God has not existed before His decrees, and can never exist without them. But it is said that although it be supposed that God had made the nature of things different from that which it is, or that from eternity He had decreed something else about nature and her order, it would not thence follow that any imperfection exists in God. But if this be said, it must at the same time be allowed that God can change His decrees. For if God had decreed something about nature and her order other than that which He has decreed—that is to say, if He had willed and conceived something else about nature—He would necessarily have had an intellect and a will different from those which He now has. And if it be allowed to assign to God another intellect and another will without any change of His essence and of His perfections, what is the reason why He cannot now change His decrees about creation and nevertheless remain equally perfect? For His intellect and will regarding created things and their order remain the same in relationship to His essence and perfection in whatever manner His intellect and will are conceived. Moreover, all the philosophers whom I have seen admit that there is no such thing as an intellect existing potentially in God, but only an intellect existing actually. But since His intellect and His will are not distinguishable from His essence, as all admit, it follows from this also that if God had had another intellect actually and another will, His essence would have been necessarily different, and hence, as I showed at the beginning, if things had been produced by God in a manner different from that in which they now exist, God's intellect and will, that is to say, His essence (as has been granted), must have been different, which is absurd.

Since, therefore, things could have been produced by God in no other manner or order, this being a truth which follows from His absolute perfection, there is no sound reasoning which can persuade us to believe that God was unwilling to create all things which are in His intellect with the same perfection as that in which they exist in His intellect. But we shall be told that there is no perfection nor imperfection in things, but that that which is in them by reason of which they are perfect or imperfect and are said to be good or evil depends upon the will of God alone, and therefore if God had willed He could have effected that that which is now perfection should have been the extreme of imperfection, and *vice versa*. But what else would this be than openly to affirm that God, who necessarily understands what He wills, is able by His will to understand things in a manner different from that in which He understands them, which, as I have just shown, is a great absurdity? I can therefore turn the argument on my opponents in this way. All things depend upon the power of God. In order that things may be differently constituted, it would be necessary that God's will should be differently constituted; but God's will cannot be other than it is, as we have lately most clearly deduced from His perfection. Things therefore cannot be differently constituted. I confess that this opinion, which subjects all things to a certain indifferent God's will, and affirms that all things depend upon God's good pleasure, is at a less distance from the truth than the opinion of those who affirm that God does everything for the sake of the Good. For these seem to place something outside of God which is independent of Him, to which He looks while He is at work as to a model, or at which He aims as if at a certain mark. This is indeed nothing else than to subject God to fate, the most absurd thing which can be affirmed of Him whom we have shown to be the first and only free cause of the essence of all things as well as of their existence. Therefore it is not worth while that I should waste time in refuting this absurdity.

PROP. XXXIV.—*The power of God is His essence itself.*

Demonst.—From the necessity alone of the essence of God it follows that God is the cause of Himself (Prop. 11), and (Prop. 16 and its Corol.) the cause of all things. Therefore the power of God, by which He Himself and all things are and act, is His essence itself.—Q.E.D.

PROP. XXXV.—*Whatever we conceive to be in God's power necessarily exists.*

Demonst.—For whatever is in God's power must (Prop. 34) be so comprehended in His essence that it

necessarily follows from it, and consequently exists
necessarily.—Q.E.D.

PROP. XXXVI.—*Nothing exists from whose nature an
effect does not follow.*

Demonst.—Whatever exists expresses the nature or
the essence of God in a certain and determinate manner
(Corol. Prop. 25); that is to say (Prop. 34), whatever
exists expresses the power of God, which is the cause of
all things, in a certain and determinate manner, and
therefore (Prop. 16) some effect must follow from it.

APPENDIX

Prejudices of men

I have now explained the nature of God and its properties. I have shown that He necessarily exists; that
He is one God; that from the necessity alone of His
own nature He is and acts; that He is, and in what way
He is, the free cause of all things; that all things are in
Him, and so depend upon Him that without Him they
can neither be nor can be conceived; and, finally, that
all things have been predetermined by Him, not indeed
from freedom of will or from absolute good pleasure,
but from His absolute nature or infinite power.

Moreover, wherever an opportunity was afforded, I
have endeavoured to remove prejudices which might
hinder the perception of the truth of what I have demonstrated; but because not a few still remain which have
been and are now sufficient to prove a very great hindrance to the comprehension of the connection of things
in the manner in which I have explained it, I have
thought it worth while to call them up to be examined

by reason. But all these prejudices which I here undertake to point out depend upon this solely: that it is commonly supposed that all things in nature, like men, work to some end; and indeed it is thought to be certain that God Himself directs all things to some sure end, for it is said that God has made all things for man, and man that he may worship God. This, therefore, I will first investigate by inquiring, firstly, why so many rest in this prejudice, and why all are so naturally inclined to embrace it? I shall then show its falsity, and, finally, the manner in which there have arisen from it prejudices concerning *good* and *evil, merit* and *sin, praise* and *blame, order* and *disorder, beauty* and *deformity,* and so forth. This, however, is not the place to deduce these things from the nature of the human mind. It will be sufficient if I here take as an axiom that which no one ought to dispute, namely, that man is born ignorant of the causes of things, and that he has a desire, of which he is conscious, to seek that which is profitable to him. From this it follows, firstly, that he thinks himself free because he is conscious of his wishes and appetites, whilst at the same time he is ignorant of the causes by which he is led to wish and desire, not dreaming what they are; and, secondly, it follows that man does everything for an end, namely, for that which is profitable to him, which is what he seeks. Hence it happens that he attempts to discover merely the final causes of that which has happened; and when he has heard them he is satisfied, because there is no longer any cause for further uncertainty. But if he cannot hear from another what these final causes are, nothing remains but to turn to himself and reflect upon the ends which usually determine him to the like actions, and thus by his own mind he necessarily judges that of another. Moreover. since he discovers, both within and without himself, a multitude of means which contribute not a little to the attainment of what is profitable to himself——for example, the eyes, which are useful for seeing, the teeth for mastication, plants and animals for nourishment, the sun for giving light, the sea for feeding fish, &c.—it comes to pass that all natural objects are considered as means for obtaining what is profitable. These too being evidently discovered and not created by man, hence he has a cause for believing that some other person exists, who has prepared them for man's use. For having considered them as means it was impossible to believe that they had created themselves, and so he was obliged to infer from the means which he was in the habit of providing for himself that some ruler or rulers of nature exist, endowed with human liberty, who have taken care of all things for him, and have made all things for his use. Since he never heard anything about the mind of these rulers, he was compelled to judge of it from his own, and hence he affirmed that the gods direct everything for his advantage, in order that he may be bound to them and hold them in the highest honour. This is the reason why each man has devised for himself, out of his own brain, a different mode of worshipping God, so that God might love him above others, and direct all nature to the service of his blind cupidity and insatiable avarice.

Thus has this prejudice been turned into a superstition and has driven deep roots into the mind—a prejudice which was the reason why every one has so eagerly tried to discover and explain the final causes of things. The attempt, however, to show that nature does nothing in vain (that is to say, nothing which is not profitable to man), seems to end in showing that nature, the gods, and man are alike mad.

Do but see, I pray, to what all this has led. Amidst

so much in nature that is beneficial, not a few things must have been observed which are injurious, such as storms, earthquakes, diseases, and it was affirmed that these things happened either because the gods were angry because of wrongs which had been inflicted on them by man, or because of sins committed in the method of worshipping them; and although experience daily contradicted this, and showed by an infinity of examples that both the beneficial and the injurious were indiscriminately bestowed on the pious and the impious, the inveterate prejudices on this point have not therefore been abandoned. For it was much easier for a man to place these things aside with others of the use of which he was ignorant, and thus retain his present and inborn state of ignorance, than to destroy the whole superstructure and think out a new one. Hence it was looked upon as indisputable that the judgments of the gods far surpass our comprehension; and this opinion alone would have been sufficient to keep the human race in darkness to all eternity, if mathematics, which does not deal with ends, but with the essences and properties of forms, had not placed before us another rule of truth. In addition to mathematics, other causes also might be assigned, which it is superfluous here to enumerate, tending to make men reflect upon these universal prejudices, and leading them to a true knowledge of things.

I have thus sufficiently explained what I promised in the first place to explain. There will now be no need of many words to show that nature has set no end before herself, and that all final causes are nothing but human fictions. For I believe that this is sufficiently evident both from the foundations and causes of this prejudice, and from Prop. 16 and Corol. Prop. 32, as well as from all those propositions in which I have shown that all things are begotten by a certain eternal necessity of

nature and in absolute perfection. Thus much, nevertheless, I will add, that this doctrine concerning an end
altogether overturns nature. For that which is in truth
the cause it considers as the effect, and *vice versa.*
Again, that which is first in nature it puts last; and,
finally, that which is supreme and most perfect it makes
the most imperfect. For (passing by the first two assertions as self-evident) it is plain from Props. 21, 22,
and 23, that that effect is the most perfect which is
immediately produced by God, and in proportion as
intermediate causes are necessary for the production of
a thing is it imperfect. But if things which are immediately produced by God were made in order that He
might obtain the end He had in view, then the last
things for the sake of which the first exist, must be the
most perfect of all. Again, this doctrine does away with
God's perfection. For if God works to obtain an end,
He necessarily seeks something of which he stands in
need. And although theologians and metaphysicians distinguish between the end of want and the end of assimi-
lation (*finem indegentiæ et finem assimilationis*), they
confess that God has done all things for His own sake,
and not for the sake of the things to be created, because
before the creation they can assign nothing excepting
God for the sake of which God could do anything; and
therefore they are necessarily compelled to admit that
God stood in need of and desired those things for which
He determined to prepare means. This is self-evident.
Nor is it here to be overlooked that the adherents of
this doctrine, who have found a pleasure in displaying
their ingenuity in assigning the ends of things, have
introduced a new species of argument, not the *reductio
ad impossibile,* but the *reductio ad ignorantiam,* to
prove their position, which shows that it had no other
method of defence left. For, by way of example, if a

stone has fallen from some roof on somebody's head and killed him, they will demonstrate in this manner that the stone has fallen in order to kill the man. For if it did not fall for that purpose by the will of God, how could so many circumstances concur through chance (and a number often simultaneously do concur)? You will answer, perhaps, that the event happened because the wind blew and the man was passing that way. But, they will urge, why did the wind blow at that time, and why did the man pass that way precisely at the same moment? If you again reply that the wind rose then because the sea on the preceding day began to be stormy, the weather hitherto having been calm, and that the man had been invited by a friend, they will urge again— because there is no end of questioning—But why was the sea agitated? why was the man invited at that time? And so they will not cease from asking the causes of causes, until at last you fly to the will of God, the refuge for ignorance.

So, also, when they behold the structure of the human body, they are amazed; and because they are ignorant of the causes of such art, they conclude that the body was made not by mechanical but by a supernatural or divine art, and has been formed in such a way so that the one part may not injure the other. Hence it happens that the man who endeavours to find out the true causes of miracles, and who desires as a wise man to understand nature, and not to gape at it like a fool, is generally considered and proclaimed to be a heretic and impious by those whom the vulgar worship as the interpreters both of nature and the gods. For these know that if ignorance be removed, amazed stupidity, the sole ground on which they rely in arguing or in defending their authority, is taken away also. But these things I leave and pass on to that which I determined to do in the third place.

After man has persuaded himself that all things which exist are made for him, he must in everything adjudge that to be of the greatest importance which is most useful to him, and he must esteem that to be of surpassing worth by which he is most beneficially affected. In this way he is compelled to form those notions by which he explains nature; such, for instance, as *good, evil, order, confusion, heat, cold, beauty,* and *deformity,* &c.; and because he supposes himself to be free, notions like those of *praise* and *blame, sin* and *merit,* have arisen. These latter I shall hereafter explain when I have treated of human nature; the former I will here briefly unfold.

It is to be observed that man has given the name *good* to everything which leads to health and the worship of God; on the contrary, everything which does not lead thereto he calls *evil.* But because those who do not understand nature affirm nothing about things themselves, but only imagine them, and take the imagination to be understanding, they therefore, ignorant of things and their nature, firmly believe an *order* to be in things; for when things are so placed that, if they are represented to us through the senses, we can easily imagine them, and consequently easily remember them, we call them well arranged; but if they are not placed so that we can imagine and remember them, we call them badly arranged or *confused.* Moreover, since those things are more especially pleasing to us which we can easily imagine, men therefore prefer order to confusion, as if order were something in nature apart from our own imagination; and they say that God has created everything in order, and in this manner they ignorantly attribute imagination to God, unless they mean perhaps

that God, out of consideration for the human imagination, has disposed things in the manner in which they
can most easily be imagined. No hesitation either seems
to be caused by the fact that an infinite number of
things are discovered which far surpass our imagination, and very many which confound it through its weakness. But enough of this. The other notions which I
have mentioned are nothing but modes in which the
imagination is affected in different ways, and nevertheless they are regarded by the ignorant as being specially
attributes of things, because, as we have remarked, men
consider all things as made for themselves, and call the
nature of a thing good, evil, sound, putrid, or corrupt,
just as they are affected by it. For example, if the
motion by which the nerves are affected by means of
objects represented to the eye conduces to well-being,
the objects by which it is caused are called *beautiful*;
while those exciting a contrary motion are called *de-
formed*. Those things, too, which stimulate the senses
through the nostrils are called sweet-smelling or thinking; those which act through the taste are called sweet
or bitter, full-flavoured or insipid; those which act
through the touch, hard or soft, heavy or light; those,
lastly, which act through the ears are said to make a
noise, sound, or harmony, the last having caused men to
lose their senses to such a degree that they have believed
that God even is delighted with it. Indeed, philosophers
may be found who have persuaded themselves that the
celestial motions beget a harmony. All these things
sufficiently show that every one judges things by the
constitution of his brain, or rather accepts the affections of his imagination in the place of things. It is
not, therefore, to be wondered at, as we may observe
in passing, that all those controversies which we see
have arisen amongst men, so that at last scepticism has

been the result. For although human bodies agree in many things, they differ in more, and therefore that which to one person is good will appear to another evil, that which to one is well arranged to another is confused, that which pleases one will displease another, and so on in other cases which I pass by both because we cannot notice them at length here, and because they are within the experience of every one. For every one has heard the expressions: So many heads, so many ways of thinking; Every one is satisfied with his own way of thinking; Differences of brains are not less common than differences of taste;—all which maxims show that men decide upon matters according to the constitution of their brains, and imagine rather than understand things. If men understood things, they would, as mathematics prove, at least be all alike convinced if they were not all alike attracted. We see, therefore, that all those methods by which the common people are in the habit of explaining nature are only different sorts of imaginations, and do not reveal the nature of anything in itself, but only the constitution of the imagination; and because they have names as if they were entities existing apart from the imagination, I call them entities not of the reason but of the imagination. All argument, therefore, urged against us based upon such notions can be easily refuted. Many people, for instance, are accustomed to argue thus:—If all things have followed from the necessity of the most perfect nature of God, how is it that so many imperfections have arisen in nature—corruption, for instance, of things till they stink; deformity, exciting disgust; confusion, evil, crime, &c.? But, as I have just observed, all this is easily answered. For the perfection of things is to be judged by their nature and power alone; nor are they more or less perfect because they delight or offend the human senses, or because they are beneficial or prejudicial to human nature. But to those who ask why God has not created all men in such a manner that they might be controlled by the dictates of reason alone, I give but this answer: Because to Him material was not wanting for the creation of everything, from the highest down to the very lowest grade of perfection; or, to speak more properly, because the laws of His nature were so ample that they sufficed for the production of everything which can be conceived by an infinite intellect, as I have demonstrated in Prop. 16.

These are the prejudices which I undertook to notice here. If any others of a similar character remain, they can easily be rectified with a little thought by any one.

SECOND PART

OF THE NATURE AND ORIGIN OF THE MIND

I PASS on now to explain those things which must necessarily follow from the essence of God or the Being eternal and infinite; not indeed to explain all these things, for we have demonstrated (Prop. 16, pt. 1) that an infinitude of things must follow in an infinite number of ways,—but to consider those things only which may conduct us as it were by the hand to a knowledge of the human mind and its highest happiness.

DEFINITIONS

I. By body, I understand a mode which expresses in a certain and determinate manner the essence of God in so far as He is considered as the thing extended. (See Corol. Prop. 25, pt. 1.)

II. I say that to the essence of anything pertains that, which being given, the thing itself is necessarily posited, and being taken away, the thing is necessarily taken; or, in other words, that, without which the thing can neither be nor be conceived, and which in its turn cannot be nor be conceived without the thing.

III. By idea, I understand a conception of the mind which the mind forms because it is a thinking thing.

Explanation.—I use the word conception rather than perception because the name perception seems to indicate that the mind is passive in its relation to the object. But the word conception seems to express the action of the mind.

IV. By adequate idea, I understand an idea which, in so far as it is considered in itself, without reference to the object, has all the properties or internal signs (*denominationes intrinsecas*) of a true idea.

Explanation.—I say internal, so as to exclude that which is external, the agreement, namely, of the idea with its object.

V. Duration is the indefinite continuation of existence.

Explanation.—I call it indefinite because it cannot be determined by the nature itself of the existing thing nor by the efficient cause, which necessarily posits the existence of the thing but does not take it away.

VI. By reality and perfection I understand the same thing.

VII. By individual things I understand things which are finite and which have a determinate existence; and if a number of individuals so unite in one action that they are all simultaneously the cause of one effect, I consider them all, so far, as a one individual thing.

AXIOMS

I. The essence of man does not involve necessary existence; that is to say, the existence as well as the non-existence of this or that man may or may not follow from the order of nature.

II. Man thinks.

III. Modes of thought, such as love, desire, or the affections of the mind, by whatever name they may be called, do not exist, unless in the same individual the idea exist of a thing loved, desired, &c. But the idea may exist although no other mode of thinking exist.

IV. We perceive that a certain body is affected in many ways.

V. No individual things are felt or perceived by us excepting bodies and modes of thought.

The postulates will be found after Proposition 13.

PROP. I.—*Thought is an attribute of God, or God is a thinking thing.*

Demonst.—Individual thoughts, or this and that thought, are modes which express the nature of God in a certain and determinate manner (Corol. Prop. 25, pt. 1). God therefore possesses an attribute (Def. 5, pt. 1), the conception of which is involved in all individual thoughts, and through which they are conceived. Thought, therefore, is one of the infinite attributes of God which expresses the eternal and infinite essence of God (Def. 6, pt. 1), or, in other words, God is a thinking thing.—Q.E.D.

Schol.—This proposition is plain from the fact that we can conceive an infinite thinking Being. For the more things a thinking being can think, the more reality or perfection we conceive it to possess, and therefore the being which can think an infinitude of things in infinite ways is necessarily infinite by his power of thinking. Since, therefore, we can conceive an infinite Being by attending to thought alone, thought is necessarily one of the infinite attributes of God (Defs. 4 and 6, pt. 1), which is the proposition we wished to prove.

PROP. II.—*Extension is an attribute of God, or God is an extended thing.*

Demonst.—The demonstration of this proposition is of the same character as that of the last.

PROP. III.—*In God there necessarily exists the idea of His essence, and of all things which necessarily follow from His essence.*

Demonst.—For God (Prop. 1, pt. 2) can think an infinitude of things in infinite ways, or (which is the same thing, by Prop. 16, pt. 1) can form an idea of His essence and of all the things which necessarily follow from it. But everything which is in the power of God is necessary (Prop. 35, pt. 1), and therefore this idea necessarily exists, and (Prop. 15, pt. 1) it cannot exist unless in God.

Schol.—The common people understand by God's power His free will and right over all existing things, which are therefore commonly looked upon as contingent; for they say that God has the power of destroying everything and reducing it to nothing. They very frequently, too, compare God's power with the power of kings. That there is any similarity between the two we have disproved in the first and second Corollaries of Prop. 32, pt. 1, and in Prop. 16, pt. 1, we have shown that God does everything with that necessity with which He understands Himself; that is to say, as it follows from the necessity of the divine nature that God understands Himself (a truth admitted by all, so by the same necessity it follows that God does an infinitude of things in infinite ways. Moreover, in Prop. 34, pt. 1, we have shown that the power of God is nothing but the active essence of God, and therefore it is as impossible for us to conceive that God does not act as that He does not exist. If it pleased me to go farther, I could show besides that the power which the common people ascribe to God is not only a human power (which shows that they look upon God as a man, or as being like a man), but that it also involves a weakness. But I do not care to talk so much upon the same subject. Again and again I ask the reader to consider and reconsider what is said upon this subject in the first part, from Prop. 16 to the end. For it is not possible for any one properly to understand the things which I wish to prove unless he takes great care not to confound the power of God with the human power and right of kings.

PROP. IV.—*The idea of God,*[1] *from which infinite numbers of things follow in infinite ways, can be one only.*

Demonst.—The infinite intellect comprehends nothing but the attributes of God and His affections (Prop. 30, pt. 1). But God is one (Corol. 1, Prop. 14, pt. 1). Therefore the idea of God, from which infinite numbers of things follow in infinite ways, can be only one.—Q.E.D.

PROP. V.—*The formal*[2] *Being of ideas recognises God for its cause in so far only as He is considered as a thinking thing, and not in so far as He is manifested by any other attribute; that is to say, the ideas both of God's attributes and of individual*

[1] Or God's idea (*Idea Dei*).—TR.

[2] "Formal"="objective," as now understood, but it does not necessarily mean materially objective. The "formal Being of ideas"=the mind.—TR.

*things do not recognise as their efficient cause the
objects of the ideas or the things which are perceived, but God Himself in so far as He is a thinking thing.*

Demonst.—This is plain, from Prop. 3, pt. 2; for we
there demonstrated that God can form an idea of His
own essence, and of all things which necessarily follow
from it, solely because He is a thinking thing, and not
because He is the object of His idea. Therefore the
formal Being of ideas recognises God as its cause in
so far as He is a thinking thing. But the proposition
can be proved in another way. The formal Being of ideas
is a mode of thought (as is self-evident); that is to say,
(Corol. Prop. 25, pt. 1), a mode which expresses in a
certain manner the nature of God in so far as He is a
thinking thing. It is a mode, therefore (Prop. 10, pt. 1)
that involves the conception of no other attribute of
God, and consequently is the effect (Ax. 4, pt. 1) of
no other attribute except that of thought; therefore the
formal Being of ideas, &c.—Q.E.D.

PROP. VI.—*The modes of any attribute have God for
a cause only in so far as He is considered under
that attribute of which they are modes, and not
in so far as He is considered under any other
attribute.*

Demonst.—Each attribute is conceived by itself and
without any other (Prop. 10, pt. 1). Therefore the
modes of any attribute involve the conception of that
attribute and of no other, and therefore (Ax. 4, pt. 1)
have God for a cause in so far as He is considered under
that attribute of which they are modes, and not so far
as He is considered under any other attribute.—Q.E.D.

Corol.—Hence it follows that the formal Being of things which are not modes of thought does not follow from the divine nature because of His prior knowledge of these things, but, as we have shown, just as ideas follow from the attribute of thought, in the same manner and with the same necessity the objects of ideas follow and are concluded from their attributes.

PROP. VII.—*The order and connection of ideas is the same as the order and connection of things.*

This is evident from Ax. 4, pt. 1. For the idea of anything caused depends upon a knowledge of the cause of which the thing caused is the effect.

Corol.—Hence it follows that God's power of thinking is equal to His actual power of acting; that is to say, whatever follows *formally* from the infinite nature of God, follows from the idea of God [idea Dei], in the same order and in the same connection *objectively* in God.

Schol.—Before we go any farther, we must here recall to our memory what we have already demonstrated, that everything which can be perceived by the infinite intellect as constituting the essence of substance pertains entirely to the one sole substance only, and consequently that substance thinking and substance extended are one and the same substance, which is now comprehended under this attribute and now under that. Thus, also, a mode of extension and the idea of that mode are one and the same thing expressed in two different ways—a truth which some of the Hebrews appear to have seen as if through a cloud, since they say that God, the intellect of God, and the things which are the objects of that intellect are one and the same thing. For example, the circle existing in nature and the idea that is in God of an existing circle are one and the same thing, which is manifested through different attributes; and, therefore, whether we think of nature under the attribute of extension, or under the attribute of thought, or under any other attribute whatever, we shall discover one and the same order, or one and the same connection of causes; that is to say, in every case the same sequence of things. Nor have I had any other reason for saying that God is the cause of the idea, for example, of the circle in so far only as He is a thinking thing, and of the circle itself in so far as He is an extended thing, but this, that the formal Being of the idea of a circle can only be perceived through another mode of thought, as its proximate cause, and this again must be perceived through another, and so on *ad infinitum*. So that when things are considered as modes of thought, we must explain the order of the whole of nature or the connection of causes by the attribute of thought alone, and when things are considered as modes of extension, the order of the whole of nature must be explained through the attribute of extension alone, and so with other attributes. Therefore God is in truth the cause of things as they are in themselves in so far as He consists of infinite attributes, nor for the present can I explain the matter more clearly.

PROP. VIII.—*The ideas of non-existent individual things or modes are comprehended in the infinite idea of God, in the same way that the formal essences of individual things or modes are contained in the attributes of God.*

Demonst.—This proposition is evident from the preceding proposition, but it is to be understood more clearly from the preceding scholium.

Corol.—Hence it follows that when individual things do not exist unless in so far as they are comprehended in the attributes of God, their objective Being or ideas do not exist unless in so far as the infinite idea of God exists; and when individual things are said to exist, not only in so far as they are included in God's attributes, but in so far as they are said to have duration, their ideas involve the existence through which they are said to have duration.

Schol.—If any one desires an instance in order that what I have said may be more fully understood, I cannot give one which will adequately explain what I have been saying, since an exact parallel does not exist: nevertheless, I will endeavour to give as good an illustration as can be found.

The circle, for example, possesses this property, that the rectangles contained by the segments of all straight lines cutting one another in the same circle are equal; therefore in a circle there is contained an infinite number of rectangles equal to one another, but none of them can be said to exist unless in so far as the circle exists, nor can the idea of any one of these rectangles be said to exist unless in so far as it is comprehended in the idea of the circle. Out of this infinite number of rectangles, let two only, E and D, be conceived to exist. The ideas of these two rectangles do not now exist merely in so far as they are comprehended in the idea of the circle, but because they involve the existence of their rectangles, and it is this which distinguishes them from the other ideas of the other rectangles.

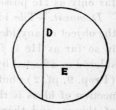

Prop. IX.—*The idea of an individual thing actually existing has God for a cause, not in so far as He is infinite, but in so far as He is considered to be affected by another idea of an individual thing actually existing, of which idea also He is the cause in so far as He is affected by a third, and so on* ad infinitum.

Demonst.—The idea of any individual thing actually existing is an individual mode of thought, and is distinct from other modes of thought (Corol. and Schol. Prop. 8, pt. 2), and therefore (Prop. 6, pt. 2) has God for a cause in so far only as He is a thinking thing; not indeed as a thinking thing absolutely (Prop. 28, pt. 1), but in so far as He is considered as affected by another mode of thought. Again, He is the cause of this latter mode of thought in so far as He is considered as affected by another, and so on *ad infinitum.* But the order and connection of ideas (Prop. 7, pt. 2) is the same as the order and connection of causes; therefore every individual idea has for its cause another idea, that is to say, God in so far as He is affected by another idea; while of this second idea God is again the cause in the same way, and so on *ad infinitum.*—Q.E.D.

Corol.—A knowledge of everything which happens in the individual object of any idea exists in God in so far only as He possesses the idea of that object.

Demonst.—The idea of everything which happens in the object of any idea exists in God (Prop. 3, pt. 2), not in so far as He is infinite, but in so far as He is considered as affected by another idea of an individual thing (Prop. 9, pt. 2); but (Prop. 7, pt. 2) the order and connection of ideas is the same as the order and connection of things, and therefore the knowledge of that which happens in any individual object will exist in God in so far only as He has the idea of that object.

PROP. X.—*The Being of substance does not pertain to the essence of man, or, in other words, substance does not constitute the form of man.*

Demonst.—The Being of substance involves necessary existence (Prop. 7, pt. 1). If, therefore, the Being of substance pertained to the essence of man, the existence of man would necessarily follow from the existence of substance (Def. 2, pt. 2), and consequently he would necessarily exist, which (Ax. 1, pt. 2) is an absurdity. Therefore the Being of substance does not pertain, &c. —Q.E.D.

Schol.—This proposition may be demonstrated from Prop. 5, pt. 1, which proves that there are not two substances of the same nature. For since it is possible for more men than one to exist, therefore that which constitutes the form of man is not the Being of substance. This proposition is evident also from the other properties of substance; as, for example, that it is by its nature infinite, immutable, indivisible, &c., as any one may easily see.

Corol.—Hence it follows that the essence of man consists of certain modifications of the attributes of God; for the Being of substance does not pertain to the essence of man (Prop. 10, pt. 2). It is therefore something (Prop. 15, pt. 1) which is in God, and which without God can neither be nor be conceived, or (Corol. Prop. 25, pt. 1) an affection or mode which expresses the nature of God in a certain and determinate manner.

Schol.—Every one must admit that without God nothing can be nor be conceived; for every one admits that God is the sole cause both of the essence and of the existence of all things; that is to say, God is not only the cause of things, to use a common expression, *secundum fieri*, but also *secundum esse*. But many people say that that pertains to the essence of a thing without which the thing can neither be nor can be conceived, and they therefore believe either that the nature of God belongs to the essence of created things, or that created things can be or can be conceived without God; or, which is more probable, there is no consistency in their thought. I believe that the cause of this confusion is that they have not observed a proper order of philosophic study. For although the divine nature ought to be studied first, because it is first in the order of knowledge and in the order of things, they think it last; while, on the other hand, those things which are called objects of the senses are believed to stand before everything else. Hence it has come to pass that there was nothing of which men thought less than the divine nature while they have been studying natural objects, and when they afterwards applied themselves to think about God, there was nothing of which they could think less than those prior fictions upon which they had built their knowledge of natural things, for these fictions could in no way help to the knowledge of the divine nature. It is no wonder, therefore, if we find them continually contradicting themselves. But this I pass by. For my only purpose was to give a reason why I did not say that that pertains to the essence of a thing without which the thing can neither be nor can be conceived; and my reason is, that individual things cannot be nor be conceived without God, and yet God does not pertain to their essence. I have rather, therefore, said that the essence of a thing is necessarily that which being given, the thing is posited, and being taken away, the thing is taken away, or that without which the thing can neither be nor be conceived, and which in its turn cannot be nor be conceived without the thing.

PROP. XI.—*The first thing which forms the actual Being of the human mind is nothing else than the idea of an individual thing actually existing.*

Demonst.—The essence of man is formed (Corol. Prop. 10, pt. 2) by certain modes of the attributes of God, that is to say (Ax. 2, pt. 2), modes of thought, the idea of all of them being prior by nature to the modes of thought themselves (Ax. 3, pt. 2); and if this idea exists, other modes (which also have an idea in nature prior to them) must exist in the same individual likewise (Ax. 3, pt. 2). Therefore an idea is the first thing which forms the Being of the human mind. But it is not the idea of a non-existent thing, for then the idea itself (Corol. Prop. 8, pt. 2) could not be said to exist. It will, therefore, be the idea of something actually existing. Neither will it be the idea of an infinite thing, for an infinite thing must always necessarily exist (Props. 21 and 22, pt. 1), and this (Ax. 1, pt. 2) is absurd. Therefore the first thing which forms the actual Being of the human mind is the idea of an individual thing actually existing. —Q.E.D.

Corol.—Hence it follows that the human mind is a part of the infinite intellect of God, and therefore, when we say that the human mind perceives this or that thing, we say nothing else than that God has this or that idea; not indeed in so far as He is infinite, but in so far as He is manifested through the nature of the human mind, or in so far as He forms the essence of the human mind;

and when we say that God has this or that idea, not merely in so far as He forms the nature of the human mind, but in so far as He has at the same time with the human mind the idea also of another thing, then we say that the human mind perceives the thing partially or inadequately.

Schol.—At this point many of my readers will no doubt stick fast, and will think of many things which will cause delay; and I therefore beg of them to advance slowly, step by step, with me, and not to pronounce judgment until they shall have read everything which I have to say.

PROP. XII.—*Whatever happens in the object of the idea constituting the human mind must be perceived by the human mind; or, in other words, an idea of that thing will necessarily exist in the human mind. That is to say, if the object of the idea constituting the human mind be a body, nothing can happen in that body which is not perceived by the mind.*

Demonst.—The knowledge of everything which happens in the object of any idea necessarily exists in God (Corol. Prop. 9, pt. 2), in so far as He is considered as affected with the idea of that object; that is to say (Prop. 11, pt. 2), in so far as He forms the mind of any being. The knowledge, therefore, necessarily exists in God of everything which happens in the object of the idea constituting the human mind; that is to say, it exists in Him in so far as He forms the nature of the human mind; or, in other words (Corol. Prop. 11, pt. 2), the knowledge of this thing will necessarily be in the mind, or the mind perceives it.—Q.E.D.

Schol.—This proposition is plainly deducible and

more easily to be understood from Schol. Prop. 7, pt. 2, to which the reader is referred.

Prop. XIII.—*The object of the idea constituting the human mind is a body, or a certain mode of extension actually existing, and nothing else.*

Demonst.—For if the body were not the object of the human mind, the ideas of the affections of the body would not be in God (Corol. Prop. 9, pt. 2) in so far as He has formed our mind, but would be in Him in so far as He has formed the mind of another thing; that is to say (Corol. Prop. 11, pt. 2), the ideas of the affections of the body would not be in our mind. But (Ax. 4, pt. 2) we have ideas of the affections of a body; therefore the object of the idea constituting the human mind is a body, and that too (Prop. 11, pt. 2) actually existing. Again, if there were also any other object of the mind besides a body, since nothing exists from which some effect does not follow (Prop. 36, pt. 1), the idea of some effect produced by this object would necessarily exist in our mind (Prop. 11, pt. 2). But (Ax. 5, pt. 2) there is no such idea, and therefore the object of our mind is a body existing, and nothing else.—Q.E.D.

Corol.—Hence it follows that man is composed of mind and body, and that the human body exists as we perceive it.

Schol.—Hence we see not only that the human mind is united to the body, but also what is to be understood by the union of the mind and body. But no one can understand it adequately or distinctly without knowing adequately beforehand the nature of our body; for those things which we have proved hitherto are altogether general, nor do they refer more to man than to other individuals, all of which are animate, although in different degrees. For of everything there necessarily exists in God an idea of which He is the cause, in the same way as the idea of the human body exists in Him; and therefore everything that we have said of the idea of the human body is necessarily true of the idea of any other thing. We cannot, however, deny that ideas, like objects themselves, differ from one another, and that one is more excellent and contains more reality than another, just as the object of one idea is more excellent and contains more reality than another. Therefore, in order to determine the difference between the human mind and other things and its superiority over them, we must first know, as we have said, the nature of its object, that is to say, the nature of the human body. I am not able to explain it here, nor is such an explanation necessary for what I wish to demonstrate.

This much, nevertheless, I will say generally, that in proportion as one body is better adapted than another to do or suffer many things, in the same proportion will the mind at the same time be better adapted to perceive many things, and the more the actions of a body depend upon itself alone, and the less other bodies co-operate with it in action, the better adapted will the mind be for distinctly understanding. We can thus determine the superiority of one mind to another; we can also see the reason why we have only a very confused knowledge of our body, together with many other things which I shall deduce in what follows. For this reason I have thought it worth while more accurately to explain and demonstrate the truths just mentioned, to which end it is necessary for me to say beforehand a few words upon the nature of bodies.

AXIOM 1.—All bodies are either in a state of motion or rest.

Axiom 2.—Every body moves, sometimes slowly, sometimes quickly.

Lemma I.—*Bodies are distinguished from one another in respect of motion and rest, quickness and slowness, and not in respect of substance.*

Demonst.—I suppose the first part of this proposition to be self-evident. But it is plain that bodies are not distinguished in respect of substance, both from Prop. 5, pt. 1, and Prop. 8, pt. 1, and still more plainly from what I have said in the scholium to Prop. 15, pt. 1.

Lemma II.—*All bodies agree in some respects.*

Demonst.—For all bodies agree in this, that they involve the conception of one and the same attribute (Def. 1, pt. 2). They have, moreover, this in common, that they are capable generally of motion and of rest, and of motion at one time quicker and at another slower.

Lemma III.—*A body in motion or at rest must be determined to motion or rest by another body, which was also determined to motion or rest by another, and that in its turn by another, and so on ad infinitum.*

Demonst.—Bodies (Def. 1, pt. 2) are individual things, which (Lem. 1) are distinguished from one another in respect of motion and rest, and therefore (Prop. 28, pt. 1) each one must necessarily be determined to motion or rest by another individual thing; that is to say (Prop. 6, pt. 1), by another body which (Ax. 1) is also either in motion or at rest. But this body, by the same reasoning, could not be in motion or at rest unless it had been determined to motion or rest by another body, and this again, by the same reasoning, must have been determined by a third, and so on *ad infinitum*.—Q.E.D.

Corol.—Hence it follows that a body in motion will continue in motion until it be determined to a state of rest by another body, and that a body at rest will continue at rest until it be determined to a state of motion by another body. This indeed is self-evident. For if I suppose that a body, A, for example, is at rest, if I pay no regard to other bodies in motion, I can say nothing about the body A except that it is at rest. If it should afterwards happen that the body A should move, its motion could not certainly be a result of its former rest, for from its rest nothing could follow than that the body A should remain at rest. If, on the other hand, A be supposed to be in motion, so long as we regard A alone, the only thing we can affirm about it is that it moves. If it should afterwards happen that A should be at rest, the rest could not certainly be a result of the former motion, for from its motion nothing could follow but that A should move; the rest must therefore be a result of something which was not in A, that is to say, of an external cause by which it was determined to rest.

AXIOM 1.—All the modes by which one body is affected by another follow from the nature of the body affected, and at the same time from the nature of the affecting body, so that one and the same body may be moved in different ways according to the diversity of the nature of the moving bodies, and, on the other hand, different bodies may be moved in different ways by one and the same body.

AXIOM 2.—When a body in motion strikes against another which is at rest and immovable, it is reflected, in order that it may continue its motion, and the angle of the line of reflected motion with the plane of the body at rest against which it struck will be equal to the angle which the line of the motion of incidence makes with the same plane.

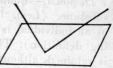

Thus much for simplest bodies which are distinguished from one another by motion and rest, speed and slowness alone; let us now advance to composite bodies.

DEF.—When a number of bodies of the same or of different magnitudes are pressed together by others, so that they lie one upon the other, or if they are in motion with the same or with different degrees of speed, so that they communicate their motion to one another in a certain fixed proportion, these bodies are said to be mutually united, and taken altogether they are said to compose one body or individual, which is distinguished from other bodies by this union of bodies.

AXIOM 3.—Whether it is easy or difficult to force the parts composing an individual to change their situation, and consequently whether it is easy or difficult for the individual to change its shape, depends upon whether the parts of the individual or of the compound body lie with less, or whether they lie with greater surfaces upon one another. Hence bodies whose parts lie upon each other with greater surfaces I will call hard; those soft, whose parts lie on one another with smaller surfaces; and those fluid, whose parts move amongst each other.

LEMMA IV.—*If a certain number of bodies be separated from the body or individual which is composed of a number of bodies, and if their place be supplied by the same number of other bodies of the same nature, the individual will retain the nature which it had before without any change of form.*

Demonst.—Bodies are not distinguished in respect of substance (Lem. 1); but that which makes the form of an individual is the union of bodies (by the preceding definition). This form, however (by hypothesis), is retained, although there may be a continuous change of the bodies. The individual, therefore, will retain its nature, with regard both to substance and to mode, as before.

LEMMA V.—*If the parts composing an individual become greater or less proportionately, so that they preserve towards one another the same kind of motion and rest, the individual will also retain the nature which it had before without any change of form.*

Demonst.—The demonstration is of the same kind as that immediately preceding.

LEMMA VI.—*If any number of bodies composing an individual are compelled to divert into one direction the motion they previously had in another, but are nevertheless able to continue and reciprocally communicate their motions in the same manner as before, the individual will then retain its nature without any change of form.*

Demonst.—This is self-evident, for the individual is supposed to retain everything which, according to the definition, constitutes its form.

LEMMA VII.—*The individual thus composed will, moreover, retain its nature whether it move as a whole or be at rest, or whether it move in this or that direction, provided that each part retain its own motion and communicate it as before to the rest.*

Demonst.—The proof is evident from the definition preceding Lemma 4.

Schol.—We thus see in what manner a composite individual can be affected in many ways and yet retain its nature. Up to this point we have conceived an individual to be composed merely of bodies which are distinguished from one another solely by motion and rest, speed and slowness, that is to say, to be composed of the most simple bodies. If we now consider an individual of another kind, composed of many individuals of diverse natures, we shall discover that it may be affected in many other ways, its nature nevertheless being preserved. For since each of its parts is composed of a number of bodies, each part (by the preceding Lemma), without any change of its nature, can move more slowly or more quickly, and consequently can communicate its motion more quickly or more slowly to the rest. If we now imagine a third kind of individual composed of these of the second kind, we shall discover that it can be affected in many other ways without any change of form. Thus, if we advance *ad infinitum*, we may easily conceive the whole of nature to be one individual, whose parts, that is to say, all bodies, differ in infinite ways without any change of the whole individual.[1] If it had been my object to consider specially the question of a body, I should have had to explain and demonstrate these things more fully. But, as I have already said, I

[1] The passage is most important as indicating how Spinoza conceived that change could occur *within* a changeless whole. [Ed.]

have another end in view, and I have noticed them only because I can easily deduce from them those things which I have proposed to demonstrate.

Postulate 1.—The human body is composed of a number of individuals of diverse nature, each of which is composite to a high degree.

Postulate 2.—Of the individuals of which the human body is composed, some are fluid, some soft, and some hard.

Postulate 3.—The individuals composing the human body, and consequently the human body itself, are affected by external bodies in many ways.

Postulate 4.—The human body needs for its preservation many other bodies by which it is, as it were, continually regenerated.

Postulate 5.—When a fluid part of the human body is determined by an external body, so that it often strikes upon another which is soft, the fluid part changes the plane of the soft part, and leaves upon it, as it were, some traces of the impelling external body.

Postulate 6.—The human body can move and arrange external bodies in many ways.

PROP. XIV.—*The human mind is adapted to the perception of many things, and its aptitude increases in proportion to the number of ways in which its body can be disposed.*

Demonst.—The human body is affected (Post. 3 and 6) in many ways by external bodies, and is so disposed as to affect external bodies in many ways. But the human mind must perceive (Prop. 12, pt. 2) everything which happens in the human body. The human mind is therefore adapted, &c.—Q.E.D.

PROP. XV.—*The idea which constitutes the formal Being of the human mind is not simple, but is composed of a number of ideas.*

Demonst.—The idea which constitutes the formal Being of the human mind is the idea of a body (Prop. 13, pt. 2) which (Post. 1) is composed of a number of individuals composite to a high degree. But an idea of each individual composing the body must necessarily exist in God (Corol. Prop. 8, pt. 2); therefore (Prop. 7, pt. 2) the idea of the human body is composed of these several ideas of the component parts.—Q.E.D.

PROP. XVI.—*The idea of every way in which the human body is affected by external bodies must involve the nature of the human body, and at the same time the nature of the external body.*

Demonst.—All the ways in which any body is affected follow at the same time from the nature of the affected body, and from the nature of the affecting body (Ax. 1, following Corol. Lem. 3); therefore the idea of these affections (Ax. 4, pt. 1) necessarily involves the nature of each body, and therefore the idea of each way in which the human body is affected by an external body involves the nature of the human body and of the external body.—Q.E.D.

Corol. 1.—Hence it follows, in the first place, that the human mind perceives the nature of many bodies together with that of its own body.

Corol. 2.—It follows, secondly, that the ideas we have of external bodies indicate the constitution of our own body rather than the nature of external bodies. This I have explained in the Appendix of the First Part by many examples.

PROP. XVII.—*If the human body be affected in a way which involves the nature of any external body, the human mind will contemplate that external body as actually existing or as present, until the human body be affected by an affect which excludes the existence or presence of the external body.*

Demonst.—This is evident. For so long as the human body is thus affected, so long will the human mind (Prop. 12, pt. 2) contemplate this affection of the external body, that is to say (Prop. 16, pt. 2), it will have an idea of a mode actually existing which involves the nature of the external body, that is to say, an idea which does not exclude the existence or presence of the nature of the external body, but posits it; and therefore the mind (Corol. 1, Prop. 16, pt. 2) will contemplate the external body as actually existing, &c.—Q.E.D.

Corol.—The mind is able to contemplate external things by which the human body was once affected as if they were present, although they are not present and do not exist.

Demonst.—When external bodies so determine the fluid parts of the human body that they often strike upon the softer parts, the fluid parts change the plane of the soft parts (Post. 5); and thence it happens that the fluid parts are reflected from the new planes in a direction different from that in which they used to be reflected (Ax. 2, following Corol. Lem. 3), and that also afterwards when they strike against these new planes by their own spontaneous motion, they are reflected in the same way as when they were impelled towards those planes by external bodies. Consequently those fluid bodies produce an affection in the human body while they keep up this reflex motion similar to that produced by the presence of an external body. The mind, therefore (Prop. 12,

pt. 2), will think as before, that is to say, it will again
contemplate the external body as present (Prop. 17,
pt. 2). This will happen as often as the fluid parts of
the human body strike against those planes by their
own spontaneous motion. Therefore, although the external bodies by which the human body was once affected
do not exist the mind will perceive them as if they were
present so often as this action is repeated in the body.

Schol.—We see, therefore, how it is possible for us to
contemplate things which do not exist as if they were
actually present. This may indeed be produced by other
causes, but I am satisfied with having here shown one
cause through which I could explain it, just as if I had
explained it through the true cause. I do not think
however, that I am far from the truth, since no postulate
which I have assumed contains anything which is not
confirmed by an experience that we cannot mistrust after
we have proved the existence of the human body as we
perceive it (Corol. following Prop. 13, pt. 2). Moreover
(Corol. Prop. 17, pt. 2, and Corol. 2, Prop. 16, pt. 2),
we clearly see what is the difference between the idea,
for example, of Peter, which constitutes the essence of
the mind itself of Peter, and the idea of Peter himself
which is in another man; for example, in Paul. For the
former directly manifests the essence of the body of
Peter himself, nor does it involve existence unless so long
as Peter exists; the latter, on the other hand, indicates
rather the constitution of the body of Paul than the
nature of Peter; and therefore so long as Paul's body
exists with that constitution, so long will Paul's mind
contemplate Peter as present, although he does not exist.
But in order that we may retain the customary phraseology, we will give to those affections of the human body,
the ideas of which represent to us external bodies as
if they were present, the name of *images of things*, al-

though they do not actually reproduce the forms of the things. When the mind contemplates bodies in this way, we will say that it imagines. Here I wish it to be observed, in order that I may begin to show what *error* is, that these imaginations of the mind, regarded by themselves, contain no error, and that the mind is not in error because it imagines, but only in so far as it is considered as wanting in an idea which excludes the existence of those things which it imagines as present. For if the mind, when it imagines non-existent things to be present, could at the same time know that those things did not really exist, it would think its power of imagination to be a virtue of its nature and not a defect, especially if this faculty of imagining depended upon its own nature alone, that is to say (Def. 7, pt. 1), if this faculty of the mind were free.

Prop. XVIII.—*If the human body has at any time been simultaneously affected by two or more bodies, whenever the mind afterwards imagines one of them, it will also remember the others.*

Demonst.—The mind imagines a body (Corol. Prop. 17, pt. 2) because the human body is affected and disposed by the impressions of an external body, just as it was affected when certain of its parts received an impulse from the external body itself. But by hypothesis, the body was at that time disposed in such a manner that the mind imagined two bodies at once; therefore it will imagine two at once now, and whenever it imagines one, it will immediately recollect the other.—q.e.d.

Schol.—We clearly understand by this what memory is. It is nothing else than a certain concatenation of ideas, involving the nature of things which are outside the human body, a concatenation which corresponds in the mind to the order and concatenation of the affections of the human body. I say, firstly, that it is a concatenation of those ideas only which involve the nature of things which are outside the human body, and not of those ideas which explain the nature of those things, for there are in truth (Prop. 16, pt. 2) ideas of the affections of the human body, which involve its nature as well as the nature of external bodies. I say, in the second place, that this concatenation takes place according to the order and concatenation of the affections of the human body, that I may distinguish it from the concatenation of ideas which takes place according to the order of the intellect, and enables the mind to perceive things through their first causes, and is the same in all men. Hence we can clearly understand how it is that the mind from the thought of one thing at once turns to the thought of another thing which is not in any way like the first. For example, from the thought of the word *pomum* a Roman immediately turned to the thought of the fruit, which has no resemblance to the articulate sound *pomum*, nor anything in common with it, excepting this, that the body of that man was often affected by the thing and the sound; that is to say, he often heard the word *pomum* when he saw the fruit. In this manner each person will turn from one thought to another according to the manner in which the habit of each has arranged the images of things in the body. The soldier, for instance, if he sees the footsteps of a horse in the sand, will immediately turn from the thought of a horse to the thought of a horseman, and so to the thought of war. The countryman, on the other hand, from the thought of a horse will turn to the thought of his plough, his field, &c.; and thus each person will turn from one thought to this or that thought, according

to the manner in which he has been accustomed to connect and bind together the images of things in his mind.

PROP. XIX.—*The human mind does not know the human
body itself, nor does it know that the body exists,
except through ideas of affections by which the
body is affected.*

Demonst.—The human mind is the idea itself or the
knowledge of the human body (Prop. 13, pt. 2). This
knowledge (Prop. 9, pt. 2) is in God in so far as He is
considered as affected by another idea of an individual
thing. But because (Post. 4) the human body needs a
number of bodies by which it is, as it were, continually
regenerated, and because the order and connection of
ideas is the same as the order and connection of causes
(Prop. 7, pt. 2), this idea will be in God in so far as
He is considered as affected by the ideas of a multitude
of individual things.

God, therefore, has the idea of the human body or
knows the human body in so far as He is affected by
a multitude of other ideas, and not in so far as He
forms the nature of the human mind; that is to say
(Corol. 11, pt. 2), the human mind does not know the
human body. But the ideas of the affections of the
body are in God in so far as He forms the nature
of the human mind; that is to say (Prop. 12, pt. 2), the
human mind perceives these affections, and consequently
(Prop. 16, pt. 2) the human body itself actually existing
(Prop. 17, pt. 2). The human mind, therefore, perceives
the human body, &c.—Q.E.D.

PROP. XX.—*There exists in God the idea or knowledge
of the human mind, which follows in Him, and is*

*related to Him in the same way as the idea or
knowledge of the human body.*

Demonst.—Thought is an attribute of God (Prop. 1,
pt. 2), and therefore there must necessarily exist in God
an idea of Himself (Prop. 3, pt. 2), together with an
idea of all His affections, and consequently (Prop. 11,
pt. 2) an idea of the human mind. Moreover, this idea or
knowledge of the mind does not exist in God in so far as
He is infinite, but in so far as He is affected by another
idea of an individual thing (Prop. 9, pt. 2). But the
order and connection of ideas is the same as the order
and connection of causes (Prop. 7, pt. 2). This idea or
knowledge of the mind, therefore, follows in God, and
is related to God in the same manner as the idea or
knowledge of the body.—Q.E.D.

PROP. XXI.—*This idea of the mind is united to the
mind in the same way as the mind itself is united
to the body.*

Demonst.—We have shown that the mind is united
to the body because the body is the object of the
mind (Props. 12 and 13, pt. 2), therefore, by the same
reasoning, the idea of the mind must be united with its
object, the mind itself, in the same way as the mind
itself is united to the body.—Q.E.D.

Schol.—This proposition is to be understood much
more clearly from what has been said in the scholium
to Prop. 7, pt. 2, for we have here shown that the idea
of the body and the body, that is to say (Prop. 13,
pt. 2), the mind and the body, are one and the same
individual, which at one time is considered under the
attribute of thought, and at another under that of extension: the idea of the mind, therefore, and the mind

itself are one and the same thing, which is considered under one and the same attribute, that of thought. It follows, I say, that the idea of the mind and the mind itself exist in God from the same necessity and from the same power of thought. For, indeed, the idea of the mind, that is to say, the idea of the idea, is nothing but the form of the idea in so far as this is considered as a mode of thought and without relation to the object, just as a person who knows anything, by that very fact knows that he knows, and knows that he knows that he knows, and so *ad infinitum*. But more on this subject afterwards.

Prop. XXII.—*The human mind not only perceives the affections of the body, but also the ideas of these affections.*

Demonst.—The ideas of the ideas of affections follow in God and are related to God in the same way as the ideas themselves of affections. This is demonstrated like Prop. 20, pt. 2. But the ideas of the affections of the body are in the human mind (Prop. 12, pt. 2), that is to say, in God (Corol. Prop. 11, pt. 2), in so far as He constitutes the essence of the human mind; therefore, the ideas of these ideas will be in God in so far as He has the knowledge or idea of the human mind; that is to say (Prop. 21, pt. 2), they will be in the human mind itself, which, therefore, not only perceives the affections of the body, but also the ideas of these affections.—Q.E.D.

Prop. XXIII.—*The mind does not know itself except in so far as it perceives the ideas of the affections of the body.*

Demonst.—The idea or knowledge of the mind (Prop. 20, pt. 2) follows in God and is related to God in the same way as the idea or knowledge of the body. But since (Prop. 19, pt. 2) the human mind does not know the human body itself, that is to say (Corol. Prop. 11, pt. 2), since the knowledge of the human body is not related to God in so far as He constitutes the nature of the human mind, therefore the knowledge of the mind is not related to God in so far as He constitutes the essence of the human mind; and therefore (Corol. Prop. 11, pt. 2) the human mind so far does not know itself. Moreover, the ideas of the affections by which the body is affected involve the nature of the human body itself (Prop. 16, pt. 2), that is to say (Prop. 13, pt. 2), they agree with the nature of the mind; therefore a knowledge of these ideas will necessarily involve a knowledge of the mind. But (Prop. 22, pt. 2) the knowledge of these ideas is in the human mind itself, and therefore the human mind so far only has a knowledge of itself.—Q.E.D.

PROP. XXIV.—*The human mind does not involve an adequate knowledge of the parts composing the human body.*

Demonst.—The parts composing the human body pertain to the essence of the body itself only in so far as they communicate their motions to one another by some certain method (see Def. following Corol. Lem. 3), and not in so far as they can be considered as individuals without relation to the human body. For the parts of the human body are individuals (Post. 1), composite to a high degree, parts of which (Lem. 4) can be separated from the human body and communicate their motions (Ax. 1, following Lem. 3) to other bodies in another way, although the nature and form of the human body itself is closely preserved. Therefore (Prop. 3, pt. 2) the idea or knowledge of each part will be in God in so far as He is considered as affected (Prop. 9, pt. 2) by another idea of an individual thing, which individual thing is prior to the part itself in the order of nature (Prop. 7, pt. 2). The same thing may be said of each part of the individual itself composing the human body, and therefore the knowledge of each part composing the human body exists in God in so far as He is affected by a number of ideas of things, and not in so far as He has the idea of the human body only; that is to say (Prop. 13, pt. 2), the idea which constitutes the nature of the human mind; and therefore (Corol. Prop. 11, pt. 2) the human mind does not involve an adequate knowledge of the parts composing the human body.—Q.E.D.

PROP. XXV.—*The idea of each affection of the human body does not involve an adequate knowledge of an external body.*

Demonst.—We have shown that the idea of an affection of the human body involves the nature of an external body so far as (Prop. 16, pt. 2) the external body determines the human body in some certain manner. But in so far as the external body is an individual which is not related to the human body, its idea or knowledge is in God (Prop. 9, pt. 2) in so far as He is considered as affected by the idea of another thing, which idea (Prop. 7, pt. 2) is prior by nature to the external body itself. Therefore the adequate knowledge of an external body is not in God in so far as He has the idea of the affection of the human body, or, in other words, the idea of the affection of the human body does not involve an adequate knowledge of an external body.—Q.E.D.

PROP. XXVI.—*The human mind perceives no external body as actually existing, unless through the ideas of the affections of its body.*

Demonst.—If the human body is in no way affected by any external body, then (Prop. 7, pt. 2) the idea of the human body, that is to say (Prop. 13, pt. 2), the human mind, is not affected in any way by the idea of the existence of that body, nor does it in any way perceive the existence of that external body. But in so far as the human body is affected in any way by any external body, so far (Prop. 16, pt. 2, with its Corol.) does it perceive the external body.—Q.E.D.

Corol.—In so far as the human mind imagines an external body, so far it has not an adequate knowledge of it.

Demonst.—When the human mind through the ideas of the affections of its body contemplates external bodies, we say that it then imagines (Schol. Prop. 17, pt. 2), nor can the mind (Prop. 26, pt. 2) in any other way imagine external bodies as actually existing. Therefore (Prop. 25, pt. 2) in so far as the mind imagines external bodies it does not possess an adequate knowledge of them.—Q.E.D.

PROP. XXVII.—*The idea of any affection of the human body does not involve an adequate knowledge of the human body itself.*

Demonst.—Every idea of any affection of the human body involves the nature of the human body in so far as the human body itself is considered as affected in a cer-

tain manner (Prop. 16, pt. 2). But in so far as the
human body is an individual which can be affected in a
multitude of other ways, its idea, &c. (See Demonst.
Prop. 25, pt. 2.)

Prop. XXVIII.—*The ideas of the affections of the
human body, in so far as they are related only to the
human mind, are not clear and distinct, but confused.*

Demonst.—The ideas of the affections of the human
body involve the nature both of external bodies and
of the human body itself (Prop. 16, pt. 2), and must
involve the nature not only of the human body, but
of its parts, for the affections are ways (Post. 3) in
which the parts of the human body, and consequently
the whole body, is affected. But (Props. 24 and 25, pt.
2) an adequate knowledge of external bodies and of the
parts composing the human body does not exist in God
in so far as He is considered as affected by the human
mind, but in so far as He is affected by other ideas.
These ideas of affections, therefore, in so far as they are
related to the human mind alone, are like conclusions
without premises, that is to say, as is self-evident, they
are confused ideas.—Q.E.D.

Schol.—The idea which forms the nature of the mind
is demonstrated in the same way not to be clear and
distinct when considered in itself. So also with the
idea of the human mind, and the ideas of the ideas
of the affections of the human body, in so far as they are
related to the mind alone, as every one may easily see.

Prop. XXIX.—*The idea of the idea of any affection of
the human body does not involve an adequate knowledge of the human mind.*

Demonst.—The idea of an affection of the human body (Prop. 27, pt. 2) does not involve an adequate knowledge of the body itself, or, in other words, does not adequately express its nature, that is to say (Prop. 13, pt. 2), it does not correspond adequately with the nature of the human mind, and therefore (Ax. 6, pt. 1) the idea of this idea does not adequately express the nature of the human mind, nor involve an adequate knowledge of it.—Q.E.D.

Corol.—From this it is evident that the human mind, when it perceives things in the common order of nature, has no adequate knowledge of itself nor of its own body, nor of external bodies, but only a confused and mutilated knowledge; for the mind does not know itself unless in so far as it perceives the ideas of the affections of the body (Prop. 23, pt. 2). Moreover (Prop. 19, pt. 2), it does not perceive its body unless through those same ideas of the affections by means of which alone (Prop. 26, pt. 2) it perceives external bodies. Therefore in so far as it possesses these ideas it possesses an adequate knowledge neither of itself (Prop. 29, pt. 2), nor of its body (Prop. 27, pt. 2), nor of external bodies (Prop. 25, pt. 2), but merely (Prop. 28, pt. 2, together with the scholium) a mutilated and confused knowledge. —Q.E.D.

Schol.—I say expressly that the mind has no adequate knowledge of itself, nor of its body, nor of external bodies, but only a confused knowledge, as often as it perceives things in the common order of nature, that is to say, as often as it is determined to the contemplation of this or that *externally*—namely, by a chance coincidence, and not as often as it is determined *internally*—for the reason that it contemplates [1] several things at once, and is determined to understand in what they

[1] In this latter case.—Tr.

differ, agree, or oppose one another; for whenever it is internally disposed in this or in any other way, it then contemplates things clearly and distinctly, as I shall show presently.

PROP. XXX.—*About the duration of our body we can have but a very inadequate knowledge.*

Demonst.—The duration of our body does not depend upon its essence (Ax. 1, pt. 2), nor upon the absolute nature of God (Prop. 21, pt. 1), but (Prop. 28, pt. 1) the body is determined to existence and action by causes which also are determined by others to existence and action in a certain and determinate manner, whilst these, again, are determined by others, and so on *ad infinitum.* The duration, therefore, of our body depends upon the common order of nature and the constitution of things. But an adequate knowledge of the way in which things are constituted, exists in God in so far as He possesses the ideas of all things, and not in so far as He possesses only the idea of the human body (Corol. Prop. 9, pt. 2). Therefore the knowledge of the duration of our body is altogether inadequate in God, in so far as He is only considered as constituting the nature of the human mind, that is to say (Corol. Prop. 11, pt. 2), this knowledge in our mind is altogether inadequate.— Q.E.D.

PROP. XXXI.—*About the duration of individual things which are outside us we can have but a very inadequate knowledge.*

Demonst.—Each individual thing, like the human body, must be determined to existence and action by another individual thing in a certain and determinate manner, and this again by another, and so on *ad infinitum* (Prop. 28, pt. 1). But we have demonstrated in the preceding proposition, from this common property of individual things, that we have but a very inadequate knowledge of the duration of our own body; therefore the same conclusion is to be drawn about the duration of individual things, that is to say, that we can have but a very inadequate knowledge of it.—Q.E.D.

Corol.—Hence it follows that all individual things are contingent and corruptible, for we can have no adequate knowledge concerning their duration (Prop. 31, pt. 2), and this is what is to be understood by us as their contingency and capability of corruption (Schol. 1, Prop. 33, pt. 1); for (Prop. 29, pt. 1) there is no other contingency but this.

PROP. XXXII.—*All ideas, in so far as they are related to God, are true.*

Demonst.—All the ideas which are in God always agree with those things of which they are the ideas (Corol. Prop. 7, pt. 2), and therefore (Ax. 6, pt. 1) they are all true.—Q.E.D.

PROP. XXXIII.—*In ideas there is nothing positive on account of which they are called false.*

Demonst.—If the contrary be asserted, conceive, if it be possible, a positive mode of thought which shall constitute the form or error of falsity. This mode of thought cannot be in God (Prop. 32, pt. 2), but outside God it can neither be nor be conceived (Prop. 15, pt. 1), and therefore in ideas there is nothing positive on account of which they are called false.—Q.E.D.

PROP. XXXIV.—*Every idea which in us is absolute, that is to say, adequate and perfect, is true.*

Demonst.—When we say that an adequate and perfect idea is in us, we say nothing else than (Corol. Prop. 11, pt. 2) that an adequate and perfect idea exists in God in so far as He constitutes the essence of the human mind, and consequently (Prop. 32, pt. 2) we say nothing else than that this idea is true.—Q.E.D.

PROP. XXXV.—*Falsity consists in the privation of knowledge, which inadequate, that is to say, mutilated and confused ideas involve.*

Demonst.—There is nothing positive in ideas which can constitute a form of falsity (Prop. 33, pt. 2). But falsity cannot consist in absolute privation (for we say that minds and not bodies err and are mistaken); nor can it consist in absolute ignorance, for to be ignorant and to be in error are different. Falsehood, therefore, consists in the privation of knowledge which is involved by inadequate knowledge of things or by inadequate and confused ideas.—Q.E.D.

Schol.—In the scholium of Prop. 17, pt. 2, I have explained how error consists in the privation of knowledge; but for the sake of fuller explanation, I will give an example. For instance, men are deceived because they think themselves free, and the sole reason for thinking so is that they are conscious of their own actions, and ignorant of the causes by which those actions are determined. Their idea of liberty therefore is this—that they know no cause for their own actions; for as to saying that their actions depend upon their will, these are words to which no idea is attached. What the will is, and in what manner it moves the body, every one is igno-

rant, for those who pretend otherwise, and devise seats
and dwelling-places of the soul, usually excite our laughter or disgust. Just in the same manner, when we look
at the sun, we imagine his distance from us to be about
200 feet; the error not consisting solely in the imagination, but arising from our not knowing what the true
distance is when we imagine, and what the causes of
our imagination. For although we may afterwards know
that the sun is more than 600 diameters of the earth
distant from us, we still imagine it near us, since we
imagine it to be so near, not because we are ignorant
of its true distance, but because an affection of our body
involves the essence of the sun, in so far as our body
itself is affected by it.

PROP. XXXVI.—*Inadequate and confused ideas follow
by the same necessity as adequate or clear and
distinct ideas.*

Demonst.—All ideas are in God (Prop. 15, pt. 1), and
in so far as they are related to God are true (Prop. 32,
pt. 2) and (Corol. Prop. 7, pt. 2) adequate. No ideas,
therefore, are inadequate or confused unless in so far as
they are related to the individual mind of some person
(see Props. 24 and 28, pt. 2). All ideas, therefore, both
adequate and inadequate, follow by the same necessity
(Corol. Prop. 6, pt. 2).

PROP. XXXVII.—*That which is common to everything
(see Lemma 2), and which is equally in the part
and in the whole, forms the essence of no individual
thing.*

Demonst.—For if this be denied, let that which is
common be conceived, if possible, to constitute the

essence of some individual thing,—the essence, for example, of B. Without B, therefore (Def. 2, pt. 2), that which is common can neither be nor be conceived. But this is contrary to the hypothesis. Therefore that which is common does not pertain to the essence of B, nor does it form the essence of any other individual thing.

PROP. XXXVIII.—*Those things which are common to everything, and which are equally in the part and in the whole, can only be adequately conceived.*

Demonst.—Let there be something A, which is common to all bodies, and which is equally in the part of each body and in the whole. I say that A can only be adequately conceived. For the idea of A (Corol. Prop. 7, pt. 2) will necessarily be adequate in God, both in so far as He has the idea of the human body and in so far as He has the idea of its affections, which (Props. 16, 25, and 27, pt. 2) involve the nature of the human body, and partly also the nature of external bodies; that is to say (Props. 12 and 13, pt. 2), this idea will necessarily be adequate in God in so far as He constitutes the human mind, or in so far as He has ideas which are in the human mind. The mind, therefore (Corol. Prop. 11, pt. 2), necessarily perceives A adequately, both in so far as it perceives itself or its own or any external body; nor can A be conceived in any other manner.—Q.E.D.

Corol.—Hence it follows that some ideas or notions exist which are common to all men, for (Lem. 2) all bodies agree in some things; which (Prop. 38, pt. 2) must be adequately, that is to say, clearly and distinctly, perceived by all.

PROP. XXXIX.—*There will exist in the human mind an adequate idea of that which is common and proper*

to the human body, and to any external bodies by
which the human body is generally affected—of that
which equally in the part of each of these external
bodies and in the whole is common and proper.

Demonst.—Let A be something which is common and
proper to the human body and certain external bodies;
let it exist equally in the human body and in those external bodies, and let it exist equally in the part of each
external body and in the whole. An adequate idea of
A itself will exist in God (Corol. Prop. 7, pt. 2), both
in so far as He has the idea of the human body and in
so far as He has the idea of the given external bodies.
Let it be supposed that the human body is affected by
an external body through that which it has in common
with the external body, that is to say, by A. The idea of
this affection will involve the property of A (Prop. 16,
pt. 2), and therefore (Corol. Prop. 7, pt. 2) the idea
of this affection, in so far as it involves the property
of A, will exist adequately in God in so far as He is
affected by the idea of the human body, that is to say
(Prop. 13, pt. 2), in so far as He constitutes the nature
of the human mind. Therefore (Corol. Prop. 11, pt. 2)
this idea is also adequate in the human mind.—Q.E.D.

Corol.—Hence it follows that the more things the
body has in common with other bodies, the more things
will the mind be adapted to perceive.

PROP. XL.—*Those ideas are also adequate which follow*
in the mind from ideas which are adequate in it.

Demonst.—This is evident. For when we say that
an idea follows in the human mind from ideas which
are adequate in it, we do but say (Corol. Prop. 11,
pt. 2) that in the divine intellect itself an idea exists

of which God is the cause, not in so far as He is infinite, nor in so far as He is affected by the ideas of a multitude of individual things, but in so far only as He constitutes the essence of the human mind.

Schol. 1.—I have thus explained the origin of those notions which are called common, and which are the foundations of our reasoning; but of some axioms or notions other causes exist which it would be advantageous to explain by our method, for we should thus be able to distinguish those notions which are more useful than others, and those which are scarcely of any use; those which are common; those which are clear and distinct only to those persons who do not suffer from prejudice; and, finally, those which are ill-founded. Moreover, it would be manifest whence these notions which are called *second*, and consequently the axioms founded upon them, have taken their origin, and other things, too, would be explained which I have thought about these matters at different times. Since, however, I have set apart this subject for another treatise, and because I do not wish to create disgust with excessive prolixity, I have determined to pass by this matter here. But not to omit anything which is necessary for us to know, I will briefly give the causes from which terms called *Transcendental*, such as *Being, Thing, Something*, have taken their origin. These terms have arisen because the human body, inasmuch as it is limited, can form distinctly in itself a certain number only of images at once. (For the explanation of the word *image*, see Schol. Prop. 17, pt. 2.) If this number be exceeded, the images will become confused; and if the number of images which the body is able to form distinctly be greatly exceeded, they will all run one into another. Since this is so, it is clear (Corol. Prop. 17, and Prop. 18, pt. 2) that in proportion to the number of images which can be formed at the same time in the body will be the number of bodies which the human mind can imagine at the same time. If the images in the body, therefore, are all confused, the mind will confusedly imagine all the bodies without distinguishing the one from the other, and will include them all, as it were, under one attribute, that of being or thing. The same confusion may also be caused by lack of uniform force in the images and from other analogous causes, which there is no need to discuss here, the consideration of one cause being sufficient for the purpose we have in view. For it all comes to this, that these terms signify ideas in the highest degree confused. It is in this way that those notions have arisen which are called *Universal,* such as, *Man, Horse, Dog,* &c.; that is to say, so many images of men, for instance, are formed in the human body at once, that they exceed the power of the imagination, not entirely, but to such a degree that the mind has no power to imagine the determinate number of men and the small differences of each, such as colour and size, &c. It will therefore distinctly imagine that only in which all of them agree in so far as the body is affected by them, for by that the body was chiefly affected, that is to say, by each individual, and this it will express by the name *man,* covering thereby an infinite number of individuals; to imagine a determinate number of individuals being out of its power. But we must observe that these notions are not formed by all persons in the same way, but that they vary in each case according to the thing by which the body is more frequently affected, and which the mind more easily imagines or recollects. For example, those who have more frequently looked with admiration upon the stature of men, by the name *man* will understand an animal of erect stature, while those who have been in the habit of fixing their thoughts on something else, will form another common image of men, describing man, for instance, as an animal capable of laughter, a biped without feathers, a rational animal, and so on; each person forming universal images of things according to the temperament of his own body. It is not therefore to be wondered at that so many controversies have arisen amongst those philosophers who have endeavoured to explain natural objects by the images of things alone.

Schol. 2.—From what has been already said, it clearly appears that we perceive many things and form universal ideas:

1. From individual things, represented by the senses to us in a mutilated and confused manner, and without order to the intellect (Corol. Prop. 29, pt. 2). These perceptions I have therefore been in the habit of calling knowledge from vague experience.

2. From signs; as, for example, when we hear or read certain words, we recollect things and form certain ideas of them similar to them, through which ideas we imagine things (Schol. Prop. 18, pt. 2). These two ways of looking at things I shall hereafter call knowledge of the first kind, opinion or imagination.

3. From our possessing common notions and adequate ideas of the properties of things (Corol. Prop. 38, Prop. 39, with Corol. and Prop. 40, pt. 2). This I shall call reason and knowledge of the second kind.

Besides these two kinds of knowledge, there is a third, as I shall hereafter show, which we shall call intuitive science. This kind of knowing advances from an adequate idea of the formal essence of certain attributes of God to the adequate knowledge of the essence of things. All this I will explain by one example. Let there be three numbers given through which it is required to discover a fourth which shall be to the third as the second is to the first. A merchant does not hesitate to multiply the second and third together and divide the product by the first, either because he has not yet forgotten the things which he heard without any demonstration from his schoolmaster, or because he has seen the truth of the rule with the more simple numbers, or because from the 19th Prop. in the 7th book of Euclid he understands the common property of all proportionals.

But with the simplest numbers there is no need of all this. If the numbers 1, 2, 3, for instance, be given, every one can see that the fourth proportional is 6 much more clearly than by any demonstration, because from the ratio in which we see by one intuition that the first stands to the second we conclude the fourth.

PROP. XLI.—*Knowledge of the first kind alone is the cause of falsity; knowledge of the second and third orders is necessarily true.*

Demonst.—To knowledge of the first kind we have said, in the preceding scholium, that all those ideas belong which are inadequate and confused, and, therefore (Prop. 35, pt. 2), this knowledge alone is the cause of falsity. Moreover, to knowledge of the second and third kind we have said that those ideas belong which are adequate, and therefore this knowledge (Prop. 34, pt. 2) is necessarily true.

PROP. XLII.—*It is the knowledge of the second and third, and not that of the first kind, which teaches us to distinguish the true from the false.*

Demonst.—This proposition is self-evident. For he who knows how to distinguish between the true and the

false must have an adequate idea of the true and the
false, that is to say (Schol. 2, Prop. 40, pt. 2), he
must know the true and the false by the second or third
kind of knowledge.

PROP. XLIII.—*He who has a true idea knows at the
same time that he has a true idea, nor can he doubt
the truth of the thing.*[1]

Demonst.—A true idea in us is that which in God
is adequate, in so far as He is manifested by the nature
of the human mind (Corol. Prop. 11, pt. 2). Let us
suppose, therefore, that there exists in God, in so far as
He is manifested by the nature of the human mind, an
adequate idea, A. Of this idea there must necessarily
exist in God an idea, which is related to Him in the
same way as the idea A (Prop. 20, pt. 2, the demonstration of which is universal). But the idea A is supposed
to be related to God in so far as He is manifested by
the nature of the human mind. The idea of the idea A
must therefore be related to God in the same manner,
that is to say (Corol. Prop. 11, pt. 2), this adequate
idea of the idea A will exist in the mind itself which
has the adequate idea A. He therefore who has an adequate idea, that is to say (Prop. 34, pt. 2), he who knows
a thing truly, must at the same time have an adequate
idea or a true knowledge of his knowledge, that is to
say (as is self-evident) he must be certain.—Q.E.D.

Schol.—In the scholium to Prop. 21, pt. 2, I have
explained what is the idea of an idea, but it is to be
observed that the preceding proposition is evident by
itself. For no one who has a true idea is ignorant

[1] Here as always in connection with Spinoza's underlying
rationalism, the *Improvement of the Understanding* will prove
illuminating. [Ed.]

that a true idea involves the highest certitude; to have
a true idea signifying just this, to know a thing perfectly or as well as possible. No one, in fact, can doubt
this, unless he supposes an idea to be something dumb,
like a picture on a tablet, instead of being a mode of
thought, that is to say, intelligence itself. Moreover, I
ask who can know that he understands a thing unless
he first of all understands that thing? that is to say,
who can know that he is certain of anything unless he is
first of all certain of that thing? Then, again, what can
be clearer or more certain than a true idea as the standard of truth? Just as light reveals both itself and the
darkness, so truth is the standard of itself and of the
false. I consider what has been said to be a sufficient
answer to the objection that if a true idea is distinguished from a false idea only in so far as it is said
to agree with that of which it is the idea, the true idea
therefore has no reality nor perfection above the false
idea (since they are distinguished by an external sign
alone), and consequently the man who has true ideas
will have no greater reality or perfection than he who
has false ideas only. I consider, too, that I have already
replied to those who inquire why men have false ideas,
and how a man can certainly know that he has ideas
which agree with those things of which they are the
ideas. For with regard to the difference between a true
and a false idea, it is evident from Prop. 35, pt. 2,
that the former is related to the latter as being is to
non-being. The causes of falsity, too, I have most clearly
shown in Props. 19-35, including the scholium to
the last. From what has there been said, the nature of
the difference between a man who has true ideas and one
who has only false ideas is clear. With regard to the
last-mentioned point—how a man can know that he
has an idea which agrees with that of which it is the

idea—I have shown almost more times than enough
that he knows it simply because he has an idea which
agrees with that of which it is the idea, that is to say,
because truth is its own standard. We must remember,
besides, that our mind, in so far as it truly perceives
things, is a part of the infinite intellect of God (Corol.
Prop. 11, pt. 2), and therefore it must be that the clear
and distinct ideas of the mind are as true as those of
God.

PROP. XLIV.—*It is not of the nature of reason to consider things as contingent but as necessary.*

Demonst.—It is in the nature of reason to perceive
things truly (Prop. 41, pt. 2), that is to say (Ax. 6,
pt. 1), as they are in themselves, that is to say (Prop.
29, pt. 1), not as contingent but as necessary.—Q.E.D.

Corol. 1.—Hence it follows that it is through the
imagination alone that we look upon things as contingent both with reference to the past and the future.

Schol.—How this happens I will explain in a few
words. We have shown above (Prop. 17, pt. 2, with
Corol.) that unless causes occur preventing the present
existence of things, the mind always imagines them
present before it, even if they do not exist. Again (Prop.
18, pt. 2), we have shown that if the human body has
once been simultaneously affected by two external bodies,
whenever the mind afterwards imagines one it will immediately remember the other; that is to say, it will look
upon both as present before it, unless causes occur which
prevent the present existence of the things. No one
doubts, too, that we imagine time because we imagine
some bodies to move with a velocity less, or greater than,
or equal to that of others. Let us therefore suppose
a boy who yesterday, for the first time, in the morning

saw Peter, at midday Paul, in the evening Simeon, and to-day in the morning again sees Peter. It is plain from Prop. 18, pt. 2, that as soon as he sees the morning light he will imagine the sun passing through the same part of the sky as on the day preceding; that is to say, he will imagine the whole day, and at the same time Peter will be connected in his imagination with the morning, Paul with midday, and Simeon with the evening. In the morning, therefore, the existence of Paul and Simeon will be imagined in relation to future time, while in the evening, if the boy should see Simeon, he will refer Peter and Paul to the past, since they will be connected with the past in his imagination. This process will be constant in proportion to the regularity with which he sees Peter, Paul, and Simeon in this order. If it should by some means happen that on some other evening, in the place of Simeon, he should see James, on the following morning he will connect in his imagination with the evening at one time Simeon and at another James, but not both together. For he is supposed to have seen one and then the other in the evening, but not both together. His imagination will therefore fluctuate, and he will connect with a future evening first one and then the other; that is to say, he will consider neither as certain, but both as a contingency in the future.

This fluctuation of the imagination will take place in the same way if the imagination is dealing with things which we contemplate in the same way with reference to past or present time, and consequently we imagine things related to time past, present, or future as contingent.

Corol 2.—It is of the nature of reason to perceive things under a certain form of eternity.

Demonst.—It is of the nature of reason to consider

things as necessary and not as contingent (Prop. 44, pt. 2). This necessity of things it perceives truly (Prop. 41, pt. 2); that is to say (Ax. 6, pt. 1), as it is in itself. But (Prop. 16, pt. 1) this necessity of things is the necessity itself of the eternal nature of God. Therefore it is of the nature of reason to consider things under this form of eternity. Moreover, the foundations of reason are notions which explain those things which are common to all (Prop. 38, pt. 2), and these things explain the essence of no individual thing (Prop. 37, pt. 2), and must therefore be conceived without any relation to time, but under a certain form of eternity. —Q.E.D.

PROP. XLV.—*Every idea of any body or actually existing individual thing necessarily involves the eternal and infinite essence of God.*

Demonst.—The idea of an individual thing actually existing necessarily involves both the essence and existence of the thing itself (Corol. Prop. 8, pt. 2). But individual things (Prop. 15, pt. 1) cannot be conceived without God, and since (Prop. 6, pt. 2) God is their cause in so far as He is considered under that attribute of which they are modes, their ideas (Ax. 4, pt. 1) must necessarily involve the conception of that attribute, or, in other words (Def. 6, pt. 1), must involve the eternal and infinite essence of God.—Q.E.D.

Schol.—By existence is to be understood here not duration, that is, existence considered in the abstract, as if it were a certain kind of quantity, but I speak of the nature itself of the existence which is assigned to individual things, because from the eternal necessity of the nature of God infinite numbers of things follow in infinite ways (Prop. 16, pt. 1). I repeat, that I speak of the existence itself of individual things in so far as they are in God. For although each individual thing is determined by another individual thing to existence in a certain way, the force nevertheless by which each thing perseveres in its existence follows from the eternal necessity of the nature of God (see Corol. Prop. 24, pt. 1).

PROP. XLVI.—*The knowledge of the eternal and infinite essence of God which each idea involves is adequate and perfect.*

Demonst.—The demonstration of the preceding proposition is universal, and whether a thing be considered as a part or as a whole, its idea, whether it be of a part or whole, will involve the eternal and infinite essence of God (Prop. 45, pt. 2). Therefore that which gives a knowledge of the eternal and infinite essence of God is common to all, and is equally in the part and in the whole. This knowledge therefore (Prop. 38, pt. 2) will be adequate.—Q.E.D.

PROP. XLVII.—*The human mind possesses an adequate knowledge of the eternal and infinite essence of God.*

Demonst.—The human mind possesses ideas (Prop. 22, pt. 2) by which (Prop. 23, pt. 2) it perceives itself and its own body (Prop. 19, pt. 2), together with (Corol. 1, Prop. 16, and Prop. 17, pt. 2) external bodies, as actually existing. Therefore (Props. 45 and 46, pt. 2) it possesses an adequate knowledge of the eternal and infinite essence of God.—Q.E.D.

Schol.—Hence we see that the infinite essence and the eternity of God are known to all; and since all things are in God and are conceived through Him, it follows that we can deduce from this knowledge many things which we can know adequately, and that we can thus form that third sort of knowledge mentioned in Schol. 2, Prop. 40, pt. 2, of whose excellence and value the Fifth Part will be the place to speak. The reason why we do not possess a knowledge of God as distinct as that which we have of common notions is, that we cannot imagine God as we can bodies; and because we have attached the name God to the images of things which we are in the habit of seeing, an error we can hardly avoid, inasmuch as we are continually affected by external bodies. Many errors, of a truth, consist merely in the application of the wrong names to things. For if a man says that the lines which are drawn from the centre of the circle to the circumference are not equal, he understands by the circle, at all events for the time, something else than mathematicians understand by it. So when men make errors in calculation, the numbers which are in their minds are not those which are upon the paper. As far as their mind is concerned there is no error, although it seems as if there were, because we think that the numbers in their minds are those which are upon the paper. If we did not think so, we should not believe them to be in error. For example, when I lately heard a man complaining that his court had flown into one of his neighbour's fowls, I understood what he meant, and therefore did not imagine him to be in error. This is the source from which so many controversies arise—that men either do not properly explain their own thoughts, or do not properly interpret those of other people; for, in truth, when they most contradict one another, they either think the same things or something different, so that those things which they suppose to be errors and absurdities in another person are not so.

PROP. XLVIII.—*In the mind there is no absolute or free will, but the mind is determined to this or that volition by a cause, which is also determined by another cause, and this again by another, and so on* ad infinitum.

Demonst.—The mind is a certain and determinate mode of thought (Prop. 11, pt. 2), and therefore (Corol. 2, Prop. 17, pt. 1) it cannot be the free cause of its own actions, or have an absolute faculty of willing or not willing, but must be determined to this or that volition (Prop. 28, pt. 1) by a cause which is also determined by another cause, and this again by another, and so on *ad infinitum.*—Q.E.D.

Schol.—In the same manner it is demonstrated that in the mind there exists no absolute faculty of understanding, desiring, loving, &c. These and the like faculties, therefore, are either altogether fictitious, or else are nothing but metaphysical or universal entities, which we are in the habit of forming from individual cases. The intellect and will, therefore, are related to this or that idea or volition as rockiness is related to this or that rock, or as man is related to Peter or Paul. The reason why men imagine themselves to be free we have explained in the Appendix to the First Part. Before, however, I advance any farther, I must observe that by the will I understand a faculty of affirming or denying, but not a desire; a faculty, I say, by which the mind affirms or denies that which is true or false, and not a desire by which the mind seeks a thing or turns away from it. But now that we have demonstrated that these faculties are universal notions which are not distinguishable from the individual notions from which they are formed, we must now inquire whether the volitions themselves are anything more than the ideas of things. We must inquire, I say, whether in the mind there exists any other affirmation or negation than that which the idea involves in so far as it is an idea. For this purpose see the following proposition, together with Def. 3, pt. 2, so that thought may not fall into pictures. For by ideas I do not understand the images which are formed at the back of the eye, or, if you please, in the middle of the brain, but rather the conceptions of thought.

PROP. XLIX.—*In the mind there is no volition or affirmation and negation excepting that which the idea, in so far as it is an idea, involves.*

Demonst.—In the mind there exists (Prop. 48, pt. 2) no absolute faculty of willing or not willing. Only individual volitions exist, that is to say, this and that affirmation and this and that negation. Let us conceive therefore, any individual volition, that is, any mode of thought, by which the mind affirms that the three angles of a triangle are equal to two right angles. This affirmation involves the conception or idea of the triangle, that is to say, without it the affirmation cannot be conceived. For to say that A must involve the conception B, is the same as saying that A cannot be conceived without B. Moreover, without the idea of the triangle this affirmation (Ax. 3, pt. 2) cannot be, and it can therefore neither be nor be conceived without that idea. But this idea of the triangle must involve this same affirmation that its three angles are equal to two right angles. Therefore also, *vice versa,* this idea of the triangle without this affirmation can neither be nor be conceived. Therefore (Def. 2, pt. 2) this affirmation pertains to the essence of the idea of the triangle, nor is it anything else besides this. Whatever too we have said of this volition (since it has been taken arbitrarily) applies to all other volitions, that is to say, they are nothing but ideas.—Q.E.D.

Corol.—The will and the intellect are one and the same.

Demonst.—The will and the intellect are nothing but the individual volitions and ideas themselves (Prop. 48, pt. 2, and its Schol.) But the individual volition and idea (Prop. 49, pt. 2) are one and the same. Therefore the will and the intellect are one and the same.—Q.E.D.

Schol.—I have thus removed what is commonly thought to be the cause of error. It has been proved above that falsity consists solely in the privation which mutilated and confused ideas involve. A false idea, therefore, in so far as it is false, does not involve certitude. Consequently, when we say that a man assents to what is false and does not doubt it, we do not say that he is certain, but merely that he does not doubt, that is to say, that he assents to what is false, because there are no causes sufficient to make his imagination waver (Schol. Prop. 44, pt. 2). Although, therefore, a man may be supposed to adhere to what is false, we shall never on that account say that he is certain. For by certitude we understand something positive (Prop. 43, pt. 2, with the Schol.), and not the privation of doubt; but by the privation of certitude we understand falsity. If the preceding proposition, however, is to be more clearly comprehended, a word or two must be added; it yet remains also that I should answer the objections which may be brought against our doctrine, and finally, in order to remove all scruples, I have thought it worth while to indicate some of its advantages. I say some, as the principal advantages will be better understood when we come to the Fifth Part. I begin, therefore, with the first, and I warn my readers carefully to distinguish between an idea or conception of the mind and the images of things formed by our imagination. Secondly, it is necessary that we should distinguish between ideas and the words by which things are signified. For it is because these three things, images, words, and ideas, are by many people either altogether confounded or not distinguished with sufficient accuracy and care that such ignorance exists about this doctrine of the will, so necessary to be known both for the purposes of speculation and for the wise government of life. Those who think that ideas consist of images, which are formed in us by meeting with external bodies, persuade themselves that those ideas of things of which we can form no similar image are not ideas, but mere fancies constructed by the free power of the will. They look upon ideas, therefore, as dumb pictures on a tablet, and being prepossessed with this prejudice, they do not see that an idea, in so far as it is an idea, involves affirmation or negation. Again, those who confound words with the idea, or with the affirmation itself which the idea involves, think that they can will contrary to their perception, because they affirm or deny something in words alone contrary to their perception. It will be easy for us, however, to divest ourselves of these prejudices if we attend to the nature of thought, which in no way involves the conception of extension, and by doing this we clearly see that an idea, since it is a mode of thought, is not an image of anything, nor does it consist of words. For the essence of words and images is formed of bodily motions alone, which involve in no way whatever the conception of thought.

Let thus much suffice under this head. I pass on now to the objections to which I have already alluded.

The first is, that it is supposed to be certain that the will extends itself more widely than the intellect, and is therefore different from it. The reason why men suppose that the will extends itself more widely than the intellect is because they say they have discovered that they do not need a larger faculty of assent—that is to say, of affirmation—and denial than that which they now have for the purpose of assenting to an infinite number of other things which we do not perceive, but that they do need a greater faculty for understanding them. The will, therefore, is distinguished from the intellect, the latter being finite, the former infinite. The second objection which can be made is that there is nothing which experience seems to teach more clearly than the possibility of suspending our judgment, so as not to assent to the things we perceive; and we are strengthened in this opinion because no one is said to be deceived in so far as he perceives a thing, but only in so far as he assents to it or dissents from it. For example, a man who imagines a winged horse does not therefore admit the existence of a winged horse; that is to say, he is not necessarily deceived, unless he grants at the same time that a winged horse exists. Experience, therefore, seems to show nothing more plainly than that the will or faculty of assent is free, and different from the faculty of the intellect.

Thirdly, it may be objected that one affirmation does not seem to contain more reality than another; that is to say, it does not appear that we need a greater power for affirming a thing to be true which is true than for affirming a thing to be true which is false. Nevertheless, we observe that one idea contains more reality or perfection than another, for as some objects are nobler than others, in the same proportion are their ideas more perfect. It appears indisputable, therefore, that there is a difference between the will and the intellect.

Fourthly, it may be objected that if a man does not act from freedom of the will, what would he do if he were in a state of equilibrium, like the ass of Buridanus? Would he not perish from hunger and thirst? and if this is granted, do we not seem to conceive him as a statue of a man or as an ass? If I deny that he would thus perish, he will consequently determine himself and possess the power of going where he likes and doing what he likes.

There may be other objections besides these, but as I am not bound to discuss what every one may dream, I shall therefore make it my business to answer as briefly as possible those only which I have mentioned. In reply to the first objection, I grant that the will extends itself more widely than the intellect, if by the intellect we understand only clear and distinct ideas; but I deny that the will extends itself more widely than the perceptions or the faculty of conception; nor, indeed, do I see why the faculty of will should be said to be infinite any more than the faculty of feeling; for as by the same faculty of will we can affirm an infinite number of things (one after the other, for we cannot affirm an infinite number of things at once), so also by the same faculty of feeling we can feel or perceive (one after another) an infinite number of bodies. If it be said that there are an infinite number of things which we cannot perceive, I reply that such things as these we can reach by no thought, and consequently by no faculty of will. But it is said that if God wished us to perceive those things, it would be necessary for Him to give us a larger faculty of perception, but not a larger faculty of will than He has already given us, which is the same thing as saying that if God wished us to understand an infinite number of other beings, it would be necessary for Him to give us a greater intellect, but not a more universal idea of being (in order to embrace that infinite number of beings), than He has given us. For we have shown that the will is a Universal, or the idea by which we explain all individual volitions, that is to say, that which is common to them all. It is not to be wondered at, therefore, that those who believe this common or universal idea of all the volitions to be a faculty should say that it extends itself infinitely beyond the limits of the intellect. For the universal is predicated of one or of many, or of an infinite number of individuals.

The second objection I answer by denying that we have free power of suspending judgment. For when we say that a person suspends judgment, we only say in other words that he sees that he does not perceive the thing adequately. The suspension of the judgment, therefore, is in truth a perception and not free will. In order that this may be clearly understood, let us take the case of a boy who imagines a horse and perceives nothing else. Since this imagination involves the existence of the horse (Corol. Prop. 17, pt. 2), and the boy does not perceive anything which negates its existence, he will necessarily contemplate it as present, nor will he be able to doubt its existence although he may not be certain of it. This is a thing which we daily experience in dreams, nor do I believe that there is any one who thinks that he has the free power during dreams of suspending his judgment upon those things which he dreams, and of causing himself not to dream those things which he dreams that he sees; and yet in dreams it nevertheless happens that we suspend our judgment, for we dream that we dream.

I grant, it is true, that no man is deceived in so far as he perceives; that is to say, I grant that mental images considered in themselves involve no error (Schol. Prop. 17, pt. 2); but I deny that a man in so far as he perceives affirms nothing. For what else is it to perceive a winged horse than to affirm of the horse that it has wings? For if the mind perceived nothing else but this winged horse, it would regard it as present, nor would it have any reason for doubting its existence, nor any power of refusing assent to it, unless the image of the winged horse be joined to an idea which negates its existence, or the mind perceives that the idea of the winged horse which it has is inadequate. In either of the two latter cases it will necessarily deny or doubt the existence of the horse.

With regard to the third objection, what has been said will perhaps be a sufficient answer,—namely, that the will is something universal, which is predicated of all ideas, and that it signifies that only which is common to them all, that is to say, affirmation. Its adequate essence, therefore, in so far as it is thus considered in the abstract, must be in every idea, and in this sense only must it be the same in all; but not in so far as it is considered as constituting the essence of an idea, for so far, the individual affirmations differ just as the ideas differ. For example, the affirmation which the idea of a circle involves differs from that which the idea of a triangle involves, just as the idea of a circle differs from the idea of a triangle. Again, I absolutely deny that we need a power of thinking in order to affirm that to be true which is true, equal to that which we need in order to affirm that to be true which is false. For these two affirmations, if we look to the mind, are related to one another as being and non-being, for there is nothing positive in ideas which constitutes a form of falsity (Prop. 35, pt. 2, with its Schol., and Schol. to Prop. 47, pt. 2).

Here therefore particularly is it to be observed how easily we are deceived when we confuse universals with individuals, and the entities of reason and abstractions with realities.

With regard to the fourth objection, I say that I entirely grant that if a man were placed in such a state of equilibrium he would perish of hunger and thirst, supposing he perceived nothing but hunger and thirst, and the food and drink which were equidistant from him. If you ask me whether such a man would not be thought an ass rather than a man, I reply that I do not know; nor do I know what ought to be thought of a man who hangs himself, or of children, fools, and madmen.

It remains for me now to show what service to our own lives a knowledge of this doctrine is. This we shall easily understand from the remarks which follow. Notice—

1. It is of service in so far as it teaches us that we do everything by the will of God alone, and that we are partakers of the divine nature in proportion as our actions become more and more perfect and we more and more understand God. This doctrine, therefore, besides giving repose in every way to the soul, has also this advantage, that it teaches us in what our highest happiness or blessedness consists, namely, in the knowledge of God alone, by which we are drawn to do those things only which love and piety persuade. Hence we clearly see how greatly those stray from the true estimation of virtue who expect to be distinguished by God with the highest regards for virtue and the noblest actions as if for the completest servitude, just as if virtue itself and the service of God were not happiness itself and the highest liberty.

2. It is of service to us in so far as it teaches us how we ought to behave with regard to the things of fortune, or those which are not in our power, that is to say, which do not follow from our own nature; for it teaches us with equal mind to wait for and bear each form of fortune, because we know that all things follow from

the eternal decree of God, according to that same necessity by which it follows from the essence of a triangle that its three angles are equal to two right angles.

3. This doctrine contributes to the welfare of our social existence, since it teaches us to hate no one, to despise no one, to mock no one, to be angry with no one, and to envy no one. It teaches every one, moreover, to be content with his own, and to be helpful to his neighbour, not from any womanish pity, from partiality, or superstition, but by the guidance of reason alone, according to the demand of time and circumstance, as I shall show in the Third Part.

4. This doctrine contributes not a little to the advantage of common society, in so far as it teaches us by what means citizens are to be governed and led; not in order that they may be slaves, but that they may freely do those things which are best.

Thus I have discharged the obligation laid upon me in this scholium, and with it I make an end of the Second Part, in which I think that I have explained the nature of the human mind and its properties at sufficient length, and, considering the difficulties of the subject, with sufficient clearness. I think, too, that certain truths have been established, from which much that is noble, most useful, and necessary to be known can be deduced, as we shall partly see from what follows.

THIRD PART

ON THE ORIGIN AND NATURE OF THE AFFECTS

MOST persons who have written about the affects and man's conduct of life seem to discuss, not the natural things which follow the common laws of nature, but things which are outside her. They seem indeed to con-

sider man in nature as a kingdom within a kingdom.
For they believe that man disturbs rather than follows
her order; that he has an absolute power over his own
actions; and that he is altogether self-determined. They
then proceed to attribute the cause of human weakness
and changeableness, not to the common power of nature,
but to some vice of human nature, which they therefore
bewail, laugh at, mock, or, as is more generally the case,
detest; whilst he who knows how to revile most elo-
quently or subtilly the weakness of the mind is looked
upon as divine. It is true that very eminent men have
not been wanting, to whose labour and industry we
confess ourselves much indebted, who have written many
excellent things about the right conduct of life, and
who have given to mortals counsels full of prudence,
but no one so far as I know has determined the nature
and strength of the affects, and what the mind is able
to do towards controlling them. I remember, indeed, that
the celebrated Descartes, although he believed that the
mind is absolute master over its own actions, tried nevertheless to explain by their first causes human affects, and
at the same time to show the way by which the mind
could obtain absolute power over them; but in my opinion
he has shown nothing but the acuteness of his great
intellect, as I shall make evident in the proper place,
for I wish to return to those who prefer to detest and
scoff at human affects and actions than understand
them. To such as these it will doubtless seem a mar-
vellous thing for me to endeavour to treat by a geometrical method the vices and follies of men, and to
desire by a sure method to demonstrate those things
which these people cry out against as being opposed
to reason, or as being vanities, absurdities, and mon-
strosities. The following is my reason for so doing.
Nothing happens in nature which can be attributed to

any vice of nature, for she is always the same and everywhere one. Her virtue is the same, and her power of acting; that is to say, her laws and rules, according to which all things are and are changed from form to form, are everywhere and always the same; so that there must also be one and the same method of understanding the nature of all things whatsoever, that is to say, by the universal laws and rules of nature. The affects, there-fore, of hatred, anger, envy, considered in themselves, follow from the same necessity and virtue of nature as other individual things; they have therefore certain causes through which they are to be understood, and certain properties which are just as worthy of being known as the properties of any other thing in the contemplation alone of which we delight. I shall, therefore, pursue the same method in considering the nature and strength of the affects and the power of the mind over them which I pursued in our previous discussion of God and the mind, and I shall consider human actions and appetites just as if I were considering lines, planes, or bodies.

Def. I.—I call that an adequate cause whose effect can be clearly and distinctly perceived by means of the cause. I call that an inadequate or partial cause whose effect cannot be understood by means of the cause alone.

Def. II.—I say that we act when anything is done, either within us or without us, of which we are the adequate cause, that is to say (by the preceding Def.), when from our nature anything follows, either within us or without us, which by that nature alone can be clearly and distinctly understood. On the other hand, I say that we suffer when anything is done within us, or when any-thing follows from our nature, of which we are not the cause excepting partially.

DEF. III.—By affect I understand the affections of the body, by which the power of acting of the body itself is increased, diminished, helped, or hindered, together with the ideas of these affections.

If, therefore, we can be the adequate cause of any of these affections, I understand the affect to be an action, otherwise it is a passion.

Postulate 1.—The human body can be affected in many mays by which its power of acting is increased or diminished, and also in other ways which make its power of acting neither greater nor less.

This postulate or axiom is based upon Post. 1 and Lems. 5 and 7, following Prop. 13, pt. 2.

Postulate 2.—The human body is capable of suffering many changes, and, nevertheless, can retain the impressions or traces of objects (Post. 5, pt. 2), and consequently the same images of things. (For the definition of images see Schol. Prop. 17, pt. 2.)

PROP. I.—*Our mind acts at times and at times suffers: in so far as it has adequate ideas, it necessarily acts; and in so far as it has inadequate ideas, it necessarily suffers.*

Demonst.—In every human mind some ideas are adequate, and others mutilated and confused (Schol. Prop. 40, pt. 2). But the ideas which in any mind are adequate are adequate in God in so far as He forms the essence of that mind (Corol. Prop. 11, pt. 2), while those again which are inadequate in the mind are also adequate in God (by the same Corol.), not in so far as He contains the essence of that mind only, but in so far as He contains the ideas [1] of other things at the same time in

[1] "Mentes," both in Paulus, Bruder, and Van Vloten and Land, but obviously a mistake for "ideas," as a reference tu

Himself. Again, from any given idea some effect must necessarily follow (Prop. 36, pt. 1), of which God is the adequate cause (Def. 1, pt. 3), not in so far as He is infinite, but in so far as He is considered as affected with the given idea (Prop. 9, pt. 2). But of that effect of which God is the cause, in so far as He is affected by an idea which is adequate in any mind, that same mind is the adequate cause (Corol. Prop. 11, pt. 2). Our mind, therefore (Def. 2, pt. 3), in so far as it has adequate ideas, necessarily at times acts, which is the first thing we had to prove. Again, if there be anything which necessarily follows from an idea which is adequate in God, not in so far as He contains within Himself the mind of one man only, but also, together with this, the ideas [1] of other things, then the mind of that man (Corol. Prop. 11, pt. 2) is not the adequate cause of that thing, but is only its partial cause, and therefore (Def. 2, pt. 3), in so far as the mind has inadequate ideas, it necessarily at times suffers. This was the second thing to be proved. Therefore our mind, &c.—Q.E.D.

Corol.—Hence it follows that the mind is subject to passions in proportion to the number of inadequate ideas which it has, and that it acts in proportion to the number of adequate ideas which it has.

PROP. II.—*The body cannot determine the mind to thought, neither can the mind determine the body to motion nor rest, nor to anything else, if there be anything else.*

Demonst.—All modes of thought have God for a cause in so far as He is a thinking thing, and not in

Corol. Prop. 11, pt. 2, will show. Kirchmann's translation omits "mentes" in the first passage marked, and renders, "insofern er andere Dinge in sich enthält."

[1] See footnote, p. 207.

so far as He is manifested by any other attribute (Prop. 6, pt. 2). That which determines the mind to thought, therefore, is a mode of thought and not of extension, that is to say (Def. 1, pt. 2), it is not the body. This is the first thing which was to be proved. Again, the motion and rest of the body must be derived from some other body, which has also been determined to motion or rest by another, and, absolutely, whatever arises in the body must arise from God, in so far as He is considered as affected by some mode of extension, and not in so far as He is considered as affected by any mode of thought (Prop. 6, pt. 2), that is to say, whatever arises in the body cannot arise from the mind, which is a mode of thought (Prop. 11, pt. 2). This is the second thing which was to be proved. Therefore, the body cannot determine, &c.—Q.E.D.

Schol.—This proposition will be better understood from what has been said in the scholium of Prop. 7, pt. 2, that is to say, that the mind and the body are one and the same thing, conceived at one time under the attribute of thought, and at another under that of extension. For this reason, the order or concatenation of things is one, whether nature be conceived under this or under that attribute, and consequently the order of the actions and passions of our body is coincident in nature with the order of the actions and passions of the mind. This is also plain from the manner in which we have demonstrated Prop. 12, pt. 2.

Although these things are so, and no ground for doubting remains, I scarcely believe, nevertheless, that, without a proof derived from experience, men will be induced calmly to weigh what has been said, so firmly are they persuaded that, solely at the bidding of the mind, the body moves or rests, and does a number of things which depend upon the will of the mind alone, and upon the power of thought. For what the body can do no one has hitherto determined, that is to say, experience has taught no one hitherto what the body, without being determined by the mind, can do and what it cannot do from the laws of nature alone, in so far as nature is considered merely as corporeal. For no one as yet has understood the structure of the body so accurately as to be able to explain all its functions, not to mention the fact that many things are observed in brutes which far surpass human sagacity, and that sleep-walkers in their sleep do very many things which they dare not do when awake; all this showing that the body itself can do many things from the laws of its own nature alone at which the mind belonging to that body is amazed. Again, nobody knows by what means or by what method the mind moves the body, nor how many degrees of motion it can communicate to the body, nor with what speed it can move the body. So that it follows that when men say that this or that action of the body springs from the mind which has command over the body, they do not know what they say, and they do nothing but confess with pretentious words that they know nothing about the cause of the action, and see nothing in it to wonder at. But they will say, that whether they know or do not know by what means the mind moves the body, it is nevertheless in their experience that if the mind were not fit for thinking the body would be inert. They say, again, it is in their experience that the mind alone has power both to speak and be silent, and to do many other things which they therefore think to be dependent on a decree of the mind. But with regard to the first assertion, I ask them if experience does not also teach that if the body be sluggish the mind at the same time is not fit for thinking? When the body is asleep, the mind slumbers with it, and has not the power to think, as it has when the body is awake. Again, I believe that all have discovered that the mind is not always equally fitted for thinking about the same subject, but in proportion to the fitness of the body for this or that image to be excited in it will the mind be better fitted to contemplate this or that object. But my opponents will say, that from the laws of nature alone, in so far as it is considered to be corporeal merely, it cannot be that the causes of architecture, painting, and things of this sort, which are the results of human art alone, could be deduced, and that the human body, unless it were determined and guided by the mind, would not be able to build a temple. I have already shown, however, that they do not know what the body can do, nor what can be deduced from the consideration of its nature alone, and that they find that many things are done merely by the laws of nature which they would never have believed to be possible without the direction of the mind, as, for example, those things which sleep-walkers do in their sleep, and at which they themselves are astonished when they wake. I adduce also here the structure itself of the human body, which so greatly surpasses in workmanship all those things which are constructed by human art, not to mention what I have already proved, that an infinitude of things follows from nature under whatever attribute it may be considered.

With regard to the second point, I should say that human affairs would be much more happily conducted if it were equally in the power of men to be silent and to speak; but experience shows over and over again that there is nothing which men have less power over than the tongue, and that there is nothing which they are less able to do than to govern their appetites, so that many persons believe that we do those things only with freedom which we seek indifferently; as the desire for such things can easily be lessened by the recollection of another thing which we frequently call to mind; it being impossible, on the other hand, to do those things with freedom which we seek with such ardour that the recollection of another thing is unable to mitigate it. But if, however, we had not found out that we do many things which we afterwards repent, and that when agitated by conflicting affects we see that which is better and follow that which is worse, nothing would hinder us from believing that we do everything with freedom. Thus the infant believes that it is by free will that it seeks the breast; the angry boy believes that by free will he wishes vengeance; the timid man thinks it is with free will he seeks flight; the drunkard believes that by a free command of his mind he speaks the things which when sober he wishes he had left unsaid. Thus the madman, the chatterer, the boy, and others of the same kind, all believe that they speak by a free command of the mind, whilst, in truth, they have no power to restrain the impulse which they have to speak, so that experience itself, no less than reason, clearly teaches that men believe themselves to be free simply because they are conscious of their own actions, knowing nothing of the causes by which they are determined: it teaches, too, that the decrees of the mind are nothing but the appetites themselves, which differ, therefore, according to the different temper of the body. For every man determines all things from his affect; those who are agitated by contrary affects do not know what they want, whilst those who are agitated by no affect are easily driven hither and thither. All this plainly shows that the decree of the mind, the appetite, and determination of the body are coincident in nature, or rather that they are one and the same thing, which, when it is considered under the attribute of thought and manifested by that, is called a decree, and when it is considered under the attribute of extension and is deduced from the laws of motion and rest, is called a determination. This, however, will be better understood as we go on, for there is another thing which I wish to be observed here—that we cannot by a mental decree do a thing unless we recollect it. We cannot speak a word, for instance, unless we recollect it. But it is not in the free power of the mind either to recollect a thing or to forget it. It is believed, therefore, that the power of the mind extends only thus far—that from a mental decree we can speak or be silent about a thing only when we recollect it. But when we dream that we speak, we believe that we do so from a free decree of the mind; and yet we do not speak, or, if we do, it is the result of a spontaneous motion of the body. We dream, again, that we are concealing things, and that we do this by virtue of a decree of the mind like that by which, when awake, we are silent about things we know. We dream, again, that, from a decree of the mind, we do some things which we should not dare to do when awake. And I should like to know, therefore, whether there are two kinds of decrees in the mind—one belonging to dreams and the other free. If this be too great nonsense, we must necessarily grant that this decree of the mind, which is believed to be free, is not distinguishable from the imagination or memory, and is nothing but the affirmation which the idea necessarily involves in so far as it is an idea (Prop. 49, pt. 2). These decrees of the mind, therefore, arise in the mind by the same necessity as the ideas of things actually existing. Consequently, those who believe that they speak, or are silent, or do anything else from a free decree of the mind, dream with their eyes open.

PROP. III.—*The actions of the mind arise from adequate ideas alone, but the passions depend upon those alone which are inadequate.*

Demonst.—The first thing which constitutes the essence of the mind is nothing but the idea of an actually existing body (Props. 11 and 13, pt. 2). This idea is composed of a number of others (Prop. 15, pt. 2), some of which are adequate and others inadequate (Corol. Prop. 38, pt. 2, and Corol. Prop. 29, pt. 2). Everything, therefore, of which the mind is the proximate cause, and which follows from the nature of the mind, through which it must be understood, must necessarily follow from an adequate or from an inadequate idea. But in so far as the mind (Prop. 1, pt. 3) has inadequate ideas, so far it necessarily suffers; therefore the actions of the mind follow from adequate ideas alone, and the mind therefore suffers only because it has inadequate ideas.

Schol.—We see, therefore, that the passions are not related to the mind, unless in so far as it possesses something which involves negation; in other words, unless in so far as it is considered as a part of nature, which by itself and without the other parts cannot be clearly and distinctly perceived. In the same way I could show that passions are related to individual things, just as they are related to the mind, and that they cannot be perceived in any other way; but my purpose is to treat of the human mind alone.

PROP. IV.—*A thing cannot be destroyed except by an external cause.*

Demonst.—This proposition is self-evident, for the definition of any given thing affirms and does not deny the existence of the thing; that is to say, it posits the essence of the thing and does not negate it. So long, therefore, as we attend only to the thing itself, and not to external causes, we shall discover nothing in it which can destroy it.—Q.E.D.

PROP. V.—*In so far as one thing is able to destroy another are they of contrary natures; that is to say, they cannot exist in the same subject.*

Demonst.—If it were possible for them to come together, or to coexist in the same subject, there would then be something in that subject able to destroy it, which (Prop. 4, pt. 3) is absurd. Therefore, in so far, &c.—Q.E.D.

PROP. VI.—*Each thing, in so far as it is in itself, endeavours to persevere in its being.* ✓

Demonst.—Individual things are modes by which the attributes of God are expressed in a certain and determinate manner (Corol. Prop. 25, pt. 1); that is to say (Prop. 34, pt. 1), they are things which express in a certain and determinate manner the power of God, by which He is and acts. A thing, too, has nothing in itself through which it can be destroyed, or which can negate its existence (Prop. 4, pt. 3), but, on the contrary, it is opposed to everything which could negate its existence (Prop. 5, pt. 3). Therefore, in so far as it can and is in itself, it endeavours to persevere in its own being.—Q.E.D.

PROP. VII.—*The effort by which each thing endeavours to persevere in its own being is nothing but the actual essence of the thing itself.* ✓

Demonst.—From the given essence of anything certain things necessarily follow (Prop. 36, pt. 1); nor are things able to do anything else than what necessarily follows from their determinate nature (Prop. 29, pt. 1). Therefore, the power of a thing, or the effort by means of which it does or endeavours to do anything, either by itself or with others—that is to say (Prop. 6, pt. 3), the power or effort by which it endeavours to persevere in its being—is nothing but the given or actual essence of the thing itself.—Q.E.D.

PROP. VIII.—*The effort by which each thing endeavours to persevere in its own being does not involve finite but indefinite time.*

Demonst.—If it involved a limited time, which would determine the duration of the thing, then from that power alone by which the thing exists it would follow that, after that limited time, it could not exist but must be destroyed. But this (Prop. 4, pt. 3) is absurd. The effort, therefore, by which a thing exists does not involve definite time, but, on the contrary (Prop. 4, pt. 3), if the thing be destroyed by no external cause, by the same power by which it now exists it will always continue to exist, and this effort, therefore, by which it endeavours to persevere, &c.—Q.E.D.

PROP. IX.—*The mind, both in so far as it has clear and distinct ideas, and in so far as it has confused ideas, endeavours to persevere in its being for an indefinite time, and is conscious of this effort.*

Demonst.—The essence of the mind is composed of adequate and inadequate ideas (as we have shown in Prop. 3, pt. 3), and therefore (Prop. 7, pt. 3), both in so

far as it has the former and in so far as it has the latter,
it endeavours to persevere in its being, and endeavours
to persevere in it for an indefinite time (Prop. 8, pt. 3).
But since the mind (Prop. 23, pt. 2), through the ideas
of the affections of the body, is necessarily conscious of
itself, it is therefore conscious (Prop. 7, pt. 3) of its
effort.

Schol.—This effort *conatus* when it is related to the mind
alone, is called *will,* but when it is related at the same
time both to the mind and the body, is called *appetite,*
which is therefore nothing but the very essence of man,
from the nature of which necessarily follow those things
which promote his preservation, and thus he is determined to do those things. Hence there is no difference
between appetite and desire, unless in this particular,
that desire is generally related to men in so far as they
are conscious of their appetites, and it may therefore be
defined as appetite of which we are conscious. From
what has been said it is plain, therefore, that we neither
strive for, wish, seek, nor desire anything because we
think it to be good, but, on the contrary, we adjudge
a thing to be good because we strive for, wish, seek, or
desire it.

PROP. X.—*There can be no idea in the mind which excludes the existence of the body, for such an idea is
contrary to the mind.*

Demonst.—There can be nothing in our body which
is able to destroy it (Prop. 5, pt. 3), and there cannot
be, therefore, in God an idea of any such thing in so
far as He has the idea of the body (Corol. Prop. 9,
pt. 2); that is to say (Props. 11 and 13, pt. 2), no
idea of any such thing can exist in our mind, but, on
the contrary, since (Props. 11 and 13, pt. 2) the first

thing which constitutes the essence of the mind is the
idea of a body actually existing, the first and chief thing
belonging to our mind is the effort (Prop. 7, pt. 3) to
affirm the existence of our body, and therefore the idea
which denies the existence of our body is contrary to
our mind.—Q.E.D.

PROP. XI.—*If anything increases, diminishes, helps, or
limits our body's power of action, the idea of that
thing increases, diminishes, helps, or limits our
mind's power of thought.*

Demonst.—This proposition is evident from Prop. 7,
pt. 2, and also from Prop. 14, pt. 2.

Schol.—We thus see that the mind can suffer great
changes, and can pass now to a greater and now to a
lesser perfection; these passions explaining to us the
affects of joy and sorrow. By *joy*, therefore, in what
follows, I shall understand the passion by which the
mind passes to a greater perfection; by *sorrow*, on the
other hand, the passion by which it passes to a less
perfection. The affect of joy, related at the same time
both to the mind and the body, I call *pleasurable excitement (titillatio)* or *cheerfulness*; that of sorrow I call
pain or *melancholy*. It is, however, to be observed that
pleasurable excitement and pain are related to a man
when one of his parts is affected more than the others;
cheerfulness and melancholy, on the other hand, when
all parts are equally affected. What the nature of desire
is I have explained in the scholium of Prop. 9, pt. 3;
and besides these three—joy, sorrow, and desire—I
know of no other primary affect, the others springing
from these, as I shall show in what follows. But before I
advance any farther, I should like to explain more fully

Prop. 10, pt. 3, so that we may more clearly understand in what manner one idea is contrary to another.

In the scholium of Prop. 17, pt. 2, we have shown that the idea which forms the essence of the mind involves the existence of the body so long as the body exists. Again, from Corol. Prop. 8, pt. 2, and its scholium, it follows that the present existence of our mind depends solely upon this—that the mind involves the actual existence of the body. Finally, we have shown that the power of the mind by which it imagines and remembers things also depends upon this—that it involves the actual existence of the body (Props. 17 and 18, pt. 2, with the Schol.) From these things it follows, that the present existence of the mind and its power of imagination are negated as soon as the mind ceases to affirm the present existence of the body. But the cause by which the mind ceases to affirm this existence of the body cannot be the mind itself (Prop. 4, pt. 2), nor can it be the body's ceasing to be; for (Prop. 6, pt. 2) the mind does not affirm the existence of the body because the body began to exist, and therefore, by the same reasoning, it does not cease to affirm the existence of the body because the body ceases to be, but (Prop. 17, pt. 2) because of another idea excluding the present existence of our body, and consequently of our mind, and contrary, therefore, to the idea which forms the essence of our mind.

PROP. XII.—*The mind endeavours as much as possible to imagine those things which increase or assist the body's power of acting.*

Demonst.—The human mind will contemplate any external body as present so long as the human body is affected in a way which involves the nature of that external body (Prop. 17, pt. 2), and consequently (Prop. 7, pt. 2) as long as the human mind contemplates any external body as present, that is to say (Schol. Prop. 17, pt. 2), imagines it, so long is the human body affected in a way which involves the nature of that external body. Consequently as long as the mind imagines those things which increase or assist our body's power of action, so long is the body affected in a way which increases or assists that power (Post. 1, pt. 3), and consequently (Prop. 11, pt. 3) so long the mind's power of thought is increased or assisted; therefore (Props. 6 and 9, pt. 3) the mind endeavours as much as possible to imagine those things.—Q.E.D.

PROP. XIII.—*Whenever the mind imagines those things which lessen or limit the body's power of action, it endeavours as much as possible to recollect what excludes the existence of these things.*

Demonst.—So long as the mind imagines anything of this sort, the power of the body and of the mind is lessened or limited (as we have shown in the preceding proposition). Nevertheless the mind will continue to imagine these things until it imagines some other thing which will exclude their present existence (Prop. 17, pt. 2); that is to say, as we have just shown, the power of the mind and of the body is diminished or limited until the mind imagines something which excludes the existence of these things. This, therefore (Prop. 9, pt. 3), the mind will endeavour to imagine or recollect as much as possible.—Q.E.D.

Corol.—Hence it follows that the mind is averse to imagine those things which lessen or hinder its power and that of the body.

Schol.—From what has been said we can clearly see

what love is and what hatred is. *Love* is nothing but joy accompanied with the idea of an external cause, and *hatred* is nothing but sorrow with the accompanying idea of an external cause. We see too that he who loves a thing necessarily endeavours to keep it before him and to preserve it, and, on the other hand, he who hates a thing necessarily endeavours to remove and destroy it. But we shall speak at greater length upon these points in what follows.

PROP. XIV.—*If the mind at any time has been simultaneously affected by two affects, whenever it is afterwards affected by one of them, it will also be affected by the other.*

Demonst.—If the human body has at any time been simultaneously affected by two bodies, whenever the mind afterwards imagines one of them, it will immediately remember the other (Prop. 18, pt. 2). But the imaginations of the mind indicate rather the affects of our body than the nature of external bodies (Corol. 2, Prop. 16, pt. 2), and therefore if the body, and consequently the mind (Def. 3, pt. 3), has been at any time, &c.—Q.E.D.

PROP. XV.—*Anything may be accidentally the cause of joy, sorrow, or desire.*

Demonst.—Let the mind be supposed to be affected at the same time by two affects, its power of action not being increased or diminished by one, while it is increased or diminished by the other (Post 1, pt. 3). From the preceding proposition it is plain that when the mind is afterwards affected by the first affect through its true cause, which (by hypothesis) of itself neither increases nor diminishes the mind's power of thinking, it will at the same time be affected by the other affect, which does increase or diminish that power, that is to say (Schol. Prop. 11, pt. 3), it will be affected with joy or sorrow; and thus the thing itself will be the cause of joy or of sorrow, not of itself, but accidentally. In the same way it can easily be shown that the same thing may accidentally be the cause of desire.—Q.E.D.

Corol.—The fact that we have contemplated a thing with an affect of joy or sorrow, of which it is not the efficient cause, is a sufficient reason for being able to love or hate it.

Demonst.—For this fact alone is a sufficient reason (Prop. 14, pt. 3) for its coming to pass that the mind in imagining the thing afterwards is affected with the affect of joy or sorrow, that is to say (Prop. 11, pt. 3), that the power of the mind and of the body is increased or diminished, &c., and, consequently (Prop. 12, pt. 3), that the mind desires to imagine the thing or (Corol. Prop. 13, pt. 3) is averse to doing so, that is to say (Schol. Prop. 13, pt. 3), that the mind loves the thing or hates it.

Schol.—We now understand why we love or hate certain things from no cause which is known to us, but merely from sympathy or antipathy, as they say. To this class, too, as we shall show in the following propositions, are to be referred those objects which affect us with joy or sorrow solely because they are somewhat like objects which usually affect us with those affects. I know indeed that the writers who first introduced the words "Sympathy" and "Antipathy" desired thereby to signify certain hidden qualities of things, but nevertheless I believe that we shall be permitted to understand by those names qualities which are plain and well known.

PROP. XVI.—*If we imagine a certain thing to possess something which resembles an object which usually affects the mind with joy or sorrow, although the quality in which the thing resembles the object is not the efficient cause of these affects, we shall nevertheless, by virtue of the resemblance alone, love or hate the thing.*

Demonst.—The quality in which the thing resembles the object we have contemplated in the object itself (by hypothesis) with the affect of joy or sorrow, and since (Prop. 14, pt. 3), whenever the mind is affected by the image of this quality, it is also affected by the former or latter affect, the thing which is perceived by us to possess this quality will be (Prop. 15, pt. 3) accidentally the cause of joy or sorrow. Therefore (by the preceding Corol.), although the quality in which the thing resembles the object is not the efficient cause of these affects, we shall nevertheless love the thing or hate it.

PROP. XVII.—*If we imagine that a thing that usually affects us with the affect of sorrow has any resemblance to an object which usually affects us equally with a great affect of joy, we shall at the same time hate the thing and love it.*

Demonst.—This thing (by hypothesis) is of itself the cause of sorrow, and (Schol. Prop. 13, pt. 3) in so far as we imagine it with this affect we hate it; but in so far as we imagine it to resemble an object which usually affects us equally with a great affect of joy do we love it with an equally great effort of joy (Prop. 16, pt. 3), and so we shall both hate it and love it at the same time.—Q.E.D.

Schol.—This state of mind, which arises from two contrary affects, is called *vacillation of the mind*. It is related to affect as doubt is related to the imagination (Schol. Prop. 44, pt. 2). Nor do vacillation and doubt differ from one another except as greater and less. It is to be observed that in the preceding proposition I have deduced these vacillations of the mind from causes which occasion the one affect directly and the other contingently. This I have done because the affects could thus be more easily deduced from what preceded, and not because I deny that these vacillations often originate from the object itself which is the efficient cause of both affects. For the human body (Post. 1, pt. 2) is composed of a number of individuals of different natures, and therefore (Ax. 1, after Lem. 3, following Prop. 13, pt. 2) it can be affected by one and the same body in very many and in different ways. On the other hand, the same object can be affected in a number of different ways, and consequently can affect the same part of the body in different ways. It is easy, therefore, to see how one and the same object may be the cause of many and contrary affects.

PROP. XVIII.—*A man is affected by the image of a past or future thing with the same affect of joy or sorrow as that with which he is affected by the image of a present thing.*

Demonst.—As long as a man is affected by the image of anything, he will contemplate the thing as present although it does not exist (Prop. 17, pt. 2, with Corol.), nor does he imagine it as past or future, unless in so far as its image is connected with that of past or future time (Schol. Prop. 44, pt. 2). Therefore the image of the thing considered in itself alone is the same whether it

be related to future, past, or present time; that is to say
(Corol. 2, Prop. 16, pt. 2), the state of the body or the
affect is the same whether the image be that of a past,
present, or future thing. The affect, therefore, of joy
and sorrow is the same whether the image be that of a
past, present, or future thing.—Q.E.D.

Schol. 1.—I call a thing here past or future in so far
as we have been or shall be affected by it; for example,
in so far as we have seen a thing or are about to see it,
in so far as it has strengthened us or will strengthen
us; has injured or will injure us. For in so far as we
thus imagine it do we affirm its existence; that is to say,
the body is affected by no affect which excludes the
existence of the thing, and therefore (Prop. 17, pt. 2)
the body is affected by the image of the thing in the
same way as if the thing itself were present. But because
it generally happens that those who possess much experience hesitate when they think of a thing as past or
future, and doubt greatly concerning its issue (Schol.
Prop. 44, pt. 2), therefore the affects which spring
from such images of things are not so constant, but
are generally disturbed by the images of other things,
until men become more sure of the issue.

Schol. 2.—From what has now been said we under- ↘
stand the nature of Hope, Fear, Confidence, Despair,
Gladness, Remorse. *Hope* is nothing but unsteady joy,
arising from the image of a future or past thing about
whose issue we are in doubt. *Fear*, on the other hand,
is an unsteady sorrow, arising from the image of a
doubtful thing. If the doubt be removed from these
affects, then hope and fear become *Confidence* and *Despair*, that is to say, joy or sorrow, arising from the
image of a thing for which we have hoped or which
we have feared. *Gladness*, again, is joy arising from

the image of a past thing whose issues we have doubted. *Remorse* [1] is the sorrow which is opposed to gladness.

PROP. XIX.—*He who imagines that what he loves is destroyed will sorrow, but if he imagines that it is preserved he will rejoice.*

Demonst.—The mind endeavours as much as it can to imagine those things which increase or assist the body's power of action (Prop. 12, pt. 3), that is to say (Schol. Prop. 13, pt. 3), to imagine those things which it loves. But the imagination is assisted by those things which posit the existence of the object and is restrained by those which exclude its existence (Prop. 17, pt. 2). Therefore the images of things which posit the existence of the beloved object assist the mind's effort to imagine it, that is to say (Schol. Prop. 11, pt. 3), they affect the mind with joy; whilst those, on the other hand, which exclude the existence of the beloved object restrain that same effort of the mind, that is to say (Schol. Prop. 11, pt. 3), they affect the mind with sorrow. He, therefore, who imagines that what he loves is destroyed, &c.—Q.E.D.

PROP. XX.—*He who imagines that what he hates is destroyed will rejoice.*

Demonst.—The mind (Prop. 13, pt. 3) endeavours to imagine those things which exclude the existence of whatever lessens or limits the body's power of action; that is to say (Schol. Prop. 13, pt. 3), it endeavours to imagine those things which exclude the existence of what it hates, and therefore the image of the thing

---

[1] *Conscientiæ morsus.* So also on pp. 271 and 329 (*Gewissensibiss,* Auerbach.) But remorse is something more than is given in this definition, and is more nearly akin to *poenitentia,* repentance, as defined on p. 273.

which excludes the existence of what the mind hates assists this endeavour of the mind, that is to say (Schol. Prop. 11, pt. 3), affects the mind with joy. He, therefore, who imagines that what he hates is destroyed will rejoice.—Q.E.D.

PROP. XXI.—*He who imagines that what he loves is affected with joy or sorrow will also be affected with joy or sorrow, and these affects will be greater or less in the lover as they are greater or less in the thing loved.*

Demonst.—The images of things (Prop. 19, pt. 5) which posit the existence of the beloved object assist the effort of the mind to imagine it; but joy posits the existence of the thing which rejoices, and the greater the joy the more is existence posited, for (Schol. Prop. 11, pt. 3) joy is the transition to a greater perfection. The image, therefore, in the lover of the joy of the beloved object assists the effort of his mind to imagine the object, that is to say (Schol. Prop. 11, pt. 3), affects the lover with joy proportionate to the joy of the object he loves. This was the first thing to be proved. Again, in so far as anything is affected with sorrow, so far is it destroyed, and the destruction is greater as the sorrow with which it is affected is greater (Schol. Prop. 11, pt. 3). Therefore (Prop. 19, pt. 3) he who imagines that what he loves is affected with sorrow will also be affected with sorrow, and it will be greater as this affect shall have been greater in the object beloved.

PROP. XXII.—*If we imagine that a person affects with joy a thing which we love, we shall be affected with love towards him. If, on the contrary, we imagine that he affects it with sorrow, we shall also be affected with hatred towards him.*

Demonst.—He who affects with joy or sorrow the thing we love affects us also with joy or sorrow whenever we imagine the beloved object so affected (Prop. 21, pt. 3). But this joy or sorrow is supposed to exist in us accompanied with the idea of an external cause; therefore (Schol. Prop. 13, pt. 3) if we imagine that a person affects with joy or sorrow a thing which we love, we shall be affected with love or hatred towards him.—Q.E.D.

Schol.—Prop. 21 explains to us what *commiseration* is, which we may define as sorrow which springs from another's loss. By what name the joy is to be called which springs from another's good I do not know. Love toward the person who has done good to another we shall call *favour* (*favor*), whilst hatred towards him who has done evil to another we shall call *indignation* (*indignatio*). It is to be observed, too, that we not only feel pity for the object which we have loved, as we showed in Prop. 21, but also for that to which we have been attached by no affect; provided only we adjudge it to be like ourselves (as I shall show hereafter), and so we shall regard with favour him who has done any good to the object which is like us, and, on the contrary, be indignant with him who has done it any harm.

PROP. XXIII.—*He who imagines that what he hates is affected with sorrow will rejoice; if, on the other hand, he imagines it to be affected with joy he will be sad; and these affects will be greater or less in him in proportion as their contraries are greater or less in the object he hates.*

Demonst.—In so far as the hated thing is affected with sorrow is it destroyed, and the destruction is greater as the sorrow is greater (Schol. Prop. 11, pt. 3). He, therefore (Prop. 20, pt. 3), who imagines that the thing which he hates is affected with sorrow will on the contrary be affected with joy, and the joy will be the greater in proportion as he imagines the hated thing to be affected with a greater sorrow. This was the first thing to be proved. Again, joy posits the existence of the thing which rejoices (Schol. Prop. 11, pt. 3), and it does so the more in proportion as the joy is conceived to be greater. If a person, therefore, imagines that he whom he hates is affected with joy, this idea (Prop. 13, pt. 3) will restrain the effort of the mind of him who hates, that is to say (Schol. Prop. 11, pt. 3), he will be affected with sorrow.—Q.E.D.

Schol.—This joy can hardly be solid and free from any mental conflict. For, as I shall show directly in Prop. 27, in so far as we imagine that what is like ourselves is affected with sorrow, we must be sad; and, on the contrary, if we imagine it to be affected with joy, we rejoice. Here, however, we are considering merely hatred.

PROP. XXIV.—*If we imagine that a person affects with joy a thing which we hate, we are therefore affected with hatred towards him. On the other hand, if we imagine that he affects it with sorrow, we are therefore affected with love towards him.*

Demonst.—This proposition is proved in the same manner as Prop. 22, pt. 3, which see.

Schol.—These and the like affects of hatred are related to *envy*, which is therefore nothing but hatred in so far as it is considered to dispose a man so that he rejoices over the evil and is saddened by the good which befalls another.

PROP. XXV.—*We endeavour to affirm everything, both concerning ourselves and concerning the beloved object which we imagine will affect us or the object with joy, and, on the contrary, we endeavour to deny everything that will affect either it or ourselves with sorrow.*

Demonst.—Everything which we imagine as affecting the beloved object with joy or sorrow affects us also with joy or sorrow (Prop. 21, pt. 3). But the mind (Prop. 12, pt. 3) endeavours as much as it can to imagine those things which affect us with joy, that is to say, Prop. 17, pt. 2 and its Corol.), it endeavours to consider them as present. On the contrary (Prop. 13, pt. 3), it endeavours to exclude the existence of what affects us with sorrow: therefore we endeavour to affirm everything both concerning ourselves and concerning the beloved object which we imagine will affect us or it with joy, &c.—Q.E.D.

PROP. XXVI.—*If we hate a thing, we endeavour to affirm concerning it everything which we imagine will affect it with sorrow, and, on the other hand, to deny everything concerning it which we imagine will affect it with joy.*

Demonst.—This proposition follows from Prop. 23, as the preceding proposition follows from Prop. 21.

Schol.—We see from this how easily it may happen, that a man should think too much of himself or of the beloved object, and, on the contrary, should think too little of what he hates. When a man thinks too much of himself, this imagination is called *pride*, and is a kind of delirium, because he dreams with his eyes open, that he is able to do all those things to which he attains in imagination alone, regarding them therefore as realities, and rejoicing in them so long as he cannot imagine anything to exclude their existence and limit his power of action. Pride, therefore, is that joy which arises from a man's thinking too much of himself. The joy which arises from thinking too much of another is called overestimation, and that which arises from thinking too little of another is called contempt.

PROP. XXVII.—*Although we may not have been moved towards a thing by any affect, yet if it is like ourselves, whenever we imagine it to be affected by any affect we are therefore affected by the same.*

Demonst.—The images of things are affections of the human body, and the ideas of these affections represent to us external bodies as if they were present (Schol. Prop. 17, pt. 2), that is to say (Prop. 16, pt. 2), these ideas involve both the nature of our own body and at the same time the present nature of the external body. If, therefore, the nature of the external body be like that of our body, then the idea of the external body which we imagine will involve an affection of our body like that of the external body. Therefore, if we imagine any one who is like ourselves to be affected with any affect, this imagination will express an affection of our body like that affect, and therefore we shall be affected with a similar affect ourselves, because we imagine something like us to be affected with the same. If, on the other hand, we hate a thing which is like ourselves, we shall so far (Prop. 23, pt. 3) be affected with an affect contrary and not similar to that with which it is affected.—Q.E.D.

Schol.—This imitation of affects, when it is connected with sorrow, is called *commiseration* (see Schol. Prop. 22, pt. 3), and where it is connected with desire is called *emulation*, which is nothing else than the desire which is engendered in us for anything, because we imagine that other persons, who are like ourselves, possess the same desire.

Corol. 1.—If we imagine that a person to whom we have been moved by no affect, affects with joy a thing which is like us, we shall therefore be affected with love towards him. If, on the other hand, we imagine that he affects it with sorrow, we shall be affected with hatred towards him.

Demonst.—This Corol. follows from the preceding proposition, just as Prop. 22, pt. 3, follows from Prop. 21, pt. 3.

Corol. 2.—If we pity a thing, the fact that its misery affects us with sorrow will not make us hate it.

Demonst.—If we could hate the thing for this reason, we should then (Prop. 23, pt. 3) rejoice over its sorrow, which is contrary to the hypothesis.[1]

Corol. 3.—If we pity a thing, we shall endeavour as much as possible to free it from its misery.

Demonst.—That which affects with sorrow the thing that we pity, affects us likewise with the same sorrow (Prop. 27, pt. 3), and we shall, therefore, endeavour to devise every means by which we may take away or destroy the existence of the cause of the sorrow (Prop. 13, pt. 3); that is to say (Schol. Prop. 9, pt. 3), we shall seek to destroy it, or shall be determined thereto,

---

[1] This indicates that Spinoza, like Hume, finds evidence for direct social sentiments even at the level of passion. [Ed.]

and therefore we shall endeavour to free from its misery
the thing we pity.

Schol.—This will or desire of doing good, arising
from our pity for the object which we want to benefit, is
called *benevolence*, which is, therefore, simply the desire
which arises from commiseration. With regard to the
love or hatred towards the person who has done good or
evil to the thing we imagine to be like ourselves, see
Schol. Prop. 22, pt. 3.

PROP. XXVIII.—*We endeavour to bring into existence
everything which we imagine conduces to joy, and
to remove or destroy everything opposed to it, or
which we imagine conduces to sorrow.*

Demonst.—We endeavour to imagine as much as possible all those things which we think conduce to joy
(Prop. 12, pt. 3), that is to say (Prop. 17, pt. 2), we
strive as much as possible to perceive them as present or
actually existing. But the mind's effort or power in
thinking is equal to and correspondent with the body's
effort or power in acting, as clearly follows from Corol.
Prop. 7, pt. 2, and Corol. Prop. 11, pt. 2, and therefore
absolutely whatever conduces to joy we endeavour to
make exist, that is to say (Schol. Prop. 9, pt. 3), we
seek after it and aim at it. This is the first thing which
was to be proved. Again, if we imagine that a thing
which we believe causes us sorrow, that is to say (Schol.
Prop. 13, pt. 3), which we hate is destroyed, we shall
rejoice (Prop. 20, pt. 3), and therefore (by the first
part of this demonstration) we shall endeavour to destroy it, or (Prop. 13, pt. 3) to remove it from us, so
that we may not perceive it as present. This is the
second thing which was to be proved. We endeavour,
therefore, to bring into existence, &c.—Q.E.D.

PROP. XXIX.—*We shall endeavour to do everything which we imagine men* [1] *will look upon with joy, and, on the contrary, we shall be averse to doing anything to which we imagine men are averse.*

Demonst.—If we imagine men to love or hate a thing, we shall therefore love or hate it (Prop. 27, pt. 3); that is to say (Schol. Prop. 13, pt. 3), we shall therefore rejoice or be sad at the presence of the thing, and therefore (Prop. 28, pt. 3) everything which we imagine that men love or look upon with joy, we shall endeavour to do, &c.—Q.E.D.

Schol.—This effort to do some things and omit doing others, solely because we wish to please men, is called *ambition*, especially if our desire to please the common people is so strong that our actions or omissions to act are accompanied with injury to ourselves or to others. Otherwise this endeavour is usually called *humanity.* Again, the joy with which we imagine another person's action, the purpose of which is to delight us, I call *praise*, and the sorrow with which we turn away from an action of a contrary kind I call *blame*.

PROP. XXX.—*If a person has done anything which he imagines will affect others with joy, he also will be affected with joy, accompanied with an idea of himself as its cause; that is to say, he will look upon himself with joy. If, on the other hand, he has done anything which he imagines will affect others with sorrow, he will look upon himself with sorrow.*

Demonst.—He who imagines that he affects others with joy or sorrow will necessarily be affected with joy

---

[1] Both here and in what follows I understand by the word *men*, men to whom we are moved by no affect. (Sp.)

or sorrow (Prop. 27, pt. 3). But since man is conscious of himself (Props. 19 and 23, pt. 2) by means of the affections by which he is determined to act; therefore he who has done anything which he imagines will affect others with joy will be affected with joy accompanied with a consciousness of himself as its cause; that is to say, he will look upon himself with joy, and, on the other hand, &c.—Q.E.D.

Schol.—Since love (Schol. Prop. 13, pt. 3) is joy attended with the idea of an external cause, and hatred is sorrow attended with the idea of an external cause, the joy and sorrow spoken of in this proposition will be a kind of love and hatred. But because love and hatred are related to external objects, we will therefore give a different name to the affects which are the subject of this proposition, and we will call this kind of joy which is attended with the idea of an external cause *self-exaltation*, and the sorrow opposed to it we will call *shame*. The reader is to understand that this is the case in which joy or sorrow arises because the man believes that he is praised or blamed, otherwise I shall call this joy accompanied with the idea of an external cause *contentment with one's-self*, and the sorrow opposed to it *repentance*. Again, since (Corol. Prop. 17, pt. 2) it may happen that the joy with which a person imagines that he affects other people is only imaginary, and since (Prop. 25, pt. 3) every one endeavours to imagine concerning himself what he supposes will affect himself with joy, it may easily happen that the self-exalted man becomes proud, and imagines that he is pleasing everybody when he is offensive to everybody.

PROP. XXXI.—*If we imagine that a person loves, desires, or hates a thing which we ourselves love, desire, or hate, we shall on that account love, de-*

*sire, or hate the thing more steadily. If, on the
other hand, we imagine that he is averse to the
thing we love or loves the thing to which we are
averse, we shall then suffer vacillation of mind.*

Demonst.—If we imagine that another person loves a
thing, on that very account we shall love it (Prop. 27,
pt. 3). But we are supposed to love it independently
of this, and a new cause for our love is therefore added,
by which it is strengthened, and consequently the object
we love will be loved by us on this account the more
steadily. Again, if we imagine that a person is averse
to a thing, on that very account we shall be averse to it
(Prop. 27, pt. 3); but if we suppose that we at the
same time love it, we shall both love the thing and be
averse to it, that is to say (Schol. Prop. 17, pt. 3), we
shall suffer vacillation of mind.—Q.E.D.

Corol.—It follows from this proposition and from
Prop. 28, pt. 3, that every one endeavours as much as
possible to make others love what he loves, and to hate
what he hates. Hence the poet says—

> "Speremus pariter, pariter metuamus amantes;
> Ferreus est, si quis, quod sinit alter, amat."[1]

This effort to make every one approve what we love or
hate is in truth ambition (Schol. Prop. 29, pt. 3), and
so we see that each person by nature desires that other
persons should live according to his way of thinking;
but if every one does this, then all are a hindrance to one
another, and if every one wishes to be praised or beloved
by the rest, then they all hate one another.

PROP. XXXII.—*If we imagine that a person enjoys a
thing which only one can possess, we do all we can
to prevent his possessing it.*

[1] Ovid, Amor. ii. 19: Spinoza has, however, transposed the
lines.—TR.

Demonst. If we imagine that a person enjoys a thing, that will be a sufficient reason (Prop. 27, pt. 3, with Corol. 1) for making us love the thing and desiring to enjoy it. But (by hypothesis) we imagine that his enjoyment of the thing is an obstacle to our joy, and therefore (Prop. 28, pt. 3) we endeavour to prevent his possessing it.—Q.E.D.

Schol.—We see, therefore, that the nature of man is generally constituted so as to pity those who are in adversity and envy those who are in prosperity, and (Prop. 32, pt. 3) he envies with a hatred which is the greater in proportion as he loves what he imagines another possesses. We see also that from the same property of human nature from which it follows that men pity one another it also follows that they are envious and ambitious.[1] If we will consult experience, we shall find that she teaches the same doctrine, especially if we consider the first years of our life. For we find that children, because their body is, as it were, continually in equilibrium, laugh and cry merely because they see others do the same; whatever else they see others do they immediately wish to imitate; everything which they think is pleasing to other people they want. And the reason is, as we have said, that the images of things are the affections themselves of the human body, or the ways in which it is affected by external causes and disposed to this or that action.

PROP. XXXIII.—*If we love a thing which is like ourselves, we endeavour as much as possible to make it love us in return.*

[1] This is a quite typical revelation of Spinoza's deductive method as applied to the realm of psychology. Two passions seemingly opposed turn out to arise from the same source. Cf. the Freudian psychology. [Ed.]

Demonst.—We endeavour as much as possible to imagine before everything else the thing we love (Prop. 12, pt. 3). If, therefore, it be like ourselves, we shall endeavour to affect it with joy before everything else (Prop. 29, pt. 3); that is to say, we shall endeavour as much as possible to cause the beloved object to be affected with joy attended with the idea of ourselves, or, in other words (Schol. Prop. 13, pt. 3), we try to make it love us in return.—Q.E.D.

PROP. XXXIV.—*The greater the affect with which we imagine that a beloved object is affected towards us, the greater will be our self-exaltation.*

Demonst.—We endeavour as much as possible to make a beloved object love us in return (Prop. 33, pt. 3), that is to say (Schol. Prop. 13, pt. 3), to cause it to be affected with joy attended with the idea of ourselves. In proportion, therefore, as we imagine the beloved object to be affected with a joy of which we are the cause, will our endeavour be assisted, that is to say (Prop. 11, pt. 3 with Schol.), will be the greatness of the joy with which we are affected. But since we rejoice because we have affected with joy another person like ourselves, we shall look upon ourselves with joy (Prop. 30, pt. 3); and therefore the greater the affect with which we imagine that the beloved object is affected towards us, the greater will be the joy with which we shall look upon ourselves, that is to say (Schol. Prop. 30, pt. 3), the greater will be our self-exaltation.—Q.E.D.

PROP. XXXV.—*If I imagine that an object beloved by me is united to another person by the same, or by a closer bond of friendship than that by which I myself alone held the object, I shall be affected*

with hatred towards the beloved object itself, and
shall envy that other person.

Demonst.—The greater the love with which a person
imagines a beloved object to be affected towards him,
the greater will be his self-exaltation (Prop. 34, pt. 3),
that is to say (Schol. Prop. 30, pt. 3), the more will he
rejoice. Therefore (Prop. 28, pt. 3) he will endeavour
as much as he can to imagine the beloved object united
to him as closely as possible, and this effort or desire
is strengthened if he imagines that another person
desires for himself the same object (Prop. 31, pt. 3).
But this effort or desire is supposed to be checked by
the image of the beloved object itself attended by the
image of the person whom it connects with itself. Therefore (Schol. Prop. 11, pt. 3) the lover on this account
will be affected with sorrow attended with the idea of the
beloved object as its cause together with the image of
another person; that is to say (Schol. Prop. 13, pt. 3),
he will be affected with hatred towards the beloved
object and at the same time towards this other person
(Corol. Prop. 15, pt. 3), whom he will envy (Prop. 23,
pt. 3) as being delighted with it.—Q.E.D.

Schol.—This hatred towards a beloved object when
joined with envy is called Jealousy, which is therefore
nothing but a vacillation of the mind springing from
the love and hatred both felt together, and attended with
the idea of another person whom we envy. Moreover,
this hatred towards the beloved object will be greater in
proportion to the joy with which the jealous man has
been usually affected from the mutual affection between
him and his beloved, and also in proportion to the affect
with which he had been affected towards the person who
is imagined to unite to himself the beloved object. For if
he has hated him, he will for that very reason hate the

beloved object (Prop. 24, pt. 3), because he imagines it
to affect with joy that which he hates, and also (Corol.
Prop. 15, pt. 3) because he is compelled to connect the
image of the beloved object with the image of him whom
he hates. This feeling is generally excited when the
love is love towards a woman. The man who imagines
that the woman he loves prostitutes herself to another is
not merely troubled because his appetite is restrained,
but he turns away from her because he is obliged to
connect the image of a beloved object with the privy
parts and with what is excremental in another man; and
in addition to this, the jealous person is not received
with the same favour which the beloved object formerly
bestowed on him,—a new cause of sorrow to the lover,
as I shall show.

Prop. XXXVI.—*He who recollects a thing with which
he has once been delighted, desires to possess it with
every condition which existed when he was first
delighted with it.*

Demonst.—Whatever a man has seen together with an
object which has delighted him will be (Prop. 15, pt. 3)
contingently a cause of joy, and therefore (Prop. 28,
pt. 3) he will desire to possess it all, together with the
object which has delighted him, that is to say, he will
desire to possess the object with every condition which
existed when he was first delighted with it.—Q.E.D.

Corol.—If, therefore, the lover discovers that one of
these conditions be wanting, he will be sad.

Demonst.—For in so far as he discovers that any one
condition is wanting does he imagine something which
excludes the existence of the object. But since (Prop.
36, pt. 3) he desires the object or condition from love,

he will therefore be sad (Prop. 19, pt. 3) in so far as he imagines that condition to be wanting.—Q.E.D.

Schol.—This sorrow, in so far as it is related to the absence of what we love, is called *longing*.

PROP. XXXVII.—*The desire which springs from sorrow or joy, from hatred or love, is greater in proportion as the affect is greater.*

Demonst.—Sorrow lessens or limits a man's power of action (Schol. Prop. 11, pt. 3), that is to say (Prop. 7, pt. 3), it lessens or limits the effort by which a man endeavours to persevere in his own being, and therefore (Prop. 5, pt. 3) it is opposed to this effort; consequently, if a man be affected with sorrow, the first thing he attempts is to remove that sorrow; but (by the definition of sorrow) the greater it is, the greater is the human power of action to which it must be opposed, and so much the greater, therefore, will be the power of action with which the man will endeavour to remove it; that is to say (Schol. Prop. 9, pt. 3), with the greater eagerness or desire will he struggle to remove it. Again, since joy (Schol. Prop. 11, pt. 3) increases or assists a man's power of action, it is easily demonstrated, by the same method, that there is nothing which a man who is affected with joy desires more than to preserve it, and his desire is in proportion to his joy. Again, since hatred and love are themselves affects either of joy or sorrow, it follows in the same manner that the effort, desire, or eagerness which arises from hatred or love will be greater in proportion to the hatred or love.—Q.E.D.

PROP. XXXVIII.—*If a man has begun to hate a beloved thing, so that his love to it is altogether destroyed, he will for this very reason hate it more than he would have done if he had never loved it, and his hatred will be in greater proportion to his previous love.*

Demonst.—If a man begins to hate a thing which he loves, a constraint is put upon more appetites than if he had never loved it. For love is joy (Schol. Prop. 13, pt. 3), which a man endeavours to preserve as much as possible (Prop. 28, pt. 3), both by looking on the beloved object as present (Schol. Prop. 13, pt. 3), and by affecting it with joy as much as possible (Prop. 21, pt. 3); this effort (Prop. 37, pt. 3) to preserve the joy of love being the greater in proportion as his love is greater, and so also is the effort to bring the beloved object to love him in return (Prop. 33, pt. 3). But these efforts are restrained by the hatred towards the beloved object (Corol. Prop. 13, and Prop. 23, pt. 3); therefore the lover (Schol. Prop. 11, pt. 3) for this reason also will be affected with sorrow, and that the more as the love had been greater; that is to say, in addition to the sorrow which was the cause of the hatred there is another produced by his having loved the object, and consequently he will contemplate with a greater affect of sorrow the beloved object; that is to say (Schol. Prop. 13, pt. 3), he will hate it more than he would have done if he had not loved it, and his hatred will be in proportion to his previous love.—Q.E.D.

PROP. XXXIX.—*If a man hates another, he will endeavour to do him evil, unless he fears a greater evil will therefrom arise to himself; and, on the other hand, he who loves another will endeavour to do him good by the same rule.*

Demonst.—To hate a person (Schol. Prop. 13, pt. 3) is to imagine him as a cause of sorrow, and therefore (Prop. 28, pt. 3) he who hates another will endeavour to remove or destroy him. But if he fears lest a greater grief, or, which is the same thing, a greater evil, should fall upon himself, and one which he thinks he can avoid by refraining from inflicting the evil he meditated, he will desire not to do it (Prop. 28, pt. 3); and this desire will be stronger than the former with which he was possessed of inflicting the evil, and will prevail over it (Prop. 37, pt. 3). This is the first part of the proposition. The second is demonstrated in the same way. Therefore if a man hates another, &c.—q.e.d.

Schol.—By *good,* I understand here every kind of joy and everything that conduces to it; chiefly, however, anything that satisfies longing, whatever that thing may be. By *evil,* I understand every kind of sorrow, and chiefly whatever thwarts longing. For we have shown above (Schol. Prop. 9, pt. 3) that we do not desire a thing because we adjudge it to be good, but, on the contrary, we call it good because we desire it, and consequently everything to which we are averse we call evil. Each person, therefore, according to his affect judges or estimates what is good and what is evil, what is better and what is worse, and what is the best and what is the worst. Thus the covetous man thinks plenty of money to be the best thing and poverty the worst. The ambitious man desires nothing like glory, and on the other hand dreads nothing like shame. To the envious person, again, nothing is more pleasant than the misfortune of another, and nothing more disagreeable than the prosperity of another. And so each person according to his affect judges a thing to be good or evil, useful or useless. We notice, moreover, that this affect, by which a man is so disposed as not to will the thing he wills, and to will that which he does not will, is called *fear*, which may therefore be defined as that *apprehension* which leads a man to avoid an evil in the future by incurring a lesser evil (Prop. 28, pt. 3). If the evil feared is shame, then the fear is called *modesty*. If the desire of avoiding the future is restrained by the fear of another evil, so that the man does not know what he most wishes, then this apprehension is called *consternation*, especially if both the evils feared are very great.

PROP. XL.—*If we imagine that we are hated by another without having given him any cause for it, we shall hate him in return.*

Demonst.—If we imagine that another person is affected with hatred, on that account we shall also be affected with it (Prop. 27, pt. 3); that is to say, we shall be affected with sorrow (Schol. Prop. 13, pt. 3), accompanied with the idea of an external cause. But (by hypothesis) we imagine no cause for this sorrow excepting the person himself who hates us, and therefore, because we imagine ourselves hated by another, we shall be affected with sorrow accompanied with the idea of him who hates us; that is to say (Schol. Prop. 18, pt. 3), we shall hate him.—Q.E.D.

Schol.—If we imagine that we have given just cause for the hatred, we shall then (Prop. 30, pt. 3, with its Schol.) be affected with shame. This, however (Prop. 25, pt. 3), rarely happens.

This reciprocity of hatred may also arise from the fact that hatred is followed by an attempt to bring evil upon him who is hated (Prop. 39, pt. 3). If, therefore, we imagine that we are hated by any one else, we shall imagine him as the cause of some evil or sorrow, and thus we shall be affected with sorrow or apprehension accompanied with the idea of the person who hates us as a cause; that is to say, we shall hate him in return, as we have said above.

Corol. 1.—If we imagine that the person we love is affected with hatred towards us, we shall be agitated at the same time both with love and hatred. For in so far as we imagine that we are hated are we determined (Prop. 40, pt. 3) to hate him in return. But (by hypothesis) we love him notwithstanding, and therefore we shall be agitated both by love and hatred.

Corol. 2.—If we imagine that an evil has been brought upon us through the hatred of some person towards whom we have hitherto been moved by no affect, we shall immediately endeavour to return that evil upon him.

Demonst.—If we imagine that another person is affected with hatred towards us, we shall hate him in return (Prop. 40, pt. 3), and (Prop. 26, pt. 3) we shall endeavour to devise and (Prop. 39, pt. 3) bring upon him everything which can affect him with sorrow. But (by hypothesis) the first thing of this kind we imagine is the evil brought upon ourselves, and therefore we shall immediately endeavour to bring that upon him.—Q.E.D.

Schol.—The attempt to bring evil on those we hate is called *anger,* and the attempt to return the evil inflicted on ourselves is called *vengeance.*

PROP. XLI.—*If we imagine that we are beloved by a person without having given any cause for the love (which may be the case by Corol. Prop. 15, pt. 3, and by Prop. 16, pt. 3), we shall love him in return.*

Demonst.—This proposition is demonstrated in the same way as the preceding, to the scholium of which the reader is also referred.

Schol.—If we imagine that we have given just cause for love, we shall pride ourselves upon it (Prop. 30, pt. 3, with its Schol.). This frequently occurs (Prop. 25, pt. 3), and we have said that the contrary takes place when we believe that we are hated by another person (Schol. Prop. 40, pt. 3). This reciprocal love, and consequently (Prop. 39, pt. 3) this attempt to do good to the person who loves us, and who (by the same Prop. 39, pt. 3) endeavours to do good to us, is called *thankfulness* or *gratitude*, and from this we can see how much readier men are to revenge themselves than to return a benefit.

Corol.—If we imagine that we are loved by a person we hate, we shall at the same time be agitated both by love and hatred. This is demonstrated in the same way as the preceding proposition.

Schol.—If the hatred prevail, we shall endeavour to bring evil upon the person by whom we are loved. This affect is called Cruelty, especially if it is believed that the person who loves has not given any ordinary reason for hatred.

PROP. XLII.—*If, moved by love or hope of self-exaltation, we have conferred a favour upon another person, we shall be sad if we see that the favour is received with ingratitude.*

Demonst.—If we love a thing which is of the same nature as ourselves, we endeavour as much as possible to cause it to love us in return (Prop. 33, pt. 3). If we confer a favour, therefore, upon any one because of our love towards him, we do it with a desire by which we are possessed that we may be loved in return; that is to say (Prop. 34, pt. 3), from the hope of self-exaltation, or (Schol. Prop. 30, pt. 3) of joy, and we shall consequently (Prop. 12, pt. 3) endeavour as much as possible to imagine this cause of self-exaltation, or to contemplate it as actually existing. But (by hypothesis) we imagine something else which excludes the existence of that cause, and, therefore (Prop. 19, pt. 3), this will make us sad.—Q.E.D.

PROP. XLIII.—*Hatred is increased through return of hatred, but may be destroyed by love.*

Demonst.—If we imagine that the person we hate is affected with hatred towards us, a new hatred is thereby produced (Prop. 40, pt. 3), the old hatred still remaining (by hypothesis). If, on the other hand, we imagine him to be affected with love towards us, in so far as we imagine it (Prop. 30, pt. 3) shall we look upon ourselves with joy, and endeavour (Prop. 29, pt. 3) to please him; that is to say (Prop. 41, pt. 3), in so far shall we endeavour not to hate him nor to affect him with sorrow. This effort (Prop. 37, pt. 3) will be greater or less as the affect from which it arises is greater or less, and, therefore, should it be greater than that which springs from hatred, and by which (Prop. 26, pt. 3) we endeavour to affect with sorrow the object we hate, then it will prevail and banish hatred from the mind. —Q.E.D.

PROP. XLIV.—*Hatred which is altogether overcome by love passes into love, and the love is therefore greater than if hatred had not preceded it.*

Demonst.—The demonstration is of the same kind as that of Prop. 38, pt. 3. For if we begin to love a thing which we hated, or upon which we were in the habit of looking with sorrow, we shall rejoice for the very reason that we love, and to this joy which love involves (see its definition in the Schol. of Prop. 13, pt. 3) a new joy is added, which springs from the fact that the effort to remove the sorrow which hatred involves (Prop. 37, pt. 3) is so much assisted, there being also present before us as the cause of our joy the idea of the person whom we hated.

Schol.—Notwithstanding the truth of this proposition, no one will try to hate a thing or will wish to be affected with sorrow in order that he may rejoice the more; that is to say, no one will desire to inflict loss on himself in the hope of recovering the loss, or to become ill in the hope of getting well, inasmuch as every one will always try to preserve his being and to remove sorrow from himself as much as possible. Moreover, if it can be imagined that it is possible for us to desire to hate a person in order that we may love him afterwards the more, we must always desire to continue the hatred. For the love will be the greater as the hatred has been greater, and therefore we shall always desire the hatred to be more and more increased. Upon the same principle we shall desire that our sickness may continue and increase in order that we may afterwards enjoy the greater pleasure when we get well, and therefore we shall always desire sickness, which (Prop. 6, pt. 3) is absurd.

PROP. XLV.—*If we imagine that any one like ourselves is affected with hatred towards an object like ourselves which we love, we shall hate him.*

Demonst.—The beloved object hates him who hates it (Prop. 40, pt. 3), and therefore we who love it, who imagine that any one hates it, imagine also that it is affected with hatred; that is to say, with sorrow (Schol.

Prop. 13, pt. 3), and consequently (Prop. 21, pt. 3) we are sad, our sadness being accompanied with the idea of the person, as the cause thereof, who hates the beloved object; that is to say (Schol. Prop. 13, pt. 3), we shall hate him.—Q.E.D.

PROP. XLVI.—*If we have been affected with joy or sorrow by any one who belongs to a class or nation different from our own, and if our joy or sorrow is accompanied with the idea of this person as its cause, under the common name of his class or nation, we shall not love or hate him merely, but the whole of the class or nation to which he belongs.*

Demonst.—This proposition is demonstrated in the same way as Prop. 16, pt. 3.

PROP. XLVII.—*The joy which arises from our imagining that what we hate has been destroyed or has been injured is not unaccompanied with some sorrow.*

Demonst.—This is evident from Prop. 27, pt. 3; for in so far as we imagine an object like ourselves affected with sorrow shall we be sad.

Schol.—This proposition may also be demonstrated from Corol. Prop. 17, pt. 2. For as often as we recollect the object, although it does not actually exist, we contemplate it as present, and the body is affected in the same way as if it were present. Therefore, so long as the memory of the object remains, we are so determined as to contemplate it with sorrow, and this determination, while the image of the object abides, is restrained by the recollection of those things which exclude the existence of the object, but is not altogether removed. Therefore we rejoice only so far as the determination is restrained, and hence it happens that the joy which springs from the misfortune of the object we hate is renewed as often as we recollect the object. For, as we have already shown, whenever its image is excited, inasmuch as this involves the existence of the object, we are so determined as to contemplate it with the same sorrow with which we were accustomed to contemplate it when it really existed. But because we have connected with this image other images which exclude its existence, the determination to sorrow is immediately restrained, and we rejoice anew; and this happens as often as this repetition takes place. This is the reason why we rejoice as often as we call to mind any evil that is past, and why we like to tell tales about the dangers we have escaped, since whenever we imagine any danger, we contemplate it as if it were about to be, and are so determined as to fear it—a determination which is again restrained by the idea of freedom, which we connected with the idea of the danger when we were freed from it, and this idea of freedom again makes us fearless, so that we again rejoice.

PROP. XLVIII.—*Love and hatred towards any object, for example, towards Peter, are destroyed if the joy and the sorrow which they respectively involve be joined to the idea of another cause; and they are respectively diminished in proportion as we imagine that Peter has not been their sole cause.*

Demonst.—This is plain from the very definition of love and hatred (see Schol. Prop. 13, pt. 3), joy being called love to Peter and sorrow being called hatred to him, solely because he is considered to be the cause of this or that affect. Whenever, therefore, we can no longer consider him either partially or entirely its cause, the affect towards him ceases or is diminished.—Q.E.D.

PROP. XLIX.—*For the same reason, love or hatred towards an object we imagine to be free must be greater than towards an object which is under necessity.*

Demonst.—An object which we imagine to be free must (Def. 7, pt. 1) be perceived through itself and without others. If, therefore, we imagine it to be the cause of joy or sorrow, we shall for that reason alone love or hate it (Schol. Prop. 13, pt. 3), and that too with the greatest love or the greatest hatred which can spring from the given affect (Prop. 48, pt. 3). But if we imagine that the object which is the cause of that effect is necessary, then (by the same Def. 7, pt. 1) we shall imagine it as the cause of that affect, not alone, but together with other causes, and so (Prop. 48, pt. 3) our love or hatred towards it will be less.—Q.E.D.

Schol.—Hence it follows that our hatred or love towards one another is greater than towards other things, because we think we are free. We must take into account also the imitation of affects which we have discussed in Props. 27, 34, 40, and 43, pt. 3.

PROP. L.—*Anything may be accidentally the cause either of hope or fear.*

This proposition is demonstrated in the same way as Prop. 15, pt. 3, which see, together with Schol. 2, Prop. 18, pt. 3.

Schol.—Things which are accidentally the causes either of hope or fear are called good or evil omens. In so far as the omens are the cause of hope and fear

(by the Def. of hope and fear in Schol. 2, Prop. 18,
pt. 3) are they the cause of joy or of sorrow, and consequently (Corol. Prop. 15, pt. 3) so far do we love
them or hate them, and (Prop. 28, pt. 3) endeavour to
use them as means to obtain those things for which we
hope, or to remove them as obstacles or causes of fear.
It follows, too, from Prop. 25, pt. 3, that our natural
constitution is such that we easily believe the things we
hope for, and believe with difficulty those we fear, and
that we think too much of the former and too little of
the latter. Thus have superstitions arisen, by which men
are everywhere disquieted. I do not consider it worth
while to go any farther, and to explain here all those
vacillations of mind which arise from hope and fear,
since it follows from the definition alone of these affects
that hope cannot exist without fear, nor fear without
hope (as we shall explain more at length in the proper
place). Besides, in so far as we hope for a thing or
fear it, we love it or hate it, and therefore everything
which has been said about hatred and love can easily be
applied to hope and fear.

PROP. LI.—*Different men may be affected by one and
the same object in different ways, and the same
man may be affected by one and the same object in
different ways at different times.*

Demonst.—The human body (Post. 3, pt. 2) is affected by external bodies in a number of ways. Two
men, therefore, may be affected in different ways at the
same time, and, therefore (Ax. 1, after Lemma 3, following Prop. 13, pt. 2), they can be affected by one
and the same object in different ways. Again (Post. 3,
pt. 2), the human body may be affected now in this and
now in that way, and consequently (by the axiom just

‑quoted) it may be affected by one and the same object in different ways at different times.—Q.E.D.

Schol.—We thus see that it is possible for one man to love a thing and for another man to hate it; for this man to fear what this man does not fear, and for the same man to love what before he hated, and to dare to do what before he feared. Again, since each judges according to his own affect what is good and what is evil, what is better and what is worse (Schol. Prop. 39, pt. 3), it follows that men may change in their judgment as they do in their affects,[1] and hence it comes to pass that when we compare men, we distinguish them solely by the difference in their affects, calling some brave, others timid, and others by other names. For example, I shall call a man *brave* who despises an evil which I usually fear, and if, besides this, I consider the fact that his desire of doing evil to a person whom he hates or doing good to one whom he loves is not restrained by that fear of evil by which I am usually restrained, I call him *audacious*. On the other hand, the man who fears an evil which I usually despise will appear *timid*, and if, besides this, I consider that his desire is restrained by the fear of an evil which has no power to restrain me, I call him *pusillanimous*; and in this way everybody will pass judgment. Finally, from this nature of man and the inconstancy of his judgment, in consequence of which he often judges things from mere effect, and the things which he believes contribute to his joy or his sorrow, and which, therefore, he endeavours to bring to pass or remove (Prop. 28, pt. 3), are often only imaginary—to say nothing about what we have demonstrated in the Second Part of this book about

[1] That this may be the case, although the human mind is part of the divine intellect, we have shown in Corol. Prop. 11, pt. 2 (Sp.).

the uncertainty of things—it is easy to see that a man
may often be himself the cause of his sorrow or his joy,
or of being affected with sorrow or joy accompanied
with the idea of himself as its cause, so that we can
easily understand what repentance and what self-
approval are. Repentance is sorrow accompanied with
the idea of one's self as the cause, and self-approval is
joy accompanied with the idea of one's self as the
cause; and these affects are very intense because men
believe themselves free (Prop. 49, pt. 3).

PROP. LII.—*An object which we have seen before together with other objects, or which we imagine
possesses nothing which is not common to it with
many other objects, we shall not contemplate so
long as that which we imagine possesses something
peculiar.*

Demonst.—Whenever we imagine an object which we
have seen with others, we immediately call these to mind
(Prop. 18, pt. 2, with Schol.), and thus from the contemplation of one object we immediately fall to contemplating another. This also is our way with an object
which we imagine to possess nothing except what is
common to a number of other objects. For this is the
same thing as supposing that we contemplate nothing in
it which we have not seen before with other objects.
On the other hand, if we suppose ourselves to imagine in
an object something peculiar which we have never seen
before, it is the same as saying that the mind, while it
contemplates that object, holds nothing else in itself to
the contemplation of which it can pass, turning away
from the contemplation of the object, and therefore it is
determined to the contemplation solely of the object.
Therefore an object, &c.—Q.E.D.

Schol.—This affection of the mind or imagination of a particular thing, in so far as it alone occupies the mind, is called *astonishment,* and if it is excited by an object we dread, we call it *consternation,* because astonishment at the evil so fixes us in the contemplation of itself, that we cannot think of anything else by which we might avoid the evil. On the other hand, if the objects at which we are astonished are human wisdom, industry, or anything of this kind, inasmuch as we consider that their possessor is by so much superior to ourselves, the astonishment goes by the name of *veneration*; whilst, if the objects are human anger, envy, or anything of this sort, it goes by the name of *horror.* Again, if we are astonished at the wisdom of industry of a man we love, then our love on that account (Prop. 12, pt. 3) will be greater, and this love, united to astonishment or veneration, we call *devotion.* In the same manner it is possible to conceive of hatred, hope, confidence, and other affects being joined to astonishment, so that more affects may be deduced than are indicated by the words in common use. From this we see that names have been invented for affects from common usage, rather than from accurate knowledge of them.

To astonishment is opposed contempt, which is usually caused, nevertheless, by our being determined to astonishment, love, or fear towards an object either because we see that another person is astonished at, loves or fears this same object, or because at first sight it appears like other objects, at which we are astonished or which we love or fear (Prop. 15, with Corol. pt. 3, and Prop. 27, pt. 3). But if the presence of the object or a more careful contemplation of it should compel us to deny that there exists in it any cause for astonishment, love, fear, &c., then from its presence itself, the mind remains determined to think rather of those things which are

not in it than of those which are in it, although from
the presence of an object the mind is accustomed to
think chiefly about what is in the object. We may also
observe that as devotion springs from astonishment at
a thing we love, so *derision* springs from the contempt
of a thing we hate or fear, whilst *scorn* arises from the
contempt of folly, as veneration arises from astonishment at wisdom. We may also conceive of love, hope,
glory, and other affects being joined to contempt, and
thus deduce other affects which also we are not in the
habit of distinguishing by separate words.

PROP. LIII.—*When the mind contemplates itself and
its own power of acting it rejoices, and it rejoices
in proportion to the distinctness with which it
imagines itself and its power of action.*

Demonst.—Man has no knowledge of himself except
through the affections of his own body and their ideas
(Props. 19 and 23, pt. 2); whenever, therefore, it happens that the mind is able to contemplate itself, it is
thereby supposed to pass to a greater perfection, that
is to say (Schol. Prop. 11, pt. 3), it is supposed to be
affected with joy, and the joy is greater in proportion
to the distinctness with which it imagines itself and its
power of action.—Q.E.D.

Corol.—The more a man imagines that he is praised
by other men, the more is this joy strengthened; for the
more a man imagines that he is praised by others, the
more does he imagine that he affects others with joy
accompanied by the idea of himself as a cause (Schol.
Prop. 29, pt. 3), and therefore (Prop. 27, pt. 3)
he is affected with greater joy accompanied with the
idea of himself.—Q.E.D.

PROP. LIV.—*The mind endeavours to imagine those things only which posit its power of acting.*

Demonst.—The effort or power of the mind is the essence of the mind itself (Prop. 7, pt. 3), but the essence of the mind, as is self-evident, affirms only that which the mind is and is able to do, and does not affirm that which the mind is not and cannot do, and therefore the mind endeavours to imagine those things only which affirm or posit its power of acting.—Q.E.D.

PROP. LV.—*When the mind imagines its own weakness it necessarily sorrows.*

Demonst.—The essence of the mind affirms only that which the mind is and is able to do, or, in other words, it is the nature of the mind to imagine those things only which posit its power of acting (Prop. 54, pt. 3). If we say, therefore, that the mind, while it contemplates itself, imagines its own weakness, we are merely saying in other words that the effort of the mind to imagine something which posits its power of acting is restrained, that is to say (Schol. Prop. 11, pt. 3), the mind is sad. —Q.E.D.

Corol.—This sorrow is strengthened in proportion as the mind imagines that it is blamed by others. This is demonstrated in the same way as Corol. Prop. 53, pt. 3.

Schol.—This sorrow, accompanied with the idea of our own weakness, is called *humility*, and the joy which arises from contemplating ourselves is called *self-love* or *self-approval*. Inasmuch as this joy recurs as often as a man contemplates his own virtues or his own power of acting, it comes to pass that every one loves to tell of his own deeds, and to display the powers both of his body and mind; and that for this reason men become

an annoyance to one another. It also follows that men
are naturally envious (Schol. Prop. 24, and Schol. Prop.
32, pt. 3), that is to say, they rejoice over the weaknesses of their equals and sorrow over their strength.
For whenever a person imagines his own actions he is
affected with joy (Prop. 53, pt. 3), and his joy is the
greater in proportion as he imagines that his actions
express more perfection, and he imagines them more
distinctly; that is to say (by what has been said in
Schol. 1, Prop. 40, pt. 2), in proportion as he is able
to distinguish them from others, and to contemplate
them as individual objects. A man's joy in contemplating himself will therefore be greatest when he contemplates something in himself which he denies of
other people. For if he refers that which he affirms of
himself to the universal idea of man or of animal
nature, he will not so much rejoice; on the other hand,
he will be sad if he imagines that his own actions when
compared with those of other people are weaker than
theirs, and this sorrow he will endeavour to remove
(Prop. 28, pt. 3), either by misinterpreting the actions
of his equals, or giving as great a lustre as possible to
his own. It appears, therefore, that men are by nature
inclined to hatred and envy, and we must add that their
education assists them in this propensity, for parents
are accustomed to excite their children to follow virtue by the stimulus of honour and envy alone. But an
objection perhaps may be raised that we not unfrequently venerate men and admire their virtues. In order
to remove this objection I will add the following
corollary.

Corol.—No one envies the virtue of a person who is
not his equal.

Demonst.—Envy is nothing but hatred (Schol. Prop.
24, pt 3), that is to say (Schol. Prop. 13, pt. 3), sorrow,

or, in other words (Schol. Prop. 11, pt. 3), an affection by which the effort of a man or his power of action is restrained. But (Schol. Prop. 9, pt. 3) a man neither endeavours to do nor desires anything excepting what can follow from his given nature, therefore a man will not desire to affirm of himself any power of action, or, which is the same thing, any virtue which is peculiar to another nature and foreign to his own. His desire, therefore, cannot be restrained, that is to say (Schol. Prop. 11, pt. 3), he cannot feel any sorrow because he contemplates a virtue in another person altogether unlike himself, and consequently he cannot envy that person, but will only envy one who is his own equal, and who is supposed to possess the same nature.

Schol.—Since, therefore, we have said in Schol. Prop. 52, pt. 3, that we venerate a man because we are astonished at his wisdom and bravery, &c., this happens because (as is evident from the proposition itself) we imagine that he specially possesses these virtues, and that they are not common to our nature. We therefore envy them no more than we envy trees their height or lions their bravery.

PROP. LVI.—*Of joy, sorrow, and desire, and consequently of every effort which either, like vacillation of mind, is compounded of these, or, like love, hatred, hope, and fear, is derived from them, there are just as many kinds as there are kinds of objects by which we are affected.*

Demonst.—Joy and sorrow, and consequently the affects which are compounded of these or derived from them, are passions (Schol. Prop. 11, pt. 3). But (Prop. 1, pt. 3) we necessarily suffer in so far as we have inadequate ideas, and (Prop. 3, pt. 3) only in so far as we have them; that is to say (see Schol. Prop. 40, pt. 2), we necessarily suffer only in so far as we imagine, or (see Prop. 17, pt. 2, with its Schol.) in so far as we are affected with an affect which involves the nature of our body and that of an external body. The nature, therefore, of each passion must necessarily be explained in such a manner, that the nature of the object by which we are affected is expressed. The joy, for example, which springs from an object A. involves the nature of that object A., and the joy which springs from B. involves the nature of that object B., and therefore these two affects of joy are of a different nature. In like manner the affect of sorrow which arises from one object is of a different kind from that which arises from another cause, and the same thing is to be understood of love, hatred, hope, fear, vacillation of mind, &c.; so that there are necessarily just as many kinds of joy, sorrow, love, hatred, &c., as there are kinds of objects by which we are affected. But desire is the essence itself or nature of a person in so far as this nature is conceived from its given constitution as determined towards any action (Schol. Prop. 9, pt. 3), and therefore as a person is affected by external causes with this or that kind of joy, sorrow, love, hatred, &c., that is to say, as his nature is constituted in this or that way, so must his desire vary and the nature of one desire differ from that of another, just as the affects from which each desire arises differ. There are as many kinds of desires, therefore, as there are kinds of joy, sorrow, love, &c., and, consequently (as we have just shown), as there are kinds of objects by which we are affected.—Q.E.D.

Schol.—Amongst the different kinds of affects, which (by the preceding Prop.) must be very great in number, the most remarkable are *voluptuousness, drunkenness, lust, avarice,* and *ambition,* which are nothing but notions of love or desire, which explain the nature of this or that affect through the objects to which they are related. For by *voluptuousness, drunkenness, lust, avarice,* and *ambition* we understand nothing but an immoderate love or desire for good living, for drinking, for women, for riches, and for glory. It is to be observed that these affects, in so far as we distinguish them by the object alone to which they are related, have no contraries. For *temperance, sobriety,* and *chastity,* which we are in the habit of opposing to voluptuousness, drunkenness, and lust, are not affects nor passions: but merely indicate the power of the mind which restrains these affects.[1]

The remaining kinds of affects I cannot explain here (for they are as numerous as are the varieties of objects), nor, if I could explain them, is it necessary to do so. For it is sufficient for the purpose we have in view, the determination, namely, of the strength of the affects and the mind's power over them, to have a general definition of each kind of affect. It is sufficient for us, I say, to understand the common properties of the mind and the affects, so that we may determine what and how great is the power of the mind to govern and constrain the affects. Although, therefore, there is a great difference between this or that affect of love, of hatred, or of desire—for example, between the love towards children and the love towards a wife—it is not worth while for us to take cognisance of these differences, or to investigate the nature and origin of the affects any further.

[1] Thus Spinoza, like Plato, tends to amalgamate the virtues into "power of mind" or knowledge. [Ed.]

Prop. LVII.—*The affect of one person differs from the corresponding affect of another as much as the essence of the one person differs from that of the other.*

Demonst.—This proposition is evident from Ax. 1, following Lem. 3, after Schol. Prop. 13, pt. 2. Nevertheless, we will demonstrate it from the definitions of the three primitive affects. All affects are related to desire, joy, or sorrow, as the definitions show which we have given of those affects. But desire is the very nature or essence of a person (Schol. Prop. 9, pt. 3), and therefore the desire of one person differs from the desire of another as much as the nature or essence of the one differs from that of the other. Again, joy and sorrow are passions by which the power of a person or his effort to persevere in his own being is increased or diminished, helped, or limited (Prop. 11, pt. 3, with its Schol.). But by the effort to persevere in his own being, in so far as it is related at the same time to the mind and the body, we understand appetite and desire (Schol. Prop. 9, pt. 3), and therefore joy and sorrow are desire or appetite in so far as the latter is increased, diminished, helped, or limited by external causes; that is to say (Schol. Prop. 9, pt. 3), they are the nature itself of each person.

The joy or sorrow of one person therefore differs from the joy or sorrow of another as much as the nature or essence of one person differs from that of the other, and consequently the affect of one person differs from the corresponding affect of another, &c.—Q.E.D.

Schol.—Hence it follows that the affects of animals which are called irrational (for after we have learnt the origin of the mind we can in no way doubt that brutes feel) differ from human affects as much as the nature of a brute differs from that of a man. Both the man and the horse, for example, are swayed by the lust to propagate, but the horse is swayed by equine lust and the man by that which is human. The lusts and appetites of insects, fishes, and birds must vary in the same way; and so, although each individual lives contented with its own nature and delights in it, nevertheless the life with which it is contented and its joy are nothing but the idea or soul of that individual, and so the joy of one differs in character from the joy of the other as much as the essence of the one differs from the essence of the other. Finally, it follows from the preceding proposition that the joy by which the drunkard is enslaved is altogether different from the joy which is the portion of the philosopher,—a thing I wished just to hint in passing. So much, therefore, for the affects which are related to man in so far as he suffers. It remains that I should say a few words about those things which are related to him in so far as he acts.

PROP. LVIII.—*Besides the joys and ~~sorrows~~ desires which are passions, there are other affects of joy and ~~sorrow~~ desire which are related to us in so far as we act.*

Demonst.—When the mind conceives itself and its own power of acting, it is rejoiced (Prop. 53, pt. 3). But the mind necessarily contemplates itself whenever it conceives a true or adequate idea (Prop. 43, pt. 2); and as (Schol. 2, Prop. 40, pt. 2) it does conceive some adequate ideas, it is rejoiced in so far as it conceives them, or, in other words (Prop. 1, pt. 3), in so far as it acts. Again, the mind, both in so far as it has clear and distinct ideas and in so far as it has confused ideas, endeavours to persevere in its own being (Prop. 9, pt. 3). But by this effort we understand desire (Schol. Prop. 9, pt. 3), and therefore desire also is related to us in so far as we think; that is to say (Prop. 1, pt. 3), in so far as we act.—Q.E.D.

PROP. LIX.—*Amongst all the affects which are related to the mind in so far as it acts, there are none which are not related to joy or desire.*

Demonst.—All the affects are related to desire, joy, or sorrow, as the definitions we have given of them show. By sorrow, however, we understand that the mind's power of acting is lessened or limited (Prop. 11, pt. 3, and its Schol.), and therefore, in so far as the mind suffers sorrow is its power of thinking, that is to say (Prop. 1, pt. 3), its power of acting, lessened or limited. Therefore no affects of sorrow can be related to the mind in so far as it acts, but only affects of joy and desire, which (by the preceding Prop.) are also so far related to the mind.—Q.E.D.

Schol.—All the actions which follow from the affects which are related to the mind in so far as it thinks I ascribe to *fortitude*, which I divide into *strength of mind* (*animositas*) and *generosity*. By *strength of mind*, I mean the desire by which each person endeavours from the dictates of reason alone to preserve his own being. By *generosity*, I mean the desire by which from the dictates of reason alone each person endeavours to help other people and to join them to him in friendship. Those actions, therefore, which have for their aim the advantage only of the doer I ascribe to strength of mind, whilst those which aim at the advantage of others I ascribe to generosity. Temperance, therefore, sobriety, and presence of mind in danger, are a species of strength of mind, while moderation and mercy are a species of generosity.

I have now, I think, explained the principal affects and vacillations of the mind which are compounded of the three primary affects, desire, joy, and sorrow, and have set them forth through their first causes. From what has been said it is plain that we are disturbed by external causes in a number of ways, and that, like the waves of the sea agitated by contrary winds, we fluctuate in our ignorance of our future and destiny. I have said, however, that I have only explained the principal mental complications, and not all which may exist. For by the same method which we have pursued above it would be easy to show that love unites itself to repentance, scorn, shame, &c.; but I think it has already been made clear to all that the affects can be combined in so many ways, and that so many variations can arise, that no limits can be assigned to their number. It is sufficient for my purpose to have enumerated only those which are of consequence; the rest, of which I have taken no notice, being more curious than important. There is one constantly recurring characteristic of love which I have yet to notice, and that is, that while we are enjoying the thing which we desired, the body acquires from that fruition a new disposition by which it is otherwise determined, and the images of other things are excited in it, and the mind begins to imagine and to desire other things. For example, when we imagine anything which usually delights our taste, we desire to enjoy it by eating it. But whilst we enjoy it the stomach becomes full, and the constitution of the body becomes altered. If, therefore, the body being now otherwise disposed, the image of the food, in consequence of its being present, and therefore also the effort or desire to eat it, become more intense, then this new disposition of the body will oppose this effort or desire, and consequently the presence of the food which we desired will become hateful to us, and this hatefulness is what we call loathing or disgust. As for the external affections of the body which are observed in the affects, such as trembling, paleness, sobbing, laughter, and the like, I have neglected to notice them, because they belong to the body alone without any relationship to the mind. A few things remain to be said about the definitions of the affects, and I will therefore here repeat the definitions in order, appending to them what is necessary to be observed in each.

THE AFFECTS.—DEF. I.—*Desire* is the essence itself of man in so far as it is conceived as determined to any action by any one of his affections.

Explanation.—We have said above, in the Schol. of Prop. 9, pt. 3, that desire is appetite which is self-conscious, and that appetite is the essence itself of man in so far as it is determined to such acts as contribute to his preservation. But in the same scholium I have taken care to remark that in truth I cannot recognise any difference between human appetite and desire. For whether a man be conscious of his appetite or not, it remains one and the same appetite, and so, lest I might appear to be guilty of tautology, I have not explained desire by appetite, but have tried to give such a definition of desire as would include all the efforts of human nature to which we give the name of appetite, desire, will, or impulse. For I might have said that desire is the essence itself of man in so far as it is considered as determined to any action; but from this definition it would not follow (Prop. 23, pt. 2) that the mind could be conscious of its desire or appetite, and therefore, in order that I might include the cause of this consciousness, it was necessary (by the same proposition) to add the words, *in so far as it is conceived as determined to any action by any one of his affections.* For by an affection of the human essence we understand any constitution of that essence, whether it be innate, whether it be conceived through the attribute of thought alone or of extension alone, or whether it be related to both. By the word "desire," therefore, I understand all the efforts, impulses, appetites, and volitions of a man, which vary according to his changing disposition, and not unfrequently are so opposed to one another that he is drawn hither and thither, and knows not whither he ought to turn.

II. *Joy* is man's passage from a less to a greater perfection.

III. *Sorrow* is man's passage from a greater to a less perfection.

Explanation.—I say passage, for joy is not perfection itself. If a man were born with the perfection to which he passes, he would possess it without the affect of joy; a truth which will appear the more clearly from the affect of sorrow, which is the opposite to joy. For that sorrow consists in the passage to a less perfection, but not in the less perfection itself, no one can deny, since in so far as a man shares any perfection he cannot be sad. Nor can we say that sorrow consists in the privation of a greater perfection, for privation is nothing. But the affect of sorrow is a reality, and it therefore must be the reality of the passage to a lesser perfection, or the reality by which man's power of acting is diminished or limited (Schol. Prop. 11, pt. 3). As for the definitions of cheerfulness, pleasurable excitement, melancholy, and grief, I pass these by, because they are related rather to the body than to the mind, and are merely different kinds of joy or of sorrow.

IV. *Astonishment* is the imagination of an object in

which the mind remains fixed because this particular imagination has no connection with others.

Explanation.—In the Schol. of Prop. 18, pt. 2, we have shown that that which causes the mind from the contemplation of one thing immediately to pass to the thought of another is that the images of these things are connected one with the other, and are so arranged that the one follows the others; a process which cannot be conceived when the image of the thing is new, for the mind will be held in the contemplation of the same object until other causes determine it to think of other things. The imagination, therefore, considered in itself, of a new object is of the same character as other imaginations; and for this reason I do not class astonishment among the affects, nor do I see any reason why I should do it, since this abstraction of the mind arises from no positive cause by which it is abstracted from other things, but merely from the absence of any cause by which from the contemplation of one thing the mind is determined to think other things. I acknowledge, therefore (as I have shown in Schol. Prop. 11, pt. 3), only three primitive or primary affects, those of joy, sorrow, and desire; and the only reason which has induced me to speak of astonishment is, that it has been the custom to give other names to certain affects derived from the three primitives whenever these affects are related to objects at which we are astonished. This same reason also induces me to add the definition of contempt.

V. *Contempt* is the imagination of an object which so little touches the mind that the mind is moved by the presence of the object to imagine those qualities which are not in it rather than those which are in it. (See Schol. Prop. 52, pt. 3.)

The definitions of veneration and scorn I pass by

here, because they give a name, so far as I know, to none of the affects.

VI. *Love* is joy with the accompanying idea of an external cause.

Explanation.—This definition explains with sufficient clearness the essence of love; that which is given by some authors, who define love to be the will of the lover to unite himself to the beloved object, expressing not the essence of love but one of its properties, and in as much as these authors have not seen with sufficient clearness what is the essence of love, they could not have a distinct conception of its properties, and consequently their definition has by everybody been thought very obscure. I must observe, however, when I say that it is a property in a lover to will a union with the beloved object, that I do not understand by a will a consent or deliberation or a free decree of the mind (for that this is a fiction we have demonstrated in Prop. 48, pt. 2), nor even a desire of the lover to unite himself with the beloved object when it is absent, nor a desire to continue in its presence when it is present, for love can be conceived without either one or the other of these desires; but by will I understand the satisfaction that the beloved object produces in the lover by its presence, by virtue of which the joy of the lover is strengthened, or at any rate supported.

VII. *Hatred* is sorrow with the accompanying idea of an external cause.

Explanation.—What is to be observed here will easily be seen from what has been said in the explanation of the preceding definitions. (See, moreover, Schol. Prop. 13, pt. 3.)

VIII. *Inclination* (*propensio*) is joy with the accompanying idea of some object of being accidentally the cause of the joy.

IX. *Aversion* is sorrow with the accompanying idea of some object which is accidentally the cause of the sorrow. (See Schol. Prop. 15, pt. 3.)

X. *Devotion* is love towards an object which astonishes us.

Explanation.—That astonishment arises from the novelty of the object we have shown in Prop. 52, pt. 3. If, therefore, it should happen that we often imagine the object at which we are astonished, we shall cease to be astonished at it, and hence we see that the affect of devotion easily degenerates into simple love.

XI. *Derision* is joy arising from the imagination that something we despise is present in an object we hate.

Explanation.—In so far as we despise a thing we deny its existence (Schol. Prop. 52, pt. 3), and so far (Prop. 20, pt. 3) do we rejoice. But inasmuch as we suppose that a man hates what he ridicules, it follows that this joy is not solid. (See Schol. Prop. 47, pt. 3.)

XII. *Hope* is a joy not constant, arising from the idea of something future or past, about the issue of which we sometimes doubt.

XIII. *Fear* is a sorrow not constant, arising from the idea of something future or past, about the issue of which we sometimes doubt. (See Schol. 2, Prop. 18, pt. 3.)

Explanation.—From these definitions it follows that there is no hope without fear nor fear without hope, for the person who wavers in hope and doubts concerning the issue of anything is supposed to imagine something which may exclude its existence, and so far, therefore, to be sad (Prop. 19, pt. 3), and consequently while he wavers in hope, to fear lest his wishes should not be accomplished. So also the person who fears, that is to say, who doubts whether what he hates will not come to pass, imagines something which excludes the existence of what he hates, and therefore (Prop. 20, pt. 3) is rejoiced, and consequently so far hopes that it will not happen.

XIV. *Confidence* is joy arising from the idea of a past or future object from which cause for doubting is removed.

XV. *Despair* is sorrow arising from the idea of a past or future object from which cause for doubting is removed.

Explanation.—Confidence, therefore, springs from hope and despair from fear, whenever the reason for doubting the issue is taken away; a case which occurs either because we imagine a thing past or future to be present and contemplate it as present, or because we imagine other things which exclude the existence of those which made us to doubt.

For although we can never be sure about the issue of individual objects (Corol. Prop. 31, pt. 2), it may nevertheless happen that we do not doubt it. For elsewhere we have shown (Schol. Prop. 49, pt. 2) that it is one thing not to doubt and another to possess certitude, and so it may happen that from the image of an object either past or future we are affected with the same affect of joy or sorrow as that by which we should be affected from the image of an object present, as we have demonstrated in Prop. 18, pt. 3, to which, together with the scholium, the reader is referred.

XVI. *Gladness* (*gaudium*) is joy with the accompanying idea of something past, which, unhoped for, has happened.

XVII. *Remorse* is sorrow with the accompanying idea of something past, which, unhoped for, has happened.

XVIII. *Commiseration* is sorrow with the accompanying idea of evil which has happened to some one whom we imagine like ourselves (Schol. Prop. 22, and Schol. Prop. 27, pt. 3).

Explanation.—Between commiseration and compassion there seems to be no difference, excepting perhaps that commiseration refers rather to an individual affect and compassion to it as a habit.

XIX. *Favour* is love towards those who have benefited others.

XX. *Indignation* is hatred towards those who have injured others.

Explanation.—I am aware that these names in common bear a different meaning. But my object is not to explain the meaning of words but the nature of things, and to indicate them by words whose customary meaning shall not be altogether opposed to the meaning which I desire to bestow upon them. I consider it sufficient to have said this once for all. As far as the cause of these affects is concerned, see Corol. 1, Prop. 27, pt. 3, and Schol. Prop. 22, pt. 3.

XXI. *Over-estimation* consists in thinking too highly of another person in consequence of our love for him.

XXII. *Contempt* consists in thinking too little of another person in consequence of our hatred for him.

Explanation.—Over-estimation and contempt are therefore respectively effects or properties of love or hatred, and so over-estimation may be defined as love in so far as it affects a man so that he thinks too much of the beloved object; and, on the contrary, contempt may be defined as hatred in so far as it affects a man so that he thinks too little of the object he hates. (See Schol. Prop. 26, pt. 3.)

XXIII. *Envy* is hatred in so far as it affects a man so that he is sad at the good fortune of another person and is glad when any evil happens to him.

Explanation.—To envy is generally opposed compassion (*misericordia*), which may therefore be defined as follows, notwithstanding the usual signification of the word:—

XXIV. *Compassion* is love in so far as it affects a man so that he is glad at the prosperity of another person and is sad when any evil happens to him.

Explanation.—With regard to the other properties of envy, see Schol. Prop. 24, and Schol. Prop. 32, pt. 3. These are affects of joy and sorrow which are attended by the idea of an external object as their cause, either of itself or accidentally. I pass now to consider other affects which are attended by the idea of something within us as the cause.

XXV. *Self-satisfaction* is the joy which is produced by contemplating ourselves and our own power of action.

XXVI. *Humility* is the sorrow which is produced by contemplating our impotence or helplessness.

Self-satisfaction is opposed to humility in so far as we understand by the former the joy which arises from contemplating our power of action, but in so far as we understand by it joy attended with the idea of something done, which we believe has been done by a free decree of our mind, it is opposed to repentance, which we may thus define:—

XXVII. *Repentance* is sorrow accompanied with the idea of something done which we believe has been done by a free decree of our mind.

Explanation.—We have shown what are the causes of these affects in Schol. Prop. 51, pt. 3, Props. 53 and 54, pt. 3, and Prop. 55, pt. 3, together with its Schol. With regard to a free decree of the mind, see Schol. Prop. 35, pt. 2. Here, however, I must observe, that it is not to be wondered at that sorrow should always follow all those actions which are from custom called wicked, and that joy should follow those which are called good. But that this is chiefly the effect of education will be evident from what we have before said. Parents, by reprobating what are called bad actions, and frequently blaming their children whenever they commit them, while they persuade them to what are called good actions, and praise their children when they perform them, have caused the emotions of sorrow to connect themselves with the former, and those of joy with the latter. Experience proves this, for custom and religion are not the same everywhere; but, on the contrary, things which are sacred to some are profane to others, and what are honourable with some are disgraceful with others. Education alone, therefore, will determine whether a man will repent of any deed or boast of it.

XXVIII. *Pride* is thinking too much of ourselves, through self-love.

Explanation.—Pride differs, therefore, from over-estimation, inasmuch as the latter is related to an external object, but pride to the man himself who thinks of himself too highly. As over-estimation, therefore, is an effect or property of love, so pride is an effect or property of self-love, and it may therefore be defined as love of ourselves or self-satisfaction, in so far as it affects us so that we think too highly of ourselves. (See Schol. Prop. 26, pt. 3.)

To this affect a contrary does not exist, for no one, through hatred of himself, thinks too little of himself; indeed, we may say that no one thinks too little of himself, in so far as he imagines himself unable to do this or that thing. For whatever he imagines that he cannot do, that thing he necessarily imagines, and by his imagination is so disposed that he is actually incapable of doing what he imagines he cannot do. So long, therefore, as he imagines himself unable to do this or that thing, so long is he not determined to do it, and consequently so long it is impossible for him to do it. If, however, we pay attention to what depends upon opinion alone, we shall be able to conceive it possible for a man to think too little of himself, for it may happen that while he sorrowfully contemplates his own weakness he will imagine himself despised by everybody, although nothing could be further from their thoughts than to despise him. A man may also think too little of himself if in the present he denies something of himself in relation to a future time of which he is not sure; for example, when he denies that he can conceive of nothing with certitude, and that he can desire and do nothing which is not wicked and base. We may also say that a man thinks too little of himself when we see that, from an excess of fear or shame, he does not dare to do what others who are his equals dare to do. This affect, to which I will give the name of Despondency, may therefore be opposed to pride; for as self-satisfaction springs from pride, so despondency springs from humility, and it may therefore be defined thus:—

XXIX. *Despondency* is thinking too little of ourselves through sorrow.

Explanation.—We are, nevertheless, often in the habit of opposing humility to pride, but only when we attend to their effects rather than to their nature. For we are accustomed to call a man proud who boasts too much (Schol. Prop. 30, pt. 3), who talks about nothing but his own virtues and other people's vices, who wishes to be preferred to everybody else, and who marches along with that stateliness and pomp which belong to others whose position is far above his. On the other hand, we call a man humble who often blushes, who confesses his own faults and talks about the virtues of others, who yields to every one, who walks with bended head, and who neglects to adorn himself. These affects, humility and despondency, are very rare, for human nature, considered in itself, struggles against them as much as it can (Props. 13 and 54, pt. 3), and hence those who have the most credit for being abject and humble are generally the most ambitious and envious.

XXX. *Self-exaltation* is joy with the accompanying idea of some action we have done, which we imagine people praise.

XXXI. *Shame* is sorrow, with the accompanying idea of some action which we imagine people blame.

Explanation.—With regard to these affects see Schol. Prop. 30, pt. 3. A difference, however, is here to be observed between shame and modesty. Shame is sorrow which follows a deed of which we are ashamed. Modesty is the dread or fear of shame, which keeps a man from committing any disgraceful act. To modesty is usually opposed impudence, which indeed is not an affect, as I shall show in the proper place; but the names of affects, as I have already said, are matters rather of custom than indications of the nature of the affects. I have thus discharged the task which I set myself of explaining the affects of joy and sorrow. I will advance now to those which I ascribe to desire.

XXXII. *Regret* is the desire or longing to possess something, the affect being strengthened by the memory of the object itself, and at the same time being restrained by the memory of other things which exclude the existence of the desired object.

Explanation.—Whenever we recollect a thing, as we have often said, we are thereby necessarily disposed to contemplate it with the same affect as if it were present before us. But this disposition or effort, while we are awake, is generally restrained by the images of things which exclude the existence of the thing which we

recollect. Whenever, therefore, we recollect a thing
which affects us with any kind of joy, we thereby
endeavour to contemplate it with the same affect of
joy as if it were present,—an attempt which is, however, immediately restrained by the memory of that
which excludes the existence of the thing. Regret, therefore, is really a sorrow which is opposed to the joy
which arises from the absence of what we hate. (See
Schol. Prop. 47, pt. 3.) But because the name *regret*
seems to connect this affect with desire, I therefore
ascribe it to desire.

XXXIII. *Emulation* is the desire which is begotten in
us of a thing because we imagine that other persons have
the same desire.

Explanation.—He who seeks flight because others
seek it, he who fears because he sees others fear, or even
he who withdraws his hand and moves his body as if his
hand were burning because he sees that another person
has burnt his hand, such as these, I say, although they
may indeed imitate the affect of another, are not said to
emulate it; not because we have recognised one cause
for emulation and another for imitation, but because it
has been the custom to call that man only emulous
who imitates what we think noble, useful, or pleasant.
With regard to the cause of emulation, see also Prop. 27,
pt. 3, with the Schol. For the reason why envy is generally connected with this affect, see Prop. 32, pt. 3,
with its Schol.

XXXIV. *Thankfulness* or *gratitude* is the desire or
endeavour of love with which we strive to do good to
others who, from a similar affect of love, have done good
to us (Prop. 39, with Schol. Prop. 41, pt. 3).

XXXV. *Benevolence* is the desire to do good to those
whom we pity (Schol. Prop. 27, pt. 3).

XXXVI. *Anger* is the desire by which we are impelled, through hatred, to injure those whom we hate (Prop. 39, pt. 3).

XXXVII. *Vengeance* is the desire which, springing from mutual hatred, urges us to injure those who, from a similar affect, have injured us (Corol. 2, Prop. 40, pt. 3, with Schol.).

XXXVIII. *Cruelty* or *ferocity* is the desire by which a man is impelled to injure any one whom we love or pity.

Explanation.—To cruelty is opposed mercy, which is not a passion, but a power of the mind by which a man restrains anger and vengeance.

XXXIX. *Fear* is the desire of avoiding the greater of two dreaded evils by the less (Schol. Prop. 39, pt. 3).

XL. *Audacity* is the desire by which we are impelled to do something which is accompanied with a danger which our equals fear to meet.

XLI. A person is said to be *pusillanimous* whose desire is restrained by the fear of a danger which his equals dare to meet.

Explanation.—Pusillanimity, therefore, is nothing but the dread of some evil which most persons do not usually fear, and therefore I do not ascribe it to the affects of desire. I wished, notwithstanding, to explain it here, because in so far as we attend to desire, pusillanimity is the true opposite of the affect of audacity.

XLII. *Consternation* is affirmed of the man whose desire of avoiding evil is restrained by astonishment at the evil which he fears.

Explanation.—Consternation is therefore a kind of pusillanimity. But because consternation springs from a double fear, it may be more aptly defined as that dread which holds a man stupefied or vacillating, so that he cannot remove an evil. I say *stupefied,* in so far as we understand his desire of removing the evil to be restrained by his astonishment. I say also *vacillating*, in so far as we conceive the same desire to be restrained by the fear of another evil which equally tortures him, so that he does not know which of the two evils to avoid. See Schol. Prop. 39, and Schol. Prop. 52, pt. 3. With regard to pusillanimity and audacity, see Schol. Prop. 51, pt. 3.

XLIII. *Courtesy* or *moderation* is the desire of doing those things which please men and omitting those which displease them.

XLIV. *Ambition* is the immoderate desire of glory.

Explanation.—Ambition is a desire which increases and strengthens all the affects (Props. 27 and 31, pt. 3), and that is the reason why it can hardly be kept under control. For so long as a man is possessed by any desire, he is necessarily at the same time possessed by this. *Every noble man*, says Cicero, *is led by glory, and even the philosophers who write books about despising glory place their names on the title-page.*[1]

XLV. *Luxuriousness* is the immoderate desire or love of good living.

XLVI. *Drunkenness* is the immoderate desire and love of drinking.

XLVII. *Avarice* is the immoderate desire and love of riches.

XLVIII. *Lust* is the immoderate desire and love of sexual intercourse.

Explanation.—This desire of sexual intercourse is usually called lust, whether it be held within bounds or not. I may add that the five last-mentioned affects (as we have shown in Schol. Prop. 56, pt. 3) have no contraries, for moderation is a kind of ambition (see Schol. Prop. 29, pt. 3), and I have already observed that

[1] Pro Archia.

temperance, sobriety, and chastity show a power and not a passion of the mind. Even supposing that an avaricious, ambitious, or timid man refrains from an excess of eating, drinking, or sexual intercourse, avarice, ambition, and fear are not therefore the opposites of voluptuousness, drunkenness, or lust. For the avaricious man generally desires to swallow as much meat and drink as he can, provided only it belong to another person. The ambitious man, too, if he hopes he can keep it a secret, will restrain himself in nothing, and if he lives amongst drunkards and libertines, will be more inclined to their vices just because he is ambitious. The timid man, too, does what he does not will; and although, in order to avoid death, he may throw his riches into the sea, he remains avaricious; nor does the lascivious man cease to be lascivious because he is sorry that he cannot gratify his desire. Absolutely, therefore, these affects have reference not so much to the acts themselves of eating and drinking as to the appetite and love itself. Consequently nothing can be opposed to these affects but nobility of soul and strength of mind, as we shall see afterwards.

The definitions of jealousy and the other vacillations of the mind I pass over in silence, both because they are compounded of the affects which we have already defined, and also because many of them have no names, —a fact which shows that, for the purposes of life, it is sufficient to know these combinations generally. Moreover, it follows from the definitions of the affects which we have explained that they all arise from desire, joy, or sorrow, or rather that there are none but these three, which pass under names varying as their relations and external signs vary. If, therefore, we attend to these primitive affects and to what has been said above about the nature of the mind, we shall be able here to define the affects in so far as they are related to the mind alone.

General definition of the affects.—Affect, which is called *animi pathema*, is a confused idea by which the mind affirms of its body, or any part of it, a greater or less power of existence than before; and this increase of power being given, the mind itself is determined to one particular thought rather than to another.

Explanation.—I say, in the first place, that an affect or passion of the mind *is a confused idea.* For we have shown (Prop. 3, pt. 3) that the mind suffers only in so far as it has inadequate or confused ideas. I say again, *by which the mind affirms of its body, or any part of it, a greater or less power of existence than before.* For all ideas which we possess of bodies indicate the actual constitution of our body rather than the nature of the external body (Corol. 2, Prop. 16, pt. 2); but this idea, which constitutes the form of an affect, must indicate or express the constitution of the body, or of some part of it; which constitution the body or any part of it possesses from the fact that its power of action or force of existence is increased or diminished, helped or limited. But it is to be observed, that when I say *a greater or less power of existence than before,* I do not mean that the mind compares the present with the past constitution of the body, but that the idea which constitutes the form of affect affirms something of the body which actually involves more or less reality than before. Moreover, since the essence of the mind (Props. 11 and 13, pt. 2) consists in its affirmation of the actual existence of its body, and since we understand by perfection the essence itself of the thing, it follows that the mind passes to a greater or less perfection when it is able to affirm of its body, or some part of it, something which involves a greater or less reality than before. When, therefore, I have said that the mind's power of thought is increased or diminished, I have wished to be understood as meaning nothing else than that the mind has formed an idea of its body, or some part of its body, which expresses more or less reality than it had hitherto affirmed of the body. For the value of ideas and the actual power of thought are measured by the value of the object. Finally, I added, *which being given, the mind itself is determined to one particular thought rather than to another*, that I might also express the nature of desire in addition to that of joy and sorrow, which is explained by the first part of the definition.

FOURTH PART

OF HUMAN BONDAGE OR OF THE STRENGTH OF THE AFFECTS

PREFACE

THE impotence of man to govern or restrain the affects I call bondage, for a man who is under their control is not his own master, but is mastered by fortune, in whose power he is, so that he is often forced to follow the worse, although he sees the better before him. I propose in this part to demonstrate why this is, and also to show what of good and evil the affects possess. But before I begin I should like to say a few words about perfection and imperfection, and about good and evil. If a man has proposed to do a thing and has accomplished it, he calls it perfect, and not only he, but every one else who has really known or has believed that he has known the mind and intention of the author of that work will call it perfect too. For example, having seen some work (which I suppose to be as yet not finished), if we know that the intention of the author of that work is to build a house, we shall call the house imperfect; while, on the other hand, we shall call it perfect as soon as we see the work has been brought to the end which the author had determined for it. But if we see any work such as we have never seen before, and if we do not know the mind of the workman, we shall then not be able to say whether the work is perfect or imperfect.[1] This seems to have been the first signification of these words; but afterwards men began to form universal ideas, to think out for themselves types of houses, buildings, castles, and to prefer some types of things to others; and so it happened that each person called a thing perfect which seemed to agree with the universal idea which he had formed of that thing, and, on the other hand, he called a thing imperfect which seemed to agree less with his typical conception, although, according to the intention of the workman, it had been entirely completed. This appears to be the only reason why the words *perfect* and *imperfect* are commonly applied to natural objects which are not made with human hands; for men are in the habit of forming, both of natural as well as of artificial objects, universal ideas which they regard as types of things, and which they think nature has in view, setting them before herself as types too; it being the common opinion that she does nothing except for the sake of some end. When, therefore, men see something done by nature which does not altogether answer to that typal conception which they have of the thing, they think that nature herself

---

[1] A translation cannot show the etymology of the word *perfect* as it is shown in the original Latin, so that this passage may perhaps seem rather obscure. It is only necessary, however, to bear in mind that *perfect* and *accomplished* are expressible by the same word in Latin, and that *accomplish* is the primary meaning of *perficere*.—TRANS.

has failed or committed an error, and that she has left the thing imperfect. Thus we see that the custom of applying the words *perfect* and *imperfect* to natural objects has arisen rather from prejudice than from true knowledge of them. For we have shown in the Appendix to the First Part of this work that nature does nothing for the sake of an end, for that eternal and infinite Being whom we call God or Nature acts by the same necessity by which He exists; for we have shown that He acts by the same necessity of nature as that by which He exists (Prop. 16, pt. 1). The reason or cause, therefore, why God or nature acts and the reason why He exists are one and the same. Since, therefore, He exists for no end, He acts for no end; and since He has no principle or end of existence, He has no principle or end of action. A final cause, as it is called, is nothing, therefore, but human desire, in so far as this is considered as the principle or primary cause of anything. For example, when we say that the having a house to live in was the final cause of this or that house, we merely mean that a man, because he imagined the advantages of a domestic life, desired to build a house. Therefore, having a house to live in, in so far as it is considered as a final cause, is merely this particular desire, which is really an efficient cause, and is considered as primary, because men are usually ignorant of the causes of their desires; for, as I have often said, we are conscious of our actions and desires, but ignorant of the causes by which we are determined to desire anything. As for the vulgar opinion that nature sometimes fails or commits an error, or produces imperfect things, I class it amongst those fictions mentioned in the Appendix to the First Part.

Perfection, therefore, and imperfection are really only modes of thought; that is to say, notions which we are

in the habit of forming from the comparison with one
another of individuals of the same species or genus, and
this is the reason why I have said, in Def. 6, pt. 2, that
by reality and perfection I understand the same thing;
for we are in the habit of referring all individuals in
nature to one genus, which is called the most general;
that is to say, to the notion of being, which embraces
absolutely all the individual objects in nature. In so far,
therefore, as we refer the individual objects in nature
to this genus, and compare them one with another, and
discover that some possess more being or reality than
others, in so far do we call some more perfect than
others; and in so far as we assign to the latter anything
which, like limitation, termination, impotence, &c., involves negation, shall we call them imperfect, because
they do not affect our minds so strongly as those we
call perfect, but not because anything which really belongs to them is wanting, or because nature has committed an error. For nothing belongs to the nature of
anything excepting that which follows from the necessity
of the nature of the efficient cause, and whatever follows
from the necessity of the nature of the efficient cause
necessarily happens.

With regard to good and evil, these terms indicate
nothing positive in things considered in themselves, nor
are they anything else than modes of thought, or notions
which we form from the comparison of one thing with
another. For one and the same thing may at the same
time be both good and evil or indifferent. Music, for example, is good to a melancholy person, bad to one mourn-
ing, while to a deaf man it is neither good nor bad. But
although things are so, we must retain these words. For
since we desire to form for ourselves an idea of man
upon which we may look as a model of human nature,
it will be of service to us to retain these expressions

in the sense I have mentioned. By *good,* therefore, I understand in the following pages everything which we are certain is a means by which we may approach nearer and nearer to the model of human nature we set before us. By *evil,* on the contrary, I understand everything which we are certain hinders us from reaching that model. Again, I shall call men more or less perfect or imperfect in so far as they approach more or less nearly to this same model. For it is to be carefully observed, that when I say that an individual passes from a less to a greater perfection and *vice versa,* I do not understand that from one essence or form he is changed into another (for a horse, for instance, would be as much destroyed if it were changed into a man as if it were changed into an insect), but rather we conceive that his power of action, in so far as it is understood by his own nature, is increased or diminished. Finally, by perfection generally, I understand as I have said, reality; that is to say, the essence of any object in so far as it exists and acts in a certain manner, no regard being paid to its duration. For no individual thing can be said to be more perfect because for a longer time it has persevered in existence; inasmuch as the duration of things cannot be determined by their essence, the essence of things involving no fixed or determined period of existence; any object, whether it be more or less perfect, always being able to persevere in existence with the same force as that with which it commenced existence. All things, therefore, are equal in this respect.

DEFINITIONS

I.—By good, I understand that which we certainly know is useful to us.

II. By evil, on the contrary, I understand that which we certainly know hinders us from possessing anything that is good.

With regard to these two definitions, see the close of the preceding preface.

III. I call individual things contingent in so far as we discover nothing, whilst we attend to their essence alone, which necessarily posits their existence or which necessarily excludes it.

IV. I call these individual things possible, in so far as we are ignorant, whilst we attend to the causes from which they must be produced, whether these causes are determined to the production of these things. In Schol. 1, Prop. 33, pt. 1, I made no difference between possible and contingent, because there was no occasion there to distinguish them accurately.

V. By contrary affects, I understand in the following pages those which, although they may be of the same kind, draw a man in different directions; such as voluptuousness and avarice, which are both a species of love, and are not contrary to one another by nature, but only by accident.

VI. What I understand by affect towards a thing future, present, and past, I have explained in Schol. 1 and 2, Prop. 18, pt. 3, to which the reader is referred.

Here, however, it is to be observed that it is the same with time as it is with place; for as beyond a certain limit we can form no distinct imagination of distance—that is to say, as we usually imagine all objects to be equally distant from us, and as if they were on the same plane, if their distance from us exceeds 200 feet, or if their distance from the position we occupy is greater than we can distinctly imagine—so we imagine all objects to be equally distant from the present time, and refer them as if to one moment, if the period to which their existence belongs is separated from the present by a longer interval than we can usually imagine distinctly.

VII. By end for the sake of which we do anything, I understand appetite.

VIII. By virtue and power, I understand the same thing; that is to say (Prop. 7, pt. 3), virtue, in so far as it is related to man, is the essence itself or nature of the man in so far as it has the power of affecting certain things which can be understood through the laws of its nature alone.

AXIOM

There is no individual thing in nature which is not surpassed in strength and power by some other thing, but any individual thing being given, another and a stronger is also given, by which the former can be destroyed.

PROP. I.—*Nothing positive contained in a false idea is removed by the presence of the true in so far as it is true.*

Demonst.—Falsity consists in nothing but the privation of knowledge which inadequate ideas involve (Prop. 35, pt. 2), nor do they possess anything positive on account of which they are called false (Prop. 33, pt. 2); on the contrary, in so far as they are related to God, they are true (Prop. 32, pt. 2). If, therefore, anything positive contained in a false idea were removed by the presence of the true in so far as it is true, a true idea would be removed by itself, which (Prop. 4, pt. 3) is absurd. Nothing positive, therefore, &c.—Q.E.D.

Schol.—This proposition can be understood more

clearly from Corol. 2, Prop. 16, pt. 2. For an imagination is an idea which indicates the present constitution
of the human body rather than the nature of an external body, not indeed distinctly but confusedly, so that
the mind is said to err. For example, when we look
at the sun, we imagine his distance from us to be about
200 feet, and in this we are deceived so long as we
remain in ignorance of the true distance. When this is
known, the error is removed, but not the imagination,
that is to say, the idea of the sun which manifests his
nature in so far only as the body is affected by him;
so that although we know his true distance, we nevertheless imagine him close to us. For, as we have shown in
Schol. Prop. 35, pt. 2, it is not because we are ignorant
of the sun's true distance that we imagine him to be so
close to us, but because the mind conceives the magnitude of the sun just in so far as the body is affected
by him. So when the rays of the sun falling upon a sur-
face of water are reflected to our eyes, we imagine
him to be in the water, although his true place is known
to us. So with the other imaginations by which the mind
is deceived; whether they indicate the natural constitution of the body or an increase or diminution in its
power of action, they are not opposed to the truth, nor
do they disappear with the presence of the truth. We
know that when we groundlessly fear any evil, the fear
vanishes when we hear correct intelligence; but we also
know, on the other hand, that when we fear an evil
which will actually come upon us, the fear vanishes
when we hear false intelligence, so that the imaginations do not disappear with the presence of the truth,
in so far as it is true, but because other imaginations
arise which are stronger, and which exclude the present
existence of the objects we imagine, as we have shown in
Prop. 17, pt. 2.

PROP. II.—*We suffer in so far as we are a part of nature, which part cannot be conceived by itself nor without the other parts.*

Demonst.—We are said to suffer when anything occurs in us of which we are only the partial cause (Def. 2, pt. 3), that is to say (Def. 1, pt. 3), anything which cannot be deduced from the laws of our own nature alone; we suffer, therefore, in so far as we are a part of nature, which part cannot be conceived by itself nor without the other parts.—Q.E.D.

PROP. III.—*The force by which man perseveres in existence is limited, and infinitely surpassed by the power of external causes.*

Demonst.—This is evident from the Axiom, pt. 4. For any man being given, there is given something else—for example, A—more powerful than he is, and A being given, there is again given something, B, more powerful than A, and so on *ad infinitum*. Hence the power of man is limited by the power of some other object, and is infinitely surpassed by the power of external causes.—Q.E.D.

PROP. IV.—*It is impossible that a man should not be a part of nature, and that he should suffer no changes but those which can be understood through his own nature alone, and of which he is the adequate cause.*

Demonst.—The power by which individual things and consequently man preserve their being is the actual power of God or nature (Corol. Prop. 24, pt. 1), not in so far as it is infinite, but in so far as it can be manifested by the actual essence of man (Prop. 7, pt. 3).

The power therefore of man, in so far as it is manifested by his actual essence, is part of the infinite power of God or nature, that is to say (Prop. 34, pt. 1), part of His essence. This was the first thing to be proved. Again, if it were possible that man could suffer no changes but those which can be understood through his nature alone, it would follow (Props. 4 and 6, pt. 3) that he could not perish, but that he would exist for ever necessarily; and this necessary existence must result from a cause whose power is either finite or infinite, that is to say, either from the power of man alone, which would be able to place at a distance from himself all other changes which could take their origin from external causes, or it must result from the infinite power of nature by which all individual things would be so directed that man could suffer no changes but those tending to his preservation. But the first case (by the preceding proposition, whose demonstration is universal and capable of application to all individual objects) is absurd; therefore if it were possible for a man to suffer no changes but those which could be understood through his own nature alone, and consequently (as we have shown) that he should always necessarily exist, this must follow from the infinite power of God; and therefore (Prop. 16, pt. 1) from the necessity of the divine nature, in so far as it is considered as affected by the idea of any one man, the whole order of nature, in so far as it is conceived under the attributes of thought and extension, would have to be deduced. From this it would follow (Prop. 21, pt. 1) that man would be infinite, which (by the first part of this demonstration) is an absurdity. It is impossible, therefore, that a man can suffer no changes but those of which he is the adequate cause.—Q.E.D.

Corol.—Hence it follows that a man is necessarily always subject to passions, and that he follows and obeys the common order of nature, accommodating himself to it as far as the nature of things requires.

PROP. V.—*The force and increase of any passion and its perseverance in existence are not limited by the power by which we endeavour to persevere in existence, but by the power of an external cause compared with our own power.*

Demonst.—The essence of a passion cannot be explained by our essence alone (Defs. 1 and 2, pt. 3); that is to say (Prop. 7, pt. 3), the power of a passion cannot be limited by the power by which we endeavour to persevere in our being, but (as has been shown in Prop. 16, pt. 2) must necessarily be limited by the power of an external cause compared with our own power.—Q.E.D.

PROP. VI.—*The other actions or power of a man may be so far surpassed by force of some passion or affect, that the affect may obstinately cling to him.*

Demonst.—The force and increase of any passion and its perseverance in existence are limited by the power of an external cause compared with our own power (Prop. 5, pt. 4), and therefore (Prop. 3, pt. 4) may surpass the power of man.—Q.E.D.

PROP. VII.—*An affect cannot be restrained nor removed unless by an opposed and stronger affect.*

Demonst.—An affect, in so far as it is related to the mind, is an idea by which the mind affirms a greater or lesser power of existence for its body than the body possessed before (by the general definition of affects at the end of Third Part). Whenever, therefore, the mind is agitated by any affect, the body is at the same time affected with an affection by which its power of action is increased or diminished. Again, this affection of the body (Prop. 5, pt. 4) receives from its own cause a power to persevere in its own being, a power, therefore, which cannot be restrained nor removed unless by a bodily cause (Prop. 6, pt. 2) affecting the body with an affection contrary to the first (Prop. 5, pt. 3), and stronger than it (Ax. 1, pt. 4). Thus the mind (Prop. 12, pt. 2) is affected by the idea of an affection stronger than the former and contrary to it; that is to say (by the general definition of the affects), it will be affected with an affect stronger than the former and contrary to it, and this stronger affect will exclude the existence of the other or remove it. Thus an affect cannot be restrained nor removed unless by an opposed and stronger affect.—Q.E.D.

Corol.—An affect, in so far as it is related to the mind, cannot be restrained nor removed unless by the idea of a bodily affection opposed to that which we suffer and stronger than it. For the affect which we suffer cannot be restrained nor removed unless by an opposed and stronger affect (Prop. 7, pt. 4); that is to say (by the general definition of the affects), it cannot be removed unless by the idea of a bodily affection stronger than that which affects us, and opposed to it.

PROP. VIII.—*Knowledge of good or evil is nothing but an affect of joy or sorrow in so far as we are conscious of it.*

Demonst.—We call a thing good which contributes to the preservation of our being, and we call a thing evil if

it is an obstacle to the preservation of our being (Defs.
1 and 2, pt. 4); that is to say (Prop. 7, pt. 3), a thing
is called by us good or evil as it increases or diminishes,
helps or restrains, our power of action. In so far, therefore (Defs. of *joy* and *sorrow* in Schol. Prop. 11, pt. 3),
as we perceive that any object affects us with joy or
sorrow do we call it good or evil, and therefore the
knowledge of good or evil is nothing but an idea of joy
or sorrow which necessarily follows from the affect
itself of joy or sorrow (Prop. 22, pt. 2). But this idea
is united to the affect in the same way as the mind is
united to the body (Prop. 21, pt. 2), or, in other words
(as we have shown in the Schol. to Prop. 21, pt. 2),
this idea is not actually distinguished from the affect
itself; that is to say (by the general definition of the
affects), it is not actually distinguished from the idea
of the affection of the body unless in conception alone.
This knowledge, therefore, of good and evil is nothing
but the affect itself of joy and sorrow in so far as we
are conscious of it.—Q.E.D.

PROP. IX.—*If we imagine the cause of an affect to be
actually present with us, that affect will be stronger
than if we imagined the cause not to be present.*

Demonst.—The imagination is an idea by which the
mind contemplates an object as present (see the definition of the imagination in Schol. Prop. 17, pt. 2), an
idea which nevertheless indicates the constitution of the
human body rather than the nature of the external object
(Corol. 2, Prop. 16, pt. 2). Imagination, therefore (by
the general definition of the affects), is an affect in so
far as it indicates the constitution of the body. But the
imagination (Prop. 17, pt. 2) increases in intensity in

proportion as we imagine nothing which excludes the present existence of the external object. If, therefore, we imagine the cause of an affect to be actually present with us, that affect will be intenser or stronger than if we imagined the cause not to be present.—Q.E.D.

Schol.—When I said (in Prop. 18, pt. 3) that we are affected by the image of an object in the future or the past with the same affect with which we should be affected if the object we imagined were actually present, I was careful to warn the reader that this was true in so far only as we attend to the image alone of the object itself, for the image is of the same nature whether we have imagined the object or not; but I have not denied that the image becomes weaker when we contemplate as present other objects which exclude the present existence of the future object. This exception I neglected to make, because I had determined to treat in this part of my work of the strength of the affects.

Corol.—The image of a past or future object, that is to say, of an object which we contemplate in relation to the past or future to the exclusion of the present, other things being equal, is weaker than the image of a present object, and consequently the affect towards a future or past object, other things being equal, is weaker then than the affect towards a present object.

PROP. X.—*We are affected with regard to a future object which we imagine will soon be present more powerfully than if we imagine that the time at which it will exist is further removed from the present, and the memory of an object which we imagine has but just passed away also affects us more powerfully than if we imagine the object to have passed away some time ago.*

Demonst.—In so far as we imagine that an object will quickly be present or has not long since passed away, do we imagine something which excludes the presence of the object less than if we imagine that the time of its existence is at a great distance from the present, either in the future or the past (as is self-evident), and therefore (Prop. 9, pt. 4) so far shall we be affected more strongly with regard to it.—Q.E.D.

Schol.—From the observations which we made upon Def. 6, pt. 4, it follows that all objects which are separated from the present time by a longer interval than our imagination has any power to determine affect us equally slightly, although we know them to be separated from one another by a large space of time.

PROP. XI.—*The affect towards an object which we imagine as necessary, other things being equal, is stronger than that towards an object that is possible, contingent, or not necessary.*

Demonst.—In so far as we imagine any object to be necessary do we affirm its existence, and, on the other hand, we deny its existence in so far as we imagine it to be not necessary (Schol. 1, Prop. 33, pt. 1), and therefore (Prop. 9, pt. 4) the affect towards a necessary object, other things being equal, is stronger than that which we feel towards one that is not necessary.

PROP. XII.—*The affect towards an object which we know does not exist in the present, and which we imagine as possible, other things being equal, is stronger than the affect towards a contingent object.*

Demonst.—In so far as we imagine an object as contingent, we are not affected by the image of any other object which posits the existence of the first (Def. 3, pt. 4), but, on the contrary (by hypothesis), we imagine some things which exclude its present existence. But in so far as we imagine any object in the future to be possible do we imagine some things which posit its existence (Def. 4, pt. 4), that is to say (Schol. 2, Prop. 18, pt. 3), things which foster hope or fear, and therefore the affect towards a possible object is stronger, &c.—Q.E.D.

Corol.—The affect towards an object which we know does not exist in the present, and which we imagine as contingent, is much weaker than if we imagined that the object were present to us.

Demonst.—The affect towards an object which we imagine to exist in the present is stronger than if we imagined it as future (Corol. Prop. 9, pt. 4), and is much stronger if we imagine the future to be at a great [1] distance from the present time (Prop. 10, pt. 4). The affect, therefore, towards an object which we imagine will not exist for a long time is so much feebler than if we imagined it as present, and nevertheless (Prop. 12, pt. 4) is stronger than if we imagined it as contingent; and therefore the affect towards a contingent object is much feebler than if we imagined the object to be present to us.—Q.E.D.

PROP. XIII.—*The affect towards a contingent object which we know does not exist in the present, other things being equal, is much weaker than the affect towards a past object.*

Demonst.—In so far as we imagine an object as contingent, we are affected with no image of any other

---

[1] *Non multum distare.* Ed. Pr. Corrected from Dutch version.—Tr.

object which posits the existence of the first (Def. 3, pt. 4). On the contrary, we imagine (by hypothesis) certain things which exclude its present existence. But in so far as we imagine it in relationship to past time are we supposed to imagine something which brings it back to the memory or which excites its image (Prop. 18, pt. 2, with the Schol.), and therefore so far causes us to contemplate it as present (Corol. Prop. 17, pt. 2). Therefore (Prop. 9, pt. 4), the affect towards a contingent object which we know does not exist in the present, other things being equal, will be weaker than the affect towards a past object.—Q.E.D.

PROP. XIV.—*No affect can be restrained by the true knowledge of good and evil in so far as it is true, but only in so far as it is considered as an affect.*

Demonst.—An affect is an idea by which the mind affirms a greater or less power of existence for the body than it possessed before (by the general definition of the affects); and therefore (Prop. 1, pt. 4) this idea has nothing positive which can be removed by the presence of the truth, and consequently the true knowledge of good and evil, in so far as it is true, can restrain no affect. But in so far as it is an affect (see Prop. 8, pt. 4) will it restrain any other affect, provided that the latter be the weaker of the two (Prop. 7, pt. 4). —Q.E.D.

PROP. XV.—*Desire which arises from a true knowledge of good and evil can be extinguished or restrained by many other desires which take their origin from the affects by which we are agitated.*

Demonst.—From the true knowledge of good and evil, in so far as this (Prop. 8, pt. 4) is an affect, necessarily arises desire (Def. 1 of the affects, pt. 3), which is greater in proportion as the affect from which it springs is greater (Prop. 37, pt. 3). But this desire (by hypothesis), because it springs from our understanding something truly, follows therefore in us in so far as we act (Prop. 1, pt. 3), and therefore must be understood through our essence alone (Def. 2, pt. 3), and consequently its strength and increase must be limited by human power alone (Prop. 7, pt. 3). But the desires which spring from the affects by which we are agitated are greater as the affects themselves are greater, and therefore their strength and increase (Prop. 5, pt. 4) must be limited by the power of external causes, a power which, if it be compared with our own, indefinitely surpasses it (Prop. 3, pt. 4). The desires, therefore, which take their origin from such affects as these may be much stronger than that which takes its origin from a true knowledge of good and evil, and the former (Prop. 7, pt. 4) may be able to restrain and extinguish the latter. —Q.E.D.

PROP. XVI.—*The desire which springs from a knowledge of good and evil can be easily extinguished or restrained, in so far as this knowledge is connected with the future, by the desire of things which in the present are sweet.*

Demonst.—The affect towards an object which we imagine as future is weaker than towards that which we imagine as present (Corol. Prop. 9, pt. 4). But the desire which springs from a true knowledge of good and evil, even although the knowledge be of objects which are good at the present time, may be extinguished or restrained by any casual desire (Prop. 15, pt. 4, the demonstration of this proposition being universal), and therefore the desire which springs from a knowledge of good and evil, in so far as this knowledge is connected with the future, can be easily restrained or extinguished.—q.e.d.

PROP. XVII.—*The desire which springs from a true knowledge of good and evil can be still more easily restrained, in so far as this knowledge is connected with objects which are contingent, by the desire of objects which are present.*

Demonst.—This proposition is demonstrated in the same way as the preceding proposition from Corol. Prop. 12, pt. 4.

Schol.—In these propositions I consider that I have explained why men are more strongly influenced by an opinion than by true reason, and why the true knowledge of good and evil causes disturbance in the mind, and often gives way to every kind of lust, whence the saying of the poet, *"Video meliora proboque, deteriora sequor."* The same thought appears to have been in the mind of the Preacher when he said, *"He that increaseth knowledge increaseth sorrow."* I say these things not because I would be understood to conclude, therefore, that it is better to be ignorant than to be wise, or that the wise man in governing his passions is nothing better than the fool, but I say them because it is necessary for us to know both the strength and weakness of our nature, so that we may determine what reason can do and what it cannot do in governing our affects. This, moreover, let it be remembered, is the Part in which I meant to treat of human weakness alone, all consideration of the power of reason over the passions being reserved for a future portion of the book.

Prop. XVIII.—*The desire which springs from joy, other things being equal, is stronger than that which springs from sorrow.*

Demonst.—Desire is the very essence of man (Def. 1 of the Affects, pt. 3), that is to say (Prop. 7, pt. 3), the effort by which a man strives to persevere in his being. The desire, therefore, which springs from joy, by that very affect of joy (by the definition of joy in Schol. Prop. 11, pt. 3) is assisted or increased, while that which springs from sorrow, by that very affect of sorrow (by the same Schol.) is lessened or restrained, and so the force of the desire which springs from joy must be limited by human power, together with the power of an external cause, while that which springs from sorrow must be limited by human power alone. The latter is, therefore, weaker than the former.—Q.E.D.

Schol.—I have thus briefly explained the causes of human impotence and want of stability, and why men do not obey the dictates of reason. It remains for me now to show what it is which reason prescribes to us, which affects agree with the rules of human reason, and which, on the contrary, are opposed to these rules. Before, however, I begin to demonstrate these things by our full geometrical method, I should like briefly to set forth here these dictates of reason, in order that what I have in my mind about them may be easily comprehended by all. Since reason demands nothing which is opposed to nature, it demands, therefore, that every person should love himself, should seek his own profit,—what is truly profitable to him, should desire everything that really leads man to greater perfection, and absolutely that every one should endeavour, as far as in him lies, to preserve his own being. This is all true as necessarily as that the whole is greater than its part (Prop. 6, pt.

*Rational nature

3). Again, since virtue (Def. 8, pt. 4) means nothing but acting according to the laws of our own nature, and since no one endeavours to preserve his being (Prop. 7, pt. 3) except in accordance with the laws of his own nature, it follows *Firstly,* That the foundation of virtue is that endeavour itself to preserve our own being, and that happiness consists in this—that a man can preserve his own being. *Secondly,* It follows that virtue is to be desired for its own sake, nor is there anything more excellent or more useful to us than virtue, for the sake of which virtue ought to be desired. *Thirdly,* It follows that all persons who kill themselves are impotent in mind, and have been thoroughly overcome by external causes opposed to their nature. Again, from Post. 4, pt. 2, it follows that we can never free ourselves from the need of something outside us for the preservation of our being, and that we can never live in such a manner as to have no intercourse with objects which are outside us. Indeed, so far as the mind is concerned, our intellect would be less perfect if the mind were alone, and understood nothing but itself. There are many things, therefore, outside us which are useful to us, and which, therefore, are to be sought. Of all these, none more excellent can be discovered than those which exactly agree with our nature. If, for example, two individuals of exactly the same nature are joined together, they make up a single individual, doubly stronger than each alone. Nothing, therefore, is more useful to man than man. Men can desire, I say, nothing more excellent for the preservation of their being than that all should so agree at every point that the minds and bodies of all should form, as it were, one mind and one body; that all should together endeavour as much as possible to preserve their being, and that all should together seek the common good of all. From this it follows that men who are governed by reason,—that is to say, men who, under the guidance of reason, seek their own profit,—desire nothing for themselves which they do not desire for other men, and that, therefore, they are just, faithful, and honourable.

These are those dictates of reason which I purposed briefly to set forth before commencing their demonstration by a fuller method, in order that, if possible, I might win the attention of those who believe that this principle,—that every one is bound to seek his own profit,—is the foundation of impiety, and not of virtue and piety. Having now briefly shown that this belief of theirs is the contrary of the truth, I proceed, by the same method as that which we have hitherto pursued, to demonstrate what I have said.

PROP. XIX.—*According to the laws of his own nature each person necessarily desires that which he considers to be good, and avoids that which he considers to be evil.*

Demonst.—The knowledge of good and evil (Prop. 8, pt. 4), is the affect itself of joy or sorrow, in so far as we are conscious of it, and, therefore (Prop. 28, pt. 3), each person necessarily desires that which he considers to be good, and avoids that which he considers to be evil. But this desire is nothing but the essence itself or nature of man (Def. of appetite in Schol. Prop. 9, pt. 3, and Def. 1 of the Affects, pt. 3). Therefore, according to the laws of his own nature alone, he necessarily desires or avoids, &c.—Q.E.D.

PROP. XX.—*The more each person strives and is able to seek his own profit, that is to say, to preserve his being, the more virtue does he possess; on the other hand, in so far as each person neglects his own profit, that is to say, neglects to preserve his own being, is he impotent.*

Demonst.—Virtue is human power itself, which is limited by the essence alone of man (Def. 8, pt. 4), that is to say (Prop. 7, pt. 3), which is limited by the effort alone by which man endeavours to persevere in his being. The more, therefore, each person strives and is able to preserve his being, the more virtue does he possess, and consequently (Props. 4 and 6, pt. 3), in proportion as he neglects to preserve his being is he impotent.

Schol.—No one, therefore, unless defeated by external causes and those which are contrary to his nature, neglects to seek his own profit or preserve his being. No one, I say, refuses food or kills himself from a necessity of his nature, but only when forced by external causes. The compulsion may be exercised in many ways. A man kills himself under compulsion by another when that other turns the right hand, with which the man had by chance laid hold of a sword, and compels him to direct the sword against his own heart; or the command of a tyrant may compel a man, as it did Seneca, to open his own veins, that is to say, he may desire to avoid a greater evil by a less. External and hidden causes also may so dispose his imagination and may so affect his body as to cause it to put on another nature contrary to that which it had at first, and one whose idea cannot exist in the mind (Prop. 10, pt. 3); but a very little reflection will show that it is as impossible that a man, from the necessity of his nature, should endeavour not to exist, or to be changed into some other form, as it is that something should be begotten from nothing.

PROP. XXI.—*No one can desire to be happy, to act well and live well, who does not at the same time desire to be, to act, and to live, that is to say, actually to exist.*

Demonst.—The demonstration of this proposition, or rather the proposition itself, is self-evident, and is also evident from the definition of desire. For desire (Def. 1 of the Affects, pt. 3), whether it be desire of living or acting happily or well, is the very essence of man, that is to say (Prop. 7, pt. 3), the endeavour by which every one strives to preserve his own being. No one, therefore, can desire, &c.—Q.E.D.

PROP. XXII.—*No virtue can be conceived prior to this (the endeavour, namely, after self-preservation).*

Demonst.—The endeavour after self-preservation is the essence itself of a thing (Prop. 7, pt. 3). If, therefore, any virtue could be conceived prior to this of self-preservation, the essence itself of the thing would be conceived (Def. 8, pt. 4) as prior to itself, which (as is self-evident) is absurd. No virtue, therefore, &c.—Q.E.D.

Corol.—The endeavour after self-preservation is the primary and only foundation of virtue. For prior to this principle no other can be conceived (Prop. 22, pt. 4), and without it (Prop. 21, pt. 4) no virtue can be conceived.

PROP. XXIII.—*A man cannot be absolutely said to act in conformity with virtue, in so far as he is determined to any action because he has inadequate ideas, but only in so far as he is determined because he understands.*

Demonst.—In so far as a man is determined to action because he has inadequate ideas (Prop. 1, pt. 3), he suffers, that is to say (Defs. 1 and 2, pt. 3), he does something which through his essence alone cannot be perceived, that is to say (Def. 8, pt. 4), which does not follow from his virtue. But in so far as he is determined to any action because he understands, he acts (Prop. 1, pt. 3), that is to say (Def. 2, pt. 3), he does something which is perceived through his essence alone, or (Def. 8, pt. 4) which adequately follows from his virtue.—Q.E.D.

PROP. XXIV.—*To act absolutely in conformity with virtue is, in us, nothing but acting, living, and preserving our being (these three things have the same meaning) as reason directs, from the ground of seeking our own profit.*

Demonst.—To act absolutely in conformity with virtue is nothing (Def. 8, pt. 4) but acting according to the laws of our own proper nature. But only in so far as we understand do we act (Prop. 3, pt. 3). Therefore, to act in conformity with virtue is nothing but acting, living, and preserving our being as reason directs, and doing so (Corol. Prop. 22, pt. 4) from the ground of seeking our own profit.

PROP. XXV.—*No one endeavours to preserve his own being for the sake of another object.*

Demonst.—The effort by which any object strives to persevere in its own being is limited solely by the essence of the object itself (Prop. 7, pt. 3), and from this given essence alone it necessarily follows (and not from the essence of any other object) (Prop. 6, pt. 3) that each object strives to preserve its being. This proposition is also evident from Corol. Prop. 22, pt. 4. For if a man endeavoured to preserve his being for the sake of any other object, this object would then become the primary foundation of virtue (as is self-evident), which (by the Corol. just quoted) is an absurdity. No one, therefore, endeavours to preserve his being, &c.—Q.E.D.

PROP. XXVI.—*All efforts which we make through reason are nothing but efforts to understand, and the mind, in so far as it uses reason, adjudges nothing as profitable to itself excepting that which conduces to understanding.*

Demonst.—The endeavour after self-preservation is nothing but the essence of the object itself (Prop. 7, pt. 3), which, in so far as it exists, is conceived to have power to persevere in existence (Prop. 6, pt. 3), and to do those things which necessarily follow from its given nature. (See the definition of desire in Schol. Prop. 9, pt. 3.) But the essence of reason is nothing but our mind, in so far as it clearly and distinctly understands. (See definition of clear and distinct understanding in Schol. 2, Prop. 40, pt. 2.) Therefore (Prop. 40, pt. 2), all efforts which we make through reason are nothing else than efforts to understand. Again, since this effort of the mind, by which the mind, in so far as it reasons endeavours to preserve its being, is nothing but the effort to understand (by the first part of this demonstration), it follows (Corol. Prop. 22, pt. 4), that this effort to understand is the primary and sole foundation of virtue, and that (Prop. 25, pt. 4) we do not endeavour to understand things for the sake of any end, but, on the contrary, the mind, in so far as it reasons, can conceive nothing as being good for itself except that which conduces to understanding (Def. 1, pt. 4).—Q.E.D.

PROP. XXVII.—*We do not know that anything is certainly good or evil excepting that which actually conduces to understanding, or which can prevent us from understanding.*

Demonst.—The mind, in so far as it reasons, desires nothing but to understand, nor does it adjudge anything to be profitable to itself excepting what conduces to understanding (Prop. 26, pt. 4). But the mind (Props. 41 and 43, pt. 2, with the Schol.) possesses no certitude, unless in so far as it possesses adequate ideas, or (which by Schol. Prop. 40, pt. 2, is the same thing) in so far as it reasons. We do not know, therefore, that anything is certainly good, excepting that which actually conduces to understanding, and, on the other hand, we do not know that anything is evil excepting that which can hinder us from understanding—Q.E.D.

PROP. XXVIII.—*The highest good of the mind is the knowledge of God, and the highest virtue of the mind is to know God.*

Demonst.—The highest thing which the mind can understand is God, that is to say (Def. 6, pt. 1), Being absolutely infinite, and without whom (Prop. 15, pt. 1) nothing can be nor can be conceived, and therefore (Props. 26 and 27, pt. 4) that which is chiefly profitable to the mind, or (Def. 1, pt. 4) which is the highest good of the mind, is the knowledge of God. Again, the mind acts only in so far as it understands (Props. 1 and 3, pt. 3), and only in so far (Prop. 23, pt. 4) can it be absolutely said to act in conformity with virtue. To understand, therefore, is the absolute virtue of the mind. But the highest thing which the mind can understand is God (as we have already demonstrated), and therefore the highest virtue of the mind is to understand or know God.—Q.E.D.

PROP. XXIX.—*No individual object whose nature is altogether different from our own can either help or restrain our power of acting, and absolutely nothing can be to us either good or evil unless it possesses something in common with ourselves.*

Demonst.—The power of an individual object, and consequently (Corol. Prop. 10, pt. 2) that of man, by which he exists and acts, is determined only by another individual object (Prop. 28, pt. 1), whose nature (Prop. 6, pt. 2) must be understood through the same attribute as that by means of which human nature is conceived. Our power of acting, therefore, in whatever way it may be conceived, can be determined, and consequently helped or restrained, by the power of another individual object possessing something in common with us, and cannot be thus determined by the power of an object whose nature is altogether different from ours. Inasmuch, therefore, as a thing is called good or evil because it is the cause of joy or sorrow (Prop. 8, pt. 4), that is to say (Schol. Prop. 11, pt. 3), because it increases or diminishes, helps or restrains, our power of action; an object, whose nature is altogether different from our own, cannot be either good or evil to us.—Q.E.D.

PROP. XXX.—*Nothing can be evil through that which it possesses in common with our nature, but in so far as a thing is evil to us is it contrary to us.*

Demonst.—We call that thing evil which is the cause of sorrow (Prop. 8, pt. 4), that is to say (by the definition of sorrow in Schol. Prop. 11, pt. 3), which lessens or restrains our power of action. If, therefore, any object were evil to us through that which it possesses in common with us, it could lessen or restrain what it possesses in common with us, which (Prop. 4, pt. 3) is absurd. Nothing, therefore, through that which it possesses in common with us can be evil to us, but, on the contrary, in so far as it is evil, that is to say (as we have already shown), in so far as it can lessen or restrain our power of action (Prop. 5, pt. 3), is it contrary to us.—Q.E.D.

PROP. XXXI.—*In so far as an object agrees with our nature is it necessarily good.*

Demonst.—In so far as any object agrees with our nature (Prop. 30, pt. 4) it cannot be evil. It must, therefore, necessarily be either good or indifferent. If it be supposed as indifferent, that is to say, as neither good nor evil, nothing (Ax. 3, pt. 1, and Def. 1, pt. 4) will follow from its nature which conduces to the preservation of our nature, that is to say (by hypothesis), which conduces to its own preservation. But this (Prop. 6, pt. 3) is absurd, and, therefore, in so far as the object agrees with our nature, it will necessarily be good.—Q.E.D.

Corol.—Hence it follows that the more an object agrees with our own nature, the more profitable it is to us, that is to say, the better it is for us, and, conversely, the more profitable an object is to us, the more does it agree with our own nature. For in so far as it does not agree with our nature it will necessarily be either diverse from our nature or contrary to it. If diverse, it can (Prop. 29, pt. 4) be neither good nor evil, but if contrary, it will therefore be contrary also to that which agrees with our own nature, that is to say (Prop. 31, pt. 4), contrary to the good, or, in other words, it will be evil. Nothing, therefore, can be good except in so far as it agrees with our nature, and therefore the more an object agrees with our nature the more profitable it will be, and *vice versa.*—Q.E.D.

PROP. XXXII.—*In so far as men are subject to passions, they cannot be said to agree in nature.*

Demonst.—Things which are said to agree in nature are understood to agree in power (Prop. 7, pt. 3), and not in impotence or negation, and consequently (Schol. Prop. 3, pt. 3), not in passion, and therefore men, in so far as they are subject to passion, cannot be said to agree in nature.—Q.E.D.

Schol.—This proposition is self-evident, for he who says that black and white agree solely in the fact that neither of them is red, absolutely affirms that black and white agree in nothing. So also if we say that a stone and a man agree solely in this, that they are both finite or impotent, or do not exist from the necessity of their nature, or are both to an indefinite extent dominated by external causes, we affirm that a stone and a man agree in nothing, for things which agree in negation only, or in that which they have not, really agree in nothing.

PROP. XXXIII.—*Men may differ in nature from one another in so far as they are agitated by affects which are passions, and in so far also as one and*

the same man is agitated by passions is he change-
able and inconstant.

Demonst.—The nature or essence of the affects cannot be explained through our essence or nature alone
(Defs. 1 and 2, pt. 3), but must be determined by the
power, that is to say (Prop. 7, pt. 3), the nature of
external causes compared with our own nature. Hence
it follows that there are as many kinds of each affect as
there are kinds of objects by which we are affected
(Prop. 56, pt. 3); that men are affected in different
ways by one and the same object (Prop. 51, pt. 3),
and so far differ in nature; and, finally, that one and
the same man (Prop. 51, pt. 3) is affected in different
ways towards the same object, and so far is changeable
and inconstant.—Q.E.D.

PROP. XXXIV.—*In so far as men are agitated by*
affects which are passions can they be contrary to
one another.

Demonst.—A man, Peter, for example, may be a cause
of sorrow to Paul, because he possesses something re-
sembling that which Paul hates (Prop. 16, pt. 3), or
because he alone possesses something which Paul himself also loves (Prop. 32, pt. 3, with its Schol.), or for
other reasons (the chief of which are mentioned in Schol.
Prop. 55, pt. 3). Hence it will come to pass (Def. 7 of
the affects) that Paul hates Peter, and, consequently, it
will easily happen (Prop. 40, pt. 3, with its Schol.) that
Peter in turn hates Paul, and that they endeavour (Prop.
39, pt. 3) to injure one another, or, in other words
(Prop. 30, pt. 4), that they are contrary to one another.
But the affect of sorrow is always a passion (Prop. 59,
pt. 3), and therefore men, in so far as they are agitated

by affects which are passions, can be contrary to one another.—Q.E.D.

Schol.—I have said that Paul hates Peter because he imagines that Peter possesses something which he himself loves, from which at first sight it appears to follow, that because they both love the same thing, and consequently agree in nature with one another, they are, therefore, injurious to one another; and if this be true, Props. 30 and 31, pt. 4, would be false. But if we will examine the matter impartially, we shall see that all these things are quite in accord. For Peter and Paul are not injurious to one another in so far as they agree in nature, that is to say, in so far as they both love the same object, but in so far as they differ from one another. For in so far as they both love the same object is the love of each strengthened (Prop. 31, pt. 3), that is to say (Def. 6 of the affects), so far is the joy of both increased. It is far from true, therefore, that in so far as they love the same object and agree in nature they are injurious to one another. They are injurious to one another, on the contrary, as I have said, solely because they are supposed to differ in nature. For we suppose Peter to have an idea of a beloved object which he now possesses, and Paul, on the other hand, to have an idea of a beloved object which he has lost. The former, therefore, is affected with joy, and the latter, on the contrary, with sorrow, and so far they are contrary to one another. In this manner we can easily show that the other causes of hatred depend solely on the fact that men differ by nature and not on anything in which they agree.

PROP. XXXV.—*So far as men live in conformity with the guidance of reason, in so far only do they always necessarily agree in nature.*

Demonst.—In so far as men are agitated by affects which are passions can they differ in nature (Prop. 33, pt. 4) and be contrary to one another (Prop. 34, pt. 4). But men are said to act only in so far as they live according to the guidance of reason (Prop. 3, pt. 3), and therefore, whatever follows from human nature, in so far as it is determined by reason (Def. 2, pt. 3), must be understood through human nature alone as through its proximate cause. But because every one, according to the laws of his own nature, desires that which he adjudges to be good, and endeavours to remove that which he adjudges to be evil (Prop. 19, pt. 4), and because that which from the dictates of reason we judge to be good or evil is necessarily good or evil (Prop. 41, pt. 2), it follows that men, only in so far as they live according to the guidance of reason, necessarily do those things which are good to human nature, and consequently to each man, that is to say (Corol. Prop. 31, pt. 4), which agree with the nature of each man, and therefore also men necessarily always agree with one another in so far as they live according to the guidance of reason.—Q.E.D.

Corol. 1.—There is no single thing in nature which is more profitable to man than a man who lives according to the guidance of reason. For that is most profitable to man which most agrees with his own nature (Corol. Prop. 31, pt. 4), that is to say, man (as is self-evident). But a man acts absolutely from the laws of his own nature when he lives according to the guidance of reason (Def. 2, pt. 3), and so far only does he always necessarily agree with the nature of another man (Prop. 35, pt. 4); therefore there is no single thing more profitable than man, &c.—Q.E.D.

2.—When each man seeks most that which is

profitable to himself, then are men most profitable to one another; for the more each man seeks his own profit and endeavours to preserve himself, the more virtue does he possess (Prop. 20, pt. 4), or, in other words (Def. 8, pt. 4), the more power does he possess to act according to the laws of his own nature, that is to say (Prop. 3, pt. 3), to live according to the guidance of reason. But men most agree in nature when they live according to the guidance of reason (Prop. 35, pt. 4), therefore (by the previous Corol.) men will be most profitable to one another when each man seeks most what is profitable to himself.—Q.E.D.

Schol.—To what we have just demonstrated daily experience itself testifies by so many and such striking proofs, that it is in almost everybody's mouth that man is a God to man. It is very seldom indeed that men live according to the guidance of reason; on the contrary, it so happens that they are generally envious and injurious to one another. But, nevertheless, they are scarcely ever able to lead a solitary life, so that to most men the definition of man that he is a social animal entirely commends itself, and indeed it is the case that far more advantages than disadvantages arise from the common society of men. Let satirists therefore scoff at human affairs as much as they please, let theologians denounce them, and let the melancholy praise as much as they can a life rude and without refinement, despising men and admiring the brutes, men will nevertheless find out that by mutual help they can much more easily procure the things they need, and that it is only by their united strength they can avoid the dangers which everywhere threaten them, to say nothing about its being far nobler and worthier of our knowledge to meditate upon the doings of men than upon those of brutes. But more of this elsewhere

Prop. XXXVI.—*The highest good of those who follow after virtue is common to all, and all may equally enjoy it.*

Demonst.—To act in conformity with virtue is to act according to the guidance of reason (Prop. 24, pt. 4), and every effort which we make through reason is an effort to understand (Prop. 26, pt. 4), and therefore (Prop. 28, pt. 4) the highest good of those who follow after virtue is to know God, that is to say (Prop. 47, pt. 2, with its Schol.), it is a good which is common to all men, and can be equally possessed by all men in so far as they are of the same nature.—Q.E.D.

Schol.—If anybody asks, What if the highest good of those who follow after virtue were not common to all? would it not thence follow (as above, see Prop. 34, pt. 4) that men who live according to the guidance of reason, that is to say (Prop. 35, pt. 4), men in so far as they agree in nature, would be contrary to one another? We reply that it arises from no accident, but from the nature itself of reason, that the highest good of man is common to all, inasmuch as it is deduced from the human essence itself, in so far as it is determined by reason, and also because man could not be nor be conceived if he had not the power of rejoicing in this highest good. For it pertains (Prop. 47, pt. 2) to the essence of the human mind to have an adequate knowledge of the eternal and infinite essence of God.

Prop. XXXVII.—*The good which every one who follows after virtue seeks for himself he will desire for other men; and his desire on their behalf will be greater in proportion as he has a greater knowledge of God.*

Demonst.—Men are most profitable to man in so far as they live according to the guidance of reason (Corol. 1, Prop. 35, pt. 4), and therefore (Prop. 19, pt. 4), according to the guidance of reason, we necessarily endeavour to cause men to live according to the guidance of reason. But the good which each person seeks who lives according to the dictates of reason, that is to say (Prop. 24, pt. 4), who follows after virtue, is to understand (Prop. 26, pt. 4), and therefore the good which each person seeks who follows after virtue he will also desire for other men. Again, desire, in so far as it is related to the mind, is the essence itself of the mind (Def. 1 of the Affects). But the essence of the mind consists in knowledge (Prop. 11, pt. 2), which involves the knowledge of God (Prop 47, pt. 2), and without this knowledge the essence of the mind can neither be nor be conceived (Prop. 15, pt. 1); and therefore the greater the knowledge of God which the essence of the mind involves, the greater will be the desire with which he who follows after virtue will desire for another the good which he seeks for himself.—Q.E.D.

Another Demonstration.—The good which a man seeks for himself and which he loves he will love more unchangeably if he sees that others love it (Prop. 31, pt. 3), and therefore (Corol. Prop. 31, pt. 3) he will endeavour to make others love it; and because this good (Prop. 36, pt. 4) is common to all and all can rejoice in it, he will endeavour (by the same reasoning) to cause all to rejoice in it, and (Prop. 37, pt. 3) he will do so the more, the more he rejoices in this good himself.—Q.E.D.

Schol. 1.—He who strives from an affect alone to make others love what he himself loves, and to make others live according to his way of thinking, acts from mere impulse, and is therefore hateful, especially to those who have other tastes and who therefore also desire, and by the same impulse strive to make others live according to their way of thinking.

Again, since the highest good which men seek from an affect is often such that only one person can possess it, it follows that persons who love are not consistent with themselves, and, whilst they delight to recount the praises of the beloved object, fear lest they should be believed. But he who endeavours to lead others by reason does not act from impulse, but with humanity and kindness, and is always consistent with himself.

Everything which we desire and do, of which we are the cause in so far as we possess an idea of God, or in so far as we know God, I refer to *Religion*. The desire of doing well which is born in us, because we live according to the guidance of reason, I call *Piety*. The desire to join others in friendship to himself, with which a man living according to the guidance of reason is possessed, I call *Honour*. I call that thing *Honourable* which men who live according to the guidance of reason praise; and that thing, on the contrary, I call *Base* which sets itself against the formation of friendship. Moreover, I have also shown what are the foundations of a State.

The difference also between true virtue and impotence may, from what has already been said, be easily seen to be this—that true virtue consists in living according to the guidance of reason alone; and that impotence therefore consists in this alone—that a man allows himself to be led by things which are outside himself, and by them to be determined to such actions as the common constitution of external things demands, and not to such as his own nature considered in itself alone demands. These are the things which I promised in Schol. Prop. 18, pt. 4, I would demonstrate. From them we see that the law against killing animals is based upon an empty superstition and womanish tenderness, rather than upon sound reason. A proper regard, indeed, to one's own profit teaches us to unite in friendship with men, and not with brutes, nor with things whose nature is different from human nature. It teaches us, too, that the same right which they have over us we have over them. Indeed, since the right of any person is limited by his virtue or power, men possess a far greater right over brutes than brutes possess over men. I by no means deny that brutes feel, but I do deny that on this account it is unlawful for us to consult our own profit by using them for our own pleasure and treating them as is most convenient for us, inasmuch as they do not agree in nature with us, and their affects are different from our own (Schol. Prop. 57, pt. 3).

It now remains that I should explain what are Justice, Injustice, Crime, and, finally, Merit. With regard to these, see the following scholium.

Schol. 2.—In the Appendix to the First Part I promised I would explain what are praise and blame, merit and crime, justice and injustice. I have already shown what is the meaning of praise and blame in Schol. Prop. 29, pt. 3, and this will be a fitting place for the explanation of the rest. A few words must, however, first be said about the natural and civil state of man.

It is by the highest right of nature that each person exists, and consequently it is by the highest right of nature that each person does those things which follow from the necessity of his nature; and therefore it is by the highest right of nature that each person judges what is good and what is evil, consults his own advantage as he thinks best (Props. 19 and 20, pt. 4), avenges himself (Corol. 2, Prop. 40, pt. 3), and endeavours to preserve what he loves and to destroy what he hates (**Prop.**

28, pt. 3). If men lived according to the guidance of reason, every one would enjoy this right without injuring any one else (Corol. 1, Prop. 35, pt. 4). But because men are subject to affects (Corol. Prop. 4, pt. 4), which far surpass human power or virtue (Prop. 6, pt. 4), they are often drawn in different directions (Prop. 33, pt. 4), and are contrary to one another (Prop. 34, pt. 4), although they need one another's help (Schol. Prop. 35, pt. 4).

In order, then, that men may be able to live in harmony and be a help to one another, it is necessary for them to cede their natural right, and beget confidence one in the other that they will do nothing by which one can injure the other. In what manner this can be done, so that men who are necessarily subject to affects (Corol. Prop. 4, pt. 4), and are uncertain and changeable (Prop. 33, pt. 4), can beget confidence one in the other and have faith in one another, is evident from Prop. 7, pt. 4, and Prop. 39, pt. 3. It is there shown that no affect can be restrained unless by a stronger and contrary affect, and that every one abstains from doing an injury through fear of a greater injury. By this law, therefore, can society be strengthened, if only it claims for itself the right which every individual possesses of avenging himself and deciding what is good and what is evil, and provided, therefore, that it possess the power of prescribing a common rule of life, of promulgating laws and supporting them, not by reason, which cannot restrain the affects (Schol. Prop. 17, pt. 4), but by penalties.

This society, firmly established by law and with a power of self-preservation, is called a *State*, and those who are protected by its right are called *Citizens*. We can now easily see that in the natural state there is nothing which by universal consent is good or evil, since every one in a natural state consults only his own profit; deciding according to his own way of thinking what is good and what is evil with reference only to his own profit, and is not bound by any law to obey any one but himself. Hence in a natural state sin cannot be conceived, but only in a civil state, where it is decided by universal consent what is good and what is evil, and where every one is bound to obey the State. *Sin*, therefore, is nothing but disobedience, which is punished by the law of the State alone; obedience, on the other hand, being regarded as a *merit* in a citizen, because on account of it he is considered worthy to enjoy the privileges of the State. Again, in a natural state no one by common consent is the owner of anything, nor is there anything in nature which can be said to be the rightful property of this and not of that man, but all things belong to all, so that in a natural state it is impossible to conceive a desire of rendering to each man his own or taking from another that which is his; that is to say, in a natural state there is nothing which can be called just or unjust, but only in a civil state, in which it is decided by universal consent what is one person's and what is another's. Justice and injustice, therefore, sin and merit, are external notions, and not attributes, which manifest the nature of the mind. But enough of these matters.

PROP. XXXVIII.—*That which so disposes the human body that it can be affected in many ways, or which renders it capable of affecting external bodies in many ways, is profitable to man, and is more profitable in proportion as by its means the body becomes better fitted to be affected in many ways, and to affect other bodies; on the other hand, that thing is injurious which renders the body less fitted to affect or be affected.*

Demonst.—In proportion as the body is rendered more fitted for this is the mind rendered more capable of perception (Prop. 14, pt. 2), and, therefore, whatever disposes the body in this way, and renders it fitted for this, is necessarily good or profitable (Props. 26 and 27, pt. 4), and is more profitable in proportion to its power of rendering the body more fitted for this, while, on the contrary (by Prop. 14, pt. 2, conversely, and Props. 26 and 27, pt. 4), it is injurious if it renders the body less fitted for this.—Q.E.D.

PROP. XXXIX.—*Whatever is effective to preserve the proportion of motion and rest which the parts of the human body bear to each other is good, and, on the contrary, that is evil which causes the parts of the human body to have a different proportion of motion and rest to each other.*

Demonst.—The human body needs for its preservation very many other bodies (Post. 4, pt. 2). But what constitutes the form of the human body is this, that its parts communicate their motions to one another in a certain fixed proportion (Def. preceding Lem. 4, following Prop. 13, pt. 2). Whatever, therefore, is effective to preserve the proportion of motion and rest which the parts of the human body bear to each other, preserves the form of the human body, and, consequently (Posts. 3 and 6, pt. 2), is effective to enable the body to be affected in many ways, and to affect external bodies in many ways, and, therefore (Prop. 38, pt. 4), is good. Again, whatever causes the parts of the human body to get a different proportion of motion and rest (by the definition just quoted), causes the human body to assume another form, that is to say (as is self-evident, and as we observed at the end of the preface to this part) causes the human body to be destroyed, rendering it consequently incapable of being affected in many ways, and is, therefore (Prop. 38, pt. 4,) bad.—Q.E.D.

Schol.—In what degree these things may injure or profit the mind will be explained in the Fifth Part. Here I observe merely that I understand the body to die when its parts are so disposed as to acquire a different proportion of motion and rest to each other. For I dare not deny that the human body, though the circulation of the blood and the other things by means of which it is thought to live be preserved, may, nevertheless, be changed into another nature altogether different from its own. No reason compels me to affirm that the body never dies unless it is changed into a corpse. Experience, indeed, seems to teach the contrary. It happens sometimes that a man undergoes such changes that he cannot very well be said to be the same man, as was the case with a certain Spanish poet of whom I have heard, who was seized with an illness, and although he recovered, remained, nevertheless, so oblivious of his past life that he did not believe the tales and tragedies he had composed were his own, and he might, indeed, have been taken for a grown-up child if he had also forgotten his native tongue. But if this seems incredible, what shall we say of children? The man of mature years believes the nature of children to be so different from his own, that it would be impossible to persuade him he had ever been a child, if he did not conjecture regarding himself from what he sees of others. But in order to avoid giving to the superstitious matter for new questions, I prefer to go no farther in the discussion of these matters.

PROP. XL.—*Whatever conduces to the universal fellowship of men, that is to say, whatever causes men to live in harmony with one another, is profitable, and, on the contrary, whatever brings discord into the State is evil.*

Demonst.—For whatever causes men to live in harmony with one another causes them to live according to the guidance of reason (Prop. 35, pt. 4), and, therefore (Props. 26 and 27, pt. 4), is good, and (by the same reasoning) those things are evil which excite discord.—Q.E.D.

PROP. XLI.—*Joy is not directly evil, but good; sorrow, on the other hand, is directly evil.*

Demonst.—Joy (Prop. 11, pt. 3, with its Schol.) is an affect by which the body's power of action is increased or assisted. Sorrow, on the other hand, is an affect by which the body's power of action is lessened or restrained, and, therefore (Prop. 38, pt. 4), joy is directly good.—Q.E.D.

PROP. XLII.—*Cheerfulness can never be excessive, but is always good; melancholy, on the contrary, is always evil.*

Demonst.—Cheerfulness (see its definition in Schol. Prop. 11, pt. 3) is joy, which, in so far as it is related to the body, consists in this, that all the parts of the body are equally affected, that is to say (Prop. 11, pt. 3), the body's power of action is increased or assisted, so that all the parts acquire the same proportion of motion and rest to each other. Cheerfulness, therefore (Prop. 39, pt. 4), is always good, and can never be excessive. But melancholy (see its definition in Schol. Prop. 11, pt. 3) is sorrow, which, in so far as it is related to the body, consists in this, that the body's power of action is absolutely lessened or restrained, and melancholy, therefore (Prop. 38, pt. 4), is always evil.—Q.E.D.

PROP. XLIII.—*Pleasurable excitement may be excessive and an evil, and pain may be good in so far as pleasurable excitement or joy is evil.*

Demonst.—Pleasurable excitement is joy, which, in so far as it is related to the body, consists in this, that one or some of the parts of the body are affected more than others (see Def. in Schol. Prop. 11, pt. 3). The power of this affect may, therefore, be so great as to overcome the other actions of the body (Prop. 6, pt. 4); it may cling obstinately to the body; it may impede the body in such a manner as to render it less capable of being affected in many ways, and therefore (Prop. 38, pt. 4) may be evil. Again, pain, which, on the contrary, is sorrow, considered in itself alone cannot be good (Prop. 41, pt. 4). But because its power and increase is limited by the power of an external cause compared with our own power (Prop. 5, pt. 4), we can therefore conceive infinite degrees of strength of this affect, and infinite kinds of it (Prop. 3, pt. 4), and we can therefore conceive it to be such that it can restrain an excess of pleasurable excitement, and so far (by the first part of this proposition) preventing the body from becoming less capable. So far, therefore, will pain be good.—Q.E.D.

PROP. XLIV.—*Love and desire may be excessive.*

Demonst.—Love is joy (Def. 6 of the Affects) with the accompanying idea of an external cause. Pleasurable excitement, therefore (Schol. Prop. 11, pt. 3), with the accompanying idea of an external cause, is love, and therefore love (Prop. 43, pt. 4) may be excessive. Again, desire is greater as the affect from which it springs is greater (Prop. 37, pt. 3). Inasmuch, therefore, as an affect (Prop. 6, pt. 4) may overpower the other actions of a man, so also the desire which springs from this affect may also overpower the other desires, and may therefore exist in the same excess which we have shown (in the preceding proposition) that pleasurable excitement possesses.—Q.E.D.[1]

Schol.—Cheerfulness, which I have affirmed to be good, is more easily imagined than observed; for the affects by which we are daily agitated are generally related to some part of the body which is affected more than the others, and therefore it is that the affects exist for the most part in excess, and so hold the mind down to the contemplation of one object alone, that it can think about nothing else; and although men are subject to a number of affects, and therefore few are found who are always under the control of one and the same affect, there are not wanting those to whom one and the same affect obstinately clings. We see men sometimes so affected by one object, that although it is not present, they believe it to be before them; and if this happens to a man who is not asleep, we say that he is delirious or mad. Nor are those believed to be less mad who are inflamed by love, dreaming about nothing but a mistress or harlot day and night, for they excite our laughter. But the avaricious man who thinks of nothing else but gain or money, and the ambitious man who thinks of nothing but glory, inasmuch as they do harm, and are, therefore, thought worthy of hatred, are not believed to be mad. In truth, however, avarice, ambition, lust, &c., are a kind

---

[1] The Socratic tone of this portion of the Ethic is worthy of note. Cf. prop. LXI. [Ed.]

of madness, although they are not reckoned amongst diseases.

PROP. XLV.—*Hatred can never be good.*

Demonst.—The man whom we hate we endeavour to destroy (Prop. 39, pt. 3), that is to say (Prop. 37, pt. 4), we endeavour to do something which is evil. Therefore hatred, &c.—Q.E.D.

Schol.—It is to be observed that here and in the following propositions I understand by hatred, hatred towards men only.

Corol. 1.—Envy, mockery, contempt, anger, revenge, and the other affects which are related to hatred or arise from it, are evil. This is also evident from Prop. 39, pt. 3, and Prop. 37, pt. 4.

Corol. 2.—Everything which we desire because we are affected by hatred is base and unjust in the State. This is also evident from Prop. 39, pt. 3, and from the definition in Schol. Prop. 37, pt. 4, of what is base and unjust.

Schol.—I make a great distinction between mockery (which I have said in Corol. 1 of this Prop. is bad) and laughter; for laughter and merriment are nothing but joy, and therefore, provided they are not excessive, are in themselves good (Prop. 41, pt. 4). Nothing but a gloomy and sad superstition forbids enjoyment. For why is it more seemly to extinguish hunger and thirst than to drive away melancholy? My reasons and my conclusions are these:—No God and no human being, except an envious one, is delighted by my impotence or my trouble, or esteems as any virtue in us tears, sighs, fears, and other things of this kind, which are signs of mental impotence; on the contrary, the greater the joy with which we are affected, the greater the perfection

to which we pass thereby, that is to say, the more do we
necessarily partake of the divine nature. To make use of
things, therefore, and to delight in them as much as
possible (provided we do not disgust ourselves with
them, which is not delighting in them), is the part of
a wise man. It is the part of a wise man, I say, to
refresh and invigorate himself with moderate and pleasant eating and drinking, with sweet scents and the
beauty of green plants, with ornament, with music, with
sports, with the theatre, and with all things of this
kind which one man can enjoy without hurting another.
For the human body is composed of a great number of
parts of diverse nature, which constantly need new and
varied nourishment, in order that the whole of the body
may be equally fit for everything which can follow from
its nature, and consequently that the mind may be
equally fit to understand many things at once. This
mode of living best of all agrees both with our principles
and with common practice; therefore this mode of living
is the best of all, and is to be universally commended.
There is no need, therefore, to enter more at length
into the subject.

PROP. XLVI.—*He who lives according to the guidance
of reason strives as much as possible to repay the
hatred, anger, or contempt of others towards himself with love or generosity.*

Demonst.—All affects of hatred are evil (Corol. 1,
Prop. 45, pt. 4), and, therefore, the man who lives
according to the guidance of reason will strive as much
as possible to keep himself from being agitated by the
affects of hatred (Prop. 19, pt. 4), and, consequently
(Prop. 37, pt. 4), will strive to keep others from being
subject to the same affects. But hatred is increased by

reciprocal hatred, and, on the other hand, can be extinguished by love (Prop. 43, pt. 3), so that hatred passes into love (Prop. 44, pt. 3). Therefore he who lives according to the guidance of reason will strive to repay the hatred of another, &c., with love, that is to say, with generosity (see definition of generosity in Schol. Prop. 59, pt. 3).—Q.E.D.

Schol.—He who wishes to avenge injuries by hating in return does indeed live miserably. But he who, on the contrary, strives to drive out hatred by love, fights joyfully and confidently, with equal ease resisting one man or a number of men, and needing scarcely any assistance from fortune. Those whom he conquers yield gladly, not from defect of strength, but from an increase of it. These truths, however, all follow so plainly from the definitions alone of love and the intellect, that there is no need to demonstrate them singly.

PROP. XLVII.—*The affects of hope and fear cannot be good of themselves.*

Demonst.—The affects of hope and fear cannot exist without sorrow; for fear (Def. 13 of the Affects) is sorrow, and hope (see the explanation of Defs. 12 and 13 of the Affects) cannot exist without fear. Therefore (Prop. 41, pt. 4) these affects cannot be good of themselves, but only in so far as they are able to restrain the excesses of joy (Prop. 43, pt. 4).—Q.E.D.

Schol.—We may here add that these affects indicate want of knowledge and impotence of mind, and, for the same reason, confidence, despair, gladness, and remorse are signs of weakness of mind. For although confidence and gladness are affects of joy, they nevertheless suppose that sorrow has preceded them, namely, hope or fear. In proportion, therefore, as we endeavour to live according to the guidance of reason, shall we strive as much as possible to depend less on hope, to liberate ourselves from fear, to rule fortune, and to direct our actions by the sure counsels of reason.

PROP. XLVIII.—*The affects of over-estimation and contempt are always evil.*

Demonst.—These affects (Defs. 21 and 22 of the Affects) are opposed to reason, and therefore (Props. 26 and 27, pt. 4) are evil.—Q.E.D.

PROP. XLIX.—*Over-estimation easily renders the man who is over-estimated proud.*

Demonst.—If we see that a person, through love, thinks too much of us, we shall easily glorify ourselves (Schol. 41, pt. 3), or, in other words, be affected with joy (Def. 30 of the Affects), and easily believe the good which we hear others affirm of us (Prop. 25, pt. 3), and consequently, through self-love, we shall think too much of ourselves, that is to say (Def. 28 of the Affects), we shall easily grow proud.—Q.E.D.

PROP. L.—*Pity in a man who lives according to the guidance of reason is in itself evil and unprofitable.*

Demonst.—Pity (Def. 18 of the Affects) is sorrow, and therefore (Prop. 41, pt. 4) is in itself evil. The good, however, which issues from pity, namely, that we endeavour to free from misery the man we pity (Corol. 3, Prop. 27, pt. 3), we desire to do from the dictate of reason alone (Prop. 37, pt. 4); nor can we do anything except by the dictate of reason alone, which we are sure is good (Prop. 27, pt. 4). Pity, therefore, in a man who

lives according to the guidance of reason is in itself bad
and unprofitable.—Q.E.D.

Corol.—Hence it follows that a man who lives according to the dictates of reason endeavours as much as
possible to prevent himself from being touched by pity.

Schol.—The man who has properly understood that
everything follows from the necessity of the divine
nature, and comes to pass according to the eternal
laws and rules of nature, will in truth discover nothing
which is worthy of hatred, laughter, or contempt, nor
will he pity any one, but, so far as human virtue is
able, he will endeavour to *do well,* as we say, and to
rejoice. We must add also, that a man who is easily
touched by the affect of pity, and is moved by the misery
or tears of another, often does something of which he
afterward repents, both because from an affect we do
nothing which we certainly know to be good, and also
because we are so easily deceived by false tears. But
this I say expressly of the man who lives according to
the guidance of reason. For he who is moved neither
by reason nor pity to be of any service to others is properly called inhuman; for (Prop. 27, pt. 3) he seems to
be unlike a man.

PROP. LI.—*Favour is not opposed to reason, but agrees
    with it, and may arise from it.*

Demonst.—Favour is love towards him who does good
to another (Def. 19 of the Affects), and therefore can be
related to the mind in so far as it is said to act (Prop.
59, pt. 3), that is to say (Prop. 3, pt. 3), in so
far as it understands, and therefore favour agrees with
reason.—Q.E.D.

Another Demonstration.—If we live according to the
guidance of reason, we shall desire for others the good

which we seek for ourselves (Prop. 37, pt. 4). Therefore if we see one person do good to another, our endeavour to do good is assisted, that is to say (Schol.
Prop. 11, pt. 3), we shall rejoice, and our joy (by
hypothesis) will be accompanied with the idea of the
person who does good to the other, that is to say (Def.
19 of the Affects), we shall favour him.—Q.E.D.

Schol.—Indignation, as it is defined by us (Def. 20 of
the Affects), is necessarily evil (Prop. 45, pt. 4); but it
is to be observed that when the supreme authority, constrained by the desire of preserving peace, punishes a
citizen who injures another, I do not say that it is indignant with the citizen, since it is not excited by hatred
to destroy him, but punishes him from motives of piety.

PROP. LII.—*Self-satisfaction may arise from reason,
and the self-satisfaction alone which arises from
reason is the highest which can exist.*

Demonst.—Self-satisfaction is the joy which arises
from a man's contemplating himself and his power of
action (Def. 25 of the Affects). But man's true power
of action or his virtue is reason itself (Prop. 3, pt. 3),
which he contemplates clearly and distinctly (Props. 40
and 43, pt. 2). Self-satisfaction therefore arises from
reason. Again, man, when he contemplates himself, perceives nothing clearly and distinctly or adequately, excepting those things which follow from his power of
action (Def. 2, pt. 3), that is to say (Prop. 3, pt. 3),
those things which follow from his power of understanding; and therefore from this contemplation alone the
highest satisfaction which can exist arises.—Q.E.D.

Schol.—Self-satisfaction is indeed the highest thing
for which we can hope, for (as we have shown in Prop.
25, pt. 4) no one endeavours to preserve his being for

the sake of any end. Again, because this self-satisfaction is more and more nourished and strengthened by praise (Corol. Prop. 53, pt. 3), and, on the contrary (Corol. Prop. 55, pt. 3), more and more disturbed by blame, therefore we are principally led by glory, and can scarcely endure life with disgrace.

PROP. LIII.—*Humility is not a virtue, that is to say, it does not spring from reason.*

Demonst.—Humility is sorrow, which springs from this, that a man contemplates his own weakness (Def. 26 of the Affects). But in so far as a man knows himself by true reason is he supposed to understand his essence, that is to say (Prop. 7, pt. 3), his power. If, therefore, while contemplating himself, he perceives any impotence of his, this is not due to his understanding himself, but, as we have shown (Prop. 55, pt. 3), to the fact that his power of action is restrained. But if we suppose that he forms a conception of his own impotence because he understands something to be more powerful than himself, by the knowledge of which he limits his own power of action, in this case we simply conceive that he understands himself distinctly (Prop. 26, pt. 4), and his power of action is increased. Humility or sorrow, therefore, which arises because a man contemplates his own impotence, does not spring from true contemplation or reason, and is not a virtue, but a passion.—Q.E.D.

PROP. LIV.—*Repentance is not a virtue, that is to say, it does not spring from reason; on the contrary, the man who repents of what he has done is doubly wretched or impotent.*

Demonst.—The first part of this proposition is demonstrated in the same manner as the preceding proposition. The second part follows from the definition alone of this affect (Def. 27 of the Affects). For, in the first place, we allow ourselves to be overcome by a depraved desire, and, in the second place, by sorrow.

Schol.—Inasmuch as men seldom live as reason dictates, therefore these two affects, humility and repentance, together with hope and fear, are productive of more profit than disadvantage, and therefore, since men must sin, it is better that they should sin in this way. For if men impotent in mind were all equally proud, were ashamed of nothing, and feared nothing, by what bonds could they be united or constrained? The multitude becomes a thing to be feared if it has nothing to fear. It is not to be wondered at, therefore, that the prophets, thinking rather of the good of the community than of a few, should have commended so greatly humility, repentance, and reverence. Indeed, those who are subject to these affects can be led much more easily than others, so that, at last, they come to live according to the guidance of reason, that is to say, become free men, and enjoy the life of the blessed.

PROP. LV.—*The greatest pride or the greatest despondency is the greatest ignorance of one's self.*

Demonst.—This is evident from Defs. 28 and 29 of the Affects.

PROP. LVI.—*The greatest pride or despondency indicates the greatest impotence of mind.*

Demonst.—The primary foundation of virtue is the preservation of our being (Corol. Prop. 22, pt. 4) ac-

cording to the guidance of reason (Prop. 24, pt. 4).
The man, therefore, who is ignorant of himself is ignorant of the foundation of all the virtues, and consequently is ignorant of all the virtues. Again, to act in
conformity with virtue is nothing but acting according
to the guidance of reason (Prop. 24, pt. 4), and he who
acts according to the guidance of reason must necessarily
know that he acts according to the guidance of reason
(Prop. 43, pt. 2). He, therefore, who is ignorant of
himself, and consequently (as we have just shown) altogether ignorant of all the virtues, cannot in any way act
in conformity with virtue, that is to say (Def. 8, pt 4),
is altogether impotent in mind. Therefore (Prop. 55,
pt. 4), the greatest pride or despondency indicates the
greatest impotence of mind.—Q.E.D.

Corol.—Hence follows, with the utmost clearness,
that the proud and the desponding are above all others
subject to affects.

Schol.—Despondency, nevertheless, can be corrected
more easily than pride, since the former is an affect of
sorrow, while the latter is an affect of joy, and is, therefore (Prop. 18, pt. 4), stronger than the former.

PROP. LVII.—*The proud man loves the presence of
    parasites or flatterers, and hates that of the
    noble-minded.*

Demonst.—Pride is joy arising from a man's having
too high an opinion of himself (Defs. 28 and 6 of the
Affects). This opinion a proud man will endeavour, as
much as he can, to cherish (Schol. Prop. 13, pt. 3), and,
therefore, will love the presence of parasites or flatterers
(the definitions of these people are omitted, because
they are too well known), and will shun that of the
noble-minded who think of him as is right.—Q.E.D.

Schol.—It would take too much time to enumerate here all the evils of pride, for the proud are subject to all affects, but to none are they less subject than to those of love and pity. It is necessary, however, to observe here that a man is also called proud if he thinks too little of other people, and so, in this sense, pride is to be defined as joy which arises from the false opinion that we are superior to other people, while despondency, the contrary to this pride, would be defined as sorrow arising from the false opinion that we are inferior to other people. This being understood, it is easy to see that the proud man is necessarily envious (Schol. Prop. 55, pt. 3), and that he hates those above all others who are the most praised on account of their virtues. It follows, too, that his hatred of them is not easily overcome by love or kindness (Schol. Prop. 41, pt. 3), and that he is delighted by the presence of those only who humour his weakness, and from a fool make him a madman. Although despondency is contrary to pride, the despondent man is closely akin to the proud man. For since the sorrow of the despondent man arises from his judging his own impotence by the power or virtue of others, his sorrow will be mitigated, that is to say, he will rejoice, if his imagination be occupied in contemplating the vices of others. Hence the proverb— It is a consolation to the wretched to have had companions in their misfortunes. On the other hand, the more the despondent man believes himself to be below other people, the more will he sorrow; and this is the reason why none are more prone to envy than the despondent; and why they, above all others, try to observe men's actions with a view to finding fault with them rather than correcting them, so that at last they praise nothing but despondency and glory in it; but in such a manner, however, as always to seem despondent.

These things follow from this affect as necessarily as it follows from the nature of a triangle that its three angles are equal to two right angles. It is true, indeed, that I have said that I call these and the like affects evil, in so far as I attend to human profit alone; but the laws of nature have regard to the common order of nature of which man is a part—a remark I desired to make in passing, lest it should be thought that I talk about the vices and absurdities of men rather than attempt to demonstrate the nature and properties of things. As I said in the Preface to the Third Part, I consider human affects and their properties precisely as I consider other natural objects; and, indeed, the affects of man, if they do not show his power, show, at least, the power and workmanship of nature, no less than many other things which we admire and delight to contemplate. I proceed, however, to notice those things connected with the affects which are productive either of profit or loss to man.

PROP. LVIII.—*Self-exaltation is not opposed to reason, but may spring from it.*

Demonst.—This is plain from Def. 30 of the Affects, and also from the definition of honour in Schol. 1, Prop. 37, pt. 4.

Schol.—What is called vainglory is self-satisfaction, nourished by nothing but the good opinion of the multitude, so that when that is withdrawn, the satisfaction, that is to say (Schol. Prop. 52, pt. 4), the chief good which every one loves, ceases. For this reason those who glory in the good opinion of the multitude anxiously and with daily care strive, labour, and struggle to preserve their fame. For the multitude is changeable and fickle, so that fame, if it be not preserved, soon passes

away. As every one, moreover, is desirous to catch the
praises of the people, one person will readily destroy the
fame of another; and, consequently, as the object of
contention is what is commonly thought to be the highest
good, a great desire arises on the part of every one to
keep down his fellows by every possible means, and he
who at last comes off conqueror boasts more because he
has injured another person than because he has profited
himself. This glory of self-satisfaction, therefore, is indeed vain, for it is really no glory. What is worthy of
notice with regard to shame may easily be gathered from
what has been said about compassion and repentance.
I will only add that pity, like shame, although it is not
a virtue, is nevertheless good, in so far as it shows that a
desire of living uprightly is present in the man who is
possessed with shame, just as pain is called good in so
far as it shows that the injured part has not yet putre-
fied. A man, therefore, who is ashamed of what he has
done, although he is sorrowful, is nevertheless more
perfect than the shameless man who has no desire of
living uprightly. These are the things which I undertook to establish with regard to the affects of joy and
sorrow. With reference to the desires, these are good or
evil as they spring from good or evil affects. All of
them, however, in so far as they are begotten in us of
affects which are passions, are blind (as may easily be
inferred from what has been said in Schol. Prop. 44, pt.
4), nor would they be of any use if men could be easily
persuaded to live according to the dictates of reason
alone, as I shall show in a few words.

PROP. LIX.—*To all actions to which we are determined
by an affect which is a passion we may, without the
affect, be determined by reason.*

Demonst.—To act according to reason is nothing (Prop. 3, and Def. 2, pt. 3) but to do those things which follow from the necessity of our nature considered in itself alone. But sorrow is evil so far as it lessens or restrains this power of action (Prop. 41, pt. 4); therefore we can be determined by this affect to no action which we could not perform if we were led by reason. Again, joy is evil so far only as it hinders our fitness for action (Props. 41 and 43, pt. 4); and therefore also we can so far be determined to no action which we could not do if we were led by reason. Finally, in so far as joy is good, so far it agrees with reason (for it consists in this, that a man's power of action is increased or assisted), and it is not a passion unless in so far as man's power of action is not increased sufficiently for him to conceive adequately himself and his actions (Prop. 3, pt. 3, with its Schol.). If, therefore, a man affected with joy were led to such perfection as to conceive adequately himself and his actions, he would be fitted—better even than before—for the performance of those actions to which he is now determined by the affects which are passions. But all the affects are related to joy, sorrow, or desire (see the explanation of Def. 4 of the Affects), and desire (Def. 1 of the Affects) is nothing but the endeavour itself to act; therefore to all actions to which we are determined by an affect which is a passion we may without the affect be determined by reason alone.—Q.E.D.

Another Demonstration.—Any action is called evil in so far as it arises from our being affected with hatred or some evil affect (Corol. 1, Prop. 45, pt. 4). But no action considered in itself alone is either good or evil (as we have already shown in the preface to this part), but one and the same action is sometimes good and sometimes evil. Therefore we may be led by reason (Prop.

19, pt. 4) to that same action which is sometimes evil, or which arises from some evil affect.—Q.E.D.

Schol.—This can be explained more clearly by an example. The action of striking, for instance, in so far as it is considered physically, and we attend only to the fact that a man raises his arm, closes his hand, and forcibly moves the whole arm downwards, is a virtue which is conceived from the structure of the human body. If, therefore, a man agitated by anger or hatred is led to close the fist or move the arm, this comes to pass, as we have shown in the Second Part, because one and the same action can be joined to different images of things, and therefore we may be led to one and the same action as well by the images of things which we conceive confusedly as by those which we conceive clearly and distinctly. It appears, therefore, that every desire which arises from an affect which is a passion would be of no use if men could be led by reason. We shall now see why a desire which arises from an affect which is a passion is called blind.

PROP. LX.—*The desire which arises from joy or sorrow, which is related to one or to some, but not to all, the parts of the body, has no regard to the profit of the whole man.*

Demonst.—Let it be supposed that a part of the body —A, for example—is so strengthened by the force of some external cause that it prevails over the others (Prop. 6, pt. 4). It will not endeavour, therefore, to lose its strength in order that the remaining parts of the body may perform their functions, for in that case it would have a force or power of losing its strength, which (Prop. 6, pt. 3) is absurd. It will endeavour, therefore, and consequently (Props. 7 and 12, pt. 3) the mind also will endeavour, to preserve this same state; and so the desire which arises from such an affect of joy has no regard to the whole man. If, on the other hand, it be supposed that the part A is restrained so that the other parts prevail, it can be demonstrated in the same way that the desire which springs from sorrow has no regard to the whole man.

Schol.—Since, therefore, joy is most frequently related to one part of the body (Schol. Prop. 44, pt. 4), we generally desire to preserve our being without reference to our health as a whole; and, moreover, the desires by which we are chiefly controlled (Corol. Prop. 9, pt. 4) have regard to the present only, and not to the future.

PROP. LXI.—*A desire which springs from reason can never be in excess.*

Demonst.—Desire (Def. 1 of the Affects), absolutely considered, is the very essence of man, in so far as he is conceived as determined in any way whatever to any action, and therefore the desire which springs from reason, that is to say (Prop. 3, pt. 3), which is begotten in us in so far as we act, is the very essence or nature of man in so far as it is conceived as determined to actions which are adequately conceived by the essence of man alone (Def. 2, pt. 3). If, therefore, this desire could be in excess, it would be possible for human nature, considered in itself alone, to exceed itself, or, in other words, more would be possible to it than is possible, which is a manifest contradiction, and therefore this desire can never be in excess.—Q.E.D.

PROP. LXII.—*In so far as the conception of an object is formed by the mind according to the dictate of*

reason, the mind is equally affected, whether the
idea be that of something future, past, or present.

Demonst.—Everything which the mind, under the
guidance of reason, conceives, it conceives under the
same form of eternity or necessity (Corol. 2, Prop. 44,
pt. 2), and it is affected with the same certainty (Prop.
43, pt. 2, and its Schol.). Therefore, whether the idea be
one of a future, past, or present object, the mind conceives the object with the same necessity, and is affected
with the same certainty; and whether the idea be that of
a future, past, or present object, it will nevertheless be
equally true (Prop. 41, pt. 2), that is to say (Def. 4,
pt. 2), it will always have the same properties of an
adequate idea. Therefore, in so far as the conception of
an object is formed by the mind according to the dictates of reason, the mind will be affected in the same
way whether the idea be that of something future, past,
or present.—Q.E.D.

Schol.—If it were possible for us to possess an adequate knowledge concerning the duration of things, and
to determine by reason the periods of their existence, we
should contemplate with the same affect objects future
and present, and the good which the mind conceived to
be future, it would seek just as it would seek the present
good. Consequently it would necessarily neglect the
present good for the sake of a greater future good, and
would, as we shall presently show, be very little disposed to seek a good which was present, but which would
be a cause of any future evil. But it is not possible for
us to have any other than a very inadequate knowledge
of the duration of things (Prop. 31, pt. 2), and we
determine (Schol. Prop. 44, pt. 2) the periods of the
existence of objects by the imagination alone, which is
not affected by the image of a present object in the

same way as it is by that of a future object. Hence it comes to pass that the true knowledge of good and evil which we possess is only abstract or universal, and the judgment we pass upon the order of things and the connection of causes, so that we may determine what is good for us in the present and what is evil, is rather imaginary than real. It is not, therefore, to be wondered at if the desire which arises from a knowledge of good and evil, in so far as this knowledge has regard to the future, is capable of being easily restrained by the desire of objects which are sweet to us at the present moment. (See Prop. 16, pt. 4).

PROP. LXIII.—*He who is led by fear, and does what is good in order that he may avoid what is evil, is not led by reason.*

Demonst.—All the affects which are related to the mind, in so far as it acts, that is to say (Prop. 3, pt. 3), which are related to reason, are no other than affects of joy and desire (Prop. 59, pt. 3); and therefore (Def. 13 of the Affects), he who is led by fear and does good through fear of evil is not led by reason.—Q.E.D.

Schol.—The superstitious, who know better how to rail at vice than to teach virtue, and who study not to lead man by reason, but to hold him in through fear, in order that he may shun evil rather than love virtue, aim at nothing more than that others should be as miserable as themselves, and, therefore, it is not to be wondered at if they generally become annoying and hateful to men.

Corol.—By the desire which springs from reason we follow good directly and avoid evil indirectly.

Demonst.—For the desire which springs from reason cannot spring from sorrow, but only from an affect of joy, which is not a passion (Prop. 59, pt. 3), that is to say, from joy which cannot be in excess (Prop. 61, pt. 4). This desire springs, therefore (Prop. 8, pt. 4), from the knowledge of good, and not from the knowledge of evil, and therefore, according to the guidance of reason, we seek what is good directly, and so far only do we shun what is evil.—Q.E.D.

Schol.—This corollary is explained by the example of a sick man and a healthy man. The sick man, through fear of death, eats what he dislikes; the healthy man takes a pleasure in his food, and so enjoys life more than if he feared death and directly desired to avoid it. So also the judge who condemns a guilty man to death, not from hatred or anger, but solely from love for the public welfare, is led by reason alone.

PROP. LXIV.—*The knowledge of evil is inadequate knowledge.*

Demonst.—The knowledge of evil (Prop. 8, pt. 4) is sorrow itself, in so far as we are conscious of it. But sorrow is the passage to a less perfection (Def. 3 of the Affects), and it cannot, therefore, be understood through the essence itself of man (Props. 6 and 7, pt. 3). It is, therefore (Def. 2, pt. 3), a passion which (Prop. 3, pt. 3) depends upon inadequate ideas, and consequently (Prop. 29, pt. 2) the knowledge of sorrow, that is to say, the knowledge of evil, is inadequate.—Q.E.D.

Corol.—Hence it follows that if the human mind had none but adequate ideas, it would form no notion of evil.

PROP. LXV.—*According to the guidance of reason, of two things which are good, we shall follow the*

*greater good, and of two evils, we shall follow
the less.*

Demonst.—The good which hinders us from enjoying
a greater good is really an evil, for good and evil (as we
have shown in the preface to this part) are affirmed
of things in so far as we compare them with one
another. By the same reasoning a less evil is really a
good, and therefore (Corol. Prop. 63, pt. 4), according
to the guidance of reason, we shall seek or follow the
greater good only and the lesser evil.—Q.E.D.

Corol.—According to the guidance of reason, we shall
follow a lesser evil for the sake of a greater good, and
a lesser good which is the cause of a greater evil we
shall neglect. For the evil which we here call less is
really a good, and the good, on the other hand, is evil;
and therefore (Corol. Prop. 63, pt. 4) we shall seek
the former and neglect the latter.—Q.E.D.

PROP. LXVI.—*According to the guidance of reason, we
shall seek the greater future good before that which
is less and present, and we shall seek also the less
and present evil before that which is greater and
future.*

Demonst.—If it were possible for the mind to have an
adequate knowledge of a future object, it would be
affected by the same affect towards the future object
as towards a present object (Prop. 62, pt. 4). Therefore, in so far as we attend to reason itself, as we are
supposing in this proposition that we do, it is the same
thing whether the greater good or evil be supposed to
be future or present, and therefore (Prop. 65, pt. 4)
we shall seek the greater future good before that which
is less and present, &c.—Q.E.D.

Corol.—According to the guidance of reason, we shall seek the lesser present evil which is the cause of the greater future good, and the lesser present good which is the cause of a greater future evil we shall neglect. This corollary is connected with the foregoing proposition in the same way as Corol. Prop. 65 is connected with Prop. 65.

Schol.—If what has been said here be compared with what has been demonstrated about the strength of the passions in the first eighteen Props. pt. 4, and in Schol. Prop. 18, pt. 4, it will easily be seen in what consists the difference between a man who is led by affect or opinion alone and one who is led by reason. The former, whether he wills it or not, does those things of which he is entirely ignorant, but the latter does the will of no one but himself, and does those things only which he knows are of greatest importance in life, and which he therefore desires above all things. I call the former, therefore, a slave, and the latter free.

I will add here a few words concerning the character of the free man and his manner of life.

PROP. LXVII.—*A free man thinks of nothing less than of death, and his wisdom is not a meditation upon death but upon life.*

Demonst.—A free man, that is to say, a man who lives according to the dictates of reason alone, is not led by the fear of death (Prop. 63, pt. 4), but directly desires the good (Corol. Prop. 63, pt. 4); that is to say (Prop. 24, pt. 4), desires to act, to live, and to preserve his being in accordance with the principle of seeking his own profit. He thinks, therefore, of nothing less than of death, and his wisdom is a meditation upon life.— Q.E.D.

PROP. LXVIII.—*If men were born free, they would form no conception of good and evil so long as they were free.*

Demonst.—I have said that that man is free who is led by reason alone. He, therefore, who is born free and remains free has no other than adequate ideas, and therefore has no conception of evil (Corol. Prop. 64, pt. 4), and consequently (as good and evil are correlative) no conception of good.—Q.E.D.

Schol.—It is clear from Prop. 4, pt. 4, that the hypothesis of this proposition is false, and cannot be conceived unless in so far as we regard human nature alone, or rather God, not in so far as He is infinite, but in so far only as He is the cause of man's existence. This (together with the other things we have before demonstrated) appears to have been what was meant by Moses in that history of the first man. In that history no other power of God is conceived excepting that by which He created man; that is to say, the power with which He considered nothing but the advantage of man. Therefore we are told that God forbad free man to eat of the tree of knowledge of good and evil, and warned him that as soon as he ate of it he would immediately dread death rather than desire to live. Afterwards we are told that when man found a wife who agreed entirely with his nature, he saw that there could be nothing in nature which could be more profitable to him than his wife. But when he came to believe that the brutes were like himself, he immediately began to imitate their affects (Prop. 27, pt. 3), and to lose his liberty, which the Patriarchs afterwards recovered, being led by the spirit of Christ, that is to say, by the idea of God, which alone can make a man free, and cause him to desire for other men the good he desires for himself, as (Prop. 37, pt. 4) we have already demonstrated.

PROP. LXIX.—*The virtue of a free man is seen to be as great in avoiding danger as in overcoming it.*

Demonst.—An affect cannot be restrained or removed unless a contrary and stronger affect restrains it (Prop. 7, pt. 4); but blind audacity and fear are affects which may be conceived as being equally great (Props. 5 and 3, pt. 4). The virtue or strength of mind, therefore (for the definition of this, see Schol. Prop. 59, pt. 3), which is required to restrain audacity must be equally great with that which is required to restrain fear; that is to say (Defs. 40 and 41 of the Affects), a free man avoids danger by the same virtue of the mind as that by which he seeks to overcome it.—Q.E.D.

Corol.—Flight at the proper time, just as well as fighting, is to be reckoned, therefore, as showing strength of mind in a man who is free; that is to say, a free man chooses flight by the same strength or presence of mind as that by which he chooses battle.

Schol.—What strength of mind is, or what I understand by it, I have explained in Schol. Prop. 59, pt. 3. By danger, I understand anything which may be the cause of sorrow, hatred, discord, or any other evil like them.

PROP. LXX.—*The free man who lives amongst those who are ignorant strives as much as possible to avoid their favours.*

Demonst.—Every one, according to his own disposition, judges what is good (Schol. Prop. 39, pt. 3). The ignorant man, therefore, who has conferred a favour on another person, will value it according to his own way of thinking, and he will be sad if a less value seems to be placed upon it by the person who has received it (Prop. 42, pt. 3). But a free man strives to unite other men with himself by friendship (Prop. 37, pt. 4), and not to return to them favours which they, according to their affects, may consider to be equal to those which they have bestowed. He desires rather to govern himself and others by the free decisions of reason, and to do those things only which he has discovered to be of the first importance. A free man, therefore, in order that he may not be hated by the ignorant nor yet yield to their appetites, but only to reason, will endeavour as much as possible to avoid their favours.—Q.E.D.

Schol.—I say *as much as possible.* For although men are ignorant, they are nevertheless men, who, when we are in straits, are able to afford us human assistance— the best assistance which man can receive. It is often necessary, therefore, to receive a favour from the ignorant, and to thank them for it according to their taste ; and besides this, care must be used, even in declining favours, not to seem either to despise the givers or through avarice to dread a return, so that we may not, while striving to escape their hatred, by that very act incur their displeasure. In avoiding favours, therefore, we must be guided by a consideration of what is profitable and honourable.

PROP. LXXI.—*None but those who are free are very grateful to one another.*

Demonst.—None but those who are free are very profitable to one another, or are united by the closest bond of friendship (Prop. 35, pt. 4, and Corol. 1), or with an equal zeal of love strive to do good to one another (Prop. 37, pt. 4), and therefore (Def. 34 of the Affects) none but those who are free are very grateful to one another.—Q.E.D.

Schol.—The gratitude to one another of men who are led by blind desire is generally a matter of business or a snare rather than gratitude. Ingratitude, it is to be observed, is not an affect. It is nevertheless base, because it is generally a sign that a man is too much affected by hatred, anger, pride, or avarice. For he who through stupidity does not know how to return a gift is not ungrateful; and much less is he ungrateful who is not moved by the gifts of a harlot to serve her lust, nor by those of a thief to conceal his thefts, nor by any other gifts of a similar kind. On the contrary, a man shows that he possesses a steadfast mind if he does not suffer himself to be enticed by any gifts to his own or to common ruin.

PROP. LXXII.—*A free man never acts deceitfully, but always honourably.*

Demonst.—If a free man did anything deceitfully, in so far as he is free, he would do it at the bidding of reason (for so far only do we call him free); and therefore to act deceitfully would be a virtue (Prop. 24, pt. 4), and consequently (by the same proposition) it would be more advantageous to every one, for the preservation of his being, to act deceitfully; that is to say (as is self-evident), it would be more advantageous to men to agree only in words and to be opposed in reality, which (Corol. Prop. 31, pt. 4) is absurd. A free man, therefore, &c.—Q.E.D.

Schol.—If it be asked whether, if a man by breach of faith could escape from the danger of instant death, reason does not counsel him, for the preservation of his being, to break faith; I reply in the same way, that if reason gives such counsel, she gives it to all men, and reason therefore generally counsels men to make no agreements for uniting their strength and possessing laws in common except deceitfully, that is to say, to have in reality no common laws, which is absurd.

PROP. LXXIII.—*A man who is guided by reason is freer in a State where he lives according to the common laws than he is in solitude, where he obeys himself alone.*

Demonst.—A man who is guided by reason is not led to obey by fear (Prop. 63, pt. 4), but in so far as he endeavours to preserve his being in accordance with the bidding of reason, that is to say (Schol. Prop. 66, pt. 4), in so far as he endeavours to live in freedom, does he desire to have regard for the common life and the common profit (Prop. 37, pt. 4), and consequently (as we have shown in Schol. 2, Prop. 37, pt. 4) he desires to live according to the common laws of the State. A man, therefore, who is guided by reason desires, in order that he may live more freely, to maintain the common rights of the State.—Q.E.D.

Schol.—These, and the like things which we have demonstrated concerning the true liberty of man, are related to fortitude, that is to say (Schol. Prop. 59, pt. 3), to strength of mind and generosity. Nor do I think it worth while to demonstrate here, one by one, all the properties of fortitude, and still less to show how its possessor can hate no one, be angry with no one, can neither envy, be indignant with, nor despise anybody, and can least of all be proud. For all this, together with truths of a like kind which have to do with the true life and religion, are easily deduced from

Props. 37 and 46, pt. 4, which show that hatred is to be
overcome by love, and that every one who is guided by
reason desires for others the good which he seeks
for himself. In addition, we must remember what we
have already observed in Schol. Prop. 50, pt. 4, and in
other places, that the brave man will consider above
everything that all things follow from the necessity of
the divine nature; and that, consequently, whatever he
thinks injurious and evil, and, moreover, whatever seems
to be impious, dreadful, unjust, or wicked, arises from
this, that he conceives things in a disturbed, mutilated,
and confused fashion. For this reason, his chief effort is
to conceive things as they are in themselves, and to
remove the hindrances to true knowledge, such as hatred,
anger, envy, derision, pride, and others of this kind
which we have before noticed; and so he endeavours,
as we have said, as much as possible to do well and
rejoice. How far human virtue reaches in the attainment of these things, and what it can do, I shall show
in the following part.

Appendix.

My observations in this part concerning the true
method of life have not been arranged so that they
could be seen at a glance, but have been demonstrated
here and there according as I could more easily deduce
one from another. I have determined, therefore, here
to collect them, and reduce them under principal heads.

I.

All our efforts or desires follow from the necessity of
our nature in such a manner that they can be understood

either through it alone as their proximate cause, or in so far as we are a part of nature, which part cannot be adequately conceived through itself and without the other individuals.

II.

The desires which follow from our nature in such a manner that they can be understood through it alone, are those which are related to the mind, in so far as it is conceived to consist of adequate ideas. The remaining desires are not related to the mind, unless in so far as it conceives things inadequately, whose power and increase cannot be determined by human power. but by the power of objects which are without us. The first kind of desires, therefore, are properly called actions, but the latter passions; for the first always indicate our power, and the latter, on the contrary, indicate our impotence and imperfect knowledge.

III.

Our actions, that is to say, those desires which are determined by man's power or reason, are always good; the others may be good as well as evil.

IV.

It is therefore most profitable to us in life to make perfect the intellect or reason as far as possible, and in this one thing consists the highest happiness or blessedness of man; for blessedness is nothing but the peace of mind which springs from the intuitive knowledge of God, and to perfect the intellect is nothing but to understand God, together with the attributes and actions

of God, which flow from the necessity of His nature.
The final aim, therefore, of a man who is guided by
reason, that is to say, the chief desire by which he
strives to govern all his other desires, is that by which
he is led adequately to conceive himself and all things
which can be conceived by his intelligence.

V.

There is no rational life therefore, without intelligence, and things are good only in so far as they assist
man to enjoy that life of the mind which is determined
by intelligence. Those things alone, on the other hand,
we call evil which hinder man from perfecting his
reason and enjoying a rational life.

VI.

But because all those things of which man is the efficient cause are necessarily good, it follows that no evil
can happen to man except from external causes, that is
to say, except in so far as he is a part of the whole
of nature, whose laws human nature is compelled to
obey—compelled also to accommodate himself to this
whole of nature in almost an infinite number of ways.

VII.

It is impossible that a man should not be a part of
nature and follow her common order; but if he be placed
amongst individuals who agree with his nature, his
power of action will by that very fact be assisted and
supported. But if, on the contrary, he be placed amongst
individuals who do not in the least agree with his nature,

he will scarcely be able without great change on his part to accommodate himself to them.

VIII.

Anything that exists in nature which we judge to be evil or able to hinder us from existing and enjoying a rational life, we are allowed to remove from us in that way which seems the safest; and whatever, on the other hand, we judge to be good or to be profitable for the preservation of our being or the enjoyment of a rational life, we are permitted to take for our use and use in any way we may think proper; and absolutely, every one is allowed by the highest right of nature to do that which he believes contributes to his own profit.

IX.

Nothing, therefore, can agree better with the nature of any object than other individuals of the same kind, and so (see § 7) there is nothing more profitable to man for the preservation of his being and the enjoyment of a rational life than a man who is guided by reason. Again, since there is no single thing we know which is more excellent than a man who is guided by reason, it follows that there is nothing by which a person can better show how much skill and talent he possesses than by so educating men that at last they will live under the direct authority of reason.

X.

In so far as men are carried away by envy or any affect of hatred towards one another, so far are they contrary to one another, and consequently so much the

more are they to be feared, as they have more power
than other individuals of nature.

XI.

Minds, nevertheless, are not conquered by arms, but
by love and generosity.

XII.

Above all things is it profitable to men to form
communities and to unite themselves to one another
by bonds which may make all of them as one man; and
absolutely, it is profitable for them to do whatever may
tend to strengthen their friendships.

XIII.

But to accomplish this skill and watchfulness are required; for men are changeable (those being very few
who live according to the laws of reason), and nevertheless generally envious and more inclined to vengeance
than pity. To bear with each, therefore, according to
his disposition and to refrain from imitating his affects
requires a singular power of mind. But those, on the
contrary, who know how to revile men, to denounce vices
rather than teach virtues, and not to strengthen men's
minds but to weaken them, are injurious both to themselves and others, so that many of them through an
excess of impatience and a false zeal for religion prefer
living with brutes rather than amongst men; just as
boys or youths, unable to endure with equanimity the
rebukes of their parents, fly to the army, choosing the
discomforts of war and the rule of a tyrant rather than
the comforts of home and the admonitions of a father,

suffering all kinds of burdens to be imposed upon them
in order that they may revenge themselves upon their
parents.

XIV.

Although, therefore, men generally determine everything by their pleasure, many more advantages than disadvantages arise from their common union. It is better,
therefore, to endure with equanimity the injuries inflicted
by them, and to apply our minds to those things which
subserve concord and the establishment of friendship.

XV.

The things which beget concord are those which are
related to justice, integrity, and honour; for besides
that which is unjust and injurious, men take ill also
anything which is esteemed base, or that any one should
despise the received customs of the State. But in order
to win love, those things are chiefly necessary which have
reference to religion and piety. (See Schols. 1 and 2,
Prop. 37, Schol. Prop. 46, and Schol. Prop. 73, pt. 4.)

XVI.

Concord, moreover, is often produced by fear, but it
is without good faith. It is to be observed, too, that
fear arises from impotence of mind, and therefore is of
no service to reason; nor is pity, although it seems to
present an appearance of piety.

XVII.

Men also are conquered by liberality, especially those
who have not the means wherewith to procure what

is necessary for the support of life. But to assist every
one who is needy far surpasses the strength or profit
of a private person, for the wealth of a private person
is altogether insufficient to supply such wants. Besides,
the power of any one man is too limited for him to be
able to unite every one with himself in friendship. The
care, therefore, of the poor is incumbent on the whole
of society and concerns only the general profit.

XVIII.

In the receipt of benefits and in returning thanks,
care altogether different must be taken—concerning
which see Schol. Prop. 70, and Schol. Prop. 71, pt. 4.

XIX.

The love of a harlot, that is to say, the lust of sexual
intercourse, which arises from mere external form, and
absolutely all love which recognises any other cause than
the freedom of the mind, easily passes into hatred,
unless, which is worse, it becomes a species of delirium,
and thereby discord is cherished rather than concord
(Corol. Prop. 3¹, pt. 3).

XX.

With regard to marriage, it is plain that it is in
accordance with reason, if the desire of connection is
engendered not merely by external form, but by a love
of begetting children and wisely educating them; and
if, in addition, the love both of the husband and wife
has for its cause not external form merely, but chiefly
liberty of mind.

XXI.

Flattery, too, produces concord, but only by means of the disgraceful crime of slavery or perfidy; for there are none who are more taken by flattery than the proud, who wish to be first and are not so.

XXII.

There is a false appearance of piety and religion in dejection; and although dejection is the opposite of pride, the humble dejected man is very near akin to the proud (Schol. Prop. 57, pt. 4).

XXIII.

Shame also contributes to concord, but only with regard to those matters which cannot be concealed. Shame, too, inasmuch as it is a kind of sorrow, does not belong to the service of reason.

XXIV.

The remaining affects of sorrow which have man for their object are directly opposed to justice, integrity, honour, piety, and religion; and although indignation may seem to present an appearance of equity, yet there is no law where it is allowed to every one to judge the deeds of another, and to vindicate his own or another's right.

XXV.

Affability, that is to say, the desire of pleasing men, which is determined by reason, is related to piety (Schol.

Prop. 37, pt. 4). But if affability arise from an affect, it is ambition or desire, by which men, generally under a false pretence of piety, excite discords and seditions. For he who desires to assist other people, either by advice or by deed, in order that they may together enjoy the highest good, will strive, above all things, to win their love, and not to draw them into admiration, so that a doctrine may be named after him, nor absolutely to give any occasion for envy. In common conversation, too, he will avoid referring to the vices of men, and will take care only sparingly to speak of human impotence, while he will talk largely of human virtue or power, and of the way by which it may be made perfect, so that men being moved not by fear or aversion, but solely by the affect of joy, may endeavour as much as they can to live under the rule of reason.

XXVI.

Excepting man, we know no individual thing in nature in whose mind we can take pleasure, nor anything which we can unite with ourselves by friendship or any kind of intercourse, and therefore regard to our own profit does not demand that we should preserve anything which exists in nature excepting men, but teaches us to preserve it or destroy it in accordance with its varied uses, or to adapt it to our own service in any way whatever.

XXVII.

The profit which we derive from objects without us, over and above the experience and knowledge which we obtain because we observe them and change them from their existing forms into others, is chiefly the preservation of the body, and for this reason those objects are the most profitable to us which can feed and nourish the body, so that all its parts are able properly to perform their functions. For the more capable the body is of being affected in many ways, and affecting external bodies in many ways, the more capable of thinking is the mind (Props. 38 and 39, pt. 4). But there seem to be very few things in nature of this kind, and it is consequently necessary for the requisite nourishment of the body to use many different kinds of food; for the human body is composed of a great number of parts of different nature, which need constant and varied food in order that the whole of the body may be equally adapted for all those things which can follow from its nature, and consequently that the mind also may be equally adapted to conceive many things.

XXVIII.

The strength of one man would scarcely suffice to obtain these things if men did not mutually assist one another. As money has presented us with an abstract of everything, it has come to pass that its image above every other usually occupies the mind of the multitude, because they can imagine hardly any kind of joy without the accompanying idea of money as its cause.

XXIX.

This, however, is a vice only in those who seek money not from poverty or necessity, but because they have learnt the arts of gain, by which they keep up a grand appearance. As for the body itself, they feed it in accordance with custom, but sparingly, because they believe that they lose so much of their goods as they spend upon the preservation of their body. Those, however, who know the true use of money, and regulate the measure of wealth according to their needs, live contented with few things.

xxx.

Since, therefore, those things are good which help the parts of the body to perform their functions, and since joy consists in this, that the power of man, in so far as he is made up of mind and body, is helped or increased, it follows that all those things which bring joy are good. But inasmuch as things do not work to this end —that they may affect us with joy—nor is their power of action guided in accordance with our profit, and finally, since joy is generally related chiefly to some one part of the body, it follows that generally the affects of joy (unless reason and watchfulness be present), and consequently the desires which are begotten from them, are excessive. It is to be added, that an affect causes us to put that thing first which is sweet to us in the present, and that we are not able to judge the future with an equal affect of the mind (Schol. Prop. 44, and Schol. Prop. 60, pt. 4).

xxxi.

Superstition, on the contrary, seems to affirm that what brings sorrow is good, and, on the contrary, that what brings joy is evil. But, as we have already said (Schol. Prop. 45, pt. 4), no one excepting an envious man is delighted at my impotence or disadvantage, for the greater the joy with which we are affected, the greater the perfection to which we pass, and consequently the more do we participate in the divine nature; nor can joy ever be evil which is controlled by a true consideration for our own profit. On the other hand, the man who is led by fear, and does what is good that he may avoid what is evil, is not guided by reason.

XXXII.

But human power is very limited, and is infinitely surpassed by the power of external causes, so that we do not possess an absolute power to adapt to our service the things which are without us. Nevertheless we shall bear with equanimity those things which happen to us contrary to what a consideration of our own profit demands, if we are conscious that we have performed our duty, that the power we have could not reach so far as to enable us to avoid those things, and that we are a part of the whole of nature, whose order we follow. If we clearly and distinctly understand this, the part of us which is determined by intelligence, that is to say, the better part of us, will be entirely satisfied therewith, and in that satisfaction will endeavour to persevere; for, in so far as we understand, we cannot desire anything excepting what is necessary, nor, absolutely, can we be satisfied with anything but the truth. Therefore in so far as we understand these things properly will the efforts of the better part of us agree with the order of the whole of nature.

FIFTH PART

OF THE POWER OF THE INTELLECT, OR OF HUMAN LIBERTY

PREFACE

I PASS at length to the other part of Ethic which concerns the method or way which leads to liberty. In this part, therefore, I shall treat of the power of reason, showing how much reason itself can control the affects, and then what is freedom of mind or blessedness. Thence we shall see how much stronger the wise man is than the ignorant. In what manner and in what way the intellect should be rendered perfect, and with what art the body is to be cared for in order that it may properly perform its functions, I have nothing to do with here; for all former belongs to logic, the latter to medicine. I shall occupy myself here, as I have said, solely with the power of the mind or of reason, first of all showing the extent and nature of the authority which it has over the affects in restraining them and governing them; for that we have not absolute authority over them we have already demonstrated. The Stoics indeed thought that the affects depend absolutely on our will, and that we are absolutely masters over them; but they were driven, by the contradiction of experience, though not by their own principles, to confess that not a little practice and study are required in order to restrain and govern the affects. This, one of them attempted to illustrate, if I remember rightly, by the example of two dogs, one of a domestic and the other of a hunting breed; for he was able by habit to make the house-dog hunt, and the hunting dog, on the contrary, to desist from running after hares. To the Stoical opinion Descartes much inclines. He affirms that the soul or mind is united specially to a certain part of the brain called the pineal gland, which the mind by the mere exercise of the will is able to move in different ways, and by whose help the mind perceives all the movements which are excited in the body and external objects. This gland he affirms is suspended in the middle of the brain in such a manner that it can be moved by the least motion of the animal spirits. Again, he affirms that any variation in the manner in which the animal spirits impinge upon this gland is followed by a variation in the manner in which it is suspended in the middle of the brain, and moreover that the number of different impressions on the gland is the same as that of the different external objects which propel the animal spirits towards it. Hence it comes to pass that if the gland, by the will of the soul moving it in different directions, be afterwards suspended in this or that way in which it had once been suspended by the spirits agitated in this or that way, then the gland itself will propel and determine the animal spirits themselves in the same way as that in which they had before been repelled by a similar suspension of the gland. Moreover, he affirmed that each volition of the mind is united in nature to a certain motion of the gland. For example, if a person wishes to behold a remote object, this volition will cause the pupil of the eye to dilate, but if he thinks merely of the dilation of the pupil, to have that volition will profit him nothing, because nature has not connected a motion of the gland which serves to impel the animal spirits towards the optic nerve in a way suitable for dilation or contraction of the pupil with the volition of dilation or contraction, but only with the volition of beholding objects afar off or close at hand. Finally, he maintained that although each motion of this gland appears to be connected by nature from the commencement of our life with an individual thought, these motions can nevertheless be connected by habit with other thoughts, a proposition which he attempts to demonstrate in his "Passions of the Soul," art. 50, pt. 1.

From this he concludes that there is no mind so feeble that it cannot, when properly directed, acquire absolute power over its passions; for passions, as defined by him, are "perceptions, or sensations, or emotions of the soul which are related to it specially, and which (N.B.) are

produced,[1] preserved, and strengthened by some motion
of the spirits." (See the "Passions of the Soul," art. 27,
pt. 1.) But since it is possible to join to a certain
volition any motion of the gland, and consequently of the
spirits, and since the determination of the will depends
solely on our power, we shall be able to acquire absolute mastery over our passions provided only we determine our will by fixed and firm decisions by which we
desire to direct our actions and bind with these decisions
the movements of the passions we wish to have. So far
as I can gather from his own words, this is the opinion
of that distinguished man, and I could scarcely have
believed it possible for one so great to have put it forward if it had been less subtle. I can hardly wonder
enough that a philosopher who firmly resolved to make
no deduction except from self-evident principles, and
to affirm nothing but what he clearly and distinctly perceived, and who blamed all the schoolmen because they
desired to explain obscure matters by occult qualities,
should accept a hypothesis more occult than any occult
quality. What does he understand, I ask, by the union
of the mind and body? What clear and distinct conception has he of thought intimately connected with a
certain small portion of matter? I wish that he had
explained this union by its proximate cause. But he
conceived the mind to be so distinct from the body that
he was able to assign no single cause of this union, nor
of the mind itself, but was obliged to have recourse to
the cause of the whole universe, that is to say, to God.
Again, I should like to know how many degrees of
motion the mind can give to that pineal gland, and with
how great a power the mind can hold it suspended. For

[1] After "quæque," the corrigenda to the Ed. Pr. add "ita
Auctor scripserat, N.B." The Dutch version omits the "ita
Auctor scripserat," but retains the "N.B."—TR.

I do not understand whether this gland is acted on by
the mind more slowly or more quickly than by the animal spirits, and whether the movements of the passions,
which we have so closely bound with firm decisions,
might not be separated from them again by bodily
causes, from which it would follow that although the
mind had firmly determined to meet danger, and had
joined to this decision the motion of boldness, the sight
of the danger might cause the gland to be suspended
in such a manner that the mind could think of nothing
but flight. Indeed, since there is no relation between
the will and motion, so there is no comparison between
the power or strength of the body and that of the mind,
and consequently the strength of the body can never
be determined by the strength of the mind. It is to be
remembered also that this gland is not found to be so
situated in the middle of the brain that it can be driven
about so easily and in so many ways, and that all the
nerves are not extended to the cavities of the brain.
Lastly, I omit all that Descartes asserts concerning the
will and the freedom of the will, since I have shown
over and over again that it is false. Therefore, inasmuch
as the power of the mind, as I have shown above, is
determined by intelligence alone, we shall determine by
the knowledge of the mind alone the remedies against
the affects—remedies which every one, I believe, has
experienced, although there may not have been any accurate observation or distinct perception of them, and
from this knowledge of the mind alone shall we deduce
everything which relates to its blessedness.

AXIOMS

1. If two contrary actions be excited in the same
subject, a change must necessarily take place in both,
or in one alone, until they cease to be contrary.

2. The power of an affect is limited by the power of its cause, in so far as the essence of the affect is manifested or limited by the essence of the cause itself.

This axiom is evident from Prop. 7, pt. 3.

PROP. I.—*As thoughts and the ideas of things are arranged and connected in the mind, exactly so are the affections of the body or the images of things arranged and connected in the body.*

Demonst.—The order and connection of ideas is the same (Prop. 7, pt. 2) as the order and connection of things, and *vice versa*, the order and connection of things is the same (Corol. Props. 6 and 7, pt. 2) as the order and connection of ideas. Therefore, as the order and connection of ideas in the mind is according to the order and connection of the affections of the body (Prop. 18, pt. 2), it follows, *vice versa* (Prop. 2, pt. 3), that the order and connection of the affections of the body is according to the order and connection in the mind of the thoughts and ideas of things.—Q.E.D.

PROP. II.—*If we detach an emotion of the mind or affect from the thought of an external cause and connect it with other thoughts, then the love or hatred towards the external cause and the fluctuations of the mind which arise from these affects will be destroyed.*

Demonst.—That which constitutes the form of love or hatred is joy or sorrow, accompanied with the idea of an external cause (Defs. 6 and 7 of the Affects). If this idea therefore be taken away, the form of love or hatred is also removed, and therefore these affects and any others which arise from them are destroyed.—Q.E.D.

PROP. III.—*An affect which is a passion ceases to be a passion as soon as we form a clear and distinct idea of it.*

Demonst.—An affect which is a passion is a confused idea (by the general definition of the Affects). If, therefore, we form a clear and distinct idea of this affect, the idea will not be distinguished—except by reason—from this affect, in so far as the affect is related to the mind alone (Prop. 21, pt. 2, with its Schol.), and therefore (Prop. 3, pt. 3) the affect will cease to be a passion. —Q.E.D.

Corol.—In proportion, then, as we know an affect better is it more within our control, and the less does the mind suffer from it.

PROP. IV.—*There is no affection of the body of which we cannot form some clear and distinct conception.*

Demonst.—Those things which are common to all cannot be otherwise than adequately conceived (Prop. 38, pt. 2), and therefore (Prop. 12, and Lem. 2, following Schol. Prop. 13, pt. 2) there is no affection of the body of which we cannot form some clear and distinct conception.—Q.E.D.

Corol.—Hence it follows that there is no affect of which we cannot form some clear and distinct conception. For an affect is an idea of an affection of the body (by the general definition of the Affects), and this idea therefore (Prop. 4, pt. 5) must involve some clear and distinct conception.

Schol.—Since nothing exists from which some effect does not follow (Prop. 36, pt. 1), and since we understand clearly and distinctly everything which follows from an idea which is adequate in us (Prop. 40, pt. 2),

it is a necessary consequence that every one has the
power, partly at least, if not absolutely, of understanding clearly and distinctly himself and his affects, and
consequently of bringing it to pass that he suffers less
from them. We have therefore mainly to strive to acquire
a clear and distinct knowledge as far as possible of each
affect, so that the mind may be led to pass from the affect
to think those things which it perceives clearly and distinctly, and with which it is entirely satisfied, and to
strive also that the affect may be separated from the
thought of an external cause and connected with true
thoughts. Thus not only love, hatred, &c., will be destroyed (Prop. 2, pt. 5), but also the appetites or
desires to which the affect gives rise cannot be excessive
(Prop. 61, pt. 4). For it is above everything to be
observed that the appetite by which a man is said to act
is one and the same appetite as that by which he is said
to suffer. For example, we have shown that human nature
is so constituted that every one desires that other people
should live according to his way of thinking (Schol.
Prop. 31, pt. 3), a desire which in a man who is not
guided by reason is a passion which is called ambition,
and is not very different from pride; while, on the other
hand, in a man who lives according to the dictates of
reason it is an action or virtue which is called piety
(Schol. 1, Prop. 37, pt. 4, and Demonst. 2 of the same
Prop.). In the same manner, all the appetites or desires
are passions only in so far as they arise from inadequate
ideas, and are classed among the virtues whenever they
are excited or begotten by adequate ideas; for all the
desires by which we are determined to any action may
arise either from adequate or inadequate ideas (Prop. 59,
pt. 4). To return, therefore, to the point from which
we set out: there is no remedy within our power which
can be conceived more excellent for the affects than that

which consists in a true knowledge of them, since the mind possesses no other power than that of thinking and forming adequate ideas, as we have shown above (Prop. 3, pt. 3).

Prop. V.—*An affect towards an object which we do not imagine as necessary, possible, or contingent, but which we simply imagine, is, other things being equal, the greatest of all.*

Demonst.—The affect towards an object which we imagine to be free is greater than towards one which is necessary (Prop. 49, pt. 3), and consequently still greater than towards one which we imagine as possible or contingent (Prop. 11, pt. 4). But to imagine an object as free can be nothing else than to imagine it simply, while we know not the causes by which it was determined to action. (See Schol. Prop. 35, pt. 2.) An affect, therefore, towards an object which we simply imagine is, other things being equal, greater than towards one which we imagine as necessary, possible, or contingent, and consequently greatest of all.—Q.E.D.

Prop. VI.—*In so far as the mind understands all things as necessary, so far has it greater power over the affects, or suffers less from them.*

Demonst.—The mind understands all things to be necessary (Prop. 29, pt. 1), and determined by an infinite chain of causes to existence and action (Prop. 28, pt. 1), and therefore (Prop. 5, pt. 5) so far enables itself to suffer less from the affects which arise from these things, and (Prop. 48, pt. 3) to be less affected towards them.—Q.E.D.

Schol.—The more this knowledge that things are necessary is applied to individual things which we imagine more distinctly and more vividly, the greater is this power of the mind over the affects,—a fact to which experience also testifies. For we see that sorrow for the loss of anything good is diminished if the person who has lost it considers that it could not by any possibility have been preserved. So also we see that nobody pities an infant because it does not know how to speak, walk, or reason, and lives so many years not conscious, as it were, of itself; but if a number of human beings were born adult, and only a few here and there were born infants, every one would pity the infants, because we should then consider infancy not as a thing natural and necessary, but as a defect or fault of nature. Many other facts of a similar kind we might observe.

PROP. VII.—*The affects which spring from reason or which are excited by it are, if time be taken into account, more powerful than those which are related to individual objects which we contemplate as absent.*

Demonst.—We do not contemplate an object as absent by reason of the affect by which we imagine it, but by reason of the fact that the body is affected with another affect, which excludes the existence of that object (Prop. 17, pt. 2). The affect, therefore, which is related to an object which we contemplate as absent, is not of such a nature as to overcome the other actions and power of man (concerning these things see Prop. 6, pt. 4), but, on the contrary, is of such a nature that it can in some way be restrained by those affections which exclude the existence of its external cause (Prop. 9, pt. 4). But the affect which arises from reason is necessarily related to the common properties of things (see the definition of reason in Schol. 2, Prop. 40, pt. 2), which we always contemplate as present (for nothing can exist which excludes their present existence), and which we always imagine in the same way (Prop. 38, pt. 2). This affect, therefore, always remains the same, and consequently (Ax. 1, pt. 5), the affects which are contrary to it, and which are not maintained by their external cause, must more and more accommodate themselves to it until they are no longer contrary to it. So far, therefore, the affect which springs from reason is the stronger.—Q.E.D.

PROP. VIII.—*The greater the number of the causes which simultaneously concur to excite any affect, the greater it will be.*

Demonst.—A number of simultaneous causes can do more than if they were fewer (Prop. 7, pt. 3), and therefore (Prop. 5, pt. 4) the greater the number of the simultaneous causes by which an affect is excited, the greater it is.—Q.E.D.

Schol.—This proposition is also evident from Ax. 2, pt. 5.

PROP. IX.—*If we are affected by an affect which is related to many and different causes, which the mind contemplates at the same time with the affect itself, we are less injured, suffer less from it, and are less affected therefore towards each cause than if we were affected by another affect equally great which is related to one cause only or to fewer causes.*

Demonst.—An affect is bad or injurious only in so far as it hinders the mind from thinking (Props. 26

and 27, pt. 4), and therefore that affect by which the
mind is determined to the contemplation of a number
of objects at the same time is less injurious than another
affect equally great which holds the mind in the contemplation of one object alone or of a few objects, so
that it cannot think of others. This is the first thing
we had to prove. Again, since the essence of the mind,
that is to say (Prop. 7, pt. 3), its power, consists in
thought alone (Prop. 11, pt. 2), the mind suffers less
through an affect by which it is determined to the contemplation of a number of objects at the same time
than through an affect equally great which holds it occupied in the contemplation of one object alone or of a few
objects. This is the second thing we had to prove. Finally, this affect (Prop. 48, pt. 3), in so far as it is
related to a number of external causes, is therefore less
towards each.—Q.E.D.

PROP. X.—*So long as we are not agitated by affects
which are contrary to our nature do we possess the
power of arranging and connecting the affections
of the body according to the order of the intellect.*

Demonst.—The affects which are contrary to our
nature, that is to say (Prop. 30, pt. 4), which are evil,
are evil so far as they hinder the mind from understanding (Prop. 27, pt. 4). So long, therefore, as we are not
agitated by affects which are contrary to our nature, so
long the power of the mind by which it endeavours to
understand things (Prop. 26, pt. 4) is not hindered, and
therefore so long does it possess the power of forming
clear and distinct ideas, and of deducing them the one
from the other (see Schol. 2, Prop. 40, and Schol. Prop.
47, pt. 2). So long, consequently (Prop. 1, pt. 5), do we
possess the power of arranging and connecting the affec-

tions of the body according to the order of the intellect. —Q.E.D.

Schol.—Through this power of properly arranging and connecting the affections of the body we can prevent ourselves from being easily affected by evil affects. For (Prop. 7, pt. 5) a greater power is required to restrain affects which are arranged and connected according to the order of the intellect than is required to restrain those which are uncertain and unsettled. The best thing, therefore, we can do, so long as we lack a perfect knowledge of our affects, is to conceive a right rule of life, or sure maxims (*dogmata*) of life,—to commit these latter to memory, and constantly to apply them to the particular cases which frequently meet us in life, so that our imagination may be widely affected by them, and they may always be ready to hand. For example, amongst the maxims of life we have placed this (see Prop. 46, pt. 4, with its Schol.), that hatred is to be conquered by love or generosity, and is not to be met with hatred in return. But in order that we may always have this prescript of reason in readiness whenever it will be of service, we must think over and often meditate upon the common injuries inflected by men, and consider how and in what way they may best be repelled by generosity; for thus we shall connect the image of injury with the imagination of this maxim, and (Prop. 18, pt. 2) it will be at hand whenever an injury is offered to us. If we also continually have regard to our own true profit, and the good which follows from mutual friendship and common fellowship, and remember that the highest peace of mind arises from a right rule of life (Prop. 52, pt. 4), and also that man, like other things, acts according to the necessity of nature, then the injury or the hatred which usually arises from that necessity will occupy but the least part of the imagination, and will be easily overcome: or supposing that the anger which generally arises from the greatest injuries is not so easily overcome, it will nevertheless be overcome, although not without fluctuation of mind, in a far shorter space of time than would have been necessary if we had not possessed those maxims on which we had thus meditated beforehand. This is evident from Props. 6, 7, and 8, pt. 5.

Concerning strength of mind, we must reflect in the same way for the purpose of getting rid of fear, that is to say, we must often enumerate and imagine the common dangers of life, and think upon the manner in which they can best be avoided and overcome by presence of mind and courage. It is to be observed, however, that in the ordering of our thoughts and images we must always look (Corol. Prop. 63, pt. 4, and Prop. 59, pt. 3) to those qualities which in each thing are good, so that we may be determined to action always by an affect of joy.

For example, if a man sees that he pursues glory too eagerly, let him think on its proper use, for what end it is to be followed, and by what means it can be obtained; but let him not think upon its abuse and vanity, and on the inconstancy of men and things of this sort, about which no one thinks unless through disease of mind; for with such thoughts do those who are ambitious greatly torment themselves when they despair of obtaining the honours for which they are striving; and while they vomit forth rage, wish to be thought wise. Indeed it is certain that those covet glory the most who are loudest in declaiming against its abuse and the vanity of the world. Nor is this a peculiarity of the ambitious, but is common to all to whom fortune is adverse and who are impotent in mind; for we see that a poor and avaricious man is never weary of speak-

ing about the abuse of money and the vices of the rich,
thereby achieving nothing save to torment himself and
show to others that he is unable to bear with equanimity not only his own poverty but also the wealth of
others. So also a man who has not been well received
by his mistress thinks of nothing but the fickleness of
women, their faithlessness, and their other oft-pro-
claimed failings,—all of which he forgets as soon as he
is taken into favour by his mistress again. He, therefore, who desires to govern his affects and appetites
from a love of liberty alone will strive as much as he
can to know virtues and their causes, and to fill his mind
with that joy which springs from a true knowledge of
them. Least of all will he desire to contemplate the
vices of men and disparage men, or to delight in a false
show of liberty. He who will diligently observe these
things (and they are not difficult), and will continue
to practise them, will assuredly in a short space of
time be able for the most part to direct his actions in
accordance with the command of reason.

PROP. XI.—*The greater the number of objects to which
an image is related, the more constant is it, or the
more frequently does it present itself, and the more
does it occupy the mind.*

Demonst.—The greater the number of objects to
which an image or affect is related, the greater is the
number of causes by which it can be excited and
cherished. All these causes the mind contemplates simultaneously by means of the affect (by hypothesis),
and therefore the more constant is the affect, or the
more frequently does it present itself, and the more does
it occupy the mind (Prop. 8, pt. 5).—Q.E.D.

PROP. XII.—*The images of things are more easily connected with those images which are related to things which we clearly and distinctly understand than with any others.*

Demonst.—Things which we clearly and distinctly understand are either the common properties of things or what are deduced from them (see the definition of reason in Schol. 2, Prop. 40, pt. 2), and consequently (Prop. 11, pt. 5) are more frequently excited in us; and therefore it is easier for us to contemplate other things together with these which we clearly and distinctly understand than with any others, and consequently (Prop. 18, pt. 2), it is easier to connect things with these which we clearly and distinctly understand than with any others.

PROP. XIII.—*The greater the number of other things with which any image is connected, the more frequently does it present itself.*

Demonst.—For the greater the number of other things with which an image is connected, the greater is the number of causes (Prop. 18, pt. 2) by which it may be excited.—Q.E.D.

PROP. XIV.—*The mind can cause all the affections of the body or the images of things to be related to the idea of God (ideam Dei).*

Demonst.—There is no affection of the body of which the mind cannot form some clear and distinct conception (Prop. 4, pt. 5), and therefore (Prop. 15, pt. 1) it can cause all the affections of the body to be related to the idea of God.—Q.E.D.

PROP. XV.—*He who clearly and distinctly understands himself and his affects loves God, and loves Him better the better he understands himself and his affects.*

Demonst.—He who clearly and distinctly understands himself and his affects rejoices (Prop. 53, pt. 3), and his joy is attended with the idea of God (Prop. 14, pt. 5), therefore (Def. 6 of the Affects) he loves God, and (by the same reasoning) loves Him better the better he understands himself and his affects.—Q.E.D.

PROP. XVI.—*This love to God above everything else ought to occupy the mind.*

Demonst.—For this love is connected with all the affections of the body (Prop. 14, pt. 5), by all of which it is cherished (Prop. 15, pt. 5), and therefore (Prop. 11, pt. 5) above everything else ought to occupy the mind.—Q.E.D.

PROP. XVII.—*God is free from passions, nor is He affected with any affect of joy or sorrow.*

Demonst.—All ideas, in so far as they are related to God, are true (Prop. 32, pt. 2); that is to say (Def. 4, pt. 2), are adequate, and therefore (by the general definition of the Affects) God is free from passions. Again, God can neither pass to a greater nor to a less perfection (Corol. 2, Prop. 20, pt. 1), and therefore (Defs. 2 and 3 of the Affects) He cannot be affected with any affect of joy or sorrow.—Q.E.D.

Corol.—Properly speaking, God loves no one and hates no one; for God (Prop. 17, pt. 5) is not affected with any affect of joy or sorrow, and consequently (Defs. 6 and 7 of the Affects) He neither loves nor hates any one.

PROP. XVIII.—*No one can hate God.*

Demonst.—The idea of God which is in us is adequate and perfect (Props. 46 and 47, pt. 2), and therefore in so far as we contemplate God do we act (Prop. 3, pt. 3), and consequently (Prop. 59, pt. 3) no sorrow can exist with the accompanying idea of God; that is to say (Def. 7 of the Affects), no one can hate God.—Q.E.D.

Corol.—Love to God cannot be turned into hatred.

Schol.—But some may object, that if we understand God to be the cause of all things, we do for that very reason consider Him to be the cause of sorrow. But I reply, that in so far as we understand the causes of sorrow, it ceases to be a passion (Prop. 3, pt. 5), that is to say (Prop. 59, pt. 3), it ceases to be sorrow; and therefore in so far as we understand God to be the cause of sorrow do we rejoice.

PROP. XIX.—*He who loves God cannot strive that God should love him in return.*

Demonst.—If a man were to strive after this, he would desire (Corol. Prop. 17, pt. 5) that God, whom he loves, should not be God, and consequently (Prop. 19, pt. 3) he would desire to be sad, which (Prop. 28, pt. 3) is absurd. Therefore he who loves God, &c.—Q.E.D.

PROP. XX.—*This love to God cannot be defiled either by the affect of envy or jealousy, but is the more strengthened the more people we imagine to be connected with God by the same bond of love.*

Demonst.—This love to God is the highest good which we can seek according to the dictate of reason (Prop. 28, pt. 4) ; is common to all men (Prop. 36, pt. 4) ; and we desire that all may enjoy it (Prop. 37, pt. 4). It cannot, therefore (Def. 23 of the Affects), be sullied by the affect of envy, nor (Prop. 18, pt. 5, and Def. of Jealousy in Schol. Prop. 35, pt. 3) by that of jealousy, but, on the contrary (Prop. 31, pt. 3), it must be the more strengthened the more people we imagine to rejoice in it.—Q.E.D.

Schol.—It is possible to show in the same manner that there is no affect directly contrary to this love and able to destroy it, and so we may conclude that this love to God is the most constant of all the affects, and that, in so far as it is related to the body, it cannot be destroyed unless with the body itself. What its nature is, in so far as it is related to the mind alone, we shall see hereafter.

I have, in what has preceded, included all the remedies for the affects, that is to say, everything which the mind, considered in itself alone, can do against them. It appears therefrom that the power of the mind over the affects consists—

1. In the knowledge itself of the affects. (See Schol. Prop. 4, pt. 5.)

2. In the separation by the mind of the affects from the thought of an external cause, which we imagine confusedly. (See Prop. 2, pt. 5, and Schol. Prop. 4, pt. 5.)

3. In duration, in which the affections[1] which are related to objects we understand surpass those related to objects conceived in a mutilated or confused manner. (Prop. 7, pt. 5.)

[1] *Affections.* Probably a misprint, however, for *Affectus.*

4. In the multitude of causes by which the affections[1] which are related to the common properties of things or to God are nourished. (Props. 9 and 11, pt. 5.)

5. In the order in which the mind can arrange its affects and connect them one with the other. (Schol. Prop. 10, pt. 5, and see also Props. 12, 13, and 14, pt. 5.)

But that this power of the mind over the affects may be better understood, it is to be carefully observed that we call the affects great when we compare the affect of one man with that of another, and see that one man is agitated more than another by the same affect, or when we compare the affects of one and the same man with one another, and discover that he is affected or moved more by one affect than by another.

For (Prop. 5, pt. 4) the power of any affect is limited by the power of the external cause as compared with our own power. But the power of the mind is limited solely by knowledge, whilst impotence or passion is estimated solely by privation of knowledge, or, in other words, by that through which ideas are called inadequate; and it therefore follows that that mind suffers the most whose largest part consists of inadequate ideas, so that it is distinguished rather by what it suffers than by what it does, while, on the contrary, that mind acts the most whose largest part consists of adequate ideas, so that although it may possess as many inadequate ideas as the first, it is nevertheless distinguished rather by those which belong to human virtue than by those which are a sign of human impotence. Again, it is to be observed that our sorrows and misfortunes mainly proceed from too much love towards an object which is subject to many changes, and which we can never possess. For no one is troubled or anxious about any object he does not love, neither do wrongs, suspicions, hatreds, &c., arise

[1] *Affections.* Probably a misprint, however, for *Affectus.*

except from love towards objects of which no one can be truly the possessor.

From all this we easily conceive what is the power which clear and distinct knowledge, and especially that third kind of knowledge (see Schol. Prop. 47, pt. 2) whose foundation is the knowledge itself of God, possesses over the affects; the power, namely, by which it is able, in so far as they are passions, if not actually to destroy them (see Prop. 3, pt. 5, with the Schol. to Prop. 4, pt. 5), at least to make them constitute the smallest part of the mind (see Prop. 14, pt. 5). Moreover, it begets a love towards an immutable and eternal object (see Prop. 15, pt. 5) of which we are really partakers (see Prop. 45, pt. 2); a love which therefore cannot be vitiated by the defects which are in common love, but which can always become greater and greater (Prop. 15, pt. 5), occupy the largest part of the mind (Prop. 16, pt. 5), and thoroughly affect it.

I have now concluded all that I had to say relating to this present life. For any one who will attend to what has been urged in this scholium, and to the definition of the mind and its affects, and to Props. 1 and 3, pt. 3, will easily be able to see the truth of what I said in the beginning of the scholium, that in these few words all the remedies for the affects are comprehended. It is time, therefore, that I should now pass to the consideration of those matters which appertain to the duration of the mind without relation to the body.

PROP. XXI.—*The mind can imagine nothing, nor can it recollect anything that is past, except while the body exists.*

Demonst.—The mind does not express the actual existence of its body, nor does it conceive as actual the

affections of the body, except while the body exists
(Corol. Prop. 8, pt. 2), and consequently (Prop. 26, pt.
2) it conceives no body as actually existing except while
its own body exists. It can therefore imagine nothing
(see the definition of Imagination in Schol. Prop. 17,
pt. 2), nor can it recollect anything that is past, except
while the body exists (see the definition of Memory in
Schol. Prop. 18, pt. 2).—Q.E.D.

PROP. XXII.—*In God, nevertheless, there necessarily
exists an idea which expresses the essence of this or
that human body under the form of eternity.*

Demonst.—God is not only the cause of the existence
of this or that human body, but also of its essence
(Prop. 25, pt. 1), which therefore must necessarily be
conceived through the essence of God itself (Ax. 4, pt.
1) and by a certain eternal necessity (Prop. 16, pt. 1).
This conception, moreover, must necessarily exist in God
(Prop. 3, pt. 2).—Q.E.D.

PROP. XXIII.—*The human mind cannot be absolutely
destroyed with the body, but something of it remains which is eternal.*

Demonst.—In God there necessarily exists a conception or idea which expresses the essence of the human
body (Prop. 22, pt. 5). This conception or idea is therefore necessarily something which pertains to the essence
of the human mind (Prop. 13, pt. 2). But we ascribe to
the human mind no duration which can be limited by
time, unless in so far as it expresses the actual existence
of the body, which is manifested through duration, and
which can be limited by time, that is to say (Corol.
Prop. 8, pt. 2), we cannot ascribe duration to the mind
except while the body exists.

But nevertheless, since this something is that which is conceived by a certain eternal necessity through the essence itself of God (Prop. 22, pt. 5), this something which pertains to the essence of the mind will necessarily be eternal.—Q.E.D.

Schol.—This idea which expresses the essence of the body under the form of eternity is, as we have said, a certain mode of thought which pertains to the essence of the mind and is necessarily eternal. It is impossible, nevertheless, that we should recollect that we existed before the body, because there are no traces of any such existence in the body, and also because eternity cannot be defined by time, or have any relationship to it. Nevertheless we feel and know by experience that we are eternal. For the mind is no less sensible of those things which it conceives through intelligence than of those which it remembers, for demonstrations are the eyes of the mind by which it sees and observes things.

Although, therefore, we do not recollect that we existed before the body, we feel that our mind, in so far as it involves the essence of the body under the form of eternity, is eternal, and that this existence of the mind cannot be limited by time nor manifested through duration. Only in so far, therefore, as it involves the actual existence of the body can the mind be said to possess duration, and its existence be limited by a fixed time, and so far only has it the power of determining the existence of things in time, and of conceiving them under the form of duration.

PROP. XXIV.—*The more we understand individual objects, the more we understand God.*

Demonst.—This is evident from Corol. Prop. 25, pt. 1.

Prop. XXV.—*The highest effort of the mind and its highest virtue is to understand things by the third kind of knowledge.*

Demonst.—The third kind of knowledge proceeds from an adequate idea of certain attributes of God to an adequate knowledge of the essence of things (see its definition in Schol. 2, Prop. 40, pt. 2); and the more we understand things in this manner (Prop. 24, pt. 5), the more we understand God; and therefore (Prop. 28, pt. 4) the highest virtue of the mind, that is to say (Def. 8, pt. 4), the power or nature of the mind, or (Prop. 7, pt. 3) its highest effort, is to understand things by the third kind of knowledge.—Q.E.D.

Prop. XXVI.—*The better the mind is adapted to understand things by the third kind of knowledge, the more it desires to understand them by this kind of knowledge.*

Demonst.—This is evident; for in so far as we conceive the mind to be adapted to understand things by this kind of knowledge, do we conceive it to be determined to understand things by this kind of knowledge, and consequently (Def. 1 of the Affects) the better the mind is adapted to this way of understanding things, the more it desires it.—Q.E.D.

Prop. XXVII.—*From this third kind of knowledge arises the highest possible peace of mind.*

Demonst.—The highest virtue of the mind is to know God (Prop. 28, pt. 4), or to understand things by the third kind of knowledge (Prop. 25, pt. 5). This virtue is greater the more the mind knows things by this kind of knowledge (Prop. 24, pt. 5), and therefore he who knows things by this kind of knowledge passes to the highest human perfection, and consequently (Def. 2 of the Affects) is affected with the highest joy, which is accompanied with the idea of himself and his own virtue (Prop. 43, pt. 2); and therefore (Def. 25 of the Affects) from this kind of knowledge arises the highest possible peace of mind.—Q.E.D.

PROP. XXVIII.—*The effort or the desire to know things by the third kind of knowledge cannot arise from the first kind, but may arise from the second kind of knowledge.*

Demonst.—This proposition is self-evident; for everything that we clearly and distinctly understand, we understand either through itself or through something which is conceived through itself; or, in other words, ideas which are clear and distinct in us, or which are related to the third kind of knowledge (Schol. 2, Prop. 40, pt. 2), cannot follow from mutilated and confused ideas, which (by the same scholium) are related to the first kind of knowledge, but from adequate ideas, that is to say (by the same scholium), from the second and third kinds of knowledge. Therefore (Def. 1 of the Affects) the desire of knowing things by the third kind of knowledge cannot arise from the first kind, but may arise from the second.—Q.E.D.

PROP. XXIX.—*Everything which the mind understands under the form of eternity, it understands not because it conceives the present actual existence of the body, but because it conceives the essence of the body under the form of eternity.*

Demonst.—In so far as the mind conceives the present existence of its body does it conceive duration which can be determined in time, and so far only has it the power of conceiving things in relation to time (Prop. 21, pt. 5, and Prop. 26, pt. 2). But eternity cannot be manifested through duration (Def. 8, pt. 1), and its explanation; therefore the mind so far has not the power of conceiving things under the form of eternity: but because it is the nature of reason to conceive things under the form of eternity (Corol. 2, Prop. 44, pt. 2), and because it also pertains to the nature of the mind to conceive the essence of the body under the form of eternity (Prop. 23, pt. 5), and excepting these two things nothing else pertains to the nature of the mind (Prop. 13, pt. 2), therefore this power of conceiving things under the form of eternity does not pertain to the mind except in so far as it conceives the essence of the body under the form of eternity.—Q.E.D.

Schol.—Things are conceived by us as actual in two ways; either in so far as we conceive them to exist with relation to a fixed time and place, or in so far as we conceive them to be contained in God, and to follow from the necessity of the divine nature. But those things which are conceived in this second way as true or real we conceive under the form of eternity, and their ideas involve the eternal and infinite essence of God, as we have shown in Prop. 45, pt. 2, to the scholium of which proposition the reader is also referred.

PROP. XXX.—*Our mind, in so far as it knows itself and the body under the form of eternity, necessarily has a knowledge of God, and knows that it is in God and is conceived through Him.*

Demonst.—Eternity is the very essence of God, in so far as that essence involves necessary existence (Def. 8, pt. 1). To conceive things therefore under the form of eternity, is to conceive them in so far as they are conceived through the essence of God as actually existing things, or in so far as through the essence of God they involve existence. Therefore our mind, in so far as it conceives itself and its body under the form of eternity, necessarily has a knowledge of God, and knows, &c.—Q.E.D.

PROP. XXXI.—*The third kind of knowledge depends upon the mind as its formal cause, in so far as the mind itself is eternal.*

Demonst.—The mind conceives nothing under the form of eternity, unless in so far as it conceives the essence of its body under the form of eternity (Prop. 29, pt. 5), that is to say (Props. 21 and 23, pt. 5), unless in so far as it is eternal. Therefore (Prop. 30, pt. 5) in so far as the mind is eternal it has a knowledge of God, which is necessarily adequate (Prop. 46, pt. 2), and therefore in so far as it is eternal it is fitted to know all those things which can follow from this knowledge of God (Prop. 40, pt. 2), that is to say it is fitted to know things by the third kind of knowledge (see the definition of this kind of knowledge in Schol. 2, Prop. 40, pt. 2), of which (Def. 1, pt. 3), in so far as the mind is eternal, it is the adequate or formal cause.—Q.E.D.

Schol.—As each person therefore becomes stronger in this kind of knowledge, the more is he conscious of himself and of God; that is to say, the more perfect and the happier he is, a truth which will still more clearly appear from what follows. Here, however, it is to be observed, that although we are now certain that the mind is eternal in so far as it conceives things under the form of eternity, yet, in order that what we wish to prove may be more easily explained and better understood, we shall consider the mind, as we have hitherto done, as if it had just begun to be, and had just begun to understand things under the form of eternity. This we can do without any risk of error, provided only we are careful to conclude nothing except from clear premises.

PROP. XXXII.—*We delight in whatever we understand by the third kind of knowledge, and our delight is accompanied with the idea of God as its cause.*

Demonst.—From this kind of knowledge arises the highest possible peace of mind, that is to say (Def. 25 of the Affects), the highest joy, attended moreover with the idea of one's self (Prop. 27, pt. 5), and consequently (Prop. 30, pt. 5) attended with the idea of God as its cause.—Q.E.D.

Corol.—From the third kind of knowledge necessarily springs the intellectual love of God.—For from this kind of knowledge arises (Prop. 32, pt. 5) joy attended with the idea of God as its cause, that is to say (Def. 6 of the Affects), the love of God, not in so far as we imagine Him as present (Prop. 29, pt. 5), but in so far as we understand that He is eternal; and that is what I call the intellectual love of God.

PROP. XXXIII.—*The intellectual love of God which arises from the third kind of knowledge is eternal.*

Demonst.—The third kind of knowledge (Prop. 31, pt. 5, and Ax. 3, pt. 1) is eternal, and therefore (by the same axiom) the love which springs from it is necessarily eternal.—Q.E.D.

Schol.—Although this love to God has no beginning (Prop. 33, pt. 5), it nevertheless has all the perfections of love, just as if it had originated;—as we supposed in the corollary of Prop. 32, pt. 5. Nor is there here any difference, excepting that the mind has eternally possessed these same perfections which we imagined as now accruing to it, and has possessed them with the accompanying idea of God as the eternal cause. And if joy consist in the passage to a greater perfection, blessedness must indeed consist in this, that the mind is endowed with perfection itself.

PROP. XXXIV.—*The mind is subject to affects which are related to passions only so long as the body exists.*

Demonst.—An imagination is an idea by which the mind contemplates any object as present (see its definition in Schol. Prop. 17, pt. 2). This idea nevertheless indicates the present constitution of the human body rather than the nature of the external object (Corol. 2, Prop. 16, pt. 2). An affect, therefore (by the general definition of the Affects), is an imagination in so far as it indicates the present constitution of the body, and therefore (Prop. 21, pt. 5) the mind, only so long as the body exists, is subject to affects which are related to passions.—Q.E.D.

Corol.—Hence it follows that no love except intellectual love is eternal.

Schol.—If we look at the common opinion of men, we shall see that they are indeed conscious of the eternity of their minds, but they confound it with duration, and attribute it to imagination or memory, which they believe remain after death.

PROP. XXXV.—*God loves Himself with an infinite intellectual love.*

God is absolutely infinite (Def. 6, pt. 1), that is to say (Def. 6, pt. 2), the nature of God delights in infinite perfection accompanied (Prop. 3, pt. 2) with the idea of Himself, that is to say (Prop. 11, and Def. 1, pt. 1), with the idea of Himself as cause, and this is what, in Corol. Prop. 32, pt. 5, we have called intellectual love.

PROP. XXXVI.—*The intellectual love of the mind towards God is the very love with which He loves Himself, not in so far as He is infinite, but in so far as He can be manifested through the essence of the human mind, considered under the form of eternity; that is to say, the intellectual love of the mind towards God is part of the infinite love with which God loves Himself.*

Demonst.—This love of the mind must be related to the actions of the mind (Corol. Prop. 32, pt. 5, and Prop. 3, pt. 3), and it is therefore an action by which the mind contemplates itself; and which is accompanied with the idea of God as cause (Prop. 32, pt. 5, with the Corol.); that is to say (Corol. Prop. 25, pt. 1, and Corol. Prop. 11, pt. 2), it is an action by which God, in so far as He can be manifested through the human mind, contemplates Himself, the action being accompanied with the idea of Himself; and therefore (Prop. 35, pt. 5), this love of the mind is part of the infinite love with which God loves Himself.—Q.E.D.

Corol.—Hence it follows that God, in so far as He loves Himself, loves men, and consequently that the love of God towards men and the intellectual love of the mind towards God are one and the same thing.

Schol.—Hence we clearly understand that our salvation, or blessedness, or liberty consists in a constant and eternal love towards God, or in the love of God towards men. This love or blessedness is called Glory in the sacred writings, and not without reason. For whether it be related to God or to the mind, it may properly be called repose of mind, which (Defs. 25 and 30 of the Affects) is, in truth, not distinguished from glory. For in so far as it is related to God, it is (Prop. 35, pt. 5) joy (granting that it is allowable to use this word), accompanied with the idea of Himself, and it is the same thing when it is related to the mind (Prop. 27, pt. 5). Again, since the essence of our mind consists in knowledge alone, whose beginning and foundation is God (Prop. 15, pt. 1, and Schol. Prop. 47, pt. 2), it is clear to us in what manner and by what method our mind, with regard both to essence and existence, follows from the divine nature, and continually depends upon God. I thought it worth while for me to notice this here, in order that I might show, by this example, what that knowledge of individual objects which I have called intuitive or of the third kind (Schol. 2, Prop. 40, pt. 2) is able to do, and how much more potent it is than the universal knowledge, which I have called knowledge of the second kind. For although I have shown generally in the First Part that all things, and consequently also the human mind, depend upon God both with regard to existence and essence, yet that demonstration, although legitimate, and placed beyond the possibility of a doubt, does not, nevertheless, so affect our mind as a proof from the essence itself of any individual object which we say depends upon God.

PROP. XXXVII.—*There is nothing in nature which is contrary to this intellectual love, or which can negate it.*

This intellectual love necessarily follows from the nature of the mind, in so far as it is considered, through the nature of God, as an eternal truth (Props. 33 and 29, pt. 5). If there were anything, therefore, contrary to this love, it would be contrary to the truth, and consequently whatever might be able to negate this love would be able to make the true false, which (as is self-evident) is absurd. There exists, therefore, nothing in nature, &c.—Q.E.D.

Schol.—The axiom of the Fourth Part refers only to individual objects, in so far as they are considered in relation to a fixed time and place. This, I believe, no one can doubt.

PROP. XXXVIII.—*The more objects the mind understands by the second and third kinds of knowledge, the less it suffers from those affects which are evil, and the less it fears death.*

Demonst.—The essence of the mind consists in knowledge (Prop. 11, pt. 2). The more things, therefore, the mind knows by the second and third kinds of knowledge, the greater is that part which abides (Props. 29 and 23, pt. 5), and consequently (Prop. 37, pt. 5) the greater is that part which is not touched by affects which are contrary to our nature, that is to say (Prop. 30, pt. 4), which are evil. The more things, therefore, the mind understands by the second and third kinds of knowledge, the greater is that part which remains unharmed, and the less consequently does it suffer from the affects.

Schol.—We are thus enabled to understand that which I touched upon in Schol. Prop. 39, pt. 4, and which I promised to explain in this part, namely, that death is by so much the less injurious to us as the clear and distinct knowledge of the mind is greater, and consequently as the mind loves God more. Again, since (Prop. 27, pt. 5) from the third kind of knowledge there arises the highest possible peace, it follows that it is possible for the human mind to be of such a nature that that part of it which we have shown perishes with its body (Prop. 21, pt. 5), in comparison with the part of it which remains, is of no consequence. But more fully upon this subject presently.

PROP. XXXIX.—*He who possesses a body fit for many things possesses a mind of which the greater part is eternal.*

Demonst.—He who possesses a body fitted for doing many things is least of all agitated by those affects which are evil (Prop. 38, pt. 4), that is to say (Prop. 30, pt. 4), by affects which are contrary to our nature, and therefore (Prop. 10, pt. 5) he possesses the power of arranging and connecting the affections of the body according to the order of the intellect, and consequently (Prop. 14, pt. 5) of causing all the affections of the body to be related to the idea of God (Prop. 15, pt. 5); in consequence of which he is affected with a love to God, which (Prop. 16, pt. 5) must occupy or form the greatest part of his mind, and therefore (Prop. 33, pt. 5) he possesses a mind of which the greatest part is eternal.

Schol.—Inasmuch as human bodies are fit for many things, we cannot doubt the possibility of their possessing such a nature that they may be related to minds which have a large knowledge of themselves and of God, and whose greatest or principal part is eternal, so that they scarcely fear death. To understand this more clearly, it is to be here considered that we live in con-

stant change, and that according as we change for the
better or the worse we are called happy or unhappy.
For he who passes from infancy or childhood to death
is called unhappy, and, on the other hand, we consider
ourselves happy if we can pass through the whole period
of life with a sound mind in a sound body. Moreover,
he who, like an infant or child, possesses a body fit for
very few things, and almost altogether dependent on
external causes, has a mind which, considered in itself
alone, is almost entirely unconscious of itself, of God,
and of objects. On the other hand, he who possesses
a body fit for many things possesses a mind which, considered in itself alone, is largely conscious of itself, of
God, and of objects. In this life, therefore, it is our
chief endeavour to change the body of infancy, so far as
its nature permits and is conducive thereto, into another
body which is fitted for many things, and which is related to a mind conscious as much as possible of itself,
of God, and of objects; so that everything which is
related to its memory or imagination, in comparison
with the intellect is scarcely of any moment, as I have
already said in the scholium of the preceding proposition.

PROP. XL.—*The more perfection a thing possesses, the
    more it acts and the less it suffers, and conversely
    the more it acts the more perfect it is.*

Demonst.—The more perfect a thing is, the more
reality it possesses (Def. 6, pt. 2), and consequently
(Prop. 3, pt. 3, with the Schol.) the more it acts and
the less it suffers. Inversely also it may be demonstrated in the same way that the more a thing acts the
more perfect it is.—Q.E.D.

Corol.—Hence it follows that that part of the mind
which abides, whether great or small, is more perfect

than the other part. For the part of the mind which is
eternal (Props. 23 and 29, pt. 5) is the intellect, through
which alone we are said to act (Prop. 3, pt. 3), but
that part which, as we have shown, perishes, is the
imagination itself (Prop. 21, pt. 5), through which alone
we are said to suffer (Prop. 3, pt. 3, and the general
definition of the affects). Therefore (Prop. 40, pt. 5)
that part which abides, whether great or small, is more
perfect than the latter.—Q.E.D.

Schol.—These are the things I proposed to prove concerning the mind, in so far as it is considered without
relation to the existence of the body, and from these,
taken together with Prop. 21, pt. 1, and other propositions, it is evident that our mind, in so far as it
understands, is an eternal mode of thought, which is
determined by another eternal mode of thought, and
this again by another, and so on *ad infinitum,* so that all
taken together form the eternal and infinite intellect
of God.[1]

PROP. XLI.—*Even if we did not know that our mind is
eternal, we should still consider as of primary importance Piety and Religion, and absolutely everything which in the Fourth Part we have shown to
be related to strength of mind and generosity.*

Demonst.—The primary and sole foundation of virtue
or of the proper conduct of life (by Corol. Prop. 22, and
Prop. 24, pt. 4) is to seek our own profit. But in order
to determine what reason prescribes as profitable, we
had no regard to the eternity of the mind, which we did
not recognise till we came to the Fifth Part. Therefore,

[1] Thus the modes are eternal as modes in God. This concep-
tion of a hierarchy of modes may have been suggested by
Maimonides, who, however, rejected the idea. See Letter
XXIII. [Ed.]

although we were at that time ignorant that the mind is eternal, we considered as of primary importance those things which we have shown are related to strength of mind and generosity; and therefore, even if we were now ignorant of the eternity of the mind, we should consider those commands of reason as of primary importance.—Q.E.D.

School.—The creed of the multitude seems to be different from this; for most persons seem to believe that they are free in so far as it is allowed them to obey their lusts, and that they give up a portion of their rights, in so far as they are bound to live according to the commands of divine law. Piety, therefore, and religion, and absolutely all those things that are related to greatness of soul, they believe to be burdens which they hope to be able to lay aside after death; hoping also to receive some reward for their bondage, that is to say, for their piety and religion. It is not merely this hope, however, but also and chiefly fear of dreadful punishments after death, by which they are induced to live according to the commands of divine law, that is to say, as far as their feebleness and impotent mind will permit; and if this hope and fear were not present to them, but if they, on the contrary, believed that minds perish with the body, and that there is no prolongation of life for miserable creatures exhausted with the burden of their piety, they would return to ways of their own liking; they would prefer to let everything be controlled by their own passions, and to obey fortune rather than themselves.

This seems to me as absurd as if a man, because he does not believe that he will be able to feed his body with good food to all eternity, should desire to satiate himself with poisonous and deadly drugs; or as if, because he sees that the mind is not eternal or immortal, he should therefore prefer to be mad and to live without reason,—absurdities so great that they scarcely deserve to be repeated.

PROP. XLII.—*Blessedness is not the reward of virtue, but is virtue itself; nor do we delight in blessedness because we restrain our lusts; but, on the contrary, because we delight in it, therefore are we able to restrain them.*

Demonst.—Blessedness consists in love towards God (Prop. 36, pt. 5, and its Schol.), which arises from the third kind of knowledge (Corol. Prop. 32, pt. 5), and this love, therefore (Props. 59 and 3, pt. 3), must be related to the mind in so far as it acts. Blessedness, therefore (Def. 8, pt. 4), is virtue itself, which was the first thing to be proved. Again, the more the mind delights in this divine love or blessedness, the more it understands (Prop. 32, pt. 5), that is to say (Corol. Prop. 3, pt. 5), the greater is the power it has over its affects, and (Prop. 38, pt. 5) the less it suffers from affects which are evil. Therefore, it is because the mind delights in this divine love or blessedness that it possesses the power of restraining the lusts; and because the power of man to restrain the affects is in the intellect alone, no one, therefore, delights in blessedness because he has restrained his affects, but, on the contrary, the power of restraining his lusts springs from blessedness itself.—Q.E.D.

Schol.—I have finished everything I wished to explain concerning the power of the mind over the affects and concerning its liberty. From what has been said we see what is the strength of the wise man, and how much he surpasses the ignorant who is driven forward by lust alone. For the ignorant man is not only agitated by external causes in many ways, and never enjoys true peace of soul, but lives also ignorant, as it were, both of God and of things, and as soon as he ceases to suffer ceases also to be. On the other hand, the wise man, in so far as he is considered as such, is scarcely ever moved in his mind, but, being conscious by a certain eternal necessity of himself, of God, and of things, never ceases to be, and always enjoys true peace of soul. If the way which, as I have shown, leads hither seem very difficult, it can nevertheless be found. It must indeed be difficult since it is so seldom discovered; for if salvation lay ready to hand and could be discovered without great labour, how could it be possible that it should be neglected almost by everybody? But all noble things are as difficult as they are rare.

THE LETTERS

OF CERTAIN LEARNED MEN

TO B. D. S.

AND THE AUTHOR'S REPLIES

CONTRIBUTING NOT A LITTLE TO
THE ELUCIDATION OF HIS OTHER WORKS

Letter I   HENRY OLDENBURG

TO THE VERY ILLUSTRIOUS MR. B. D. S.

(Combining God and the Errors of Descartes and Bacon.)

VERY ILLUSTRIOUS SIR, HONOURED FRIEND,

So reluctantly did I tear myself away from your side recently when I was with you in your retreat at Rhynsburg, that no sooner am I back in England than I strive, as far as possible, to rejoin you at least by an exchange of letters. Solid learning combined with humanity and refinement of character (with all of which Nature and Industry have most amply endowed you) provide such charms of their own that they win the love of all men who are open-minded and liberally educated. Come, then, most excellent Sir, and let us join our right hands in unfeigned friendship, and let us diligently cultivate it with every kind of devotion and service.

If anything from my slender store can be of service to you, consider it yours. As to the gifts of mind which you possess, allow me to claim a share of them, since this can be done without detriment to you.

At Rhynsburg we conversed about God, about infinite Extension and Thought, about the difference and the agreement of these attributes, about the nature of the union of the human soul with the body; also about the Principles of the Cartesian and the Baconian Philosophy. But as we then discoursed about problems of such moment as through a lattice and only in a hurry, and they continue to crucify my mind, let me venture to plead with you by right of the friendship begun between us, and to ask you very cordially to set forth your ideas on the above-mentioned subjects somewhat more fully, and especially not to mind instructing me in the following two points, namely, first, wherein you place the true distinction between Extension and Thought, and secondly, what defects you observe in the Philosophy of Descartes and of Bacon, and how you consider that these defects may be removed from their midst, and sounder views be substituted for them. The more freely you write to me on these and similar subjects, the more closely will you bind me to you, and you will strongly put me under an obligation to render equivalent services, if only I can.

Here there are already in the press *Certain Physiological Essays*, written by a certain English Noble, a man of excellent erudition. They treat of the nature of air and of its Elastic property, established by forty-three experiments; also of Fluidity and Firmness, and the like. As soon as they are printed I will see to it that they are delivered to you by a friend who is probably crossing the sea shortly.

Meanwhile farewell, and keep in memory your friend
who is

Yours in all love and devotion,

HENRY OLDENBURG

LONDON, $\frac{16}{26}$ *August* 1661.

Letter II   B. D. S.

TO THE VERY NOBLE AND LEARNED

MR. HENRY OLDENBURG.

(*Reply to the Preceding.*)

VERY ILLUSTRIOUS SIR,

How pleasant your friendship is to me you will be
able to judge for yourself if only you can prevail upon
your modesty to allow you to consider the excellent
qualities which you have in abundance, and although,
when I consider them, I seem to myself to be not a
little bold because assuredly I dare to enter into friendship with you, especially when I consider that all the
possessions of friends, particularly those that are spiritual, ought to be shared, yet this step will have to be
attributed to your humanity and benevolence rather than
to me. From the height of this humanity you have been
willing to lower yourself and to enrich me with the
abundance of your benevolence to such an extent that
I do not fear to enter into that close friendship which
you steadfastly offer me, and which you deign to ask
from me in return, and I will make it my earnest care
to cultivate it diligently. With regard to my mental
endowments, if I possess any, I should most willingly

allow you to make a claim upon them, even if I knew it would be to my great detriment. But lest I seem in this way to wish to decline what you ask of me by right of our friendship, I will try to set forth what I think about the subjects of which we spoke, although I do not think that this will be a means of binding you more closely to me without the intervention of your kindness.

I will begin, then, to speak briefly of God, whom I define as a Being consisting of infinite attributes of which each is infinite, or in the highest degree perfect of its kind. Here it should be noted that I understand by attribute all that which is conceived through itself, and in itself; so that its conception does not involve the conception of some other thing. For example, Extension is conceived through itself, and in itself; but not so Motion.[1] For it is conceived as in something else, and its conception involves Extension. That this is, indeed, the true definition of God is clear from the fact that we understand by God a Being supremely perfect, and absolutely infinite. That such a Being exists, it is easy to prove from this definition; but, since this is not the place for it, I will omit the proof.

But what I ought to prove here in order to satisfy your first enquiry, most illustrious Sir, are the following. First, that in nature there cannot exist two substances, unless they differ in their whole essence. Secondly, that a substance cannot be produced; but that existence pertains to the essence thereof. Thirdly, that every substance must be infinite or supremely perfect of its kind. When these points have been proved you will easily be able, most illustrious Sir, to see my

[1] Hence though eternal and following directly *from* the Attribute of Extension, Motion is only an Infinite Mode. [Ed.]

trend of thought, if only you will also pay attention
to my definition of God, so that there is no need to
speak more clearly on these matters. But in order to
prove these points clearly and briefly I could think of
nothing better than to submit for your consideration
such proofs after the manner of Geometry, and so I
send them [1] here separately, and await your verdict on
them.

You ask me, secondly, what errors I observe in the
Philosophy of Descartes and of Bacon. In this matter,
although it is not my custom to expose the errors of
others, I am nevertheless willing to gratify you. The
first, then, and greatest error, is that they have strayed
so far from the knowledge of the First Cause and of
the origin of all things. The second is that they did not
know the true nature of the human Mind. The third
is that they never arrived at the true cause of Error.
The extreme necessity of a true knowledge of these
three things is only ignored by those who are utterly
destitute of learning and training. That they have
strayed from the knowledge of the First Cause and of
the human Mind is easily gathered from the truth of
the three propositions mentioned above: wherefore I
turn to the demonstration of the third error alone. I
will say little of Bacon who speaks quite confusedly
on this subject, and proves almost nothing, but only
makes assertions. For, first, he supposes that, besides
the deception of the senses, the human intellect is fallible
by its very nature, and imagines everything after the
analogy of its own nature, and not after the analogy
of the universe, so that it is like an uneven mirror
[turned] to the rays of things, which mingles its own
nature with the nature of the things, etc. Secondly, that

[1] See *Ethics*, Part I from the beginning up to Proposition IV.

the human intellect on account of its peculiar nature is prone to make abstractions, and imagines things to be stable which are in flux, etc. Thirdly, that the human understanding is unquiet, it cannot stop or rest. And such other causes as he assigns can easily all be reduced to the single one of Descartes, namely, because the human will is free and wider in scope than the intellect, or, as Verulam [1] himself more confusedly says (Aphorism 49), because the intellect is no dry light, but receives an infusion from the will. (Here it should be noted that Verulam often uses Intellect for Mind, in which respect he differs from Descartes.) Therefore, taking little notice of the other reasons which are of no moment, I will show that this reason is false, a fact which they, too, would easily have seen if they had only paid attention to this, namely, that will differs from this or that volition in the same way as whiteness differs from this or that white thing, or humanity from this or that man; so that it is just as impossible to conceive that will is the cause of this or that volition as that humanity is the cause of Peter and Paul. Since, therefore, will is nothing but a thing of reason and cannot be said to be in any way the cause of this or that volition, and particular volitions, since they need a cause in order to exist, cannot be said to be free, but are necessarily what they are determined to be by their causes, and, lastly, since, according to Descartes, these very errors are particular volitions, it necessarily follows that errors, that is, particular volitions, are not free, but are determined by external causes, and in no way by will. This is what I promised to prove. Etc.

[RHYNSBURG, *September* 1661.]

[1] See *Novum Organum*. Book I, Aphorisms 48-51.

Letter IX (in part)   B. D. S.

TO THE VERY LEARNED YOUNG MAN SIMON
DE VRIES.

(*On the Nature of Definition and Axiom.*)

HONOURED FRIEND,

I have received your letter which I have so long
desired, and I thank you very much for it and for your
affection towards me. Your long absence has been no
less disagreeable to me than to you; meanwhile however
I am glad that my night-work is of use to you and to
our friends. For in this way I speak with you from afar
while you are absent. You have no reason to envy
Casearius. Indeed, there is no one whom I find more
disagreeable, or with whom I have been more careful
to be on my guard than with him; so that I should
like you and all our acquaintances to be warned not to
communicate my opinions to him until he shall have
attained to a riper age. He is too boyish as yet, rather
unstable, and more eager for novelty than for truth.
Yet I hope that he will cure himself of these puerile
faults in a few years. Indeed I am almost sure of
it, as far as I can judge from his nature; and so his
character makes me fond of him. * * * * *

As to your remark that you do not conceive of
Thought except under ideas, because when you take
away ideas you destroy thought, I believe that this
happens to you because while you, who are a thinking
being, do this, you set aside all your thoughts and conceptions. Therefore it is not to be wondered at that
when you have set aside all your thoughts there remains
nothing for you to think about. As regards the main

thing, I think I have sufficiently, plainly, and clearly proved that intellect, even though infinite, pertains to created Nature, not to creating Nature.

But I do not yet see what this has to do with the understanding of the third definition, nor even why it should cause difficulty. For the definition as I gave it you, unless I am mistaken, reads as follows: *By substance I mean that which is in itself and is conceived through itself, that is, whose conception does not involve the conception of some other thing. I mean the same by attribute, except that it is called attribute with respect to the intellect, which attributes such and such a nature to substance.* This definition, I say, explains clearly enough what I wish you to understand by substance or attribute. You however wish me to explain by means of an example, which it is very easy to do, how one and the same thing can be called by two names. But, not to seem niggardly, I will supply two examples. First, I say that by the name Israel I mean the third Patriarch, I also mean the same Patriarch by the name Jacob, since the name Jacob was given to him because he had seized his brother's heel. Secondly by plane I mean that which reflects all the rays of light without any change; I mean the same by white, except that it is called white in relation to a man who is looking at the plane [surface].

With this I think I have fully answered your questions. Meanwhile I shall wait to hear your judgment; and if there is yet anything which you do not consider to be well or clearly enough demonstrated, then be not shy to point it out to me, etc.

[RHYNSBURG, *March* 1663.]

Letter X   B. D. S.

To the Most Learned Young Man
Simon De Vries.

(The Limitations of Experience.)

Honoured Friend,

You ask me whether we need experience to know whether the Definition of some Attribute is true. To this I reply, that we only need Experience in the case of whatever cannot be deduced from the definition of a thing, as, for instance, the existence of Modes: for this cannot be deduced from the definition of a thing. But we do not need experience in the case of those things whose existence is not distinguished from their essence, and therefore follows from their definition.[1] Indeed, no experience will ever be able to teach us this: for experience does not teach us the essence of things; the utmost which it can effect is to determine our mind so that it only thinks of certain essences of things. Therefore, since the existence of attributes does not differ from their essence, we shall not be able to apprehend it by any kind of experience.

You ask furthermore whether even things or the states of things are eternal truths? I answer certainly. If you continue, why do I not call them eternal truths? I answer, in order that I may distinguish them, as all usually do, from those which do not explain any thing or any state of a thing, as, for instance, *nothing is produced from nothing.* This I say, and similar propositions, are called absolutely eternal truths, by which

[1] Thus Spinoza's proof of God is primarily a priori. Hence also his criticism of Boyle and empirical science in general. [Ed.]

they wish to indicate nothing else than that such things have no place outside the mind, etc.

[RHYNSBURG, *about March* 1663.]

Letter XII   B. D. S.

To the Very Learned and Very Expert

Ludovicus Meyer, p.m.q.d.

(*On the Nature of the Infinite.*)

DISTINGUISHED FRIEND,

I have received two letters from you, one dated 11 January, and delivered to me by our friend N. N.; the other dated 26 March, and sent to me by some friend, I do not know by whom, from Leyden. Both were most welcome; particularly because I gathered from them that all is very well with you and that you frequently think of me. I give you, then, my best thanks, such as I owe you, for your kindness towards me, and for the honour which you have ever deigned to do me; and I beg you at the same time to believe that I am no less devoted to you, which I shall always endeavour to show, as much as my slender powers will allow, when the opportunity is given me. And to begin, I shall be careful to reply to the question which you ask me in your letters.

You ask me, then, to communicate to you the results of my thoughts about the Infinite, which I shall most gladly do.

The question concerning the Infinite has always seemed most difficult, or rather insoluble, to all, because they did not distinguish between what must be infinite because of its own nature, or in virtue of its definition, and that which has no limits, not indeed in virtue of its essence, but in virtue of its cause. And also because they did not distinguish between that which is called infinite because it has no limits, and that whose parts we cannot equate with or explain by any number, although we know its maximum and minimum. And lastly because they did not distinguish between that which we can only understand but cannot imagine, and that which we can also imagine. I say that if they had paid attention to these distinctions, then they would not have been overwhelmed by such a vast crowd of difficulties. For they would then have clearly understood which kind of infinite cannot be divided into parts, or can have no parts, and which, on the contrary, [has parts] and that without contradiction. Moreover, they would also have understood which kind of Infinite can be conceived as greater than another Infinite, without any complication, and which cannot be so conceived; as will become clearly apparent from what I shall soon have to say.

But, first, let me in a few words explain these four, namely, Substance, Mode, Eternity, and Duration. The things that I should like to be noted about Substance are the following—First, that existence pertains to its essence, that is, that its existence follows from its mere essence and definition: this, unless my memory deceives me, I have already proved to you some time ago by word of mouth without the help of other propositions. The second point, which follows from this first one, is that substance is not one of many, but that there exists only one of the same nature. Thirdly and lastly, no substance can be conceived as other than infinite. I call the states of substance Modes, whose definition, in so far as it is not the definition of Substance, cannot involve existence. Therefore, although they exist, we can conceive them as non-existent, from which it also follows that when we are considering only the essence of Modes, and not the whole order of Nature, we cannot from the fact that they now exist deduce that they will exist or will not exist in the future, or that they existed or did not exist in the past. Hence it is clear that we conceive the existence of Substance as entirely different from the existence of Modes. Hence arises the difference between Eternity and Duration: for by means of Duration we can only explain the existence of Modes, but we can only explain the existence of Substance by means of Eternity, that is, the infinite enjoyment of existence or (in awkward Latin) *essendi.*

From all this it is clear that we can at will determine the existence and duration of Modes and conceive it as greater or less, and divide it into parts, when, as most frequently happens, we are considering their essence only and not the order of Nature. Indeed we can do so without thereby in any way destroying the conception which we have of them. But Eternity and Substance, since they cannot be conceived as other than infinite, cannot be treated thus without our destroying our conception of them at the same time. Therefore those who think that Extended Substance consists of parts, or of bodies really distinct from one another, are talking foolishly, not to say madly. For this is just as if one endeavoured, by merely adding together and accumulating many circles, to form a square, or a triangle, or something else different in its whole essence. Therefore that whole medley of arguments, by which Philosophers generally try to show that Extended Substance is finite, collapses of its own accord: for they all suppose that corporeal substance is composed of parts. In the same way others, who have persuaded themselves that a line is composed of points, could also find many arguments by which they would prove that a line is not divisible to infinity.

If however you ask why, by some natural impulse we are so prone to divide extended substance, I reply, because we conceive quantity in two ways, namely, abstractly or superficially, in so far as we have it in our imagination by the help of the senses; or as substance, which happens only through the intellect alone. And so if we consider quantity as it is in the imagination, as happens most frequently and more easily, it will be found to be divisible, finite, composed of parts, and one of many. But if we consider it as it is in our intellect, and if the thing is apprehended as it is in itself, which is very difficult to do, then, as I have sufficiently proved to you before now (if I remember rightly) it will be found to be infinite, indivisible and unique.

Moreover, because we can determine Duration and Quantity as we please, namely, when we conceive the latter abstracted from Substance and we separate the former from the mode whereby it flows from eternal things, there arise Time and Measure; Time to determine Duration and Measure to determine Quantity in such a way that, as far as possible, we may imagine them easily. Then because we separate the states of Substance from Substance itself, and reduce them to classes, so that, as far as possible, we may imagine them easily, there arises Number by which we determine them. Hence one can see clearly that Measure, Time and Number are nothing but Modes of thought or rather of imagination. Therefore it is not to be wondered at that all who have tried to understand the course of Nature by such Notions, and these moreover ill understood, should have so marvellously entangled themselves that at length they could not extricate themselves except by breaking up everything and committing even the most absurd absurdities. For since there are many things which we cannot grasp with the imagination, but only with the intellect, such as Substance, Eternity, and others—if any one tries to explain such things by Notions of this kind, which are merely aids to the imagination, he does nothing more than take pains to rave with his imagination. And even the Modes of Substance themselves can never be rightly understood if they are confused with such things of Reason or with aids of the imagination. For when we do this we separate them from Substance and from the mode by which they flow from Eternity, without which, however, they cannot be rightly understood.

In order that you may see this still more clearly take this example: if anyone conceived Duration abstractly, and, confusing it with Time, began to divide it into parts, he would never be able to understand how, for instance, an hour can pass. For in order that the hour may pass it will be necessary for the half of it to pass first, and then a half of what is left, and then a half of what remains of this remainder; and if you thus go on indefinitely, subtracting the half of what is left, you will never be able to reach the end of the hour. Therefore, many who have not got used to distinguishing the things of reason from real things, have dared to declare that Duration is composed of moments, and so have rushed upon Scylla in their desire to avoid Charybdis. For to say that Duration is composed of moments is the same as to say that Number is obtained from the mere addition of noughts.

Moreover, as is sufficiently clear from what has just been said, neither Number, nor Measure, nor Time, inasmuch as they are only aids of the imagination, can be infinite. For otherwise Number would not be number.

nor Measure measure, nor Time time. Hence one may
see clearly why many who confused these three with
real things, because they did not know the true nature
of things, actually denied that there is an Infinite. But
how lamentably they have argued let the mathematicians
judge, whom arguments of this kind could not put off
in matters which were clearly and distinctly perceived
by them. For they have not only discovered many things
which cannot be expressed by any number, which shows
sufficiently the inadequacy of numbers to determine
everything, but they also have many things which cannot
be equated with any number but exceed any number
that can be given. But they do not conclude that such
things exceed every number because of the multitude of
their parts, but because the nature of the thing cannot
admit number without manifest contradiction. For instance, all the inequalities of the
space A B C D between the two
circles and all the variations which
matter moving therein must undergo,
exceed every number. This conclusion is not drawn because of the
excessive size of the intervening
space. For however small a portion
of it we take, yet the inequalities of
this small portion will exceed every
number. Nor is this conclusion reached because, as happens in other cases, we do not know the maximum and
minimum—for we have both in this example of ours,
namely, the maximum A B, and the minimum C D.
The conclusion is only reached because the nature of
the space interposed between two circles having different centres cannot be so treated. And so if any one
wishes to determine all these inequalities by some defi-

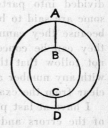

nite number, then he will, at the same time, have to bring it about that a circle should not be a circle.

Similarly, to return to our point, if any one wishes to determine all the motions of matter which have taken place hitherto, namely, by reducing them and their Duration to a definite number and time, he will be attempting nothing else than to deprive corporeal Substance, which we cannot conceive except as existing, of its states, and to bring it about that it should not have the nature which it has. This, as also many other things on which I have touched in this letter, I could clearly prove here, did I not think it superfluous.

From all that has now been said one can clearly see that certain things are infinite in their own nature, and can in no wise be conceived as finite; that some, however, are so in virtue of the cause on which they depend, yet when they are considered abstractly, they can be divided into parts and viewed as finite; lastly, that some are said to be infinite or, if you prefer, indefinite, because they cannot be equated with any number, yet they can be conceived as greater or less. For it does not follow that those things which cannot be equated with any number are necessarily equal, as is sufficiently clear from the example adduced and from many others.

I have at last put briefly before your eyes the causes of the errors and confusions which have arisen about the question of the Infinite, and, unless I am mistaken, I have thus explained them all in such a way that I do not think that there remains any question about the Infinite on which I have not touched here, or which cannot be very easily answered from what has been said. Therefore I do not think it worth while to detain you any longer with these things.

But here I should like it to be noted in passing that the more recent Peripatetics, as I at least think, misunderstood the argument of the Ancients by which they strove to prove the existence of God. For, as I find it in the works of a certain Jew, named Rab Chasdai, it reads as follows. If there is an infinite regression of causes, then all things which exist will be things that have been caused. But it cannot pertain to anything that has been caused that it should necessarily exist in virtue of its own nature. Therefore there is in Nature nothing to whose essence it pertains that it should exist necessarily. But this is absurd: and therefore also that. Therefore the force of the argument lies not in the idea that it is impossible for the Infinite actually to exist, or that a regression of causes to infinity is impossible, but only in the impossibility of supposing that things which do not exist necessarily in virtue of their own nature, are not determined to existence by something which does exist necessarily in virtue of its own nature, and which is a Cause, not an Effect.

Since time forces me to hasten, I should now like to turn to your second letter: but I shall more easily be able to reply to its contents when you have deigned to visit me. Therefore, I beg you, if it can be done, to come as soon as possible: for the time of my removal is rapidly approaching.

That is all. Farewell and remember me, who am, etc.

RHYNSBURG, 20 *April* 1663.

Letter XVIII   WILLIAM VAN BLYENBERGH

TO THE VERY ILLUSTRIOUS MR. B. D. S.

(*On God and the Nature of Good and Evil.*)

[Blyenbergh asks how it can be, since God maintains all things in their state by a continuous creation, that evil or sinful acts such as Adam's disobedience against God, occur. Ed.]

Letter XIX   B. D. S.

To the Very Learned and Prudent
Mr. William van Blyenbergh.

(*Reply to the Preceding.*)

Sir and very welcome Friend,

Your letter of the 12th December, enclosed in another of the 21st December, I only received on the 26th
of the same month, while I was at Schiedam. I gathered
from them your great love of truth, and that it alone is
the aim of all your endeavours. This made me, who also
have nothing else in view, decide not only fully to grant
your request, namely, that I should be willing to answer,
according to my understanding, the questions which you
send me now or will send me in the future, but also
on my side to do all that can promote our closer acquaintance and sincere friendship. For, of all the things which
are beyond my power nothing is more esteemed by me
than to be allowed to have the honour of entering into
the bonds of friendship with people who sincerely love
truth. For I believe that of the things beyond our power,
there is nothing in the world which we can love with
tranquillity except such men. For it is as impossible to
dissolve the love which such bear one another, since
it is founded on the love which each has for the knowledge of truth, as it is to refuse to embrace the truth
once it has been grasped. Moreover, it is the greatest
and most pleasant which can be found among things
which are not within our power; since nothing but truth
can unite together different views and dispositions. I
pass over the very great advantages which follow from
it, that I may not detain you longer with things which
no doubt you know yourself. I have done so thus far in
order the better to show you how pleasant it is to me,

and will be in future, to be allowed to have an opportunity of being able to show my ready service.

And, in order to seize the present opportunity, I will agree to answer your question which turns on this point, namely, that it seems clearly to follow from God's Providence, which is the same as His will, as well as from God's coöperation and the perpetual creation of things, either that there are no sins and no evil, or that God causes the sins and the evil. But you do not explain what you mean by evil: and, as far as I can see from the example of Adam's determined will, you seem to mean by evil the will itself in so far as it is conceived to be so *determined, or to be such as to be opposed to the command of God*; and therefore (as I should also admit, if that were so) there seems a great absurdity in asserting either of these two, namely, that God Himself brings to pass things opposed to His will, or that they are good although opposed to God's will. But I for my part cannot admit that *sins and evil are something positive, much less that anything can exist or come to pass against the will of God. On the contrary, I say that not only is sin not something positive, but also that only improperly and when speaking in human fashion can we say that we sin against God, just as when we say that men make God angry.*

For, as to the first point, we know well that everything that is, considered in itself and without regard to anything else, includes perfection, which always extends in each thing as far as does the essence of the thing itself. For it is indeed nothing different. I also take, for example, the resolution or the determined will of Adam to eat of the forbidden fruit; this resolution or determined will, considered in itself, includes as much perfection as it expresses essence. This we may understand from the fact that we cannot conceive imperfection in things unless we consider other things which have more essence. And therefore we shall be able to find no imperfection in the decision of Adam when we consider it in itself, and do not compare it with other things which are more perfect, or show a more perfect state. Yes, one can compare it with countless other things which in comparison with it are much more imperfect, such as stones, logs of wood, etc., and this everyone also admits in fact, for everyone observes with admiration and delight in animals the very things which he detests and regards with aversion in men. For example, the wars of bees, the jealousy of doves, etc., things which we detest in men and for which we nevertheless consider animals more perfect. This being so, *it clearly follows that sins, seeing that they signify nothing but imperfection, cannot consist in anything which expresses essence, like the decision of Adam or the execution thereof.*

Moreover, we also cannot say that the will of Adam opposed the will of God, and that it was evil because it displeased God. For besides the fact that it would argue a great imperfection in God if something were to happen against His will and if He were to desire something which He could not obtain, and if His nature were so determined that, like His creatures, He would have sympathy with some things and antipathy toward others, it would also be entirely opposed to the nature of God's will. For since this is not something different from His understanding, it is as impossible for anything to happen contrary to His will as it is for it to happen contrary to His understanding, that is, whatever should happen contrary to His will, would have to be by nature such as to be contrary to the understanding, like a square circle. Since, then, the will or the decision of Adam, considered in itself, was not evil, nor, properly speaking, against the will of God, so it follows that God can be, or rather, according to the argument which you mention, must be its cause, not indeed *in so far as it was evil, for the evil in it was no more than a privation of a more perfect state*, which Adam had to lose through that action. It is certain that Privation is not something positive, and that the term is only used in relation to our understanding, and not in relation to God's understanding. This comes about thus, namely, because we express by one and the same definition all individuals of the same kind, for example, all who have the external shape of men, and therefore we consider that they are all equally capable of the highest perfection which we can deduce from such a Definition, and when we find one whose deeds are incompatible with that perfection, then we consider that he is deprived thereof and that he deviates from his nature. *This we should not do, had we not brought him under such a definition, and attributed to him such a nature.* But since God neither conceives things abstractly nor makes such general definitions, and no more essence belongs to things than the Divine Understanding and power imparts to them and actually gives them, it clearly follows *that one can only speak of this privation in relation to our understanding, but not in relation to God.*

Herewith, methinks, the question is completely answered. But in order to make the path smooth and to remove every obstacle, I must still answer the following two questions, namely, first, why Scripture says that God desires the wicked to repent, and also why He forbade Adam to eat of the tree, when He had ordained the contrary; secondly, what seems to follow from what I have said, that the ungodly by their pride, avarice, desperation, etc., serve God as well as do the pious by their generosity, patience, love, etc., because they also carry out the will of God.

However, in answer to the first question I say that Scripture, since it especially serves the common people, continually speaks in human fashion, for the people are not capable of understanding high matters. And therefore, I believe that all those things which God revealed to the Prophets as necessary to salvation, are written in the form of laws, and so the Prophets composed a whole Parable, namely, first they described God as a King and Lawgiver because He revealed the means of salvation and of perdition, of which He was the cause. The means, which are no more than causes, they then called Laws, and wrote them down in the form of Laws. Salvation and perdition, which are no more than the effects which necessarily follow from these means, they represented as reward and punishment. And they adapted all their words to this parable rather than to the truth. And everywhere they described God as a man, now angry, now merciful, now desiring the future, now seized by jealousy and suspicion, and even deceived by the Devil. So that philosophers, and with them all those who are above the Law, that is, who follow virtue not as a Law but from love of it because it is the best thing, need not trouble about such words.

The prohibition to Adam, then, consisted solely in this, namely that God revealed to Adam that the eating of the fruit of the tree brought death, just as He reveals also to us through our natural understanding that poison is deadly. But if you ask to what end He revealed this to him, I answer, in order to make him thus much more perfect in knowledge. Therefore to ask God why He did not give him also a more perfect will, is just as absurd as to ask why He did not give to the circle all the properties of a sphere. This follows clearly from what was said above, and I have proved it also in the

Scholium to Proposition 15 of the First Part [of the *Principles* of Descartes proved geometrically].

With regard to the second difficulty, it is indeed true that the ungodly express the will of God according to their measure, but they are not therefore to be in any way compared to the pious. For the more perfection anything has, the more does it participate also in Deity, and the more does it express the perfection of God. Therefore since the pious have incalculably more perfection than the ungodly, their virtue cannot be compared with that of the ungodly because the ungodly lack the love of God which springs from the knowledge of Him, and whereby alone we, according to our human understanding, are said to be the servants of God. Indeed, since they know not God, they are no more than a tool in the hand of the master which serves unconsciously, and perishes in the service; on the other hand, the pious serve consciously, and become more perfect by their service.

This, Sir, is all that I can now submit in answer to your question. I wish nothing more than that it may satisfy you. But if you still find difficulty, then I beg you to let me know, in order to see if I can remove it. You on your side need not have any scruples, but as long as you do not consider yourself satisfied, I would like nothing better than to know the reasons thereof, so that truth may dawn at last. I do indeed wish that I might write in the language in which I was brought up. I might possibly express my thoughts better. But please take it in good part, and yourself correct the mistakes, and consider me.

Your devoted Friend
and servant

THE LONG ORCHARD,   B. DE SPINOZA.
5 *January* 1665.

Letter XX   WILLIAM VAN BLYENBERGH

TO THE VERY ILLUSTRIOUS MR. B. D. S.

[Blyenbergh is shocked at Spinoza's departure from Scriptural teaching. He reiterates his objection that according to Spinoza's doctrine there is no evil or God himself causes evil. He asks what is meant by a Negation in God. Ed.]

Letter XXI   B. D. S.

TO THE VERY LEARNED AND EMINENT MR. WILLIAM VAN BLYENBERGH.

(*Reply to the Preceding.*)

SIR AND FRIEND,

When I read your first letter I believed that our opinions almost coincided; but I understand from your second letter, which was delivered to me on the 21st of this month, that this is far from being so. I can see that we differ not only about the conclusions which may be ultimately derived from first principles, but also about those principles themselves. So much so that I hardly believe that our correspondence can be for our mutual instruction. For I perceive that no proof, however sound according to the Laws of Proof, avails with you, unless it agrees with that explanation which you, or other Theologians known to you, give to Holy Scripture. But if you hold that God speaks more clearly and effectively through Holy Scripture than through the light of the natural understanding, which He also gave us, and in His Divine Wisdom continually preserves firm and uncorrupted, you have strong reasons for moulding your understanding to the opinions which you attribute to Holy Scripture. I myself could not do otherwise. But as far as I am concerned, since I openly and unambiguously confess that I do not understand Holy Scripture although I have spent some years in the study of it, and since it has not escaped my notice that when I have a strong proof no such thoughts can occur to me that I can ever entertain any doubt about it, I acquiesce wholly in that which my understanding shows me, without any suspicion that I may be deceived, or that Holy Scripture, although I do not search it, can contradict it: for truth does not conflict with truth, as I have already clearly shown before in my *Appendix* (I cannot indicate the chapter, for I have not the book here with me in the country). Even if I were once to find untrue the fruits of my natural understanding, they would make me happy, since I enjoy them, and I endeavour to pass my life not in sorrow and sighing but in peace, joy and cheerfulness, and thereby I ascend a step higher. Meanwhile I know (and this gives me the greatest satisfaction and peace of mind) that all things come to pass as they do by the power of the most perfect Being, and His immutable decree.

But to return to your letter. I sincerely express my best thanks to you for having laid bare to me in time your method of philosophizing. But I give you no thanks for attributing to me such opinions as you wish to deduce from my letter. What material, I pray, did my letter provide for imputing to me these opinions, namely, that men are like unto beasts, that men die and perish after the manner of beasts, that our works are displeasing to God, etc? (It may be that we differ entirely on this last point, since I cannot but think that you conceive God as taking pleasure in our works as one who has achieved His end, inasmuch as something has succeeded according to His wish). As far as I am concerned, I have assuredly said clearly that the upright serve God, and by their continual service they become more perfect, and love God. Is this to make them like beasts, or to declare that they perish like beasts, or, lastly, that their works do not please God?

If you had read my letter with greater attention, you would have clearly perceived that our difference lay in this alone, namely, whether the perfections which the upright receive are conferred upon them by God as God, that is, absolutely, without our attributing to Him any human attributes (as I understand), or whether they are conferred on them by Him as a judge, which last is what you assert. Therefore you urge in defence of the wicked that they serve God as much as do the good, since they do what they can in accordance with the decree of God. But this by no means follows from my remarks: for I do not introduce God as a judge, and therefore I estimate works according to the quality of the work, and not according to the capacity of the workman, and the reward which follows the work follows on it as necessarily as it follows from the nature of a triangle that its three angles must be equal to two right angles. And this everyone will understand if he only considers that our greatest blessedness consists in love toward God, and that this love necessarily flows from the knowledge of God, which is so strongly commended to us. This can be easily proved in general if we will only pay attention to the nature of God's Decree, as I have explained in my *Appendix*. But I admit that all those who confuse the Divine nature with human nature are quite unable to understand this.

I had intended to end this letter here, lest I should weary you further with matters which (as is clear from the very devout addition appended at the end of your letter) serve for jest and laughter and are of no real use. But not entirely to decline your request, I will proceed further to the explanation of the words Negation and Privation, and briefly bring out what is necessary to make the meaning of my preceding letter more lucid.

I say, then, in the first place, that Privation is not an act of depriving, but only a simple and mere lack, which in itself is nothing: for it is only a thing of Reason, or a way of thinking, which we form when we compare things with each other. We say, for example, that a blind man is deprived of sight because we easily imagine him as seeing. This imagination comes about either because we compare him with others who see, or because we compare his present state with a past state when he did see. And when we consider this man in this way, that is by comparing his nature with that of others or with a former nature of his own, we affirm that sight belongs to his nature and therefore we say that he is deprived of it. But when the decree of God and His nature are considered, we cannot say of that man any more than of a stone, that he is deprived of sight, for at that time sight pertains to that man no less inconsistently than to a stone; *for to that man there pertains and belongs nothing more than the Divine understanding and will attributed to him.* And therefore God is no more the cause of his not seeing than of the stone's not seeing, which is mere Negation. *So also when we consider the nature of the man who is led by his desire for pleasure, and when we compare his present desire with that which is felt by the upright, or with that which he himself had on another occasion, we assert that the man is deprived of a better desire, because we judge that the desire of virtue then pertains to him. This we cannot do if we consider the nature of God's decree and His understanding. For in this respect the better desire belongs no more to that man's nature at that time than it does to the Nature of a Devil or of a stone*, and therefore in this respect the better desire is not Privation but Negation. So that Privation is nothing else than denying of a thing something which we judge to pertain to its nature, and Negation is nothing else than denying something of a thing because it does not belong to its nature. Hence it is clear why the desire of Adam for earthly things was evil only in relation to our understanding and not in relation to that of God. *For although God knew both the past and the present state of Adam He did not therefore conceive Adam as deprived of a past state, that is, conceive the past state as pertaining to his nature.* For then God would conceive something contrary to His will, that is, contrary to His own understanding.

If you had rightly perceived this, and also that I do not admit that liberty which Descartes ascribes to the Mind, as L. M., in my name, testified in the Preface, you would not find even the smallest contradiction in my words. But I see that I should have done much better if, in my first letter, I had replied in the words of Descartes, saying that we cannot know how our liberty, and whatever depends on it, agrees with the foresight and freedom of God (as I have done in various places in the *Appendix* to Descartes' *Principia*) so that we can find in the creation by God nothing inconsistent with our liberty, since we are unable to understand in what way God has created things, and (what is the same thing) how He preserves them. But I thought you had read the Preface and that I should be sinning against the duty of friendship, which I offered heartily, if I did not answer according to the thought that was really in my mind. But this is of no consequence.

Since, however, I see that you have not hitherto

rightly grasped the Mind of Descartes, I pray you to pay attention to these two points.

First, that neither Descartes nor I have ever said that it pertains to our nature to confine our will within the limits of our understanding, but only that God has given as a limited understanding and an unlimited will, yet in such a way that we do not know to what end He has created us; moreover that an unlimited will of this kind, or a perfect will, not only makes us more perfect, but is also very necessary for us, as I will show in what follows.

Secondly, that our liberty is placed not in a certain contingency or in a certain indifference, but in the mode of assertion or denial, so that the less indifferently we affirm or deny something the more free we are. For instance, if the nature of God is known to us, then the assertion that God exists follows as necessarily from our own nature as it follows necessarily from the nature of a triangle that its three angles are equal to two right angles. And yet we are never more free than when we assert a thing in this way. But since this necessity is nothing else than the decree of God, as I have clearly shown in my *Appendix* to Descartes' *Principles*, it may to a certain extent be understood how we do something freely, and are the cause of it, notwithstanding the fact that we do it necessarily, and according to the Decree of God. This, I say, we can understand to a certain extent, when we affirm something which we clearly and distinctly perceive; but when we assert something which we do not clearly and distinctly grasp, that is, when we suffer our will to roam beyond the limits of our understanding, then we cannot thus perceive this necessity and the Decrees of God, but only our liberty, which is always included in our will (in which respect only our actions are called good or evil). And if we then try to reconcile our liberty with God's Decree and His continual creation, we are confusing that which we clearly and distinctly understand with that which we do not perceive, and therefore our effort is vain. It is enough for us, therefore, that we know that we are free, and that we can be thus free, notwithstanding the decree of God, and that we are the cause of evil, because no action can be called evil except only in relation to our freedom. So much, then, with regard to Descartes, so that I might show that his words in this connection contain no contradiction.

I will now turn to what concerns myself, and first I will briefly call to mind the advantage which comes from my opinion, and which especially consists in this, namely, that our understanding offers Mind and Body to God without any superstition. I do not deny that prayers are very useful to us: for my understanding is too small to determine all the means which God has to lead men to the love of Him, that is, to salvation. So far is my opinion from being harmful that, on the contrary, for those who are not prepossessed by prejudices and childish superstition, it is the sole means of attaining to the highest degree of blessedness.

As to what you say, that I make men so dependent on God that I make them like the elements, plants and stones, this shows sufficiently that you most perversely misunderstand my opinion, and confuse things which concern the understanding with imagination. For if you had grasped with your pure understanding what dependence upon God is, you would certainly not think that things in so far as they depend on God, are dead, corporeal and imperfect (who ever dared to speak in so vile a fashion of the most perfect Being?). On the contrary, you would understand that for that reason, and in so far as they depend on God, they are perfect—

so much so, that we best understand this dependence and necessary operation through God's decree when we consider not logs and plants, but the most intelligible and most perfect created things, as appears clearly from what I have said before, in the second place, about the meaning of Descartes which you should have noticed.

And I cannot refrain from saying that I am very much surprised that you say: if God did not punish crime (that is, as a judge with such a punishment as the offence itself does not bring with it: for only this is in question) what consideration could restrain me from eagerly perpetrating all sorts of crimes? Surely he who only abstains from this from fear of punishment (which I hope is not so with you) in no way acts from love, and embraces virtue as little as possible. So far as I am concerned, I avoid or endeavour to avoid crimes because they are expressly repugnant to my special nature, and would make me stray from the love and the knowledge of God.

Further, if you had paid a little attention to human nature and grasped the nature of the decree of God, as I explained in my *Appendix*, and finally, if you had known how inference should proceed before a conclusion is reached, then you would not have said so boldly that this opinion makes us like logs, etc., nor would you have imputed to me the many absurdities which you imagine.

With regard to those two points which, before you proceed to your second rule, you say that you cannot understand, I reply first that Descartes is enough to enable you to arrive at your conclusion, namely, that if you will only pay attention to your own nature you will have the experience that you can suspend your judgment. But if you say that you do not find in your own experience that we have so much power over Reason to-day that we can always continue to do so, this for Descartes would be the same as saying that we cannot see to-day that as long as we exist we shall always be thinking things, or retain the nature of a thinking thing, which surely involves a contradiction.

To your second point, I say, with Descartes, that if we could not extend our will beyond the limits of our very limited understanding, we should be most wretched. It would not be in our power to eat a piece of bread, or to move a step, or to exist. For all things are uncertain and full of dangers.

I pass on now to your second Rule, and I assert that I do indeed believe that I do not attribute to Scripture that Truth which you believe to be therein, and yet I believe that I ascribe to it as much, if not more, authority, and that, far more cautiously than others, I take care not to impute to it certain childish and absurd views; and this no one can do better unless he understands Philosophy well, or has Divine revelations. So the explanations of Scripture which ordinary Theologians offer have very little influence with me, especially when they are of that kind which always take Scripture according to the letter and the external meaning. And yet I have never seen any Theologian except the Socinians, who was so dense as not to perceive that Holy Scripture very frequently speaks of God in human fashion, and expresses its meaning in Parables. As to the contradiction which you endeavour to show, in vain (in my opinion at least), I believe that you mean by Parable something entirely different from what is commonly meant. For who has ever heard that he who expresses his ideas in Parables strays from his meaning? When Micah said to King Ahab that he had seen God sitting on His throne, and the heavenly hosts standing on the right and on the left, and that God asked them who would deceive Ahab, this was certainly a Parable, by which the Prophet sufficiently expressed the chief point which he had to reveal in God's name on that occasion (which was not one for teaching sublime dogmas of Theology), so that he in no way strayed from His meaning. So also the other Prophets, at the command of God, revealed the Word of God to the people in this way, as the best means, though not as that which God enjoined, of leading the people to the primary object of Scripture, which according to the word of Christ himself consists, of course, in loving God above all things and one's neighbour as oneself. High speculations, I believe, concern Scripture least. As far as I am concerned, I have learned none of the eternal attributes of God from Holy Scripture, nor could I learn them.

As to your fifth argument (namely, that the Prophets have made manifest the Word of God in such a manner), since truth is not opposed to truth, it only remains for me to show (as anyone may judge who understands the method of proof) that Scripture, just as it is, is the true, revealed Word of God. Of this I can have no Mathematical Proof, except by Divine Revelation. For this reason I said, *I believe*, but not *I know mathematically, that all things which God revealed to the Prophets, etc.*, since I firmly believe, but I do not know mathematically, that the Prophets were the intimate counsellors and the faithful messengers of God; so that in all that I have asserted there is no contradiction whatsoever, whereas on the contrary not a few may be found on the other side.

As to the rest of your letter, namely, where you say *Lastly, the supremely perfect Being knew, etc.*, and what you then adduce against the example about the poison,

and, lastly, what concerns the *Appendix*, and what follows, I say that they do not concern the present question.

As to the Preface by L. M., it is therein certainly
shown what points Descartes should still have proved
in order to construct a sound proof of the Freedom of
the Will, and it is added that I favour the contrary
opinion, and how I do so. This perhaps I shall explain
in its proper time but I have no mind for it now.

But I have not thought about the work on Descartes,
since the time when it appeared in the Dutch language,
nor have I given it further consideration: and this not
without a reason, which it would take long to recount
here. So there remains nothing more to say but that I
am, etc.

[SCHIEDAM, 28 *Jan.* 1665.]

Letter XXII   WILLIAM VAN BLYENBERGH

TO THE VERY ILLUSTRIOUS MR. B. D. S.

[Blyenbergh expresses himself as bewildered and asks many
questions. Is murder as pleasing to God as almsgiving? Are
there not natures to which crime and pleasure-seeking appear
fitting and agreeable? Is there then no binding incentive to
virtue? If thinking men are entirely dependent on God are
they not reduced to the level of lifeless things? Ed.]

Letter XXIII   B. D. S.

TO THE VERY LEARNED AND EMINENT
WILLIAM VAN BLYENBERGH.

(Reply to the Preceding.)

SIR AND FRIEND,

I have received two letters from you this week: the
one, of the 9 March, which served merely to inform
me of the other, of the 19 February, which was sent to
me from Schiedam. In this last one I see that you
complain about what I had said *that no proof can
avail with you, etc.*, as if I had said this in reference

to my reasoning because it did not satisfy you immediately. This is far from my meaning. But I had in view your own words, which are as follows: *and if ever it happen that, after long consideration, my natural knowledge seems either to conflict with this word or not fully, etc., this word has so much authority with me that I rather doubt the conceptions which I think are clear than, etc.* Therefore, I did no more than repeat your words briefly, and I do not believe that I gave the smallest ground for offence thereby, especially as I only adduced them as an argument to show our great difference.

Moreover, since at the end of your second letter you wrote that your only wish is to continue in faith and hope, and that you were indifferent to the rest which we persuade ourselves about our natural understanding, I thought as I still think, that my writing could be of no use, and that therefore it was more advisable for me not to neglect my studies (which I must otherwise discontinue for so long) for the sake of things which can be of no use. And this does not contradict my first letter. For then I regarded you as a Philosopher pure and simple, who (as many, who consider themselves Christians, admit) has no other touchstone for truth than the natural understanding, and not theology. But you have taught me differently, and shown me that the foundation on which I meant to build our friendship, was not laid as I had thought.

Lastly, as regards the rest, this happens very commonly in the course of disputation without on that account going beyond the bounds of courtesy, and for this reason I have taken no notice of such things in your second letter and will also do likewise with this one. So much about your displeasure, in order to show that I have given no ground for it, much less for thinking that I cannot bear contradiction. I will now turn to your objections, in order to reply to them.

First then, I say that God is absolutely and effectively the cause of everything that has essence, be it what it may. Now, if you can show that Evil, Error or Villainy, etc., is something which expresses essence, then I will fully admit to you that God is the cause of villainy, evil, error, etc. I think that I have sufficiently shown that that which gives its form to evil, error, or crimes, does not consist in anything which expresses essence, and that therefore it cannot be said that God is the cause thereof. For example Nero's matricide, in so far as it contained something positive, was not a crime: for Orestes too did the same outward deed and had the same intention of killing his Mother, and yet he is not blamed, at least not in the same degree as Nero. What then was Nero's crime? Nothing else than that by this deed he showed that he was *un*grateful, *un*merciful, and *dis*obedient. And it is certain that none of these things expresses any essence, and therefore God was not the cause of them, although He was the cause of the act and the intention of Nero.

Further, I should like to remark here that while we are speaking philosophically we must not use the modes of expression of Theology. For Theology has usually, and not without reason, represented God as a perfect man; therefore it is quite appropriate in Theology that it should be said that God desires something, that God is affected with weariness at the deeds of the ungodly, and with pleasure at those of the pious. But in Philosophy, where we clearly understand that to apply to God the attributes which make a man perfect, is as bad as to want to apply to a man those which make perfect an elephant or an ass, these and similar words have no place; and we cannot use them here without thoroughly confusing our conceptions. Therefore speaking philosophically we cannot say that God demands something from someone, or that something wearies or pleases Him, for all these are human attributes, which have no place in God.

Lastly, I would like to remark that although the actions of the pious (that is, of those who have a clear idea of God, in accordance with which all their actions and thoughts are determined) and of the ungodly (that is, of those who have no idea of God, but only confused ideas of earthly things, in accordance with which all their actions and thoughts are determined) and lastly, of everything that exists, proceed necessarily from God's eternal laws and decrees, and continually depend on God, nevertheless they differ from one another not only in degree but also in essence. For although a mouse is as dependent on God as an angel is, and sadness as much as joy, yet a mouse cannot therefore be a kind of angel, or sadness a kind of joy. And herewith I think that I have answered your objections (if I have rightly understood them, for I am sometimes in doubt whether the conclusions which you draw do not differ from the Proposition which you undertake to prove).

This however will appear more clearly if, following these fundamental notions, I answer the questions which you proposed to me. The first is whether killing is as agreeable to God as alms-giving. The second is, whether in relation to God stealing is as good as being righteous. The third is whether, if there is a mind to whose especial nature the pursuit of pleasure and of crime is not repugnant but acceptable, there is any ground for virtue which would necessarily persuade it to do good and avoid evil?

To the first I say that (speaking philosophically) I do not know what you mean by *agreeable to God*. If the question is whether God does not hate the one and love the other, or whether the one has not done God harm, and the other a favour, I answer No. And if the question is this, whether men who slay and those who give alms are not equally good or perfect, I again say No.

With regard to your second, I reply, if *good in relation to God* means that the righteous man does some good to God, and the thief some evil, I answer that neither the righteous nor the thief can cause either pleasure or weariness to God. But if the question is whether both actions in so far as they are something real and caused by God, are not equally perfect, then I say that if we consider the actions alone, and in such a way, it may well be that they are equally perfect. If you then ask *whether the thief and the righteous are equally perfect and blessed, I answer No. For by a righteous man I understand one who firmly desires that each shall possess his own. I show in my Ethics (which I have not yet published) that this desire arises necessarily in the pious from the clear knowledge which they have of themselves and of God. And since the thief has no such desire, he necessarily lacks the knowledge of God and of himself, that is, the chief thing which makes us men.*[1] If you also ask what can induce you to do that action which I call virtuous rather than the other, I reply that I do not know which out of the infinite ways that there are, God makes use of in order to determine you to such actions. It may be that God has impressed upon you a clear idea of Himself so that you forget the world for love of Him, and love the rest

[1] Thus Spinoza maintains that there is an objective basis for moral judgments. The good man possesses more reality in his essence and is thus more perfect, tho the evil man is equally part of God's perfection.—See Eth. V XL. S. [Ed.]

of mankind as yourself, and it is clear that such a constitution of mind is opposed to everything else which is called evil, and therefore they cannot exist in the same subject. But this is not the place to explain the fundamentals of Ethics, or to prove all that I say, for my present object is simply to answer your objections and to defend myself against them.

Lastly as regards your third question, it supposes a contradiction, and is just as if somebody asked me if it accorded better with the nature of some one that he should hang himself, would there be any reasons why he should not hang himself? However, suppose it is possible that there is such a nature. Then I say (whether I admit the freedom of the will or not) that if some one sees that he can live better on the gallows than at his own table, he would act most foolishly if he did not go and hang himself. And he who saw clearly that he would in fact enjoy a more perfect or better life or essence by pursuing crimes rather than by following virtue, would also be a fool if he did not pursue them. For in relation to such a perverted human nature crimes would be virtuous.

As to your other question, which you added at the end of your letter, since one could ask an hundred such questions in an hour without arriving at any conclusion about anything, and since you yourself do not press for an answer I will leave it unanswered.

And for the present I will only say that I shall expect you about the time which you appointed with me, and that you will be very welcome. But I should like it to be soon, because I already intend to go to Amsterdam for a week or two. In the meantime, I remain, with cordial greetings,

Your devoted Servant,
B. DE SPINOZA.

Letter XXXII (*in part*)

To the Very Noble and Learned
Mr. Henry Oldenburg.

(*On the Whole of Nature and Its Parts.*)

Most noble Sir,

I thank you and the very Noble Mr. Boyle very
much for kindly encouraging me to go on with my
Philosophy. I do indeed proceed with it, as far as my
slender powers allow, not doubting meanwhile of your
help and goodwill.

When you ask me what I think about the question
which turns on *the Knowledge how each part of Nature
accords with the whole of it, and in what way it is connected with the other parts,* I think you mean to ask for
the reasons on the strength of which we believe that
each part of Nature accords with the whole of it, and
is connected with the other parts. For I said in my
preceding letter that I do not know how the parts
are really interconnected, and how each part accords
with the whole; for to know this it would be necessary
to know the whole of Nature and all its Parts.

I shall therefore try to show the reason which compels me to make this assertion; but I should like first
to warn you that I do not attribute to Nature beauty or
ugliness, order or confusion. For things cannot, except
with respect to our imagination, be called beautiful,
or ugly, ordered or confused.

By connection of the parts, then, I mean nothing else
than that the laws, or nature, of one part adapt themselves to the laws, or nature, of another part in such a
way as to produce the least possible opposition. With
regard to whole and parts, I consider things as parts of
some whole, in so far as their natures are mutually
adapted so that they are in accord among themselves,

as far as possible; but in so far as things differ among themselves, each produces an idea in our mind, which is distinct from the others, and is therefore considered to be a whole, not a part. For instance, since the motions of the particles of lymph, chyle, etc., are so mutually adapted in respect of magnitude and figure that they clearly agree among themselves, and all together constitute one fluid, to that extent only, chyle, lymph, etc., are considered to be parts of the blood: but in so far as we conceive the lymph particles as differing in respect of figure and motion from the particles of chyle, to that extent we consider them to be a whole, not a part.

Let us now, if you please, imagine that a small worm lives in the blood, whose sight is keen enough to distinguish the particles of blood, lymph, etc., and his reason to observe how each part on collision with another either rebounds, or communicates a part of its own motion, etc. That worm would live in this blood as we live in this part of the universe, and he would consider each particle of blood to be a whole, and not a part. And he could not know how all the parts are controlled by the universal nature of blood, and are forced, as the universal nature of blood demands, to adapt themselves to one another, so as to harmonize with one another in a certain way. For if we imagine that there are no causes outside the blood to communicate new motions to the blood, and that outside the blood there is no space, and no other bodies, to which the particles of blood could transfer their motion, it is certain that the blood would remain always in its state, and its particles would suffer no changes other than those which can be conceived from the given relation of the motion of the blood to the lymph and chyle, etc., and so blood would have to be considered always to be a whole and not a part. But, since there are very many other causes which in a certain way control the laws of the nature of blood, and are in turn controlled by the blood, hence it comes about that other motions and other changes take place in the blood, which result not only from the mere relation of the motion of its parts to one another, but from the relation of the motion of the blood and also of the external causes to one another: in this way the blood has the character of a part and not of a whole. I have only spoken of whole and part.

Now, all the bodies of nature can and should be conceived in the same way as we have here conceived the blood: for all bodies are surrounded by others, and are mutually determined to exist and to act in a definite and determined manner, while there is preserved in all together, that is, in the whole universe, the same proportion of motion and rest. Hence it follows that every body, in so far as it exists modified in a certain way, must be considered to be a part of the whole universe, to be in accord with the whole of it, and to be connected with the other parts. And since the nature of the universe is not limited, like the nature of the blood, but absolutely infinite, its parts are controlled by the nature of this infinite power in infinite ways, and are compelled to suffer infinite changes. But I conceive that with regard to substance each part has a closer union with its whole. For as I endeavoured to show in my first letter, which I wrote to you when I was still living at Rhynsburg, since it is of the nature of substance to be infinite, it follows that each part belongs to the nature of corporeal substance, and can neither exist nor be conceived without it.

You see, then, in what way and why I think that the human Body is a part of Nature. As regards the human Mind I think it too is a part of Nature: since I state that there exists in Nature an infinite power of thought,

which in so far as it is infinite, contains in itself subjectively the whole of Nature, and its thoughts proceed
in the same way as Nature, which, to be sure, is its
ideatum.

Then I declare that the human mind is this same
power, not in so far as it is infinite, and perceives the
whole of Nature, but in so far as it is finite and perceives only the human Body, and in this way I declare
that the human Mind is a part of a certain infinite
intellect.

But it would be too long a business accurately to
explain and prove here all these things, and all that
is connected with them, and I do not think that you
expect me to do so at the moment. Indeed I am not
sure that I have rightly understood your meaning, and
so have not answered something different from what
you asked. This I should like to find out from you. * *

I wrote this letter last week. But I could not send it,
because the wind prevented my going to the Hague.
That is the disadvantage of living in the country. It is
but rarely that I receive a letter when it is due, for
unless there is by chance an opportunity of sending it
here at the time, then a week or two passes before I
receive it. Then not infrequently there is a difficulty
about my being able to send it in due time. Therefore
when you see that I do not answer you as promptly as
I should, you must not think that this is due to my
forgetting you. Meanwhile time urges me to bring this
to an end. Of the rest on another occasion. Now I can
say no more than that I ask you to give a hearty
greeting from me to the very Noble Mr. Boyle, and
to remember me who am

In all affection yours

B. DE SPINOZA.

VOORBURG, 20 *November* 1665.

I desire to know whether all astronomers think that
there were two comets on the ground of their motion
or only in order to maintain Kepler's hypothesis.
Farewell.

To Mr. Henry Oldenburg,
    Secretary of the Royal Society,
        in the Pall Mall,
            in St. James's Fields,
                in London.

Letter XXXV   B. D. S.

To the Highly Esteemed and Prudent
        Mr. John Hudde.

(*The Properties of God.*)

Most Esteemed Sir,

In your last letter, written on the 30th of March,
you have made quite clear what was somewhat obscure
to me in the letter you wrote to me on the 10th of
February. Since, then, I now know what you really
think, I will put the question in the form in which you
conceive it, that is, whether there can only be one Being
which subsists in virtue of its own sufficiency or force.
I not only affirm this, but also undertake to prove it,
namely, from the fact that its nature involves necessary
existence. This can be most easily proved from the
understanding of God (as I explained in Proposition XI
of my *Geometrical Proofs of the Principles of Descartes*), or it can be proved from the other attributes of
God. In order, then, to attack this problem, let me first
briefly point out what properties must be possessed by
a Being that includes necessary existence. These are—

I. It must be eternal: for if a limited duration were

attributed to it, then that Being would be conceived as not existing, or as not involving necessary existence, beyond that limited duration. This is inconsistent with its definition.

II. It must be simple, not composed of parts. For in Nature and in our knowledge the component parts of a thing must be prior to that which is composed of them. This is out of place in that which is by its own nature eternal.

III. It cannot be conceived as limited, but only as infinite. For if the nature of this Being were limited, and were also conceived as limited, then beyond those limits that nature would be conceived as non-existent. This again is inconsistent with its definition.

IV. It must be indivisible. For if it were divisible it could be divided into parts either of the same or of a different nature. In the latter case it could be destroyed, and so not exist. This is contrary to the definition. In the former case, each part would contain necessary existence in itself, and thus one part could exist and consequently be conceived apart from another, and therefore that Nature could be understood as finite. This according to the foregoing is contrary to the definition. Hence we may see that if we want to ascribe any imperfection to a Being of this kind, we immediately fall into contradiction. For whether the imperfection which we want to impute to such a Nature consists in some defect, or in certain limitations which a nature of this kind is alleged to possess, or in some change which through lack of strength, it could suffer from external causes, we are always brought back to this, that this Nature, which involves necessary existence, does not exist, or does not exist necessarily. And therefore I conclude,

V. That everything which includes necessary existence can have in itself no imperfection, but must express pure perfection.

VI. Moreover, since it can only be the result of perfection that a Being should exist by its own sufficiency and power, it follows that if we suppose a Being which does not express all perfections to exist by its own nature, then we must also suppose that there exists also that Being which does include in itself all perfections. For if a Being which is endowed with less power exists through its own sufficiency, how much more must that exist which is endowed with the greater power.

Lastly, to come to our problem, I assert that there can only be one Being whose existence belongs to its nature, that is, that Being only which possesses all perfections in itself, and which I shall call God. For if there be assumed a Being to whose nature existence belongs, that Being must contain no imperfection, but (according to note 5) must express every perfection. And therefore the nature of that Being must belong to God (whom, according to note 6, we must also assert to exist), since He possesses in Himself all perfections and no imperfections. And it cannot exist outside God. For if it were to exist outside God, one and the same Nature, which involves necessary existence, would exist as two, which, according to our previous proof, is absurd. Therefore nothing outside God, but God alone, involves necessary existence. This is what was to be proved.

These, most esteemed Sir, are the things which I can at present contribute towards the proof of this matter. I should like to be able to prove also that I am, etc.

B. D. S.

Voorburg, 10 *April* 1666.

Letter XXXVI (*in part*)   B. D. S.

To the Very Honourable and Prudent
Mr. John Hudde.

(*The Properties of God, Especially Perfection.*)

Most Honourable Sir,

I was unable (on account of some obstacle) to reply sooner to your letter written on the nineteenth of May. But since I observe that for the most part you suspend your judgment about my proof which I sent you (I believe on account of the obscurity which you find in it), I will endeavour here to explain its meaning more clearly.

First, then, I enumerated four properties which a Being, existing in virtue of its own sufficiency or force, must possess. These four and the remaining similar properties I reduced to one in the fifth note. Then, in order to deduce all that was necessary for my proof from the single supposition, I endeavoured in the sixth note to prove the existence of God from the given supposition; and thence, lastly, assuming nothing more to be known than the simple meaning of the words, I came to the conclusion which was sought.

This, briefly, was my intention, this was my aim. Now I will explain the meaning of each link separately, and first I will begin with the assumed properties.

In the first you will find no difficulty. It, as also the second, is nothing else than an Axiom. For by simple I mean no more than that it is not composite or composed of parts which are different by nature, or of others which agree in their nature. The proof is certainly universal.

You have very well understood the meaning of the

third (namely, to this purport, that if the Being is
Thought it cannot be conceived as limited in Thought,
if the Being is Extension, it cannot be conceived as
limited in Extension, but only as unlimited). You say
however that you do not understand the conclusion
based on this, that it is a contradiction to conceive
under the negation of existence something whose definition includes existence, or (what is the same thing)
affirms existence. And since *limited* denotes nothing
positive, but only privation of the existence of the same
nature which is conceived as limited, it follows that
the definition of that which affirms existence, cannot be
conceived as limited. For instance, if the term *extension*
includes necessary existence, it will be just as impossible to conceive extension without existence, as extension
without extension. If this is granted it will also be
impossible to conceive limited extension. For if it is
conceived as limited it must be limited by its own nature,
that is, by extension; and this extension, by which it
would be limited, would have to be conceived under the
negation of existence. This, according to supposition,
is a manifest contradiction.

In the fourth I wished only to show that such a
Being cannot be divided into parts of the same nature
or into parts of a different nature, whether those which
are of a different nature involve necessary existence,
or not. For, I said, if the latter were the case, it could
be destroyed, since to destroy a thing is to resolve
it into such parts that none of them expresses the
nature of the whole; but if the former were the case, it
would be inconsistent with the three properties already
formulated.

In the fifth I only presupposed that perfection consists in being, and imperfection in the privation of being.
I say *privation*; for although, for instance, extension

negates thought of itself, this in itself is no imperfection in it. But it would argue imperfection in it, if it were to be deprived of extension, as would actually happen if it were limited, similarly if it lacked duration, position, etc.

You entirely admit the sixth: and yet you say your difficulty remains untouched (the difficulty, namely, why there cannot be several beings, existing through themselves, but differing in nature, just as thought and extension are different and can perhaps subsist through their own sufficiency). From this I can only judge that you have understood it in a very different sense from me. I am sure that I see in what sense you understand it, but in order not to lose any time, I will only explain my own meaning. I say, then, with regard to the sixth, that if we assume that something which is only unlimited and perfect of its kind exists by its own sufficiency, then we must also admit the existence of a being that is absolutely unlimited and perfect; which Being I shall call God. For if, for instance, we wish to assert that extension, or thought (which can be perfect each in its own kind, that is, in a certain kind of being) exist by their own sufficiency, we shall also have to admit the existence of God, who is absolutely perfect, that is, the existence of an absolutely unlimited being.

Here I would have you note what I have just said with regard to the word *imperfection,* namely, that this means that a thing lacks something which nevertheless belongs to its nature. For instance, Extension can only be said to be imperfect in respect of duration, position, or quantity, namely, because it does not last longer, or does not retain its position, or is not greater. But it can never be said to be imperfect because it does not think, since nothing of this kind is required by its nature, which consists only in extension, that is, in a certain kind of being, in respect of which alone it can be said to be limited or unlimited, imperfect or perfect. And since the nature of God does not consist of a certain kind of being but of absolutely unlimited being, His nature also requires all that perfectly expresses *being*; otherwise His nature would be limited and deficient. This being so, it follows that there can only exist one Being, namely God, which exists by its own force. For if, for example, we assume that extension involves existence, so that it is eternal and unlimited, it is also necessary that it should express absolutely no imperfection but only perfection: and so Extension will belong to God, or will be something which in some way expresses the nature of God, since God is a Being that is not only in a certain respect but absolutely unlimited in essence, and omnipotent. And this which is said of Extension (by way of an arbitrary illustration) will also have to be asserted of everything that we may want to set up as having such a nature. I conclude, therefore, as in my former letter, that nothing besides God, but only God, subsists by His own sufficiency. I believe that this is enough to explain the meaning of my former letter, but of this you will be the better judge. . . .

Letter XL (*in part*)   B. D. S.
TO THE VERY COURTEOUS AND PRUDENT
MR. JARIG JELLES.

(*On an Axiom of Descartes.*)

WORTHY FRIEND,
   I have duly received your last letter written on the fourteenth of this current month, but, owing to various

hindrances, I could not answer it sooner. With regard to the matter relating to Helvetius, I have spoken about it with Mr. Vossius who (not to relate in a letter all that we said to each other) ridiculed it greatly, and expressed surprise that I should inquire of him about such a trivial thing. Taking no notice of this I went nevertheless to the silversmith, named Brechtelt, who had tested the gold. But he, speaking very differently from Vossius, said that between smelting and separation the gold had increased in weight and had become heavier by as much as the weight of the silver that he had put into the smelting crucible for the purpose of the separation. Therefore he firmly believed that this gold which transmuted his silver into gold, contained something uncommon. He was not the only one who found this so, but various other men who were present at that time did so too. After this, I went to Helvetius himself, who showed me the gold and the crucible which was still gilded on the inside, and said to me that he had thrown into the melted lead not more than about one-fourth part of a grain of barley or of mustard seed. He added that within a short time he would publish an account of the whole matter, and further said that at Amsterdam a man (and he thought it was the same man as had called on him) had performed the same operation, of which you will doubtless have heard. This is all that I was able to learn about this matter.

The writer of the little book about which you write (in which he presumes to show that the arguments in Descartes' third and fifth Meditation, by which he proves the existence of God, are false) is certainly fighting his own shadow, and will harm himself more than others. Descartes' axiom is, I confess, somewhat

obscure and confused, as you have also remarked, and
he would have expressed it more clearly and truly thus:
*That the power of Thought to think about or to com-
prehend things, is not greater than the power of Nature
to exist and to act.* This is a clear and true axiom,
according to which the existence of God follows very
clearly and validly from the idea of Him. The argument of the said author of which you give an account
shows clearly enough that he does not yet understand
the matter. It is indeed true that we may go on to
infinity if thereby we would solve the question in all
its parts: but otherwise it is very silly. For example,
if some one asked by what such a finite body is set in
motion, it is possible to answer that it is determined to
such a motion by another body, and this body again
by another, and so on to infinity. This answer, I say, is
possible, because the Question is only about the motion,
and by positing each time another body, we assign a
sufficient and eternal cause of such motion. But if I see
a book containing excellent thoughts which is written
beautifully, in the hands of a common man, and I ask
him whence he has such a book, and he thereupon
answers that he has copied it from another book in the
possession of another common man who can also write
beautifully, and so on to infinity, then he does not satisfy me. For I am asking him not only about the form
and arrangement of the letters, about which alone he
answers me, but also about the thoughts and meaning
which their arrangement expresses, and this he does
not answer by thus going on to infinity. How this can
be applied to ideas may easily be understood from
what I have explained in the ninth axiom of my *Mathematical Proofs of Descartes' Principles of Philosophy.*

*　　　*　　　*

Letter L   B. D. S.

TO THE VERY COURTEOUS AND PRUDENT
MR. JARIG JELLES.

(*On Number and Figure in Relation to God.*)

WORTHY FRIEND,

With regard to Politics, the difference between Hobbes and me, about which you inquire, consists in this, that I ever preserve the natural right intact so that the Supreme Power in a State has no more right over a subject than is proportionate to the power by which it is superior to the subject. This is what always takes place in the state of Nature.

Further as regards the proof which I establish in the *Appendix to my Geometrical Proof of Descartes' Principles*, namely, that God can only very improperly be called one or single; I reply to this that a thing can only be said to be one or single in respect of its existence and not of its essence: for we do not conceive things under numbers until they have been subsumed under a common class. For example, he who holds in his hand a penny and a dollar will not think of the number two, unless he can call the penny and the dollar by one and the same name, such as pieces of money or coins: for then he can say that he has two pieces of money or two coins, because he calls the penny as well as the dollar a piece of money or a coin. Hence it seems clear that nothing can be called one or single unless some other thing has first been conceived which (as has been said) agrees with it. But since the existence of God is His essence itself, and since we can form no general idea of His essence, it is certain that he who calls God one or single has no true idea of God, or is speaking of Him inappropriately.

As regards this, that figure is a negation, and not
something positive, it is clearly evident that the totality
of matter, considered without limitation, can have no
figure and that figure has a place only in finite and
limited bodies. For he who says that he apprehends a
figure wants to express thereby nothing else than that
he is apprehending a limited thing, and how it is limited. The limitation, therefore, does not belong to the
thing in virtue of its being, but, on the contrary, it is
its not-being. Since, then, figure is nothing but limitation and limitation is negation, therefore, as has been
said, it can be nothing but negation.

The book written against mine by the Professor of
Utrecht, and published after his death, I have seen in
a bookseller's window. From the little I then read of
it I judged that it was not worth reading through, much
less worth answering. Therefore I left the book lying
there, and I left its author such as he was. I reflected
with a smile how the ignorant are always the boldest
and the most ready to write. It seemed to me that the
. . . put up their wares for sale as do the shopkeepers
who always show first what is worst. They say the
devil is a crafty fellow, but I think their spirit far surpasses his in craftiness. Farewell.

THE HAGUE, 2 *June* 1674.

Letter LVI (in part)   B. D. S.

TO THE VERY HONOURABLE AND PRUDENT
MR. HUGO BOXEL.

(On the Divine Nature and Our Conception of It.)

MOST HONOURABLE SIR,

I hasten to answer your letter, which I received yesterday, because if I go on delaying longer I shall be

compelled to postpone my reply longer than I should wish. Your health would cause me anxiety if I had not heard that you are better, and I hope you are now entirely recovered. * * *

The small compass of a letter, and limitation of time, do not permit me to explain in detail my opinion about the Divine Nature, or the other Questions which you put forward, to say nothing of the fact that to raise difficulties is not the same as to advance reasons. It is true that in the world we often act on conjecture; but it is false that our reflections are based on conjecture. In ordinary life we must follow what is most probable, but in philosophical speculations, the truth. Man would perish of thirst and hunger if he would not eat or drink until he had obtained a perfect proof that food and drink would do him good. But in contemplation this has no place. On the contrary, we must be cautious not to admit as true something which is merely probable. For when we admit one falsity, countless others follow.

Further, from the fact that divine and human sciences are full of disputes and controversies it cannot be inferred that all the things which are treated therein are uncertain: for there have been very many people who were so possessed by the love of contradiction that they laughed even at Geometrical proofs. Sextus Empiricus and other Sceptics whom you cite say that it is not true that the whole is greater than its part, and they have the same view of the other axioms.

But, putting aside and admitting the fact that in default of proofs we must be satisfied with probabilities, I say that a probable Proof ought to be such that, although we can doubt it, yet we cannot contradict it; because that which can be contradicted is not likely to be true, but likely to be false. If, for instance, I say that Peter is alive, because I saw him in good health yesterday, this is indeed likely to be true so long as no one can contradict me; but if some one else says that yesterday he saw Peter suffering from loss of consciousness, and that he believes that Peter died from it, he makes my words seem false. That your conjecture about spectres and ghosts seems false and not even probable, I have so clearly shown that I find nothing worthy of consideration in your answer.

To your question whether I have as clear an idea of God as I have of a triangle, I answer in the affirmative. But if you ask me whether I have as clear a mental image of God as I have of a triangle, I shall answer No. For we cannot imagine God, but we can, indeed, conceive Him. Here also it should be noted that I do not say that I know God entirely, but only that I understand some of His attributes, though not all, nor even **the greater** part of them, and it is certain that our ignorance of the majority of them does not hinder our having a knowledge of some of them. When I learnt Euclid's elements I first understood that the three angles of a triangle are equal to two right angles, and I clearly perceived this property of a triangle although I was ignorant of many others.

As regards spectres, or ghosts, I have never yet heard of an intelligible property of theirs, but only of Phantasies which no one can grasp. When you say that spectres, or ghosts, here in this lower region (I follow your form of expression, although I do not know that the matter here in this lower region is less valuable than that above) consist of the finest, thinnest, and most subtle substance, you seem to be speaking of spiders' webs, of air, or of vapours. To say that they are invisible means for me as much as if you said what they are not, but not what they are; unless perhaps you want to indicate that, according as they please, they make themselves now visible, now invisible, and that in these as in other impossibilities, the imagination will find no difficulty.

The authority of Plato, Aristotle, and Socrates has not much weight with me. I should have been surprised had you mentioned Epicurus, Democritus, Lucretius or any one of the Atomists, or defenders of the atoms. It is not surprising that those who invented occult Qualities, intentional Species, substantial Forms, and a thousand other trifles, should have devised spectres and ghosts, and put their faith in old women, in order to weaken the authority of Democritus, of whose good repute they were so envious that they burnt all his books, which he had published amidst so much praise. If you have a mind to put faith in them, what reasons have you for denying the miracles of the Holy Virgin, and of all the Saints, which have been described by so many very famous Philosophers, Theologians, and Historians that I can produce an hundred of them to scarcely one of the others?

Lastly, most honoured Sir, I have gone further than I intended. I do not wish to annoy you further with things which (I know) you will not admit, since you follow other principles which differ widely from my own, etc.

[THE HAGUE, *October* 1674.]

Letter LX B. D. S.

TO THE VERY NOBLE AND LEARNED MR. EHRENFRIED WALTER VON TSCHIRNHAUS.

(*On Definition and Cause.*)

MOST NOBLE SIR,

I recognize no other difference between a true and an adequate idea than that the word true refers only to the agreement of the idea with its ideatum, while the word adequate refers to the nature of the idea in itself; so that there is really no difference between a true and an adequate idea except this extrinsic relation.

But in order that I may know from which idea of a thing, out of many, all the properties of the object may be deduced, I observe one thing only, that the idea or definition of the thing should express its efficient cause.[1] For example, in order to investigate the properties of a circle, I ask whether from this idea of a circle, namely, that it is composed of innumerable right angles, I can deduce all its properties: I inquire, I say, whether this idea involves the efficient cause of a circle. Since this is not so, I seek another, namely that a circle is the space which is described by a line of which one point is fixed and the other moveable. Since this Definition expresses the efficient cause, I know that I can deduce from it all the properties of a circle, etc. So also, when I define God as the supremely perfect Being, since this definition does not express the efficient cause (for I conceive that an efficient cause can be internal as well as external) I shall not be able to discover all the properties of God from it; but when I define God as *a Being*, etc. (see Definition VI, Part I, of the *Ethics*).

As for your other problems, namely those about Motion and those which concern Method, since my views have not yet been written out in proper order, I reserve them for another occasion.

As to your assertion that he who considers the applicates of curves will deduce many things about their measurement, but that this can be done with greater ease by considering Tangents, etc., I think, on the contrary, that even by considering Tangents many other

---

[1] This passage is important as indicating the identity of essence and efficient cause for Spinoza. [Ed.]

things will be deduced with more difficulty than by considering the co-ordinates of curves; and I absolutely assert that from certain qualities of a thing (whatever the given idea) some things will be discovered more easily, others with greater difficulty (although they all concern the nature of that thing). But this only, I think, must be kept in view, that the idea to be sought is such that all the properties may be elicited from it, as has been said above. For if one is to deduce from anything all the possible properties, it necessarily follows that the last ones will be more difficult than the prior ones, etc.

[THE HAGUE, *January* 1675.]

Letter LXIII
G. H. SCHULLER

TO THE VERY DISTINGUISHED AND ACUTE PHILOSOPHER
B. D. S.

(*Concerning the Attributes of God.*)

MOST NOBLE AND DISTINGUISHED SIR,

I should blush for my long silence, for which I could be accused of ingratitude for the favour which you of your kindness have shown to me though I did not deserve it, if I did not reflect that your generous kindliness is inclined to excuse rather than to accuse, and if I did not know that, for the common good of your friends, it makes you find time for such serious reflections as it would be culpable and wrong to disturb without special cause. For this reason, then, I kept silence, and was content, in the meantime, to hear from friends of your good health. But with the present letter I want to inform you that our most noble friend Mr. von Tschirnhaus is still in England and, like us, enjoys good health, and that in his letters (which he

has sent to me) he has three times bidden me to convey
his dutiful regards, and respectful greeting to you, Sir.
He repeatedly begs me to ask you for the solution of
the following difficulties, and at the same time to beg you
to send the desired answer to them.

These are, whether you, Sir, will please convince us
by some direct proof,[1] and not by a reduction to impossibility, that we cannot know more attributes of
God than thought and extension? Further, whether it
follows from this that creatures consisting of other
attributes, cannot on the contrary conceive any extension, and that thus it would seem that there must be
constituted as many worlds as there are attributes of
God. For instance, our world of extension, so to say,
has so much amplitude; worlds consisting of other attributes would also have as much amplitude. And just
as we perceive nothing besides extension except thought,
so the creatures of those worlds must perceive nothing
but the attributes of their own world and thought.

Secondly, since the understanding of God differs
from our understanding in essence as well as in existence, it will, therefore, have nothing in common with
our understanding, and consequently (according to Book
I, Proposition III) God's understanding cannot be the
cause of our understanding.

Thirdly, in the Scholium to Proposition X, you say
that nothing in Nature is clearer than that each Being
must be conceived under some attribute (this I fully
understand) and that the more reality or being it has,
the more attributes belong to it. Hence it would seem
to follow that there exist Beings which have three, four,
or more Attributes, whereas from what has been proved
it could be inferred that each Being consists of two

---

[1] I beg you earnestly please to solve the doubts which are
raised here, and to send me your answer to them.

attributes only, namely a certain attribute of God and the idea of that attribute.

Fourthly, I should like examples of those things which are immediately produced by God, and of those which are produced by some infinite mediate modification. Thought and Extension seem to me to be of the first kind; of the second, Understanding in the case of thought, and Motion in the case of extension, etc.[1]

These are the questions which our above-mentioned Tschirnhaus desires with me to have elucidated by you, Sir, if your spare time permits. Moreover, he says that Mr. Boyle and Oldenburg had formed a strange conception of your person. Not only has he removed this, but he has added reasons which induced them not only to consider you again in a most worthy and favourable manner, but also to value very highly your *Tractatus Theologico-Politicus*. In obedience to your instructions, I dared not inform you of this. Be assured that I am at your service in every way, and that I remain,

Most noble Sir,

Your very devoted Servant

G. H. SCHULLER.

AMSTERDAM, 25 *July* 1675.

Letter LXIV B. D. S.

TO THE VERY LEARNED AND EXPERT
MR. G. H. SCHULLER.

(*Reply to the Preceding.*)

MOST EXPERT SIR,

I rejoice that at last an opportunity has presented itself to you to refresh me with one of your letters,

[1] The face of the whole of Nature which, although it varies in infinite ways remains always the same. See Scholium to Proposition XIII, Part JL

which are always most welcome to me. I earnestly beg
you to do so frequently, etc.

I turn to your doubts; and in reply to the first, I
say that the human mind can only get to know those
things which the idea of an actually existing body involves, or what can be inferred from this idea. For
the power of each thing is defined only by its essence
(according to *Ethics*, Proposition VII, Part III). But
the essence of the Mind (Proposition XIII, Part II)
consists only in this, that it is the idea of a Body actually
existing. Therefore the mind's power of understanding
only extends to those things which this idea of the Body
contains in itself, or which follow from the same. But
this idea of the Body neither involves nor expresses
any other attributes of God than Extension and
Thought. For its ideatum, namely, the Body (by Proposition VI, Part II) has God as its cause, in so far as
He is considered under the attribute of Extension and
not in so far as He is regarded under any other attribute. Therefore (by Axiom 6, Part I) this idea of
the Body involves the knowledge of God in so far only
as He is considered under the attribute of Extension.
Then, this idea, in so far as it is a mode of Thought,
also (by the same Proposition) has God for its cause
in so far as He is a thinking thing, and not in so far as
He is considered under another attribute. Therefore (by
the same Axiom) the idea of this idea involves the
knowledge of God, in so far as He is considered under
the attribute of Thought, and not in so far as He is
considered under any other attribute. Thus it is clear
that the human Mind, or the idea of the human Body,
neither involves nor expresses any other attribute of
God besides these two. Moreover (by Proposition X,
Part I) no other attribute of God can be deduced or
conceived from these two attributes or from their modi-

fications. Therefore I conclude that the human mind cannot attain to knowledge of any attribute of God except these two, as has been asserted.

As to your additional question, whether for this reason there must be constituted as many worlds as there are attributes, see *Ethics*, Scholium to Proposition VII, Part II. This proposition could also be more easily proved by reduction to absurdity. This kind of proof I am accustomed to prefer to the other, when the Proposition is negative, because it is more in accordance with the nature of such propositions. But since you demand only a positive proof, I pass on to the other, that is, whether a thing can be produced by another whose essence and existence are different: for things which are so different from one another appear to have nothing in common. But since all individual things, except those which are produced by things like themselves, differ from their causes in essence as well as in existence, I see here no reason for doubt.

In what sense I understand that God is the efficient cause of things, of their essence as well as of their existence, I believe I have sufficiently explained in the *Ethics*, Scholium and Corollary to Proposition XXV, Part I.

The axiom of the Scholium to Proposition X, Part I, as I suggested at the end of that Scholium, we form from the idea which we have of an absolutely infinite Being, and not from the fact that there are, or may be, beings which have three, four, or more attributes.

Lastly, the examples for which you ask are, of the first kind, in Thought, absolutely infinite understanding, but in Extension, motion and rest; of the second kind, the face of the whole Universe, which, although it varies in infinite modes, yet remains always the same;[1]

---

[1] This paragraph is essential in understanding the doctrine of Infinite Modes which are of two sorts: one, Intellect and Will

on this subject see Scholium 7 to the Lemma before Proposition XIV, Part II.

With these remarks, most distinguished Sir, I believe I have answered your objections and those of our friend. If, however, you consider that any doubt still remains, I beg you not to mind telling me so, in order that I may, if possible, remove it.

Farewell, etc.

THE HAGUE, 29 *July* 1675.

Letter LXV EHRENFRIED WALTER VON TSCHIRNHAUS

TO THE VERY ACUTE AND LEARNED PHILOSOPHER
B. D. S.

(Concerning Attributes.)[1]

MOST ILLUSTRIOUS SIR,

I should like from you a proof of your assertion that the soul cannot apprehend more attributes of God than Extension and Thought. Although I clearly see this, yet it seems to me that the contrary can be deduced from the Scholium to Proposition VII, Part II of the *Ethics*, perhaps only because I do not sufficiently correctly understand the meaning of this Scholium. I, therefore, decided to explain in what way I deduce this, begging you most earnestly, most illustrious Sir, to be willing to assist me with your usual kindliness whenever I do not rightly follow your meaning.

Now my arguments are in this plight. Although I gather from them that the world is certainly one, yet

---

or Motion and Rest following directly from God; and two, the face of the whole universe, following from one and consisting of finite Modes. [Ed.]

[1] This letter clearly expresses the germ of Tschirnhaus' fruitful criticism of the doctrine of Attributes. [Ed.]

it is also no less clear from them that it is expressed in infinite modes, and, therefore, that every individual thing is expressed in infinite modes. Hence it seems to follow that that Modification which constitutes my Mind, and that Modification which expresses my Body, although it is one and the same Modification, is yet expressed in infinite modes, in one mode through Thought, in another through Extension, in a third through an attribute of God unknown to me, and so on to infinity, because there are infinite Attributes of God, and the Order and Connection of the Modifications seems to be the same in all. Hence there now arises the question, why the Mind which represents a certain Modification, which same Modification is expressed not only in Extension, but in infinite other modes, why, I say, it perceives only that Modification expressed through Extension, that is, the human Body, and no other expression through other attributes.

But time does not allow me to pursue these questions at greater length. Perhaps all these doubts will be removed by continued reflection.

London, 12 *August* 1675.

Letter LXVI B. D. S.

To THE VERY NOBLE AND LEARNED
MR. EHRENFRIED WALTER VON TSCHIRNHAUS.

(*Reply to the Preceding.*)

MOST NOBLE SIR,
In answer to your objection I say that although each thing is expressed in infinite modes in the infinite understanding of God,[1] yet the infinite ideas by which it is

---

[1] Thus, as Tschirnhaus later points out (Letter LXX), the attribute of thought comes to occupy a peculiar and central

expressed cannot constitute one and the same mind of an individual thing, but an infinity of minds: seeing that each of these infinite ideas has no connection with the others, as I explained in the same Scholium to Proposition VII, Part II of the *Ethics*, and as is evident from Proposition X, Part I. If you will pay a little attention to these, you will see that no difficulty remains, etc.

THE HAGUE, 18 *August* 1675.

Letter LXX   G. H. SCHULLER, MED. DR.

TO THE VERY EMINENT AND ACUTE PHILOSOPHER
B. D. S.

(*The Unique Status of the Attribute of Thought.*)

AMSTERDAM, 14 *November* 1675.

MOST LEARNED AND EXCELLENT SIR, MOST HONOURED PATRON,

I hope that my last letter, together with the *Process* of an anonymous writer, has been duly delivered to you, and also that you are now very well, even as I am very well. I had, however, received no letter from our friend Tschirnhaus for a space of three months, whence I had made the sad conjecture that his journey from England to France was ill-starred. But now, having received a letter, I am full of joy, and in accordance with his request it is my duty to communicate it to you, Sir, to convey to you his most dutiful greetings, to inform you that he has reached Paris safely, that he has met there Mr. Huygens, as we had advised him to do, and that

---

position among all the other attributes which are contained in it. [Ed.]

for the same reason he has in every way adapted himself to his way of thinking so as to be highly esteemed by him. He mentioned that you, Sir, had advised him to associate with him (Huygens), and that you esteem his person very highly. This greatly pleased him, so that he replied that he likewise esteems your person greatly, and that he had lately obtained from you the *Tractatus Theologico-Politicus*. This is esteemed by very many there, and inquiries are eagerly made whether any other works of the same author are published. To this Mr. Tschirnhaus replied that he knew of none save the *Proofs of the First and Second Part of Descartes' Principles*. Otherwise he related nothing else about you, Sir, than the remarks just reported; hence he hopes that this will not displease you.

Huygens has recently had our Tschirnhaus summoned to him and informed him that Mr. Colbert desired some one to instruct his son in mathematics, and that if a position of this kind pleased him, he would arrange it. To this our friend replied by asking for some delay, and eventually declared that he was ready to accept. Huygens returned with the answer that the proposal pleased Mr. Colbert very much, especially as, owing to his ignorance of French, he will be compelled to speak to his son in Latin.

To the objection made most recently, he replies that the few words which I had written by your instruction, Sir, have revealed to him your meaning more deeply, and that he had already entertained these thoughts (since they chiefly admit of an explanation in these two ways) but that he has been led to follow that which was lately contained in his objection by the two following reasons. The first is that otherwise Propositions V and VII of Book II would seem to be opposed. In the former of these it is stated that the Ideata are the efficient causes of ideas, whereas the contrary seems to be shown by the proof of the latter, on account of the cited Axiom, 4, Part I. Maybe (as I rather persuade myself) I do not rightly apply the axiom in accordance with the Author's intention, which I would most willingly learn from him, if his affairs permit. The second cause which hindered me from following the given explanation was that in this way the Attribute Thought is made much more extensive than the other attributes; but since each of the Attributes constitutes the Essence of God, I certainly do not see how the one does not contradict the other. I will only add that if I may judge the minds of others by my own, then Propositions VII and VIII of Book II will be exceedingly difficult to understand, and this for no other reason than that it has pleased the Author (since I have no doubt that they seemed so clear to him) to explain the proofs added to them in such brief and sparing explanations.

He relates, moreover, that he has met in Paris a man called Leibniz, of uncommon learning, well versed in many Sciences, and free from the vulgar prejudices of Theology. He has formed an intimate friendship with him because it happens that like himself he is working at the problem of the continued perfecting of the understanding, than which, indeed, he thinks there is nothing better, and considers nothing more useful. In Morals, he says that he is perfectly disciplined, and speaks from the mere dictates of reason, without any influence of the feelings. In Physics and especially in Metaphysical studies about God and the soul, he continues, he is very expert. Lastly, he concludes that he is most worthy of having communicated to him your writings, Sir, if consent has been first obtained, since he believes that thus great advantage will come to the Author, as he promises to show more fully if it please you, Sir. But if not, then let it cause no uneasiness lest he may not keep them secret conscientiously according to the promise he gave, as he has not made the slightest mention of them. This same Leibniz thinks very highly of the *Tractatus Theologico-Politicus*, on which subject, if you remember, he once wrote a letter to you, Sir.

I would therefore pray you, Sir, unless there is some special reason against it, not to mind giving this permission, in your generous kindliness. If possible, tell me your decision as soon as you can, for as soon as I have received your reply, I shall be able to answer our friend Tschirnhaus, which I am anxious to do on Tuesday evening, unless rather weighty grounds for delay compel you, Sir, to put the matter off.

Mr. Bresser has returned from Cleves, and has sent hither a large quantity of the beer of his country. I advised him to let you, Sir, have half a barrel, which he promised to do with his most friendly greeting.

Lastly, I pray you to forgive the roughness of my style, and the haste of my pen, and to command me to do you some service, so that I may have a real opportunity of proving that I am,

Most distinguished sir,

Your most devoted servant

G. H. SCHULLER.

Letter LXXII
B. D. S.

TO THE VERY LEARNED AND EXPERT MR. G. H. SCHULLER.

(*Reply to the Preceding.*)

MOST EXPERIENCED SIR, MOST HONOURED FRIEND,

I was much pleased to understand from your letter received to-day that you are well, and that our friend

Tschirnhaus has happily accomplished his journey to France. In the conversations which he had with Huygens about me he bore himself, in my opinion, very prudently. Moreover, I greatly rejoice that he has found such a fortunate opportunity for the end which he had set himself.

I do not see what he finds in Axiom 4, Part I, to contradict Proposition V, Part II. For in this proposition it is asserted that the essence of every idea has God for its cause in so far as He is considered as a thinking thing; whereas, in that axiom, it is asserted that the knowledge or the idea of the effect depends on the knowledge or the idea of the cause. But to confess the truth, I do not sufficiently follow the meaning of your letter on this point, and I believe that either in your letter, or in the original letter, there is an error due to haste in writing. For you write that it is asserted in Proposition V that the ideata are the efficient causes of ideas, whereas this very thing is expressly denied in this proposition. Hence, I now think, arises the whole confusion, and therefore any endeavour to write more fully on this matter would be vain, and I must therefore wait until you explain to me his meaning more clearly, and I know whether the original letter is sufficiently correct.

I think I know the Leibniz of whom he writes, through his letters, but I do not know why he has gone to France, when he was a Councillor of Frankfurt. As far as I could surmise from his letters, he seemed to me a man of liberal mind, and versed in every science. But still I consider it imprudent to entrust my writings to him so soon. I should like to know first what he is doing in France, and to hear the opinion of our friend Tschirnhaus, after he has associated with him longer, and knows his character more intimately. However, greet that friend of ours most dutifully in my name, and if I can be of service to him in anything, let him say what he wants, and he will find me most ready to comply with all his wishes.

I congratulate Mr. Bresser, my most honoured friend, on his arrival or return. For the promised beer I am very grateful, and I will repay in whatever way I may.

Lastly, I have not yet attempted to make trial of the process of your kinsman, nor do I believe that I shall be able to apply my mind to the attempt. For the more I consider the thing itself, the more I am persuaded that you have not made gold, but had not sufficiently separated what was latent in the antimony. But more of this on another occasion; now I am prevented for want of time.

Meanwhile, if I can be of service to you in anything, here I am whom you will always find,

Most distinguished Sir,

Your most friendly and devoted servant,

B. DE SPINOZA.

THE HAGUE, 18 *November* 1675.
MR. G. H. SCHULLER,
DOCTOR OF MEDICINE,
IN DE KORTSTEEGH IN DE GESTOFEERDE HOET,
T'AMSTERDAM.

Letter LXXVIII   B. D. S.

TO THE VERY NOBLE AND LEARNED MR. HENRY OLDENBURG.

(On Human Evil.)

MOST NOBLE SIR,

What I said in my previous letter, that we are inexcusable because we are in the power of God as clay in the hand of the potter, I wanted to be understood in this sense, namely, that no one can blame God because He has given him an infirm nature or an impotent mind. For it would be just as absurd for a circle to complain that God has not given it the properties of a sphere, or a child who is tortured by a stone, that He has not given him a healthy body, as for a weak-minded man to complain that God has denied him strength and the true knowledge and love of God, and that He has given him a nature so weak that he cannot restrain or moderate his desires. For to the nature of each thing there belongs no more than necessarily follows from its given cause. But that it does not belong to the nature of each man to be strong-minded and that it is no more in our power to have a sound body than a sound Mind, no-one can deny, unless he wishes to contradict both experience and reason. But you will insist that if men sin from the necessity of their nature, they are excusable: but you do not explain what you want to conclude from this, whether, namely, you want to conclude that God is unable to be angry with them, or that they are worthy of blessedness, that is, of the knowledge and love of God. Now if you mean the former, I fully admit that God is not angry, and that all things come to pass according to His decision; but I deny that they ought therefore all to be blessed: for men can be excusable and nevertheless lack blessedness, and be tormented in many ways. For a horse is excusable for being a horse and not a man; nevertheless it must be a horse and not a man. He who goes mad from the bite of a dog is, indeed, to be excused, and yet is rightly suffocated, and, lastly, he who is unable to control his desires, and to restrain them through fear of the laws, although he must be excused for his weakness, is nevertheless unable to enjoy peace of mind, and the knowledge and love of God, but necessarily perishes.

I do not think it necessary to warn you here that when Scripture says that God is angry with sinners, and that He is a judge who takes cognizance of the actions of men, judges, and passes sentence, it is speaking in human fashion, and in accordance with the received opinions of the people, since its intention is not to teach Philosophy, nor to make men learned, but obedient.

Again, I do not see how, because I assume that miracles and ignorance are equivalent, I appear to confine the power of God and the knowledge of men within the same limits.

Further, I accept Christ's passion, death and burial literally, as you do, but his resurrection, allegorically. I do indeed acknowledge that this is also related by the Evangelists with so many circumstantial details that we cannot deny that the Evangelists themselves believed that Christ's body rose again, and ascended into heaven to sit at the right hand of God; and that he could also have been seen even by unbelievers if they had also been present in the places in which Christ himself appeared to his disciples; in this, however, without harm to the teaching of the gospel, they could have been deceived, as happened also to other Prophets. I gave examples of this in my previous letter. But Paul, to whom also Christ afterwards appeared, glories that he knew Christ not according to the flesh but according to the Spirit.

I thank you very much for the Catalogue of the books of the very noble Mr. Boyle. Lastly, I wait to hear from you, when you have an opportunity, about the present proceedings of the Royal Society.

Farewell, most honoured sir, and believe me yours in all love and devotion.

[THE HAGUE, 7 *February* 1676.]

Letter LXXX

EHRENFRIED WALTER VON TSCHIRNHAUS

TO THE VERY ACUTE AND LEARNED PHILOSOPHER
B. D. S.

(*The Infinite.*)

MOST ILLUSTRIOUS SIR,

First I find it exceedingly difficult to conceive how the existence of bodies having motion and figure can be proved a priori, since there is nothing of this kind in Extension when we consider it absolutely. Secondly, I should like to be informed by you in what sense is to be understood what you state in your letter on the Infinite in these words: *But they do not conclude that such things exceed every number because of the multitude of their parts.* For in fact all Mathematicians seem to me always to show with regard to such infinities that the number of the parts is so great as to exceed any assignable number, and in the example about the two circles, which is adduced there, you do not seem to prove this point, although you had undertaken to do so. For there you merely show that they do not infer this from the excessive greatness of the intervening space, and *because we do not know its maximum and minimum*; but you do not show, as you wanted to do, that they do not infer it from the multitude of the parts.

Further, I gathered from Mr. Leibniz, that the tutor of the Dauphin of France, Huet by name, a man of extraordinary learning, is going to write about the truth of human Religion, and to refute your *Tractatus Theologico-Politicus.* Farewell.

2 *May* 1676.

Letter LXXXI   B. D. S.

To the Very Noble and Learned
Mr. Ehrenfried Walter von Tschirnhaus

(*Reply to the Preceding.*)

Most Noble Sir,

What I said in my letter about the Infinite, that they do not infer the infinity of the parts from the multitude of parts, is clear from the fact that, if it were inferred from their multitude, we should not be able to conceive a greater multitude of parts, but their multitude ought to be greater than any given one, which is untrue: for in the whole space between two circles having different centres we conceive twice as many parts as in half that space, and yet the number of the parts, of the half as well as of the whole of the space, exceeds every assignable number.

Next, from extension as Descartes conceives it, that is, as a quiescent mass, it is not only, as you say, difficult to prove the existence of bodies, but absolutely impossible. For matter at rest will continue at rest as much as possible, and will not be set in motion except by some stronger external cause. For this reason I did not hesitate to say once that Descartes' principles of natural things are useless, not to say absurd.

The Hague, 5 *May* 1676.

Letter LXXXII

Ehrenfried Walter von Tschirnhaus

To the Very Acute and Learned Philosopher B. d. S.

(Extension and the Variety of Bodies.)

Most learned Sir,

I should like you to do me the favour of showing me how, according to your thoughts, the variety of things can be deduced a priori from the conception of Extension. For you remember the opinion of Descartes whereby he maintains that he can deduce this variety from Extension in no other way than by supposing that this was the effect produced in Extension by motion which was started by God. In my opinion, therefore, he does not deduce the existence of bodies from inert matter, unless perhaps you disregard the hypothesis of God as the mover; for you have not shown how that must necessarily follow a priori from the essence of God; a thing the demonstration of which Descartes believed to be beyond human comprehension. Therefore, I ask you about this subject, well knowing that you hold other views, unless perhaps there is some special reason why you did not hitherto want to make it public. That this may be so, I do not doubt, or it would not have been necessary to indicate such a thing obscurely. But you may certainly be sure that, whether you tell me something openly or whether you conceal it, my feeling for you will remain unchanged.

The reasons, however, why I should especially desire this, are these. In Mathematics I have always observed that from anything considered in itself, that is, from the definition of anything, we are able to deduce at least one property, but that if we desire more properties, then we must relate the thing defined to other things; then, if at all, from the combination of the definitions of these things new properties result. For instance, if I consider only the circumference of a circle, I shall not be able to infer anything except that it is alike at all points, or uniform, in which property it differs essentially from all other curves. But I shall never be able to deduce any other properties. If, however, I relate it to other things, say, to the radii drawn from the centre, or to two or also more intersecting lines, then I shall in this way be able to deduce some more properties. This seems to a certain extent to oppose Proposition XVI of the *Ethics*, which is almost the most important one in Book I of your Treatise. In this it is assumed as known that several properties can be deduced from the given definition of a thing. This seems to me impossible, unless we relate the defined thing to others. As a consequence of this I cannot see how from an Attribute, considered by itself, for instance from infinite Extension, there can arise a variety of bodies. If you think that this also cannot be concluded from a single attribute considered by itself, but only from all taken together, I should like to learn this from you, also how this should be conceived.

Farewell, etc.

Paris, 23 *June* 1676.

Letter LXXXIII   B. D. S.

To the Very Noble and Learned
Mr. Ehrenfried Walter von Tschirnhaus

(Reply to the Preceding.)

Most Noble Sir,

You ask whether the variety of things can be proved a priori from the conception of Extension alone. I believe I have already shown sufficiently clearly that this is impossible, and that therefore matter is badly defined by Descartes as Extension, but that it must necessarily be defined by an attribute which expresses eternal and infinite essence. But perhaps, if life lasts, I will discuss this question with you some other time more clearly. For so far I have not been able to write anything about these things in proper order.

As to what you say in addition that from the definition of each thing considered in itself we can deduce one property only, this may be true in the case of the most simple things, or in the case of things of reason (under which I also include figures) but not in the case of real beings. For from the mere fact that I define God as a Being to whose essence belongs existence I infer several of His properties, namely, that He exists necessarily, that He is unique, immutable, infinite, etc. And in this way I might adduce several other examples which I omit at present.

Lastly, I pray you to find out whether Mr. Huet's Treatise (namely, the one against the *Tractatus Theologico-Politicus*), of which you wrote before, has already been published, and whether you will be able to send